THE DEVELOPMENT OF
ATTACHMENT
AND
AFFILIATIVE SYSTEMS

Edited by
Robert N. Emde
and
Robert J. Harmon

University of Colorado Medical Center
Denver, Colorado

PLENUM PRESS • NEW YORK AND LONDON

Library of Congress Cataloging in PublicationData

Main entry under title:

The Development of attachment and affiliative systems.

    (Topics in developmental psychobiology)
    Includes bibliographical references and index.
    1. Parent and child. 2. Infant psychology. 3. Developmental psychobiology. I. Emde,
Robert N. II. Harmon, Robert John, 1946 .   . III. Series.
BF720.P37D33   115.4'22   82-3818
ISBN 0-306-40849-X   AACR2

©1982 Plenum Press, New York
A Division of Plenum Publishing Corporation
233 Spring Street, New York, N.Y. 10013

Printed in the United States of America

Contributors

Nicholas Anastasiow ● Special Education Program, Hunter College of the City of New York, New York, New York

Nancy A. Busch-Rossnagel ● Department of Human Development and Family Studies, Colorado State University, Fort Collins, Colorado

Perry M. Butterfield ● Department of Psychiatry, University of Colorado School of Medicine, Denver, Colorado

Joseph J. Campos ● Department of Psychology, University of Denver, Denver, Colorado

Thomas Z. Cassel ● Plymouth Center for Human Development, Northville, Michigan

Patricia F. Chappell ● Division of Psychiatry, Boston University Medical Center, Boston, Massachusetts

J. P. Connell ● Graduate School of Education and Human Development and Department of Psychology, University of Rochester, Rochester, New York

Linda S. Crnic ● Department of Pediatrics, University of Colorado School of Medicine, Denver, Colorado

Rex E. Culp ● Department of Human Development and Family Studies, Colorado State University, Fort Collins, Colorado

Robert N. Emde ● Department of Psychiatry, University of Colorado School of Medicine, Denver, Colorado

v

Mark Frank • Department of Psychiatry, University of Colorado School of Medicine, Denver, Colorado

Janet J. Fritz • Department of Human Development and Family Studies, Colorado State University, Fort Collins, Colorado

Ann M. Frodi • Department of Psychology, University of Rochester, Rochester, New York

Majt Frodi • Department of Psychology, University of Goteborg, Goteborg, Sweden

Theodore Gaensbauer • Department of Psychiatry, University of Colorado Health Sciences Center, Denver, Colorado

H. Hill Goldsmith • Department of Psychology, University of Texas, Austin, Texas

Marshell M. Haith • Department of Psychology, University of Denver, Denver, Colorado

Robert J. Harmon • Department of Psychiatry, University of Colorado School of Medicine, Denver, Colorado

Clare F. Haynes • C. Henry Kempe Center for the Treatment and Prevention of Child Abuse and Neglect, 1205 Oneida Street, Denver, Colorado

Carl-Phillip Hwang • Department of Psychology, University of Goteborg, Goteborg, Sweden

I. Charles Kaufman • Veterans Administration Medical Center, 4150 Clement Street, San Francisco, California

Melvin Konner • 80 Hammond Street, Cambridge, Massachusetts

Michael E. Lamb • Departments of Psychology, Psychiatry, and Pediatrics, University of Utah, Salt Lake City, Utah

George A. Morgan • Department of Human Development and Family Studies, Colorado State University, Fort Collins, Colorado

Sandy Naiman • Department of Psychiatry, University of Colorado School of Medicine, Denver, Colorado

Betty Jean Pannabecker • University of Colorado School of Medicine, Denver, Colorado

Martin L. Reite • Department of Pediatrics, University of Colorado School of Medicine, Denver, Colorado

Gene P. Sackett • Department of Psychology, Regional Primate Research Center, and Child Development and Mental Retardation Center, University of Washington, Seattle, Washington

Louis W. Sander • Division of Child Psychiatry, University of Colorado Health Sciences Center, Denver, Colorado

David W. Shucard • Department of Pediatrics, University of Colorado School of Medicine, Denver, Colorado

Patricia A. Snyder • Division of Psychiatry, Boston University Medical Center, Boston, Massachusetts

James F. Sorce • Department of Psychiatry, University of Colorado School of Medicine, Denver, Colorado

Jamie Steinberg • School of Public Health, University of Michigan, Ann Arbor, Michigan

Marilyn J. Svejda • Parent-child Nursing, School of Nursing, University of Michigan, Ann Arbor, Michigan

Katherine Tennes • Department of Psychiatry, University of Colorado School of Medicine, Denver, Colorado

Paola S. Timiras • Department of Physiology-Anatomy, University of California, Berkeley, California

Annette K. Vance • Department of Human Development and Family Studies, Colorado State University, Fort Collins, Colorado

Antonia Vernadakis • Departments of Psychiatry and Pharmacology, University of Colorado School of Medicine, Denver, Colorado

Ted D. Wade • University of Colorado Health Sciences Center, Central Laboratory, Denver, Colorado

Preface

The "Development of Attachment and Affiliative Systems" was selected as the topic for a three-day workshop held at Estes Park, Colorado, in May, 1980. The papers which resulted from this effort not only reflect a recent intensity of research in this area, but also highlight a mounting need for asking questions across disciplines and for integrating theories. The sponsor of the workshop was the Developmental Psychobiology Research Group (DPRG) of the Department of Psychiatry, University of Colorado Medical School, a group which itself is interdisciplinary and which has met regularly since 1969 to criticize research, ask questions, and discuss findings. In 1974, the Group was awarded an endowment fund by the Grant Foundation after a request for a proposal initiated by Philip Sapir and Douglas Bond. The aims of this fund are to facilitate the research of young investigators, to encourage new research, and to provide seed money for collaborative ventures. Much of what is reported here results from that support. Thus, happily, not only are the contributions timely by virtue of converging on an important topic, but they also commemorate more than five years of Grant Foundation support.

Once the topic was chosen, a small number of guests were invited to participate. The papers of Timiras, Sackett, Konner, and Lamb represent differing perspectives from neurobiology, primatology, cultural anthropology, and social psychology. Contributions from DPRG members add perspectives from psychiatry, pediatrics, developmental and clinical psychology, and behavioral genetics. According to plan, some of the papers of this interdisciplinary forum represent original work, others are theoretical, and still others suggest new approaches.

Because we have obtained volume commentaries from two senior investigators, we will not offer an overview of our own. A conceptual orientation to the topic can be found in the introductions of many of the individual chapters. Further, if we have done our editorial work appropriately, each chapter can be understood as a self-contained piece.

In addition to the Grant Foundation, we would like to acknowledge the encouragement and support of a number of key individuals. Rene Spitz was an active participant in the early days of the DPRG, and his active questioning, vigor, and enthusiasm in the last years of his life have been an inspiration for our group which persists to the present. I. Charles Kaufman, an original member of the DPRG who provided the leadership for our group in its early days, was, in many ways, its prime mover. Although he is no longer in Denver, he is still an important colleague. Donald Stilson gave invaluable statistical advice for design and data presentation on many studies reported in this volume. Finally, we would like to acknowledge the outstanding administrative and secretarial assistance of Maxine Conlon on various aspects of this volume.

ROBERT N. EMDE
ROBERT J. HARMON

Contents

PART I   PERSPECTIVES FROM PRIMATE BEHAVIOR AND NEUROBIOLOGY

Chapter 1

**Can Single Processes Explain Effects of Postnatal Influences on
Primate Development?**   3

Gene P. Sackett

Introduction   3
The Nongenerality of Isolation Rearing Effects   5
Effects of the Fetus on Its Mother   8
Conclusions   11
Abstract   11
References   11

Chapter 2

**Infant Monkeys' Achievement of Temporal Coherence with Their
Social Group**   13

Clare F. Haynes, Ted D. Wade, and Thomas Z. Cassell

Introduction   13
    The Research Problem   13
    A Primate Model   15
    The Social Group as an Organized Population   15
Method   16
    The Group and Its Environment   16
    Observational Protocol   17

Scoring of Adult Behaviors and Group State 17
Scoring of Infant Behaviors and Infant Scales 17
Results 19
Adult Group States 19
Infant Behavior Scales 21
Discussion 23
Temporal Coordination of Adult Behaviors 23
Group State Patterns 23
Infant's Achievement of Temporal Coherence with Adult
Group State 25
Research on Temporal Adaptation 27
Dyads, Subgroups, and the Overall Social Group 27
Abstract 28
References 28

Chapter 3

**Animal Models of Human Behavior: Their Application to the
Study of Attachment** 31

Linda S. Crnic, Martin L. Reite, and David W. Shucard

Are Animal Models of Attachment Necessary? 31
What Are Animal Models? A Paradox 32
Animal Models versus Animal Systems 32
Homology versus Nonhomology 33
Advantages of Animal Models 34
Risks of Animal Models 34
Minimizing the Risks 35
Animal Models Are Part of an Interactive System of Research . . 35
An Example of the Use of Animal Models: Attachment 36
Definition 36
Identification of Appropriate Species 37
Identification of Possible Neurobiological Mechanisms 38
Conclusions 39
Abstract 40
References 40

Chapter 4

Animal Models in Developmental Psychobiology 43

I. Charles Kaufman

Abstract 45
References 45

Chapter 5

**The Timing of Hormone Signals in the Orchestration of Brain
Development** 47

Paola S. Timiras

Introduction 47
Critical Periods: Vulnerability and Nurture 50
Effects of Sex Hormones 51
Effects of Thyroid Hormones 55
Timing Signals for Regulation of Growth, Development, and Aging . 59
Abstract 59
References 60

Chapter 6

**Epigenetic Factors in Neuronal Differentiation: A Review of
Recent Research** 65

Antonia Vernadakis

Introduction 65
Role of Microenvironment on Neural Differentiation 66
Hormones as Epigenetic Growth Factors 68
Neurohumor Substances as Growth Factors 69
Glial Factors in Neuronal Growth 70
Conclusions 71
Abstract 71
References 72

Chapter 7

The Role of Hormones in Mother–Infant Transactions 75

Katherine Tennes

Introduction 75
Animal Models 75

The Corticosteroid Response to Brief Separations 76
    Cortisol and the Infant's Distress 76
    Cortisol and the Mother–Infant Relationship 78
Conclusion 79
Abstract 79
References 79

PART II PERSPECTIVES FROM HUMAN STUDIES

Chapter 8

Parent-to-Infant Attachment: A Critique of the Early "Bonding"
Model 83

Marilyn J. Svejda, Betty Jean Pannabecker, and Robert N. Emde

Introduction 83
Mother-to-Infant Attachment 84
    A Review of Maternal Bonding Research 84
    Early Contact Fails to Generalize 86
    Shortcomings of the Bonding Model 87
Father-to-Infant Attachment 89
    Caregiving of the Father 89
    A Test of Father Bonding 90
Conclusion 91
    Bonding Model No Longer Useful 91
Abstract 92
References 92

Chapter 9

Silver Nitrate and the Eyes of the Newborn: Effects on Parental
Responsiveness during Initial Social Interaction 95

Perry M. Butterfield, Robert N. Emde, Marilyn Svejda, and Sandy Naiman

The First Study 96
The Second Study 99
Discussion 104
Abstract 106
References 106

Chapter 10

**Effect of Gender and Caretaking Role on Parent–Infant
Interaction**   109

*Michael E. Lamb, Ann M. Frodi, Carl-Philip Hwang, Majt Frodi, and
Jamie Steinberg*

Attitudes and Behavior of Traditional and Nontraditional Parents in
Sweden   109
   Introduction   109
   Method   111
   Results   113
   Discussion   115
Abstract   117
References   118

Chapter 11

**An Investigation of Change in the Infant–Caregiver System over
the First Week of Life**   119

Louis W. Sander, Patricia F. Chappell, and Patricia A. Snyder

Conceptual Background   119
Methods of Data Collection   123
   The Bassinet Monitor   123
   Observation and Recording of Caregiver–Infant Interaction . .   124
Results   125
   Bassinet Monitor   125
   Observation and Recording of Caregiver–Infant Interaction . .   130
Discussion   132
Abstract   135
References   136

Chapter 12

Biological Aspects of the Mother–Infant Bond   137

Melvin Konner

Consequences of Frequent Infant Nursing: A View of the Maternal
Side of the Bond   138

Foundations of Infant Social Behavior in Neurobehavioral
Growth   142
The Growth of Social Smiling   145
The Growth of the Social Fears   149
Conclusion   153
Abstract   154
References   155

Chapter 13

Toward a Theory of Infant Temperament   161

H. Hill Goldsmith and Joseph J. Campos

Relevance of Temperament to Attachment   161
Some Previous Efforts to Define Temperament   163
    Temperament in Adult Personality Theories   163
    Four Theories of Temperament with Developmental
    Orientations   163
A Behaviorally Based Definition of Infant Temperament   174
    Why Confine Our Definition to the Infancy Period?   174
    Why a Behaviorally Based Definition of Infant
    Temperament?   176
    Infant Temperament Defined   177
Implications of the Present Definition of Temperament   178
    The Relationship between Temperament and Manifest
    Behavior   178
    Temperament and Personality   179
    Contemporary Function of Temperament   179
    Cross-situational Generality of Temperament   180
    Origins of Temperament   180
    Temperament and Affect   180
    Measurement Implications of the Present Conceptualization of
    Temperament   182
    Unresolved Issues   184
Temperament and Attachment   185
    Temperament and Social Interaction: An Overview   185
    Possible Relationships between the Development of
    Temperament and Attachment   185
    Future Directions for the Study of Temperament   188
Abstract   189
References   189

Chapter 14

Parent–Infant Interaction, Attachment, and Socioemotional Development in Infancy 195

Michael E. Lamb

Introduction 195
The Development of Parent–Infant Attachments 196
    To Whom Do Attachments Form? 197
    Sex Differences 198
    Individual Differences in Parent–Infant Attachments 199
Interpreting Strange Situation Behavior 202
    Individual Differences in Strange Situation Behavior 203
    A Research Agenda 205
Predictive Validity of Security of Attachment 206
    Future Research Issues 207
Conclusion 208
Abstract 208
References 209

Chapter 15

A Structural Modeling Approach to the Study of Attachment and Strange Situation Behaviors 213

J. P. Connell and H. Hill Goldsmith

Overview 213
Previous Attachment Research: Concepts and Methodology 214
    Overview 214
    Attachment as an Organizational Construct 214
    The Strange Situation Paradigm 215
    The ABC Typology 216
Problems in Attachment Research Using the ABC Typology 216
    How Well Does the ABC System Account for Individual
    Differences in Strange Situation Behaviors 216
    The Issue of Stability of Patterns of Attachment Behaviors . . . 217
    The Issue of Predictive Validity of Patterns of Attachment
    Behaviors 218
    The Limitations of Typologies as Related to the ABC System . 219
The Structural Modeling Approach to the Study of Strange Situation
Behaviors 221

Differences between the Structural Modeling Approach and the
Traditional Approach 221
Substantive Applications of the Structural Modeling
Approach 222
Comparison of Models in Different Contexts and in Different
Groups of Subjects 228
Summary and Evaluation of the Structural Modeling Approach . . . 231
Suggested Applications 231
Disadvantages of the Approach 232
Conclusion 233
Appendix 234
Confirmatory Factor Analysis 234
Path Analysis of Functional Relationships Among Latent
Variables 237
Analysis of Latent Variable Means 240
Abstract 241
References 242

Chapter 16

**Infants' Differential Social Response to Mother and Experimenter:
Relationships to Maternal Characteristics and Quality of Infant
Play** 245

*George A. Morgan, Nancy A. Busch-Rossnagel, Rex E. Culp, Annette K.
Vance, and Janet J. Fritz*

Introduction 245
Overview 245
Strange Situation Studies 246
Reactions to Stranger and Mother, Attachment and
Competence 247
Studies of Maternal Characteristics 248
Method 249
Subjects 249
Procedure 249
Differential Social Response to Experimenter and Mother . . . 250
Maternal Characteristics 251
Quality of Infant Play 252
Results 252
Patterns of Infant Reaction to Experimenter and Mother 252
Maternal Characteristics and Infant's Differential Response . . 253

Quality of Play, Differential Response, and Maternal
Characteristics 255
Discussion 256
Differential Social Response as a Useful Way of Grouping
Infants 256
Attachment and Differential Social Response 256
Maternal and Demographic Factors 258
Differential Response as an Intervening Variable 259
Infant Effects 259
Future Research Directions 259
Abstract 260
References 260

Chapter 17

**Attachment Behavior in Abused/Neglected and Premature Infants:
Implications for the Concept of Attachment** 263

Theodore J. Gaensbauer and Robert J. Harmon

Validity of Ainsworth's Concepts of Secure versus Insecure
Attachment 265
The Strong Predisposition of Infants To Show Attachment
Behavior 268
The Specificity of Attachment Behavior 269
Stability of Attachment: Attachment Behavior as Reflecting Recent
Caretaking Experiences Rather Than Past Experiences 272
The Role of Pleasurable Interaction in Facilitating Attachment
Behavior 274
Attachment Behavior Must Be Seen in Developmental
Perspective 275
Conclusion 276
Abstract 277
References 278

Chapter 18

**Maternal Referencing in Normal and Down's Syndrome Infants: A
Longitudinal Analysis** 281

James F. Sorce, Robert N. Emde, and Mark Frank

Methods 283
    Subjects 283
    Procedure 284
Results 285
    Presence of Maternal Referencing 285
    Visual Fixation Patterns 286
    Emotional Behaviors Accompanying Referencing 287
    Emotional State Baseline 288
Discussion 289
Abstract 291
References 291

PART III COMMENTARIES

Commentary

Attachment Research and Mental Health: A Speculation 295

Nicholas Anastasiow

References 299

Commentary

Attachment Research: Prospect and Progress 301

Marshall Haith

The "System" of Infant Social Relations 302
Conceptualizing and Evaluating the Relation between the Infant and
Social Agents 305
    Attachment and Other Relations 305
    Proximity-Seeking as an Indicator of Attachment 306
Concluding Comment 307
References 308

Index 309

PART ONE

PERSPECTIVES FROM PRIMATE BEHAVIOR AND NEUROBIOLOGY

CHAPTER 1

Can Single Processes Explain Effects of Postnatal Influences on Primate Development?

Gene P. Sackett

INTRODUCTION

The modern study of behavioral development grew under the Freudian principle that early postnatal experience shapes adult human behavior. Later experience, although important for acquiring specific skills, abilities, and knowledge, does not have the primacy and permanence of early influences. This view was strengthened by Spitz (1945), who showed that human infants reared in institutions under deprived social and sensory conditions had markedly abnormal patterns of early development. Studies by Bowlby (1973) also suggested that infancy experience had a major influence on later attachment and social behavior. The pioneering experimental studies of Harry and Margaret Harlow (1965) on rhesus monkeys raised in total social isolation confirmed the results from these human studies. Rhesus isolates developed species-atypical individual and social behaviors which persisted into adulthood. With this nonhuman primate evidence, the theory that early experience is critical for species-typical primate behavior became a textbook fact.

More recently, the primacy of early experience effects has come under attack. Follow-up studies of humans reared in impoverished institutional

Gene P. Sackett • Department of Psychology, Regional Primate Research Center, and Child Development and Mental Retardation Center, University of Washington, Seattle, Washington 98195.
The research reported here was conducted between 1968 and 1978. The work was variously supported by NIH grant HD–08633 and NSF grant GB–31149 to me, and NIH grant MH–28259 and NSF grant BNS–7723660 to my colleague, William T. Greenough. NIH grants RR–00166 and RR–02274 to the Washington and Wisconsin Regional Primate Research Centers, respectively, also supported some of this effort.

conditions showed that behavioral deficits seen in infancy often disappeared later in life (Clark & Clark, 1977). Although thalidomide produced babies with drastically abnormal sensorimotor experience during infancy, many of the afflicted individuals developed normal cognitive abilities and social behavior (Decarie, 1969). Even rhesus monkeys raised in total social isolation for 6–12 months from birth developed competent social behavior with species-typical individual behavior when forced to interact with much younger "therapist" monkeys (Novak & Harlow, 1975; Suomi & Harlow, 1972). Perhaps the most compelling case for a lack of continuity between early behavior and later performance is seen in the area of human newborn assessment (Sameroff, 1978). Longitudinal retest data fail to show even modest correlations between arousal, perceptual, and motor behaviors when tests are administered only 4–5 days apart. Consistency is found only when extremely abnormal behavior is present.

Perhaps one reason for the current uncertainty about the roles of early experience is a tendency to explain primate development phenomena in terms of single processes. Cognition, caregiving, affectional relationships, social transactions, or learned motives are concepts concerning postnatal factors often used to explain various dimensions of human development. Generally, these dimensions involve social responding or problem solving, extremely variable behaviors which often exhibit low temporal correlations. On the other hand, personality and emotionality dimensions, which tend to show more stability within individuals over time, are often explained in terms of constitutional or genetic factors. However, little is known about genetic-organismic variables, and even less is known about how they interact with experience to produce changes in behavior over time. Psychobiology can contribute to an understanding of early experience effects by generating facts and concepts about actual ways in which genetic mechanisms, prenatal and perinatal variables, and postnatal conditions interact in producing the typical course of development for a species, individual differences from this time course, and deviant behavior representing abnormal developmental paths.

This chapter illustrates the idea that early experience effects cannot be explained solely by postnatal environmental conditions nor by one underlying psychobiological process. Specifically, it is proposed that (1) genotype determines the behavioral dimensions affected by variations in social-sensory experience during primate infancy; (2) at least two independent processes are needed to explain both immediate and later effects of varied social-sensory experience; and (3) some aspects of postnatal development may involve effects of the developing fetus on its mother and indirectly on her social companions. The data for these proposals come from two lines of investigation. The first involves species differences among macaque monkeys in development during and after social isolation rearing. The second concerns an epidemiological study of pregnant monkeys that were treated for bite wounds received from members of their social group.

THE NONGENERALITY OF ISOLATION REARING EFFECTS

Rhesus monkeys (*M. mulatta*) raised in total social isolation develop a syndrome of species-deviant behaviors. These include body rocking, stereotyped locomotion, self clutching, and self-directed oral activity. On social tests after the rearing period, isolates continue to show peculiar individual behavior, withdraw from social contacts, and have very low levels of environmental exploration. These characteristics usually persist into adulthood, when they are also coupled with self-directed aggression, incompetent sexual behavior, and generally inadequate maternal behavior. This syndrome has been studied in relation to human psychopathology (Harlow & Mears, 1979), and the general effects are the classic examples of how bad rearing adversely affects development (see Sackett, 1972, for a review of this literature).

Theories to explain the emergence and permanence of isolation effects in rhesus monkeys abound. They include (1) failure to develop appropriate and necessary affectional systems (Harlow & Harlow, 1965); (2) abnormal emotional responses due to the lack of stimulation in infancy (Sackett, 1965) or trauma of emergence from the isolation situation into a complex new setting (Fuller, 1967); (3) failure to learn social skills and problem-solving approaches during critical periods of infancy (Novak & Harlow, 1975); (4) biochemical deficits (McKinney, Young, Suomi, & Davis, 1973); and (5) brain anatomy abnormalities (Floeter & Greenough, 1979; Prescott, 1971).

The adequacy of some of these views was questioned in the following studies. Long-term follow-up studies of rhesus isolates showed that males were more affected in the extent and persistence of deviant behavior than were females (Sackett, Holm, & Landesman-Dwyer, 1975). On measures of exploratory behavior in a novel environment, females reared in wire cages throughout infancy were not different from socially raised controls, while males reared under the same partial isolation conditions did not differ from animals reared in total social isolation. These results suggested that there were important gender differences in risk for developing abnormal behavior following poor rearing experiences, and that the source of greater risk on the part of males might lie in processes of prenatal development. Furthermore, it seemed that a different set of principles might be needed to explain rearing-condition effects on each gender.

Another experiment further questioned the generality of the rhesus isolation syndrome. Pigtail macaques (*M. nemestrina*) were reared under conditions identical to those of rhesus isolates in prior studies (Sackett, Holm, & Ruppenthal, 1976). Pigtails are closely related to rhesus, and their general milestones of neonatal and infant development are almost identical. Our purpose was to show that pigtails responded to isolation like rhesus so that we could use pigtails to study the bases of gender differences in risk for abnormal development. However, during the rearing period, pigtails showed only low levels of isolate syndrome behavior. On social behavior tests pairing isolates with socially reared monkeys, (1) pigtails spent less than half as much time as rhesus in isolate syndrome behaviors; (2) pigtails showed no deficit in nonsocial exploration; and (3) almost every pigtail isolate engaged in some positive social interaction, while all rhesus isolates except one showed no interaction with agemate partners. A final result was especially stressful to us. For pigtails, no sex differences were found during the rearing period or on the postrearing social-behavior tests.

This study indicated that quantitative effects of isolation rearing varied between species, implicating genetic risk as a determinant of the effects of poor rearing conditions on development. Recently, we completed the study of a third species, and the results further complicate the picture (Sackett, Ruppenthal, Fahrenbruch, Holm, & Greenough, 1981). Crabeating macaques (M. fascicularis) were reared under the same isolation conditions of a visually enclosed, sound-attenuated chamber as in our previous studies of rhesus and pigtail monkeys. The main purpose of this work was to study dendritic development in the brains of monkeys reared under isolation and social conditions. All subjects were sacrificed five weeks after emergence from isolation at 7 months of age. Therefore, we could only compare the three macaque species in terms of behavior during isolation, and during the first month of social playroom testing with socially reared partners. Table I presents a summary of these comparisons.

Observations of behavior in the isolation cages were taken for 5-min daily sessions, 5–6 days per week, throughout the rearing period. The upper portion of Table I presents the emergence of session time spent in four types of behavior, averaged over the 6–month rearing period. The four categories summarize more than 95% of all activities occurring on these tests. Statistical significance was assessed by one-way ANOVAs for each category.

Passive-sleep time did not differ reliably during isolation. Pigtails spent very little time in isolate syndrome behavior. Crabeaters were reliably higher, but rhesus were extremely high in these behaviors, and differed from both of the other species. Exploration of the cage interior did not differ reliably between pigtails and crabeaters, who both exceeded rhesus. Play behavior was uniformly low and not different between the species. In sum, rhesus showed the typical isolation syndrome of low exploration and high levels of self-directed, stereotyped, and body-rocking behavior. Pigtails showed almost no isolate syndrome behavior and a great deal of exploration. Crabeaters were intermediate in isolate syndrome behavior and relatively high in exploration.

Table I. Behavioral Profiles of Three Macaque Species during and after Rearing in Total Social Isolation[a]

I. Isolation cage behavior

		Sleep passive	Isolate syndrome	Exploration	Play
Rhesus	(n = 8)	28	52	15	.5
Pigtail	(n = 16)	33	2	63	1
Crabeater	(n = 6)	22	21	52	3
p		—	<.001	<.025	—

II. Social playroom behavior

	Nonsocial			Social	
	Passive	Exploration	Isolate syndrome	Positive	Negative
Rhesus	27	5	57	.1	8
Pigtail	37	16	25	3	16
Crabeater	20	14	35	13	15
p	<.05	<.05	<.005	<.001	.10

[a]Cell entries are percentages of total test time.

Thus, even under the impoverished conditions of an isolation chamber, each species showed a different profile of behavior.

Social behavior profiles were even more revealing. The lower portion of Table I gives the percentage of test time spent in various behaviors during daily 30-min pairings of each isolate with two socially reared agemates. Statistically reliable species differences occurred for all categories except negative social behaviors involving fear and/or withdrawal from nonaggressive social contacts. Pigtails had more passive behavior than rhesus, who were not reliably different from crabeaters. Nonsocial exploration was lowest for rhesus, and did not differ between pigtails and crabeaters. Isolate syndrome behavior was highest for rhesus, intermediate for crabeaters, and reliably lower for pigtails. Of major interest, crabeaters spent 13% of their test time in positive social interactions, a value that was not significantly different from the 16% exhibited by their socially reared partners. Pigtails spent only 3% of their test time in positive social behavior, while rhesus had essentially none of these activities. Both pigtails and rhesus were reliably lower in positive social behavior than their socially raised partners. Socialized pigtails spent 23% of their time interacting, while socialized rhesus interacted 20% of the time.

These data show three different patterns of isolation effects, one for each species. Further, a dissociation occurred between isolate syndrome behavior and other major behavioral dimensions, and amount of isolate activities did not predict level of exploratory or positive social behavior. Pigtail isolates showed low levels of isolate syndrome behavior, but also had low positive social behavior. Crabeaters had higher isolate behavior levels, but also exhibited a great deal of positive social interaction as well as modest amounts of environmental exploration. Such data seem incompatible with any single theory proposed as an explanation of isolation effects. None of the species were allowed to develop affectional bonds, none experienced environmental stimulus changes during rearing, all were subjected to emergence trauma on removal from the rearing chamber, and none had the opportunity to learn social behaviors or problem-solving strategies which might help them cope with the stimulation of the postrearing environment. Yet, pigtails showed no exploratory deficits, crabeaters showed species-typical positive social behavior, and the extent of deviant individual behavior was not related to exploration or social behavior levels.

Within a given species, isolate syndrome behavior may correlate with brain cell changes or biochemical defects. However, the dissociation between behavioral dimensions found in this study suggests that a single biochemical or cellular abnormality will not explain deprived rearing-condition effects. Furthermore, the dissociation of isolate behavior from other dimensions implies that specific neurochemical factors which might underlie isolate syndrome behavior do not necessarily affect other dimensions of behavior. This analysis suggests that explaining isolation effects in primates will involve at least two independent mechanisms: one will concern the basis for genotypic differences in risk for developing isolate syndrome activities during the rearing period; the other will concern genotypic differences in the amount or quality of experience during infancy required to maintain exploratory behavior and to develop species-typical social behavior after isolation terminates.

EFFECTS OF THE FETUS ON ITS MOTHER

The idea that genetic errors and abnormal maternal processes can influence development of unborn mammals is not new (e.g., Joffee, 1969). Current extensive research on alcohol and drug use has shown that maternal influences during pregnancy can have dramatic effects on the course of offspring development (e.g., Streissguth, Landesman-Dwyer, Martin, & Smith, 1980). However, the opposite idea that the fetus can affect its pregnant mother has barely been explored. Recent studies by Gandelman and his colleagues (1977) show that rat fetuses can have important influences on each other. Female fetuses that were surrounded by male fetuses were compared with females surrounded by other females on parameters of anatomical development and behavior. Those surrounded *in utero* by males had retarded development of anatomical sex characteristics, were larger, and showed more masculine behavior than those surrounded by females. Presumably these effects were mediated by masculinization of the female fetuses from testosterone secreted into the amniotic fluid by the male fetuses.

In macaque monkeys, gender differentiation begins at about day 60 of the 165–170 day gestation period. Around day 75–80, high levels of testosterone can be measured in the mother's circulation (Resko, 1970). This heightened testosterone level remains in the mother until 2–3 days after birth of the male offspring. In a provocative study of human umbilical cord blood taken at delivery, Maccoby and her colleagues (1979) report that testosterone is higher following delivery of a male offspring, with first-born males showing a much higher level than later born males. The study described provides an example of a behavioral effect of the primate fetus on its mother, presumably mediated by a fetal hormone factor.

Over the past 15 years, the Regional Primate Research Center at the University of Washington has maintained a large colony of pigtail monkey breeders. These animals live in harem groups containing a single adult male and 6–12 females. Growth, health, and reproduction data are maintained in a computer data base, which can be used for epidemiological and demographic studies. In 1974, while studying the histories of female breeders who consistently produce poor pregnancy outcomes, I looked into a variable called "bite-wound treatments." This was an entry made in the health record of animals who were attacked and injured so badly that the veterinary staff had to remove the victim from the group for medical treatment. In this initial screening, it appeared that pregnant females who were treated for bite wounds delivered more female than male offspring. This seemed rather unlikely, but a preliminary analysis on the small sample of bitten animals supported the conclusion that females bitten during pregnancy were carrying an excessive percentage of female fetuses (Sackett et al., 1975).

Each succeeding year produced a larger sample size, and Table II summarizes the current status of the analysis (Sackett, 1981). Overall, 2,822 con-

Table II. Sex Ratios by Month of the 170 Day Gestation Period for 220 Pigtail Female Breeders Severely Bitten by Social Companions during Pregnancy

| | Days of gestation | | | | | |
	1–30	31–60	61–90	91–120	121–150	>150
N bitten	28	22	35	36	48	51
% Male	56	53	48	30	36	33
% Female	44	47	52	70	64	67
Binomial						
p	—	—	—	.011	.021	.002

ceptions from 1,308 unique breeding females were studied. Of the sex-known offspring, 51.5% were males, and this value was used as the expectation for binomial tests of the sex ratios presented in Table II. Among the total conceptions, there were 231 in which females were treated for bite wounds in the six months prior to a conception, and 220 (the total n in Table II) bitten during pregnancy. Those bitten before a pregnancy produced 55% males, a value not different from expectation. Those bitten during pregnancy yielded 57.5% females, a significant difference from expectation. In Table II, sex ratios are shown for bitten breeders by month of gestation. For the first 90 days the ratio does not differ from expectation, while after 90 days bitten breeders carrying female fetuses significantly exceed those carrying males during each gestational month. This period corresponds to the time when male fetuses masculinize their mother's blood with testosterone and suggests that this may be responsible for what appears to be protection from attack by breeders carrying male fetuses.

However, a number of other factors could be responsible for this statistical oddity (Sackett, 1981). Those ruled out by negative findings of statistical tests include (1) that females bitten during pregnancy simply produce more female offspring than breeders not attacked during pregnancy; (2) that harem group males who live with females receiving bite wounds produce more female offspring; (3) that more spontaneous abortions occur with male fetuses, especially among breeders who receive bite wounds during pregnancy; and (4) that more young and/or primiparous females are bitten and are more likely to carry female fetuses.

Another explanation could be that estrogens secreted by female fetuses, rather than testosterone by males, may somehow increase risk of attack to the mother. However, Resko, Ploem, and Stradelman (1975) did not find a difference in maternal estrogen level between rhesus monkeys carrying female and those carrying male fetuses.

Although it is not yet known exactly how this effect is mediated, some conclusions can be made. First, the sex of the fetus alters the behavior, odor, or some other aspect of its mother. Second, this alteration is perceptible, at least on some pregnancies, to the pregnant female's social companions, who behave differentially depending on the gender of the unborn offspring. More speculatively, if the causal fetal factor or factors persist for a time after birth, it seems likely that the fetus itself may affect the way its mother will behave toward it as a newborn. This could serve to set off postnatal development on a different track for males than for females, regardless of later social factors or maternal or societal expectations. In sum, this type of observation opens broader possibilities concerning the genesis of gender differences in behavior and also suggests the possibility that fetal hormones influencing the mother may be an important determinant of adequate versus inadequate care of the newborn.

CONCLUSIONS

In this chapter I have attempted to show that psychobiological investigations are required if we are to discover meaningful principles of primate behavioral development. Genetic mechanisms, as yet completely unknown, appear to determine whether an individual will be at relatively high or low risk for developing abnormally following deviant rearing experiences. There is no reason to believe that similar risk factors may not underlie vulnerability to teratogens and environmental pollutants and the probability that such physical agents will alter the course of development in individual organisms. If such genetic variance in risk is the norm, it is unlikely that the search for meaningful determinants of development in single environmental factors can lead very far. What seems to be needed, in addition to work on basic biophysical mechanisms, are multifactor studies designed to understand, rather than hide, the individual differences that we consistently ignore in our statistical "error terms." These factors may include traditional variables involving the postnatal environment, but may also involve variables that are less readily available for manipulation and measurement, such as differential effects of the fetus on its mother.

ABSTRACT

Effects of early postnatal experiences and of prenatal sex differentiation on later development have received much attention in psychobiological research. This chapter presents two studies of macaque monkeys related to these research areas. The first shows that effect of total social-isolation rearing varies markedly between three species. Genetic differences determine both the extent of isolation effects and the specific behavioral dimensions affected. The second study shows that pregnant pigtail monkeys who are attacked and wounded by their social companions are more likely to be carrying female than male fetuses. Fetal gender thus appears to influence both the mother and the social group even before birth. The implication of these results is that realistic psychobiological theory of primate development cannot ignore genetic and prenatal variables as these factors may be crucial in determining apparent environmental effects.

REFERENCES

Bowlby, J. *Separation: Anxiety and Anger.* New York: Basic Books, 1973.
Clark, A. M., & Clark, A. D. *Early experience: Myth and evidence.* New York: Free Press, 1977.

Decarie, T. G. A study of the mental and emotional development of the thalidomide child. In G. M. Foss (Ed.), *Determinants of infant behavior*, Vol. IV. London: Methuen, 1969.

Floeter M. K., & Greenough, W. T. Cerebellar plasticity: Modification of purkinje cell structure by differential rearing in monkeys. *Science*, 1979, *206*, 227–228.

Fuller, J. L. Experiential deprivation and later behavior. *Science*, 1967, *158*, 1645–1652.

Gandelman, R., Von Saal, J. M., & Reinisch, J. M. Contiguity to male fetuses effects morphology and behavior of female mice. *Nature*, 1977 *266*, 722–724.

Harlow, H. F., & Harlow, M. K. The affectional systems. In A. M. Schrier, H. F. Harlow, & F. Stollnitz (Eds.), *Behavior of nonhuman primates*, (Vol. 2). New York: Academic Press, 1965.

Harlow, H. F., & Mears, C. *The human model: Primate perspectives*. New York: Wiley, 1979.

Joffee, J. M. *Prenatal determinants of behavior*. New York: Pergamon Press, 1969.

Maccoby, E. E., Doering, C. H., Jacklin, C. N., & Kraemer, H. Concentrations of sex hormones in umbilical-cord blood: Their relation to sex and birth order of infants. *Child Development*, 1979, *50*, 632–642.

McKinney, W. T., Jr., Young, L. D., Suomi, S. J., & Davis, J. M. Chlorpromazine treatment of disturbed monkeys. *Archives of General Psychiatry*, 1973, *29*, 490–494.

Novak, M. A., and Harlow, H. F. Social recovery of monkeys isolated for the first year of life, II. Long-term assessment. *Developmental Psychology*, 1975, *15*, 50–61.

Prescott, J. W. Early somatosensory deprivation as an ontogenetic process in the abnormal development of the brain and behavior. In E. I. Goldsmith & J. Moor-Jankowski (Eds.), *Medical primatology*. Basel: S. Karger, 1971.

Resko, J. A. Androgen secretion by the fetal and neonatal rhesus monkey. *Endocrinology*, 1970, *87*, 680–687.

Resko, J. A., Ploem, J. G., & Stradelman, E. L. Estrogens in fetal and maternal plasma of the rhesus monkey. *Endocrinology*, 1975, *97*, 425–430.

Sackett, G. P. Effects of rearing conditions upon the behavior of rhesus monkeys. *Child Development*, 1965, *36*, 855–868.

Sackett, G. P. Isolation rearing in monkeys: Diffuse and specific effects on later behavior. In R. Chauvin (Ed.), *Animal models of human behavior*. Paris: Colloques Internationaux du C.N.R.S., 1972.

Sackett, G. P. Receiving severe aggression correlates with fetal gender in pregnant pigtail monkeys. *Developmental Psychobiology*, 1981, *14*, 267–272.

Sackett, G. P., Holm, R. A., & Landesman-Dwyer, S. Vulnerability for abnormal development: Pregnancy outcomes and sex differences in macaque monkeys. In N. Ellis (Ed.), *Aberrant development in infancy*. Hillsdale, N.J.: Lawrence Erlbaum, 1975.

Sackett, G. P., Holm, R. A., & Ruppenthal, G. C. Social isolation rearing: Species differences in behavior of macaque monkeys. *Developmental Psychology*, 1976, *12*, 283–288.

Sackett, G. P., Ruppenthal, G. C., Fahrenbruch, C., Holm, R. A., & Greenough, W. T. Genotype determines social isolation rearing effects in monkeys. *Developmental Psychology*, 1981, *17*, 313–318.

Sameroff, A. J. Organization and stability of newborn behavior: A commentary on the Brazelton Neonatal Behavior Assessment Scale. *Child Development Monographs*, 1978, Number 177.

Streissguth, A. P., Landesman-Dwyer, S., Martin, J., & Smith, D. W. Teratogenic effects of alcohol in humans and laboratory animals. *Science*, 1980, *209*, 353–361.

Suomi, S. J., & Harlow, H. F. Social rehabilitation of isolate-reared monkeys. *Developmental Psychology*, 1972, *6*, 487–496.

Spitz, R. Hospitalism: An inquiry into the genesis of psychiatric conditions in early childhood. *Psychoanalytic Study of the Child*, 1945, *1*, 53–74.

CHAPTER 2

Infant Monkeys' Achievement of Temporal Coherence with Their Social Group

Clare F. Haynes, Ted D. Wade, and Thomas Z. Cassel

INTRODUCTION

The Research Problem

For a socially living animal, survival requires that its actions be appropriately coordinated in both space and time with the actions of other group members. In general, the achievement of an adaptive harmony of action among members of social groups is required. The achievement of a harmony of action would presumably require the operation of psychobiological mechanisms on a variety of levels. These mechanisms give rise to the behavioral coordination characteristic of dyadic, triadic, and other subgroup relations. The coherent coordination of these social units constitutes the complex unity of the overall social group. It is to this multiform and yet unified life space that the socially living animal must adapt.

Recent research on biological rhythms has sensitized us to the salience of the rhythmical structure of any biological system. Indeed, the social group itself may be conceptualized as a biological system which exhibits a rhythmical structure. The activity rhythms of members of the social group become

Clare F. Haynes ● C. Henry Kempe Center for the Treatment and Prevention of Child Abuse and Neglect, 1205 Oneida Street, Denver, Colorado 80220.   **Ted D. Wade** ● University of Colorado Health Sciences Center, Central Laboratory, 4200 E. Ninth Avenue, Denver, Colorado 80262.   **Thomas Z. Cassel** ● Plymouth Center for Human Development, Northville, Michigan 48167. This research was supported by NIMH Post-doctoral Fellowship Grant MH–15442 and an award from the Developmental Psychobiology Research Group Endowment Fund provided by the Grant Foundation to the first author, and USPHS Grant MH–19514 to M. Reite.

coordinated in time. This coordination is necessary for the possibility of an adaptive harmony of action. Just as members of the social group are found to be distributed in space in an organized and nonrandom fashion relative to one another, so are their actions distributed in time in relation to each other. Temporal coherence refers to the pattern of these temporally organized relations: synchronization of actions and various forms of sequential coordinations would be involved.

Three questions arise from this perspective. Is there evidence for the presence of temporally coordinated activity patterns among members of social groups? If so, when do immature young come to achieve temporal coherence with their group? And by what mechanisms is this temporal coherence achieved?

Shared circadian activity rhythms constitute one form of temporally coordinated activity patterns. Various species of monkeys and apes display regular daily activity patterns (Altman & Altman, 1970; Bernstein, 1970, 1972, 1975, 1976; Chivers, 1969; Clutton-Brock, 1974; Harcourt, 1978; Kummer, 1971; Neville, 1968; Richard, 1970; Rosenblum, Kaufman, & Stynes, 1969). These patterns show some commonality across species, but there are also variations produced by specific ecological and social conditions. The presence of an habitual daily activity pattern for a social group suggests the presence of temporally coordinated activity rhythms among individual members (see Harcourt, 1978).

The survival value of coherence in activity (e.g., dispersing, converging, resting, and mating in coherent coordination) for protection from predators, for efficient foraging, and for effective distribution of functions seems self-evident (Crook, 1970; Kummer, 1971). The rapidity with which such coherence is achieved and maintained among adult dyads provides further evidence of the pervasiveness of behavioral coherence. Adult monkeys who are strangers to each other rapidly synchronize their behaviors and come to share the same cyclical patterns of activity when caged together (Bowden, Kripke, & Wyborney, 1978; Delgado-Garcia, Grau, DeFeudis, del Pozo, Jimenez, & Delgado, 1976).

In contrast to the interest in temporal coordination of adult activities, relatively little attention has been given to the achievement of temporal coherence between the activity rhythms of young offspring and adults. Although there are scattered reports of a relation between activities of infant and adult members of feral monkey groups (Altman, 1959; Harcourt, 1978; Kummer, 1971; Richard, 1970), studies which focus on variations in the behaviors of immature members as a function of the predominant adult activities (e.g., resting, grooming, feeding, and traveling) are simply not available. Generally, one finds little explicit concern in this literature with the theoretical and research problems surrounding the achievement of temporal coordination and behavioral coherence. In addition, with the interesting exception of the synchronizing and coordinating effects of pheromones, one can find no explicit concern with mechanisms which might subserve the process of temporal adaptation.

One mechanism which may underly the process of coherent temporal adaptation has been the focus of Louis W. Sander's research on the human "infant–caregiver system" (see Chapter 11, this volume; Sander, 1975, 1977; Sander & Julia, 1966; Sander, Stechler, Burns, & Julia, 1970). Sander has proposed that the interactive events of caregiving function as *Zeitgebers* to entrain the semiautonomous physiological rhythms of the infant. Through this entrainment process the infant simultaneously achieves both temporal self-coherence (as indexed by the synchronization of physiological subsystems with the clear differentiation of physiological states) and temporal coherence with the social surround (as indexed by the synchronization of activity rhythms or states with those of the social group as in day–night differentiation) (Cassel & Sander, 1975). This analysis suggests that organismic and social coherence develop together. In the absence of appropriate couplings to the social surround, organismic coherence is necessarily compromised (e.g., Harlow, 1958; Harlow & Harlow, 1962; Spitz, 1945).

Entrainment is but one of a variety of mechanisms which would be required to explain the achievement of social and organismic coherence. All such mechanisms have in common the achievement of a coupling between the activities of one system and another. The term *coupling* is employed to refer to the set of all such mechanisms, including entrainment, pheromones, shared attention, and other as yet undetermined mechanisms.

A Primate Model

In order to begin to investigate the achievement of temporal coherence on the level of the social group, we have chosen to work with a primate system because (1) the primate social group represents a model system which is amenable to continuous observation under controlled conditions; and (2) because it is assumed that some of the mechanisms for the achievement of temporal coherence may be rather general and not specific to man. The search, then, is for cross-species mechanisms with respect to which we may then discern the species-specific modulations. In light of these considerations, the present research employs a primate system to investigate the achievement of temporal coherence between infants and their social group.

The Social Group as an Organized Population

This perspective requires a shift from an exclusive concentration on the state of individuals or pairs of individuals to a concern with the state of the population of individuals (Cassel, 1980). This population, whether it be subgroups or the overall group, is viewed as a new level of organization with mechanisms and functions not reducible to the level of individuals.

This shift is formally analogous to recent trends in both neurophysiology and neuroendocrinology. For example, Erickson (1968, 1974) has argued that our understanding of many aspects of neural organization will benefit from a consideration of the patterns of activity across a population of neurons, in addition to an analysis of the activity of individual neurons. Erickson's *across-fiber pattern* theory offers a population approach to the problem of sensory encoding that is an alternative to the traditional single-unit approaches. Further, it is suggested (Cassel & Erickson, 1974; Erickson, 1978) that the population approach will be found to be of value in the analysis of more complex processes, such as memory and sensorimotor integration.

In neuroendocrinology, Mason (1968; Mason, Maher, Hartley, Mougey, Perlow, & Jones, 1976) has suggested the critical importance of looking at the *overall balance* of hormones in addition to focusing on specific, individual hormones. In both of these approaches, the state of the active population, given by the pattern of states of its members, is taken as a new level of analysis.

In the present research, the analysis is extended to the level of the social group with the question being the degree to which the state of the adult population regulates the behavioral states of infant members in a group of pigtail monkeys. To answer this question, it is first necessary to give an empirical specification of the concept of 'group state.' Here group state is defined as the state of the adult population given by the pattern of the behaviors of its members during a particular time period. Second, it is necessary to map out the relation between infant state and group state. This mapping requires the organization of infant behaviors into major categories which adequately characterize the infant's relations to the social and ecological environments. The observation of changes in any of these categories contingent on changes in adult group state would indicate the influence of group state on infant state.

METHOD

The Group and Its Environment

For this study conducted at the University of Colorado Primate Center, one harem group of 14 pigtail macaque monkeys was used. The monkeys were housed in an indoor pen which had glazed cinder block walls, a wire mesh ceiling, and bars and shelves around several walls. The group contained one adult male, seven adult females, and six infants. Three of the infants were less than a month old and three were just over a year old. The day started for the group at 07:00 hr with lights on and ended at 20:00 hr with lights out. Monkey chow and fruit were scattered over the pen floor at approximately 07:30 hr.

Observational Protocol

The group was observed every 20 min across the day during a 10 hr period. Observations commenced at 07:00 hr and ended at 17:00 hr on nine days, and commenced at 09:00 hr and ended at 19:00 hr on nine alternate days. Each individual was observed in a predetermined random order for three sequential samplings beginning at the onset of each 20-min interval. Hence, there were 31 observation sessions and 93 samplings of each member's behavior each day for a total of 18 days. The behaviors were categorized according to the taxonomy developed by Kaufman and Rosenblum (1966) for laboratory pigtail monkeys.

Scoring of Adult Behaviors and Group State

The eight adults were scored on six mutually exclusive behavioral categories. The categories were (a) resting, (b) chewing or eating, (c) foraging or drinking, (d) auto- or social grooming, (e) locomotion, and (f) other activities, primarily specific actions including stereotypic behaviors, sexual behaviors, and agonistic behaviors.

For each observation sample, an individual's behavior was scored under one of the six categories. Each such categorical score was given one point. Since the adults had their behaviors sampled three times during an observation session, each adult contributed three points to a cumulative group score. Each adult's three points could be distributed under one, two, or three behavioral categories. Since there were eight adults, the cumulative group score for an observation session would always total 24 points. For example, if all eight adults were engaged in behaviors within the same category across the three samples then one category would be scored with 24 points and the five others with 0 points.

The state of the adult population of the group for each observation session was derived from the pattern of category scores as follows. The grand mean for each category across all sessions was determined and considered to constitute a criterion level. Following this determination, the group score for each session for each of the six categories was examined to determine whether it was above or below its grand mean or criterion level. In effect, each session was classified on six nominal dimensions representing greater- or lesser-than-average scores on the six categories. Hence, each session displayed a particular criterion pattern. For example, one criterion pattern would consist of the "resting" category exceeding its criterion level with the other five categories below their criterion levels. A graphic representation of this criterion pattern would be 'R-c-f-g-l-o'—with *capital* letters representing categories which exceed criterion and *lower-case* letters categories which are below their criterion score.

Over all the observation sessions, there were 19 criterion patterns. These criterion patterns were clustered into 5 adult group states by combining those patterns which had similar transition probabilities (i.e., patterns which preceded or followed other patterns in similar ways) and which also occurred with the same relative frequency. The 5 adult group states included: (1) REST, sessions which had a criterion pattern in which only the category resting reached criterion; (2) GROOM, sessions which had criterion patterns of only the category grooming reaching criterion, or both grooming and resting categories reaching their criterion levels; (3) INGEST, sessions which had the criterion patterns of only the category chewing/eating reaching criterion, or both the categories chewing/eating and drinking/foraging reaching their criterion levels; (4) FORAGE, sessions which had the criterion patterns of only drinking/foraging reaching criterion, or both drinking/foraging and resting reaching their criterion levels; and (5) OTHER, sessions which had any other combinations of criterion patterns.

Scoring of Infant Behaviors and Infant Scales

All behaviors coded for infants were grouped into four major scales: (1) ACTIVITY, (2) PROXIMITY TO MOTHER, (3) SOCIAL ENGAGEMENT, and (4) FORAGING. Each scale represented a primary theme of infant behavior and together they described the relation of infants to their social and ecological environments.

For each observation session each infant's behavior was scored three times for each scale. Hence, each infant contributed three behaviors to each scale score each session. These behaviors were weighted and summed to produce a total score for the infant. As will be seen, the scales shared some of their component behaviors and so were necessarily correlated. Nevertheless this procedure seemed to be appropriate for our purpose of investigating the relationship between adult group state and infant state as indexed by changes in various aspects of infant behavior.

The behaviors comprising each scale were treated as points along a continuum by a numerical weighting scheme. For example, the ACTIVITY scale included all activities from resting to play. Each activity was weighted in terms of presumed activation level. The weighted activities for this scale included (a) resting or no observable activation = 0; (b) grooming of self or other = 1; (c) chewing or eating without other activation = 1; (d) passive forage, that is, sifting through the bedding material while in a sitting posture = 2; (e) manipulation of objects while in a sitting posture = 2; (f) drinking which involved movement to the site = 4; (g) active forage, that is, sifting through the bedding material with locomotion = 4; (h) locomotion about the pen = 6; and (i) play, including running, swinging, chasing, and rough and tumble = 8. Since each infant was scored on one activity at each of the three samplings during an observation session, the range of scores on this scale for a session for each infant was 0 to 24. For example, if an infant were observed to be resting at each sampling, his activity score would be 0; or if he were playing at each sampling, his score would be 24. Depending on the combination of component behaviors observed the score could fall anywhere in between these extremes.

Weights for the PROXIMITY scale reflect varying levels of contact with the mother, ranging from active contact of the infant with the mother's ventrum to a distance from the mother beyond arms reach. The component weighted behaviors for this scale included (a) cradled or enclosed at the mother's ventrum = 4; (b) passive support at the mother's ventrum or dorsal carriage = 3; (c) touching or in proximity (within arms reach) = 2; and (d) apart from mother (out of arms reach) = 0. The score range for each session on this scale for an infant was 0 to 12.

Weights for the SOCIAL ENGAGEMENT scale indicate different levels of engagement with other group members, ranging from no contact to active participation in grooming or play. The component weighted behaviors included (a) no social engagement = 0; (b) passive contact with other group members = 1; and (c) social grooming or social play = 2. An infant's score for a session ranged from 0 to 6. Contact or interactions with an infant's own mother were not included in this scale.

Weights for the FORAGING scale expressed the presence or absence, as well as the types, of food-related behaviors. The component weighted behaviors were (a) no food-related activity = 0; (b) chewing or eating = 1; (c) passive foraging = 2; (d) drinking or active foraging = 3. The scale range was 0 to 9.

RESULTS

Adult Group States

REST group states accounted for 37% of the sessions; OTHER states, for 18%; FORAGE states, for 17%; INGEST states, for 15%; and GROOM states, for 13%. Of the sessions which were lumped into the OTHER state, 43% passed criterion for such behavior as locomotion, while 19% did not exceed the criterion for any behavior.

Group state was contingent on time of day and on the preceding state. Chi-square tests for the contingency tables were significant at the .0001 level. To measure the strength of these contingencies, the asymmetric uncertainty coefficient (Nie, Hull, Jenkins, Steinbrenner, & Bent, 1975) was used. This measure gives the proportionate reduction in uncertainty about the distribution of a dependent variable when its joint occurrence with another variable is taken into account. It can be thought of as a nonparametric measure of variance accounted for by the relationship between the variables. Knowing time of day reduced the uncertainty in adult group state by 14.4%, whereas knowledge of previous group state reduced the uncertainty in state by 10.5%.

The relation between time of day and group state is shown in Figure 1. Both INGEST and OTHER states were higher in early morning. However, unlike INGEST states, sessions labelled OTHER tended to increase again toward early evening although they did not reach their early morning level. REST states rose steadily from early morning, reaching a high plateau by early afternoon and maintaining that level until observations ended in the evening. GROOM and FORAGE states rose together during the morning to early afternoon, with GROOM states peaking in late morning to early afternoon, and FORAGE states somewhat later.

A similar graph (Figure 2) shows group state as a function of previous state. The most notable features are that REST and GROOM strongly predicted REST, while INGEST strongly predicted INGEST. GROOM and FORAGE were similar in their patterns of following other group states. The OTHER state was the least predictive of, or predicted by, different states.

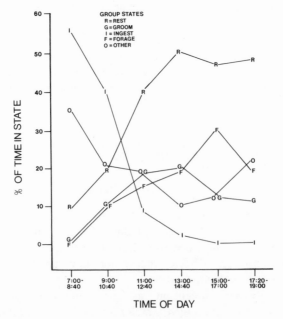

Figure 1. Percent of time the adult group was in state as a function of time of day.

Infant Behavior Scales

Data for each of the infant behavior scales was subjected to analysis of variance to determine both differences among infants and the effects of adult group state on infant behavior. Within-cell variances differed strikingly between infants less than a month old and infants more than a year old for three of the four infant scales. The first ANOVA was done for all infants on the scale, ACTIVITY. In that design, infant identity was nested under age and crossed with the factor, adult group state. Age had the largest effect, accounting for 15.7% of the variance. The state by age interaction was significant, although small.

Given the interaction, the heterogeneous variances, and the tendency of the age effect to overwhelm the other effects in magnitude, separate ANOVAs were done on each age group ($n = 3$) for each infant scale. The regression approach, in which each effect is adjusted for all other effects, was used (Nie *et al.*, 1975).

The main effect of infant identity was not significant (.01 level) for any infant variables in the young infant analysis. For older infants, the identity main effect was significant for activity, mother proximity, and foraging. Main effects of adult state were significant in all analyses except the one for forage in young infants.

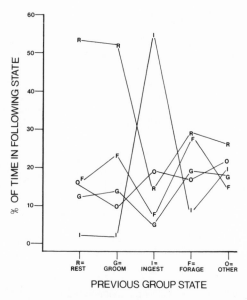

Figure 2. Percent of time the adult group was in each state as a function of the preceding state.

It was clear that group state tended to account for much more variance than infant identity. State accounted for 2.5 to 9 times more variance in all analyses except one—mother proximity in older infants—where the ratio was 0.9 to 1. The percentage of variance accounted for by state ranged from 3.7 to 6.9 for older infants and 1.1 to 5.3 for younger infants.

The interaction between state and identity was significant in only one analysis, mother proximity in older infants, and in that case the main effects each accounted for about 7% of infant state variance while the interaction accounted for 1.1%. Thus the effects of group state on infant behavior could be described as generally uniform across individuals in a given age group.

The effects of adult group state on the infant behavior scales are shown in Figure 3A for older infants and Figure 3B for younger infants. The ordinate in each figure gives the magnitude of the scale values as deviations from the overall scale mean in standard error units. In this way we facilitate comparison between and within the infant scales. Note particularly that a distance of 2.5 to 3 standard error units within a column is an approximate indication of a significant difference.

For older infants, scores on the activity and social engagement scales were elevated during adult group states FORAGE and OTHER. Their activity

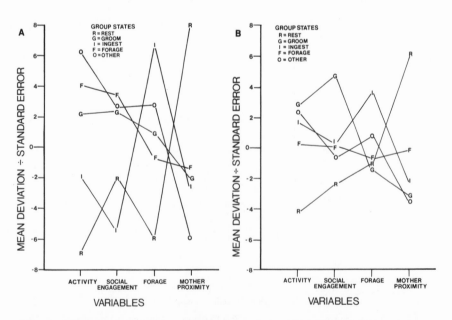

Figure 3. Mean score of infants on 4 behavior scales as a function of adult group state. (A) 3 older infants, (B) 3 younger infants. Means are expressed as deviations from the grand-mean based on all group states.

scores were most depressed during group REST, while their social engagement scores were most depressed during group state INGEST. Older infant foraging scores were higher when the adult group was ingesting, but not when the group was foraging. Group REST depressed older infant foraging. Proximity to mother scores were elevated during group REST and lowered during group state OTHER.

For younger infants, the differences in scale values as a function of group state were not as pronounced as they were for the older infants. However, the pattern of differences in scale scores for young infants is similar to that found for older infants with one major exception. Young infants had higher activity and social engagement scores during adult GROOM states, whereas mother proximity scores were lower during GROOM states. As was found for older infants, activity was depressed during group REST, although mother proximity was elevated. Foraging was higher during adult INGEST states and lower during FORAGE states.

DISCUSSION

Temporal Coordination of Adult Behaviors

Behaviors of adult members of the group were temporally coordinated within an observation session. This temporal coordination was indicated by the limited number of actual types of criterion patterns out of all the possible patterns had the behaviors of individuals been totally independent and random. Given the behaviors of some members the behaviors of other members were highly predictable.

The validity of clustering the 19 criterion patterns into five adult group states is indicated by the predictability of the temporal patterning of these states. Group state was not random, but was constrained by both the time of day and the prior group state. For example, for a late morning observation session in which the prior group state was INGEST, it was highly predictable that a combination of behaviors would be seen which would give rise to the group state label REST. Or, if the prior state were GROOM and the observation just after midday, then a REST state would be observed to follow with high probability (see Figure 1 and 2).

Group State Patterns

Although the daily pattern of activities seen in this group represents a specific adaptation to their ecological conditions, there were gross similarities to patterns observed in feral monkey groups. This suggests the influence of the phylogenetic as well as ontogenetic factors on the temporal organization of group activity rhythms.

In tropical environments groups of monkeys and apes spend a major portion of the morning and afternoon feeding and travelling. They rest at midday and engage in social grooming at this time. Social grooming also occurs in early morning prior to moving off for the day and again in the evening at the sleeping site (Altmann & Altmann, 1970; Chivers, 1969; Harcourt, 1978; Kummer, 1971).

In the present group, the major portion of the day is spent resting. This is not surprising in the light of the ecological constraints, especially in relation to the limited physical space and the absence of a need to search for food over a wide area. REST states were the most frequent types of sessions by late morning (11:00 hr), reaching a peak in early afternoon (13:00 to 14:40 hr) and remaining at that high plateau across the remainder of the observed sessions. However, the peak around midday in REST states along with the peak in GROOM states (11:00 to 14:40 hr) during roughly the same temporal period is temporally aligned with the midday rest and grooming sessions observed in feral groups.

The grooming periods seen in feral groups at the ends of the days were not observed here. Note that Bernstein (1972) also reported the highest frequency of social grooming in the middle of the day for pigtail macaques in an outdoor compound. The relatively low frequency of GROOM periods and the low probability of GROOM states perpetuating themselves across sessions (see Figure 2) are contradictory to what one might expect given that group coherence is presumably a major function of social grooming (Crook, 1970; Defler, 1976; Mitchell & Brandt, 1972). As Crook (1970) has pointed out, social grooming may be more essential as a coherence maintaining mechanism in feral groups which are required to disperse widely in order to feed. In this instance, it may function to modulate state, to consolidate alliances, and to reduce agonistic encounters.

Even under these ecological conditions where food is made available at an early morning feeding and water is available *ad lib,* there is still a rough approximation of the feeding and travel patterns observed in feral groups. INGEST and OTHER states, which are analogous to feeding and travel periods for feral animals, were the most frequent types of sessions in early to midmorning (07:00 to 10:40 hr) sessions. The early morning feeding accounts for the high frequency of INGEST states; however, OTHER states also peaked at this time. It is important to remember that 43% of the sessions lumped into the OTHER state passed the criterion for locomotion.

An afternoon increase in activity level was also seen with a peak in FORAGE states about midafternoon, and a high frequency of both OTHER and FORAGE states in late afternoon to the end of observations in early evening (17:20 to 19:00 hrs). This increase in food-related and locomotion behaviors occurred in spite of the fact that foraging in the afternoon rarely, if ever, led to the location of food—most of which had been hoarded in cheek pouches and consumed by late morning. Were the monkeys persisting in a natural pattern of a morning and afternoon increase in activity, especially food-related activity? Bernstein (1967) in his studies of pigtail monkeys noted that animals in captivity tended to show the "natural response pattern to the extent possible" under the limitations imposed on their foraging, travel, and contact patterns by the conditions of the laboratory environment (p. 228).

Infant's Achievement of Temporal Coherence with Adult Group State

The behaviors of the immature members of this group were temporally coordinated with the activities of the adult members as indexed by the group state label. Infant behaviors did not necessarily mimic the adult behaviors which gave rise to the state label; however, there was a predictable relation between the state of the adult group at a given observation session and the kinds of behaviors in which infants engaged on the four scales of activity, mother proximity, social engagement, and foraging.

For both young and old infants, activity scores were significantly depressed during adult REST states. Inspection of the data indicated that infants did rest more often during adult REST periods than they did in other group states. However, even when active in these periods, they showed subdued activity, tending to engage in less vigorous kinds of activity behaviors, such as manipulation of objects while in a sitting posture (sit movement), sifting through the bedding material (passive forage), etc. Exercise play or rough-and-tumble or chase bouts of social play were not characteristic of infants during adult REST periods.

During adult INGEST states, older infants exhibited more food-related behaviors than in other states as indicated by their higher scores on the foraging scale. When the adults were foraging but not ingesting, as in FORAGE states, the infants did not show significantly higher foraging scores. Rather in these periods social engagement appeared to be facilitated. This is an effect exactly opposite to that found in INGEST states in which social engagement was most severely depressed.

The interactive events characteristic of these periods may be hypothesized to perform two functions. First, the group state dependent activities may function as group *Zeitgebers* to entrain the infants' rhythms of state change. In this sense, group state would function in tandem with maternal state, and the infant would be coupled to the social group as well as to the mother. Second, the interactive events characteristic of any period would function to constrain the types of behavior displayed by an infant in a given state. Behavioral constraints would be achieved through a variety of mechanism, including attentional control and agonistic encounters. For example, the focused activity characteristic of the group state INGEST may synchronously activate the infants, whereas the attentional focus of this state, combined with food-related agonistic encounters, would depress play activities and even passive encounters with feeding adults.

Older infants had significantly higher activity scores during OTHER adult group states, and significantly lower mother proximity scores during these periods—again providing evidence of shared activity rhythms with high activation in the adults associated with similar activation in the infants. This pattern was not observed in young infants, for whom GROOM periods appeared to facilitate a clustering of behaviors characterized by higher activity and higher social engagement scores along with lower mother proximity scores. It may be that GROOM states are especially conducive to young infant exploratory behaviors.

The different patterns of relations between adult group state and the four infant scales for the two age groups—infants less than a month old and infants just over a year old—suggest that for the young infant the initial temporal adaptation is strongly constrained by the infant's close ventral contact with the mother, and that by one year of age the infant develops an increasingly complex kind of temporal adaptation reflecting a different level of constraint on its behaviors. Both age groups manifested lower activity and higher mother proximity scores during adult REST states, as well as higher foraging scores in adult INGEST states. However, for younger infants, the higher foraging in adult INGEST states, as well as the peak in social engagement during adult GROOM states, may represent primarily the constraint imposed on their behavior by the spatial location and activity of the mother. Because of the availability of others for social engagement in GROOM states and of bedding materials for foraging in INGEST states, what appears on the surface to be a more differentiated synchronization of younger infant and adult behaviors may be attributable primarily to maternal entrainment and constraint.

One striking difference in the patterns observed for young and old infants was the older infants' clear differentiation of adult INGEST states from other active adult states, such as GROOM, FORAGE, and OTHER. At the same time, it is evident that, behaviorally, they do not distinguish among these three active adult states and tend to be more active themselves, both individually and socially, during these states. Simply put, these states of adult activation, in contrast to adult state INGEST, are times for high-energy activities and social engagement among the older infants.

Clearly, the older infants are becoming more differentiated as individuals, as indicated by the significant main effects for individual differences on the activity, mother proximity, and foraging scales, as they develop within the same social context. At the same time, as a group, they begin to show a more differentiated relation to adult group state.

Our eventual understanding of the achievement of individuation within the context of an overall adaptive harmony of action would seem to require an understanding of the differential regulative effects of the infant's coupling to mother, to subgroup, and to the total group. For this analysis it is necessary to investigate the variety of entrainment and constraint mechanisms, to experimentally manipulate these mechanisms, and to determine their various loci and their differential contributions. By means of this approach, we may begin to trace and to understand the infant's developmental pathway of separation, individuation, and ultimate integration as a mature member of a social group.

Research on Temporal Adaptation

One clear result of the present research has been the development of methods for characterizing an adult group state at various observation moments and for assessing changes in the infant members' activity level, social engagement, proximity to mother, and foraging behaviors. The present approach allowed the demonstration of a subtle, but nevertheless real, phenomenon of temporal coherence between activity rhythms of adult and infant members of a social group. This work may help us to appreciate more fully the highly ordered nature of the social group and its function as the active context in which development and an adaptive harmony of action are achieved.

Further research is required in order to document the presence of temporal synchronization of activities of immature and adult members in other social groups. In addition, the goal of understanding the mechanisms which operate to give rise to coherence requires that we continue to investigate the contributions of maternal and group entrainment as well as the relative efficacy of maternal and group constraints.

Dyads, Subgroups, and the Overall Social Group

When we look at the human neonate, we find him in a profoundly vulnerable state. His coherent adaptation to the uterine environment has been broken. He is disconnected from his formerly sustaining environment, and has just begun to achieve connections to his new, far more complex, and far less buffered social and ecological environments.

Recent research highlights the early couplings between caregiver and infant through which the initial states of organismic and social coherence are achieved (e.g., see Chapter 11, this volume; Brazelton, Koslowski, & Main, 1974; Condon, 1977; Fogel, 1977; Stern, 1974; Trevarthen, 1977). However, the achievement of adult social coherence and organizational complexity depends not only on the maternal couplings, but on the achievement of other dyadic couplings, and future couplings with subgroups and the overall social group. Mechanisms at a variety of levels may be required to explain the achievement of adaptive coherence which allows the adult to function in adaptive harmony with a complex social system. Research on temporal adaptation is believed to be a step toward discovery of these mechanisms and toward a more full understanding of how development proceeds.

ABSTRACT

A primate system is used to investigate the achievement of temporal coherence between infants and their social group. The measurement of the "state" of the adult population at various observation moments and the measurement of contingent changes in infant members activity level, social engagement, proximity to mother, and foraging behaviors demonstrate temporal coordination between the activities of the adult population and infant members in a pigtail monkey group. Possible mechanisms through which behaviors of infants come to be temporally coherent with the activity rhythms of adults are discussed. Further research on temporal adaptation may provide a more complete understanding of the transformation in organizational complexity and social coherence which occurs in development from infancy to adulthood in socially living animals.

Acknowledgments

We thank M. Haith, A. J. Stynes, L. W. Sander and M. Reite for their critical comments on this manuscript.

REFERENCES

Altmann, S. A. Field observations of a howling monkey society. *Journal of Mammalogy,* 1959, *40,* 317–330.

Altmann, S. A., & Altmann, J. *Baboon ecology: African field research.* Chicago: University of Chicago Press, 1970.

Bernstein, I. S. A Field study of the pigtailed monkey. *Primates,* 1967, *8,* 217–228.

Bernstein, I. S. Activity patterns in pigtail monkey groups. *Folia Primatologica,* 1970, *12,* 187–198.

Bernstein, I. S. Daily activity cycles and weather influences on a pigtail monkey group. *Folia Primatologica,* 1972, *18,* 390–415.

Berbstein, I. S. Activity patterns in a gelada monkey group. *Folia Primatologica,* 1975, *23,* 50–71.

Bernstein, I. S. Activity patterns in a sooty mangabey group. *Folia Primatologica,* 1976, *26,* 185–206.

Bowden, D. M., Kripke, D. F., & Wyborney, V. G. Ultradian rhythms in waking behavior of rhesus monkeys. *Physiology and Behavior,* 1978, *21,* 929–933.

Brazelton, T. B., Koslowski, B., & Main, M. The origins of reciprocity: The early mother-infant interaction. In M. Lewis & L. A. Rosemblum (Eds.) *The effect of the infant on its caregiver*. New York: Wiley, 1974.

Cassel, T. Z. *The Trajectory of coupled organisms: Reductionism vs. systems of constraint*. Paper presented at the Annual Meeting of the American Psychological Association, Montreal, September 1980.

Cassel, T. Z., & Erickson, R. P. *On the neural basis of memory: Implications from principles of sensory neural coding*. Unpublished manuscript, 1974.

Cassel, T. Z., & Sander, L. W. *Neonatal recognition processes and attachment: Effects of masking mother's face at 7 days*. Paper presented at the Society for Research in Child Development, Denver, March 1975.

Chivers, I. J. On the daily behaviour and spacing of howling monkey groups. *Folia Primatologica*, 1969, *10*, 48–102.

Clutton-Brock, T. H. Activity patterns of red colobus (*Colobus badius tephrosceles*). *Folia Primatologica*, 1974, *21*, 161–187.

Condon, W. S. A primary phase in the organization of infant responding. In H. R. Schaffer (Ed.), *Studies in mother-infant interaction*. London: Academic Press, 1977.

Crook, J. H. The socio-ecology of primates. In J. H. Crook (Ed.). *Social behavior in birds and mammals*. New York: Academic Press, 1970.

Defler, T. R. Allogrooming in two species of macaque (*Macaca nemestrina and Macaca Radiata*). Primates, 1978, *19*, 153–167.

Delgado-Garcia, J. M., Grau, P., DeFeudis, P., del Pozo, F., Jimenez, J. M. & Delgado, J. M. R. Ultradian rhythms in the mobility and behavior of rhesus monkeys. *Experimental Brain Research*, 1976, *25*, 79–91.

Erickson, R. P. Stimulus coding in topographic and non-topographic afferent modalities: On the significance of the activity of individual sensory neurons. *Psychological Review*, 1968, *75*, 447–465.

Erickson, R. P. Parallel "population" neural coding and feature extraction. In R. O. Schmitt & F. G. Worden (Eds.), *The neurosciences: Third study program*. Cambridge: The M.I.T. Press, 1974.

Erickson, R. P. Common properties of sensory systems. In R. B. Masterton (Ed.), *Handbook of behavioral neurobiology Vol. 1: Sensory Integration*. New York: Plenum Press, 1978.

Fogel, A. Temporal organization in mother-infant face-to-face interaction. In H. B. Schaffer (Ed.) *Studies in mother-infant interaction*. London: Academic Press, 1977.

Harcourt, A. H. Activity periods and patterns of social interaction: A neglected problem. *Behaviour*, 1978, *66*, 121–135.

Harlow, H. F. The nature of love. *American Psychologist*, 1958, *13*, 673–687.

Harlow, H. F., & Harlow, M. K. Social deprivation in monkeys. *Scientific American*, 1962, *207*, 136–146.

Kaufman, I. C., & Rosenblum, L. A. A behavioral taxonomy for *Macaca nesmestrina* and *Macaca radiata*: Based on longitudinal observation of family groups in the laboratory. *Primates*, 1966, *7*, 205–258.

Kummer, H. *Primate societies*. Chicago: Aldine, 1971.

Mason, J. W. "Over-all" hormonal balance as a key to endocrine organization. *Psychosomatic medicine*, 1968, *30*, 771–808.

Mason, J. W., Maher, J. T., Hartley, L. H., Mougey, E. H., Perlow, M. J. & Jones, L. G. Selectivity of corticosteroid and catecholoamine responses to various natural stimuli. In G. Serban (Ed.), *Psychopathology of human adaptation*. New York: Plenum Press, 1976.

Mitchell, G., & Brandt, E. M. Paternal behavior in primates. In F. E. Poirier (Ed.), *Primate socialization*. New York: Random House, 1972.

Neville, M. K. Ecology and activity of Himalayan Foothill rhesus monkeys (*Macaca Mulatta*). *Ecology*, 1968, *49*, 110–123.

Nie, H. H., Hull, C. H., Jenkins, J. G., Steinbrenner, K., & Bent, D. H. *SPSS: Statistical package for the social sciences* (2nd ed.). New York: McGraw-Hill, 1975.

Richard, A. A comparative study of the activity pattern and behavior of *Alouetta villosa* and *Ateles geoffroyi. Folia Primatologica*, 1970, *12*, 241–263.

Rosenblum, L. A., Kaufman, I. C., & Stynes, A. J. Interspecfic variations in the effects of hunger on diurnally varying behavior elements in macaques. *Brain Behavioral Evolution*, 1969, *2*, 119–131.

Sander, L. W. Infant and caretaking environment: Investigation and conceptualization of adaptive behavior in a system of increasing complexity. In E. J. Anthony (Ed.), *Explorations in child psychiatry.* New York: Plenum Press, 1975.

Sander, L. W. The regulation of exchange in the infant-caretaker system and some aspects of the context-content relationship. In M. Lewis & L. A. Rosenblum (Eds.), *Interaction, conversation, and the development of language.* New York: Wiley, 1977.

Sander, L. W., & Julia, H. L. Continuous interactional monitoring in the neonate. *Psychosomatic medicine*, 1966, *28*, 822–835.

Sander, L. W., Stechler, G., Burns, P., & Julia, H. Early mother-infant interaction and 24-hour patterns of activity and sleep. *Journal of the Academy of Child Psychiatry*, 1970, *9*, 103–123.

Spitz, R. A. Hospitalism. An inquiry into the genesis of psychiatric condition in early childhood. In B. S. Eissler *et al.* (Eds.) *The psychoanalytic study of the child,* (Vol. 1). New York: International Universities Press, 1945.

Stern, D. N. Mother and infant at play: The dyadic interaction involving facial, vocal and gaze behaviors. In M. Lewis & L. A. Rosemblum (Eds.) *The effect of the infant on its caregiver.* New York: Wiley, 1974.

Trevarthen, C. Descriptive analyses of infant communicative behaviour. In H. R. Schaffer (Ed.), *Studies in mother-infant interaction.* London: Academic Press, 1977.

CHAPTER 3

Animal Models of Human Behavior

THEIR APPLICATION TO THE STUDY OF ATTACHMENT

Linda S. Crnic, Martin L. Reite, and David W. Shucard

ARE ANIMAL MODELS OF ATTACHMENT NECESSARY?

Other contributors to this volume have described intriguing evidence about possible biological substrata for attachment and affiliative behaviors. Such evidence suffers from being of necessity correlational. A statement of John Dobbing's (1968) in reference to research on the behavioral effects of malnutrition is applicable here:

> Even the most sophisticated multifactorial analysis is no substitute for the experimental testing of hypotheses, and this can only be done with animals. It should be self-evident that experimental animal and human field studies must interdigitate if any conclusions are to be reached before the end of the present interglacial period. (p. 294)

How can animal model systems be used to study attachment? We present a brief general discussion of the use of animals to model human behavior and illustrate our conclusions with examples from the study of attachment behavior.

Linda S. Crnic ● Department of Pediatrics and Psychiatry, University of Colorado School of Medicine. 4200 E. Ninth Avenue, Denver, Colorado 80262.   **Martin L. Reite** ● Department of Psychiatry, University of Colorado School of Medicine, 4200 E. Ninth Avenue, Denver, Colorado 80262.   **David W. Shucard** ● Brain Sciences Laboratories, National Jewish Hospital and Research Center, Denver, Colorado 80262.
Preparation of this chapter was supported in part by NIH grant HD–08315 to Linda Crnic, NIMH grants MH–46335 and MH–19514 to Martin Reite, and NIH grant NS–15483 to David Shucard.

What Are Animal Models? A Paradox

Models may be used at many levels in research: social interactions on a children's playground may be used to model more complex social structures; computer simulations to model psychotherapy and human social processes; abnormal animal behavior to model human psychopathology; tissue culture to model neural development. Whatever the level of complexity at which a model is used, certain requirements are the same. The model must have significant advantages of control, simplicity, ease of use, cost, or rapidity with which answers are obtained over direct study of the process modeled. If our interest is in mechanisms of control, the models must, in addition, be similar enough to the phenomenon being modeled to allow extrapolation of results to that phenomenon. Thus the value of a model lies in *both* its similarity to and difference from the process modeled. This paradox is illustrated by an example from the use of tissue culture to study neural development.

Bunge, Johnson, and Ross (1978) have found that after 8 weeks in culture, postmitotic neurons from autonomic ganglia of the perinatal rat can shift from adrenergic to cholinergic function. As discussed in Chapter 6, in this volume, this discovery has revolutionized our ideas about neuronal plasticity. A discovery of this nature was possible because of the *difference* in complexity between the system modeled (intact brain tissue) and the model (tissue culture), and it is valuable because of evidence that neural tissues in culture display processes *similar* to developmental processes in the intact organism (Arnold & Vernadakis, 1979). The essential attribute of a model lies in this balance between similarity and dissimilarity to the process being modeled.

Animal Models versus Animal Systems

It is important to distinguish research using animals to model human behavior from research using animals to study animal behavior. In animal models of human behavioral processes, the primary goal is to produce data which can be generalized to humans or hypotheses which can be tested on humans. In the study of animal behavior *per se*, direct generalizability to humans is not a primary goal. Instead, the goal is to understand the function of a system in the animal. In this approach, one might study mother–infant interaction in the rat in order to learn about the hormonal, neurochemical, or neurophysiological control of that interaction. The work of Leon and Moltz (e.g., Leon, 1974; Leon & Moltz, 1971) on the maternal pheromone in rats is an example of such research. A modeling approach, on the other hand, might involve study of the separation response of mother and infant macaques in order to devise hypotheses about the biological substrate of mother–infant interaction in humans.

The distinction between these two types of research, animal models versus animal behavior, is important because the use of models requires that the researcher have some evidence that there is homology between the animal and human processes. Basic research on animal behavior need not, and seldom does, meet this requirement. Yet, because we use the same names for behaviors and for experimental manipulations across species, research on animal processes is often mistaken for models. Pressure from funding agencies for relevance of basic research to humans contributes to the temptation to blur the distinction between these two types of research. This confusion is dangerous because it can lead to improper design of research when the rules for models are ignored and to improper generalization of findings to humans from animal research.

Homology versus Nonhomology

The term *homology* (Bock, 1969; Campbell & Hodos, 1970) implies that structures (such as anatomical entities or behavioral systems) in different species share both a common function and common underlying mechanisms because of their having evolved from a common phylogenetic ancestor. If our interest is in understanding the neurobiological mechanisms underlying a behavioral system in man, we must study an animal model with a homologous behavioral system.

The term *analogy* (Bock, 1969, prefers nonhomology) by comparison, is often used to describe a structure or behavioral system that is similar in appearance and serves a similar function in different species but cannot be traced to a common evolutionary ancestor. The fact of its having evolved independently in two different evolutionary lines may tell us about its functional significance and evolutionary survival value. But if our interest is in the neurobiological mechanisms underlying the behavior, then using a species in which the behavioral system in question is analogous (or nonhomologous) to that in the species of interest, would be a poor choice.

An example will illustrate these distinctions. As stated previously (Reite, 1977), both birds and mammals exhibit strong mother–offspring bonds. Yet birds and mammals likely shared an early reptile as a common ancestor, and from what we know of reptiles, it is unlikely that the common ancestor exhibited mother–offspring bonds. Such behavioral systems very likely evolved independently in the avian and mammalian lineages, an example of convergent evolution as described by Campbell and Hodos (1970) and based on Simpson (1961). These observations suggest that mother–offspring bonding behavior has survival value from an evolutionary standpoint, and the study of such analogous behaviors in birds and mammals may tell us how such behavioral systems evolve to fit existent ecological niches. But if our interest is in the neurobiological mechanisms underlying such behavior in man, the bird would be a poor choice as an animal model.

Advantages of Animal Models

Animal models are used because of their advantages over direct research with humans. First, some manipulations cannot ethically be performed on humans. Second, experiments with animals can be more rigorously controlled than human studies. This greatly enhances the researchers' ability to determine cause and effect relationships. Control may be exercised over the application of treatments, living conditions, early experiences, and genetic backgrounds. For example, the availability of animals of uniform genetic constitution with known single gene differences is invaluable in the study of the genetic bases of behavior (e.g., Oliverio, Eleftheriou, & Bailey, 1973). Third, the shorter life span of animals greatly facilitates developmental and especially longitudinal research, as well as research on aging. Fourth, some phenomena are simpler in animals than in man. Behaviors which share significant common neurobiological mechanisms in animals and man may be so changed and distorted in man by uniquely human social and cognitive influences that the contribution of the underlying common mechanisms may be extraordinarily difficult to dissect out. In such cases, data from appropriate animal models may be used to develop specific hypotheses that can be tested in man.

Fifth, as Hinde (1976) has noted, we may bring fewer expectations about behavior to animal research and thus rid ourselves of some bias. Unexpected similarities and differences between animal and human behavior may point to previously unrecognized phenomena in humans and lead to the development of new theoretical concepts and perspectives about human behavior. Finally, in devising new ways to observe and study animal physiology and behavior, we may develop methodologies which are useful in the study of man. An excellent example of the latter is the application of methodology developed for the study of primate social interaction to the study of occupants of group homes for the retarded (Sackett & Landesman-Dwyer, 1977).

Risks of Animal Models

The advantages of using animal models are not without cost, for, to some extent, the proper study of mankind is man. We risk the possibility that an animal model may differ too much from the human phenomenon, making extrapolation invalid. This risk must be accepted because if we knew enough about the human phenomenon and the animal model to know whether the model was perfect, we would likely know all we need to know about the phenomenon, and thus not need the animal model. In addition, as noted on

p. 32, some risk that a model is too distant from the process modeled is built into our definition of a model. We are willing to accept these risks in part because of past success with models. For example, although a good animal model of human asthma has been sought for years without finding one that exactly mimics this heterogeneous human condition, the use of animal models has resulted in progress in understanding the etiology and treatment of this disease.

Minimizing the Risks

Before models can be attempted, the phenomenon of interest must be defined in man. Thus at the very least, observational research on man must precede an attempt to develop an animal model. One of the reasons that there is skepticism about the use of animal models of human behavior, and of psychiatric disease in particular, is that the model can be no better than the definition of the phenomenon in humans. If the human phenomenon is characterized only by its symptoms, the model can only be a superficial one based upon similarity of symptoms between animals and man.

After the human phenomenon is defined, animal species which exhibit similar behaviors must be identified. One's theoretical viewpoint is important in this regard. If one believes that human behavioral aberration (psychopathology) is a function of postulated psychic structures unique to man, then by definition, animals, which (may) lack these elaborate psychic structures, cannot serve as useful models. An example of this viewpoint was developed by Kubie (1939). On the other hand, in light of recent evidence implicating biological and genetic mechanisms in human behavior (e.g., Fieve, Rosenthal, & Brill, 1975; Reite, 1981) it is likely that animal model systems may be developed which have great relevance to human behavior.

When choosing an animal model, similarity of name or appearance of the behavior must not be mistaken for similarity of underlying mechanisms. In order to decide whether the similar behavior is truly homologous to human behavior, it is necessary to analyze the presumed level of function at which the behavior is controlled, and the evolution of the behavior in both animals and humans. Thus a behavior which depends exclusively upon complex higher cognitive functions or uniquely human social–cultural structures may not be able to be modeled in animals. On the other extreme, if the presumed level of neurobiological control is cellular, even a tissue culture model may be appropriate.

Animal Models Are Part of an Interactive System of Research

It is obvious from the preceding discussion that the use of animal models must be part of a system which includes both human research and basic animal research. Research with humans is necessary to define the phenomenon in humans and to develop hypotheses about the probable level of function at which the phenomenon occurs. It is then necessary to call upon extensive knowledge of animal behavior in order to choose an appropriate model. It follows that it is impossible to know in advance the potential contribution of basic research on animal behavior to human questions.

The relationships among animal models of human processes, human research, and animal behavior research must be interactive. Human research and animal research must precede attempts to develop models. The results of research with animal models may lead to more productive research in humans, or may result in hypotheses which must be answered with further basic animal research. These in turn may lead to a refined model.

AN EXAMPLE OF THE USE OF ANIMAL MODELS: ATTACHMENT

Definition

The search for an animal model of human mother–infant attachment must begin with attempts to define attachment, and to analyze the evolutionary history of such behavior. The term *attachment* was first used in a developmental context by John Bowlby (1958), who felt it better represented his concept of a child's bonds to its mother than the term *dependency*, with its often negative clinical overtones. Since that time, its use has expanded considerably and become idiosyncratic. Sroufe and Waters (1977) have attempted to clarify its meaning. Although we will not attempt to review an extraordinarily complex field which ranges from imprinting in birds to human mother–infant attachment, we will examine several positions on the concept of mother–infant attachment in mammals.

At one end of the spectrum is Cairns (1979) who states:

> The early social development of most mammals is marked by the development of a strong emotional bond between the infant and its mother, and sometimes others. . . . The tendency to approach a specific "other" is, for altricial mammals, necessary for survival. The "attachment" arises out of the specific mutual dependence of behaviors, particularly those that are dominant in the response repertoire of the infant . . . and the mother. No single activity—such as feeding or giving tactile comfort—is necessary for the attachment to develop, even though these activities facilitate the development of specific preferences. (p. 58)

Another viewpoint is that of Rajecki, Lamb, and Obmascher (1978) who state:

> Attachment presumes at least three criteria: (1) the ability of the young to discriminate and respond differentially to the object of attachment; (2) preference for the attachment figure and differential proximity–seeking; and (3) response to removal of the attachment object, which is distinct from responses to the reduction of social stimuli per se. (p. 447)

Examining data from several animal species, including squirrel monkeys, rats, dogs, and birds, they concluded that there was no evidence that the nonprimate species exhibited attachment behavior.

Identification of Appropriate Species

Let us briefly examine some of the data for various species. Studies of mother–infant interaction have been performed in a wide variety of mammals: rodents, sheep, goats, dogs, human, and nonhuman primates. These studies are often very difficult to compare with one another because both the experimental paradigms and conceptual frameworks have varied greatly. However, sufficient evidence exists to guide us to an appropriate model of human attachment.

Rat pups show a behavioral and physiological response to removal of the mother which includes a drop in temperature, cardiac and respiratory depression, and behavioral arousal (Hofer, 1970, 1975). Hofer (1975) has shown that if these changes are prevented by providing a nonlactating female, the pups do not show a response to the removal of the mother. Thus the response is female- but not mother-specific. Likewise when we examine maternal response to pups, we see that although there is evidence for the mother's differential treatment of her own versus strange pups (Rosenblatt & Lehrman, 1963), and of male and female pups (Moore & Morelli, 1979), there is no evidence that individual recognition and preferences play a role in the mother's behavior. In addition, the adrenocortical response of a rat mother to removal of her pups is no greater than the response that would be expected on the basis of the handling involved in removing the pups (Smotherman, Wiener, Mendoza, & Levine, 1977). We do not know what this means for other physiological measures, but it suggests that the response is not specific to separation from the pups. Thus neither pups nor mothers display behavior which fits the definition of attachment of Rajecki et al..

Dogs of several breeds will exhibit separation distress upon removal from the mother, but the response does not appear to be specific to the mother, for the puppies' distress vocalizations will be equally quieted if a strange female of the same breed is brought back as if the mother is brought back (Elliot & Scott, 1961).

In goats, mothers can tell their own offspring from strange offspring, but among their own, they apparently cannot distinguish one individual from another (Klopfer, Adams, & Klopfer, 1964).

Consequently, there is little evidence that these nonprimate mammals exhibit attachment according to the criteria of Rajecki et al., (1978). In primates, on the other hand, infant monkeys of several species tested, including new world (Squirrel) monkeys, can recognize their specific mother (Harlow & Harlow, 1965; Rosemblum & Cooper, 1968). In social groups, monkey infants spend most of their time with their mothers; even at five months of age pig-tailed monkey infants spend more than 50% of their time in actual physical contact with their mothers (Reite & Short, 1980). Infant pigtailed monkeys show both behavioral depression and physiological disorganization when separated from their mothers (Reite & Short, 1978; Reite, Short, Kaufman, Stynes, & Pauley, 1978; Reite, Short, Seiler, & Pauley, 1981), even if they have been adopted by another female (Reite, Seiler, & Short, 1978). Primate behavior thus fulfills the previously mentioned criteria of attachment of Rajecki *et al.*, (1978) while nonprimate behavior does not. There may be fundamental differences in the mechanisms which underlie mother–infant attachment behavior in primate and nonprimate mammals, and scientists interested in developing animal models of human attachment should keep such a possibility in mind until definitive data become available.

Identification of Possible Neurobiological Mechanisms

We do not know very much about the neurobiological mechanisms which underlie mother–infant attachment, or, more generally, social bonding. However, it is biologically uneconomical to postulate that a new behavioral system, with unique neurobiological mechanisms, evolved *de novo* in primates. A simpler explanation is more conservative. MacLean (1973) has postulated that the primate brain has evolved through the addition of new layers to phylogenetically older layers, with the functions of the older segments of the brain preserved but modulated and controlled by the newer structures. Such a theory of brain evolution would lead us to expect that the substrata for primate-like attachment behaviors are present in nonprimate mammals and that the function of these is modulated by higher structures in primates. In rodents and ungulates, mother–infant interaction may be based primarily upon olfaction, which is related to limbic function. Kling and Steklis (1976) have recently described evidence from lesion studies that suggests that attachment or affiliative behaviors in primates are mediated by limbic regions such as the orbital frontal, medial temporal, and amygdaloid. They postulate that mother–infant bonding may be mediated by the same set of structures. Therefore, the parsimonious explanation would be that among mammals, mother–infant attachment is mediated by limbic regions common to the mammalia, and that in primates, the more highly developed discriminative functions that make possible specific attachments are subserved by the neocortical elaboration that best characterizes primate brain evolution. It is of interest that the myelination of portions of the limbic system in man, as described by Konner (Chapter 12, this volume), takes place about the time that separation stress and stranger anxiety, two milestones in attachment, appear in human infants.

CONCLUSIONS

The example of how one chooses an animal model of human attachment illustrates the major points of this chapter. The use of an animal model requires a definition of the phenomenon modeled, which is based at the very least upon observational research with humans. The choice of the species for the model calls for a tremendous amount of basic research on the behavior of various potential model species as well as for knowledge of the evolutionary history and ecological niche of these species. Thus animal models are only one part of an interactive system of research. Hypotheses derived from any model must be tested on humans, which is likely to lead to more questions to be tested on the model itself. Additional basic animal research on the physiological substrates of attachment may follow and, in turn, feed back into the model.

An important result of viewing animal models as only a part of a research system is the emphasis on the necessity for basic animal research preceding and interacting with model research. It is impossible to predict whether research on basic processes in animals will be of direct relevance to humans or to the development of animal models. An example which is relevant to the theme of this volume illustrates this. The work on maternal pheromone in rats cited earlier has led unexpectedly to the development of a potential therapy for the most frequent cause of death in prematurely born human infants, necrotizing enterocolitis (NEC). A component of the pheromone, deoxycholic acid, is consumed by the rat pups and appears to prevent the development of NEC in pups susceptible to this disease (Diaz, Samson, Kessler, Stamper, Moore, Robish, Hodson, 1980; Moltz & Kilpatrick, 1978). This substance may be of value in treating the human disease.

The primate model of attachment also illustrates the advantages of using animal models. Long-term separation of mother and infants, which is not possible in humans, can be accomplished. Similarly, implantation of devices to monitor physiological responses to separation and reunion have led to considerable knowledge of the physiological correlates of mother–infant bond separation (Reite, Short, Seiler, & Pauley, 1981).

The tension between the requirements that the model be both similar to and different from the phenomenon modeled is also illustrated in the attachment example. Because higher primates are different from man, one is able to perform the manipulations necessary to study attachment. Because they are similar to man, the results of certain studies are likely to be generalizable to man. However, because they are so similar to man, primates are more expensive and difficult to maintain, and their developmental processes are not as rapid as those of lower animals. Perhaps we need to develop an "animal" model of the nonhuman primate model of human attachment. As the previous discussion has indicated, such a model would not meet all of the criteria for the definition of attachment, but, as we have suggested, there may be sufficient continuity between nonprimate mammals and primates in the neural control of attachment behavior that some basic common processes could be explored.

ABSTRACT

Animal models of human behavioral processes present many advantages for research, especially when physiological processes are of interest. They also present risks that the model may not be homologous to the human process modeled. This chapter describes the advantages and risks of animal models and procedures which can be used to minimize those risks, using as an example the use of models of mother–infant attachment. The dependence of models upon both preliminary human research and animal research is described.

Acknowledgments

The authors thank Antonia Vernadakis for her participation in the discussions and workshop upon which this chapter is based. I. Charles Kaufman's comments on this workshop are included in Chapter 4.

REFERENCES

Arnold, E. B., & Vernadakis, A. Development of tyrosine hydroxylase activity in dissociated cell cultures. *Developmental Neuroscience, 1979, 2,* 46–50.

Bock, W. J. Discussion: The concept of homology. *Annals of the New York Academy of Sciences, 1969, 167,* 71–73.

Bowlby, J. The nature of the child's tie to his mother. *International Journal of Psychoanalysis, 1958, 39,* 350–373.

Bunge, R., Johnson, M., & Ross, C. D. Nature and nurture in development of the autonomic neuron. *Science, 1978, 199,* 1409–1416.

Cairns, R. B. *Social development.* San Francisco: W. H. Freeman, 1979.

Campbell, C. B. G., & Hodos, W. The concept of homology and the evolution of the nervous system. *Brain, Behavior and Evolution, 1970, 3,* 353–367.

Diaz, J., Samson, H., Kessler, D., Stamper, C., Moore, E., Robish, E., & Hodson, A. Experimental necrotizing enterocolitis: The possible role of bile salts in its etiology and treatment. *Pediatric Research, 1980, 14,* 595.

Dobbing, J. Vulnerable periods in developing brain. In A. Davison & J. Dobbing (Eds.), *Applied neurochemistry.* Oxford: Blackwell Scientific, 1968.

Elliot, O., & Scott, J. P. The development of emotional distress reactions to separation in puppies. *Journal of Genetic Psychology, 1961, 99,* 3–22.

Fieve, R. R., Rosenthal, D., & Brill, H. *Genetic research in psychiatry.* Baltimore: Johns Hopkins University Press, 1975.

Harlow, H. F., & Harlow, M. K. The affectional systems. In A. M. Schrier (Ed.), *The behavior of nonhuman primates.* New York: Academic Press, 1965.

Hinde, R. A. The use of differences and similarities in comparative psychopathology. In G. Serban & A. Kling (Eds.), *Animal models in human psychobiology.* New York: Plenum Press, 1976.

Hofer, M. A. Physiological responses of infant rats to separation from their mothers. *Science,* 1970, *168,* 871–873.

Hofer, M. A. Studies on how early maternal separation produces behavioral change in young rats. *Psychosomatic Medicine,* 1975, *37,* 245–264.

Kling, A., & Steklis, H. D. A neural substrate for affiliative behavior in nonhuman primates. *Brain, Behavior and Evolution,* 1976, *13,* 216–238.

Klopfer, P. H., Adams, D. K., & Klopfer, M. S. Maternal "imprinting" in goats. *Proceedings of the National Academy of Sciences,* 1964, *52,* 911–914.

Kubie, L. S. The experimental induction of neurotic reactions in man. *Yale Journal of Biology and Medicine,* 1939, *11,* 541–545.

Leon, M. Maternal pheromone. *Physiology and Behavior,* 1974, *13,* 441–453.

Leon, M., & Moltz, H. Maternal pheromone: Discrimination by pre-weanling albino rats. *Physiology and Behavior,* 1971, *7,* 265–267.

MacLean, P. D. A triune concept of the brain and behavior. In T. J. Boag & D. Campbell (Eds.), *The Clarence M. Hincks memorial lectures, 1969.* Toronto: University of Toronto Press, 1973.

Moltz, H., & Kilpatrick, S. J. Response to the maternal pheromone in the rat as protection against necrotizing enterocolitis. *Neuroscience and Biobehavioral Reviews,* 1978, *2,* 277–280.

Moore, C. L., & Morelli, G. A. Mother rats interact differently with male and female offspring. *Journal of Comparative and Physiological Psychology,* 1979, *93,* 677–684.

Oliverio, A., Eleftheriou, B. E., & Bailey, D. W. Exploratory activity: Genetic analysis of its modification by scopolamine and amphetamine. *Physiology and Behavior,* 1973, *10,* 893–899.

Rajecki, D. W., Lamb, M. E., & Obmascher, P. Toward a general theory of infantile attachment: A comparative review of aspects of the social bond. *The Behavioral and Brain Sciences,* 1978, *3,* 417–464.

Reite, M. Maternal separation in monkey infants: A model of depression. In I. Hanin & E. Usdin (Eds.), *Animal models in psychiatry and neurology.* New York: Pergamon Press, 1977.

Reite, M. Genetic factors in mental illness. In R. Simons & H. Pardes (Eds.), *Understanding human behavior in health and illness.* 2nd. ed., Baltimore: Williams and Wilkins, 1981.

Reite, M., & Short, R. Nocturnal sleep in separated monkey infants. *Archives of General Psychiatry,* 1978, *35,* 1247–1253.

Reite, M., & Short, R. A biobehavioral developmental profile (BDP) for the pigtailed monkey. *Developmental Psychobiology,* 1980, *13,* 243–285.

Reite, M. L., Seiler, C., & Short, R. Loss of your mother is more than loss of a mother. *American Journal of Psychiatry,* 1978, *135,* 370–371.

Reite, M., Short, R., Kaufman, I. C., Stynes, A. J., & Pauley, J. D. Heart rate and body temperature in separated monkey infants. *Biological Psychiatry,* 1978, *13,* 91–105.

Reite, M., Short, R., Seiler, C., & Pauley, J. D. Attachment, loss and depression. *Journal of Child Psychology and Psychiatry,* 1981, *22,* 141–169.

Rosenblum, L. A., & Cooper, R. W. *The Squirrel Monkey.* New York: Academic Press, 1968.

Rosenblatt, J. S., & Lehrman, D. S. Maternal behavior of the laboratory rat. In H. L. Rheingold (Ed.), *Maternal behavior in mammals.* New York: Wiley, 1963.

Sackett, G. P., & Landesman-Dwyer, S. Toward an ethology of mental retardation: Quantitative behavioral observation in residential settings. In P. Mittler (Ed.), *Research to practice in mental retardation: Education and training* (Vol. 2). Baltimore: University Park Press, 1977.

Simpson, G. G. *Principles of Animal Taxonomy.* New York: Columbia University Press, 1961.

Smotherman, W. P., Wiener, S., Mendoza, S. P., & Levine, S. Maternal pituitary–adrenal respon-
    siveness as a function of differential treatment of rat pups. *Developmental Psychobiology, 1977,*
    10, 113–122.
Sroufe, L. A., & Waters, E. Attachment as an organizational construct. *Child Development, 1977, 48,*
    1184–1199.

CHAPTER 4

Animal Models in Developmental Psychobiology

I. Charles Kaufman

The topic of this workshop has more than a passing interest to me since I am personally responsible for one fairly common animal model—separation of the monkey infant from its mother, but not from its home or other social companions. I think it might serve the purpose of this symposium if I were to discuss some questions about the use of that model.

Question: What human situation is being modeled?

Please note that I said "situation" advisedly because it has conceptual significance. Medical scientists generally use models to study disease or its treatment, and psychological scientists generally do likewise, A recent book by Maser and Seligman (1977) entitled *Psychopathology: Experimental Models,* says in the Preface: "A model of behavior, pathological *or normal* [my emphasis], is not necessarily identical to the behavior it models. Yet, to be useful for exploring a given phenomenon and for generating new research ideas, the model must have *symptoms* [my emphasis], causal events, and even anatomical structures in common with the *pathology* [my emphasis]." The point is that even when the model is identified with *normal* behavior, the conceptual basis is really disease-oriented. In that same book, Suomi and Harlow (1977) describe their use of the separated monkey infant model and state, "*Our choice of depression as a psychopathological disorder to model in monkeys* [my emphasis] was not made indiscriminately."

I could cite other examples in the literature that explicitly or implicitly identify depression as the human condition being modeled in the separated monkey infant and that, further, conceptualize the depressive response as a disease. I wish to disagree on both counts. It is *not* depression that is being

I. Charles Kaufman ● Veterans Administration Medical Center, 4150 Clement Street, San Francisco, California 94121

modeled, and the depressive response that occurs is *not* a disease, nor even psychopathological in and of itself. If in the past 20 years I have ever strayed from my original conceptualization, I have found my way again. My original 1959 application to NIMH was entitled, "Reactions to Separation" in infant monkeys, and all of my subsequent grants were called "The Varied Response to Mother Loss."

The human situation being modeled is that of *object loss,* a common but momentous experience of human existence, with many significant aspects, including trauma, stress, processes of adaptation, the nature of object relationship and the relation to mother as a model of object relationship, further development, predisposition to later stress responses and illness, as well as anxiety and depression. Depending on one's focus, this model may be used to study any or all of the above—that is, it becomes a gold mine for developmental psychobiology. Most investigators have chosen to study the depression that often occurs.

Question: In what ways is the mother-bereft macaque a model of human object loss?

First, the mother is the original and paradigmatic object, from whom the earliest separations occur, so that mother can indeed serve as the ideal and most pristine (i.e., uncorrupted) example of the class 'object' in an object loss study.

Second, our knowledge of evolutionary history plus our observational data strongly suggest that the infant–mother relationship and bond are *of a kind* in macaques and humans, that is, in both they develop through psychotaxic processes (directed orientations based on psychological factors) and are psychosocial in nature (the *meanings* rather than the immediate physiological stimuli are functional). Our observations make clear that both macaque and human infants care about their mothers. I have suggested that

> in view of the increasing importance of the mother (in the course of evolution) to the survival of the slower growing, more functionally dependent infant, it is understandable that natural selection favored the emergence of processes which *bind* the infant to the mother (and vice versa). . . . These include strong *feelings* toward the mother and the *wish* to remain with or near her because of the *meaning* the mother has to the infant and its emerging way of life. (Kaufman, 1978)

Third, the reaction to the loss is similar in both species, as will be described.

Question: How does the model serve the study of depression?

Human observation tells us that object loss is painful (saddening) and produces, in varying degree, withdrawal, inactivity, diminished motivation, and facial, postural, and motoric changes of the kind seen in depressive illness. The same is true of bereft monkey infants.

The reason seems obvious: because of the meaning of the object to the subject's pattern of life and the strong feelings about the object, loss of the object is disruptive and distressing.

We have already seen that the affective, affectional relationship to the mother is an evolutionary development serving survival. The depressive response to object loss also serves survival, as an adaptation to the requirement for close interpersonal bonds in higher forms of social living. The pain that follows separation acts to keep us together. (I have detailed elsewhere the adaptive functions served by the other parts of the response, i.e., the conservation–withdrawal reaction, Kaufman & Rosenblum, 1967).

All this suggests to me that depression arose as an evolutionary development that is neither psychopathological in nature nor the manifestation of a disease. As seen in the monkey infant it is an organismic reaction state, a coherent dynamic condition in which biological and psychological processes are interdependent parts—a reaction which favors survival in the ways I have mentioned. As is true of any adaptive reaction, it may fail or go awry. For example, a few monkey infants have died, probably from the hypothermia which is part of the reaction. Or, grief may surpass its appropriate bounds. Some depressive illnesses may be of this kind.

For the most part, however, to comprehend depressive illness we need to consider additional biological, psychological, and social factors to those that are involved in the depressive response to mother loss in monkey infants, although this basic organismic state is obviously utilized in the total pathological pattern. I would not be surprised if the link turns out to be the occurrence in depressive illness *also* of *some vital loss,* whether this be based on fantasy or on genetically disposed biochemical changes.

ABSTRACT

The monkey infant separated from its mother is a model of human object loss. Since object loss is a common, yet momentous experience, this model serves developmental psychobiology in numerous ways. The depressive response that occurs is not a disease nor even psychopathological in and of itself. It is an organismic reaction state selected in the course of evolution because it favors survival. To comprehend depressive *illness,* one must consider additional biological, psychological, and social factors.

REFERENCES

Kaufman, I. C. Evolution, interaction and object relationship. *Behavioral and Brain Sciences,* 1978, 3, 450–451.

Kaufman, I. C., & Rosemblum, L. A. The reaction to separation in infant monkeys: Anaclitic depression and conservation-withdrawal. *Psychosomatic Medicine, 1967, 29,* 648–675.

Maser, J. D., & Seligman, M. E. P. *Psychopathology: Experimental models.* San Francisco: W. F. Freeman, 1977.

Suomi, S. J., & Harlow, H. F. Production and alleviation of depressive behaviors in monkeys. In J. D. Maser & M. E. P. Seligman (Ed.), *Psychopathology: Experimental models.* San Francisco, W. F. Freeman, 1977.

CHAPTER 5

The Timing of Hormone Signals in the Orchestration of Brain Development

Paola S. Timiras

INTRODUCTION

During development, the entire organism as well as specific organs and systems, including the central nervous system (CNS), undergo so-called *critical periods* characterized by accelerated growth and differentiation and by great susceptibility to environmental stimuli. Among such stimuli, hormones have been shown to play roles, both organizational (i.e., to direct cell differentiation) and regulatory (i.e., to influence the rate of growth and metabolism in mammals). The most important developmental effects of major hormones are presented in Table I.

In this chapter, I will first review briefly the concept of critical periods based upon the development of the CNS and will then consider the effects of hormones on these periods. For the organizational role, I will discuss the actions of sex hormones, prenatally and at adolescence, on the development of specific brain areas—hypothalamic and limbic regions—in terms of morphologic, biochemical, and functional differentiation. For the regulatory role, I will discuss the actions of thyroid hormones on growth of specific brain components, for example, formation of synapses and development of neurotransmitters, myelinogenesis and conduction of the nerve impulse, membrane fluidity, and brain excitability.

Hormonal alterations during development result in a number of CNS abnormalities with immediate functional and behavioral impairment of the infant and child. Such developmental disturbances may also generate long-

Paola S. Timiras ● Department of Physiology–Anatomy, University of California, Berkeley, California 94720. The work conducted in Dr. Timiras's laboratory, quoted here, was supported by NIH grants AG–00043 and HD–07430.

Table I. Hormones that Affect Developmental Processes in Mammals

Source	Hormone	Main effects
Pituitary gland	Growth hormone	*Prenatally:* Unknown effects on growth
		Postnatally: Promotes growth of bone and somatic tissues. Increases protein synthesis, blood glucose concentration and free fatty acids in blood.
	ACTH	Enhances growth and steroidogenesis of adrenal cortex.
	TSH	Stimulates growth and differentiation in the thyroid gland. Increases synthesis of thyroid hormones.
	Gonadotropic hormones: FSH and LH	Stimulate the maturation and function of the testis and ovary and regulate gametogenesis and steroidogenesis in the gonads.
	Prolactin	Widespread actions on osmoregulation, metabolism, and reproduction. In humans, has been recognized as an important regulator of fertility, as well as lactation.
Thyroid gland	Thyroxine and related substances	*Prenatally:* Essential for growth and maturation of the central nervous system.
		Postnatally: Intervene in growth and maturation of bone, somatic tissues. Increase O_2 consumption (calorigenic action). Increase protein synthesis and promote the catabolism of glucose and fat. Necessary for normal lactation and reproduction.
	Calcitonin	Hormonal regulation of Ca^{++} homeostasis.
Parathyroid glands	Parathyroid hormones	Hormonal regulation of Ca^{++} homeostasis.
Pancreas	Insulin	Promotes growth postnatally and perhaps prenatally. Regulates the metabolism of carbohydrates, lipids, and proteins. Controls blood glucose concentration.
	Glucagon	Regulates blood glucose concentration.
	Somatostatin	Regulates blood glucose concentration.
Adrenal gland	Cortisol	Metabolic effects on carbohydrates, fat, and proteins. Important actions on water and electrolyte metabolism, blood cells, and

Table I. *(Continued)*

Source	Hormone	Main effects
		lymphoid tissues. Increases the excitability of the central nervous system. Necessary for adaptation.
	Aldosterone	Indispensable for life. Controls Na^+ and K^+ body content.
Ovaries	Estrogen	*Embryonic:* Appears to be essential for the full development of uterus and vagina in some species.
		May regulate CNS centers (e.g., hypothalamus and limbic system) triggering gonadotropic cyclicity, prenatally or postnatally depending on the species.
		Puberty: Appearance of female secondary sexual characters.
		Adult: Local effects in the ovary (probably exerted by diffusion) stimulating granulosa cell proliferation and antral follicle growth. Stimulates growth of the glandular epithelium of the endometrium, smooth muscle of the uterus, epithelium of the vagina, and initial changes in ductile components of the mammary gland. Controls secretion of gonadotropins.
	Progesterone	Further proliferation of uterine epithelium and acini of the mammary glands. Maintenance of pregnancy.
Testis	Testosterone	*Embryonic:* Sexual differentiation of Wolfian ducts into male gonoducts and genitalia.
		Acts on the CNS (e.g., limbic and hypothalamic structures) during the 'critical periods' inducing sexual differentiation of behavior and reproductive functions (prenatally or postnatally).
		Puberty: Development of male secondary sexual features.
		Adult: Local effect on spermatogenesis. Control of gonadotropin.
	Unknown factor	*Embryonic:* Degeneration of female ducts.
Thymus	Thymosine	Proliferation of lymphocytes. Maturation of T-lymphocytes.

term repercussions in the adult whose ability to effectively adapt to the environment depends in great measure on the functional competence established during critical maturational periods. It must also be pointed out that although the most responsive periods are at critical stages of prenatal and postnatal brain development when the brain is most plastic, hormonal and environmental stimuli continue to modify brain function, albeit to a lesser degree, during the entire life of the organism. Indeed, some of the hormones which signal the passage from one developmental stage to the other during growth and development may also operate to determine the length of the life span and to regulate physiological competence in old age.

CRITICAL PERIODS: VULNERABILITY AND NURTURE

Critical periods have been identified early during development and are characterized by differentiation and/or accelerated growth of specific organs and functions. Maturational events during these periods generally lead to functional specialization and enhanced competence. During these periods the particular developing processes are most susceptible to adverse internal and external factors, a vulnerability of which we are increasingly aware as exposure to potentially damaging agents becomes more widespread. Less well explored is the awareness that developmental processes are equally susceptible to nurturing influences and that it may be possible to promote development and enhance adult competence by providing an optimal environment, including a favorable hormonal balance, during these critical formative years.

Among the first to formulate the concept of critical periods was Stockard (1921), who found that almost any chemical was capable of producing teratogenic effects (e.g., malformations) in fish embryos if applied at the "proper" time during development. Child and his collaborates (1941) established that the most rapidly growing embryonic tissues are also the most susceptible to any change in environmental conditions, thus accounting for the specificity of effects on particular tissues. Lorenz (1935) emphasized the importance of critical periods during avian postnatal development for the formation of primary social bonds.

Although development is a process continuing until the attainment of maturity, the rate varies, through fast and slow periods, producing characteristic patterns with accelerated peaks and decelerated troughs. Should the process continue at a constant rate throughout life either no critical period would exist or its entire duration could be viewed as a critical period. Evidence indicates that this is not the case, but rather, that developmental processes undergo varying rates of growth and differentiation, the faster rates coinciding with the critical periods (Scott, 1968). Such oscillation in the pattern is evident in all aspects of physical brain development (morphological, physiological, and chemical), and also relates to behavioral functions (learning and social attachments). Even though developmental patterns lack uniformity, the programming of the sequential events that constitute each pattern is narrowly controlled and essentially predictable (Hamburger, 1968). For example, in the CNS, the spinal cord matures (e.g., shows myelin formation) before the brain, and, in the brain, the brainstem matures before the cerebral cortex. Both physical and behavioral development follow a timetable wherein the critical periods are predetermined and interruptions or deletions in the timetable have consequences not only immediate at the time of the insult but also at later ages when otherwise normal, sequentially dependent processes fail to interdigitate and thereby produce long-term irreversible dysfunctions.

Critical periods are different for each animal species; for example, rate curves of brain growth in relation to birth show that the major growth occurs at midgestation in the guinea pig, in the last trimester of pregnancy in humans, and in the first two weeks after birth in the rat (Dobbing, 1975). The effects of any agent during these periods vary with the process affected and the degree of its maturation as well as the strength of the agent and the duration of its presence. Once a system becomes organized,* whether the cells of an embryo or the behavioral patterns of a young animal, the susceptibility to environmental influences declines. Interspecies correlations are permissible only if one remembers the different developmental timetables and makes the appropriate age adjustments from one species to another. Bearing this in mind, the validity of such extrapolations has been questioned and must be balanced against the benefits of animal experimentation. In the experiments reported herein, the rat is the most used animal model because of many considerations, the foremost being easy availability, low cost, extensive documentation on endocrine function and behavioral correlates, short gestation, and feasibility of environmental control. One must remember, however, that in the rat, the main critical periods of brain development are essentially postnatal events (e.g., days 1–5 and 10–15) and their duration is telescoped compared to that in humans which is primarily prenatal and extended over a period of a few months.

EFFECTS OF SEX HORMONES

A number of sex-related differences in brain function have been reported in mammals (Harlan, Gordan, & Gorski, 1979; Levine, 1972; Reinisch,

---

* The term 'organizer' is traditionally ascribed by embryologists to chemical substances produced in specific embryonal regions and capable of inducing 'organization' of adjacent structures from previously undifferentiated tissue, irrespective of the normal end product or presumptive fate of that tissue (Spemann, 1938). This terminology has been expanded from the consideration of approximating tissues to hormones, the 'organizational' actions of which promote the differentiation and growth of nearby tissues (such as secondary sex organs by testicular hormones) as well as of distant organs such as the brain.

1974; Sawyer & Gorski, 1971; Timiras, 1972). These include, irrespective of the species, the following: regulation of the pattern of secretion of some pituitary hormones (primarily the gonadotropin, luteinizing hormone, LH, and prolactin) and their releasing or inhibitory hypothalamic hormones; activity of enzymes (peptidases) involved in pituitary hormone synthesis; female and male sexual behavior; social and play behavior; aggressive behavior; territorial marking behavior; urinating posture; learning performance; gender role; vocalization; and regulation of food intake and body weight. Given the multitude and variety of these sex-related differences, it is not surprising that a considerable amount of research both basic and clinical has been directed to a better understanding of their nature and the treatment of disorders with which they may be associated. Because sex differences are related in large part to the differential development and function of the testes or ovaries, considerable attention has been focused on the role of sex hormones in their etiophysiology and pathology. Sexual dimorphism has stimulated much interest and has given rise to two hypotheses: (1) the differences in the above-described functions and behaviors observed during childhood and adult life in humans and other animals are due to physiological factors influencing early brain development; or (2) they are the result of learning and/or socialization in later life. Verification of either of these two possibilities would have important implications for the recognition of abnormalities of development and their eventual treatment. Current evidence favors the first hypothesis, and among the physiological factors that may bring about brain sex differences, hormones, and particularly sex hormones, contribute fundamentally to the organization of neural tissues. Thus the presence or absence of sex hormones early in development will result in the differentiation—or failure to differentiate—of specific brain areas such as the hypothalamus and the limbic system. Furthermore, an optimal hormonal environment at the critical age for differentiation is necessary not only for immediate organization of a specific brain area as manifested by structural, functional, chemical, and behavioral characteristics but also for the future development of functions and behaviors that will be estblished and will mature at later ages.

The now classical experiments of Pfeiffer (1936) showed that, in the rat, modification of the hormonal environment at birth by castration and/or implantation of the gonad of the opposite sex results, at the time of puberty, in alterations in the release (cyclic in the female and acyclic or tonic in the male) of pituitary gonadotropins. Neonatal castration of males leads to a cyclic (female-type) release of gonadotropins as can be demonstrated by implanting ovarian tissue in the male and examining its gonadotropin-driven cyclicity. Conversely, females in which the testes are implanted at birth become sterile and undergo an acyclic or tonic (male-type) release of gonadotropins. Because at the time these experiments were conducted the relationship between the pituitary and the hypothalamus had not yet been demonstrated, Pfeiffer

binding estrodiol but not testosterone (Andrews & Ojeda, 1977). Some conflicting results, however, have been reported. Nonaromatizable androgens (and hence not transformable into estrogens) administered to female hamsters masculinize those neural centers which control sexual behavior, and estrogen antagonists given systemically or directly into the hypothalamus have often opposite influences on testosterone-induced neonatal brain masculinization (Martin, 1978).

From this brief discussion, it emerges irrefutably that gonadal hormones, either androgens or estrogens or both, may act at critical periods, that is, "at a limited time frame during ontogeny . . . to determine or modify in a permanent way the formation and/or the functioning" of neural centers and pathways (Harlan et al., 1979). It is unlikely, however, that the many aspects of sexual dimorphisms which are so influenced undergo precisely the same process of differentiation, temporally or mechanistically. Although we tend to search for a unified theory to encompass all the disparate dimorphic sexual functions, it may be more realistic to opt for different mechanisms acting at individual critical ages. Inasmuch as development is a continuously evolving process, the effects of hormones might depend on and vary with the unfolding maturational events occurring in any time frame. Thus hormonal actions would be multifactorial rather than unique. That this may be the case is supported by the reports that sex hormones may act on brain development and function by altering: (a) the responsiveness of specific neurons to the hormones, for example, in terms of number and binding affinity of hormone receptors (McEwen, 1979); (b) neurotransmitter production, release, or responsiveness (Vaccari et al., 1977a); (c) general metabolic activity of neurons (Harlan et al., 1979); and (d) brain structure, for example, in terms of neuronal connectivity (Dorner & Stuadt, 1969). These actions are not unique to the sex hormones but rather are indicative of those aspects of CNS development which are amenable to modification. Thus development of dendrites, of neurotransmitter substances, or of specific receptors can be influenced also by other hormones, such as thyroid hormones. The mechanisms of action of thyroid hormones have been more extensively studied in our laboratory than those of gonadal hormones and will, therefore, be discussed in the following section.

EFFECTS OF THYROID HORMONES

The role of thyroid hormones in CNS development and maturation has basic clinical importance. Hypothyroidism, when present in humans during early development, results in cretinism, an irreversible condition characterized by retarded somatic growth and development, myxedema, and severely impaired neurologic and mental competence. The "cretinous" brain can be restored to normal development with minimal, if any, long-term neurologic and intellectual deficits if the condition is diagnosed very early postnatally and replacement therapy initiated within a narrowly circumscribed period of brain maturation (i.e., first three postnatal months). Because of the potential reversibility of such otherwise extremely deleterious consequences for the hypothyroid infant, mandatory screening of all newborns for blood levels of thyroid hormones (thyroxine, T4, and triiodothyronine, T3) has recently been adopted in several states. Our own experimental studies of the effects of thyroid hormones on the development and function of the rat brain, carried out over a period of more than 20 years, have contributed significantly to legislation which will aid in the identification at an appropriate age of any potentially detrimental alteration in thyroid function. Alteration of this function in adulthood also induces psychoneurologic symptoms, for example, decreased brain excitability and somnolence in hypothyroidism, and increased convulsibility, irritability, and anxiety in hyperthyroidism.

In the rat, removal of the thyroid surgically or alteration of its function by antithyroid drugs or radioactive iodine at birth induces a significant delay in growth and development of the entire animal and most particularly of the brain (Geel & Timiras, 1967a, 1970; Geel, Valcana, & Timiras, 1967). If, however, replacement therapy with adequate doses of T3 and T4 is initiated within the first 10 postnatal days (generally therapy is initiated at the end of the first postnatal week) the animal reverts to the normal pattern of growth, and brain maturation occurs normally. However, when replacement therapy is initiated after the critical period of 10 to 12 days after birth, the animal fails to catch up and its development, particularly that of the brain, remains severely impaired. In adulthood, high doses of thyroid hormones administered to the rat made hypothyroid at birth or to the human cretin will eventually induce signs of hyperthyroidism but will not reverse intellectual deficits.

How thyroid hormones influence brain maturation has long intrigued scientists not only because of the relatively high incidence of endemic cretinism in human population but also because the hypothyroid animal (rat) represents an extremely useful model to study mental and behavioral deficits which can be reversed with appropriate treatment at the critical age. Important data describing morphological, electrophysiological, and biochemical lesions in the brain of dysthyroid rats have accumulated in the last 30 years (Grave, 1977). Only in the last 5 or 6 years, however, have we gained a better understanding of the mechanisms of thyroid hormone action on the brain with the demonstration of specific hormone receptors both in neurons and glial cells, the responsiveness of pre- and postsynaptic processes to hormonal and neurotransmitter action, and the influence on membranogenesis and membrane function.

Properties and distribution of thyroid hormone receptors have been described in selected brain areas at different ages—before, during, and after the critical period for hormonal action—and compared with adult animals and other target tissues such as the liver (Valcana & Timiras, 1979). Within the cell, thyroid hormone receptors are found primarily in the nucleus where they probably act on the genome to bring about the well-known stimulatory action of the hormones on protein synthesis (Eberhardt, Valcana, & Timiras, 1976, 1978; Naidoo, Valcana, & Timiras, 1978); they are also found in the cytosol where they may regulate the availability of free hormone to the nuclear sites (Geel, 1977; Geel, Gonzales, & Timiras, 1981); and finally, they are found in mitochondria but only until the 10th postnatal day (Sterling, Lazarus, Milch, Sakurada, & Brenner, 1978). Within the brain, their distribution varies, the highest number of binding sites being found in the cerebral hemispheres followed by the brain stem, cerebellum, and hypothalamus (Valcana, 1979). The number of these receptors in several of the brain areas studied, particularly the cerebral hemispheres, is high during late prenatal and neonatal ages, declines until 10–12 days of age at which time it stabilizes at values which appear to remain unchanged until 2 years of age (Valcana & Timiras, 1978). The high number of receptors in the immature animal is paralleled by a high number in the hypothyroid animal and may reflect either a developmental or a compensatory upward regulation of the receptors in response to low levels of the hormone. It is to be noted that thyroid hormone levels in the rat are low at birth and progressively increase within the first two postnatal weeks at the end of which the pituitary–thyroid feedback relations become well established (Dussault & Labrie, 1975).

In order to explore whether thyroid hormones directly regulate neural cells and differentially influence neuronal or glial cells, we have adopted the use of tissue culture, a relatively simple and increasingly popular model, to study properties of neural tissues. Using neuroblastoma and glioma cultures, we have demonstrated the presence of thyroid hormone receptors in both cell lines, the effectiveness of thyroid hormones in regulating transport and the balance of ions, and some differential responses between neuroblastoma and glioma cells. Indeed, our studies have shown that, with respect to all parameters investigated, the glioma cells show alterations of lesser magnitude than the neuroblastoma. This greater adaptability of the glioma cells can be interpreted as evidence for the important role (also underlined by Dr. Vernadakis in Chapter 6 of this book) of these cells in providing necessary support for optimal neuronal activity (Draves & Timiras, 1980).

One of the most striking effects of thyroid hormones is on dendritic growth. In neonatally thyroidectomized rats without replacement therapy, the development of the dendritic tree is severely stunted but is restored to normal if hormones are administered at the critical age. A classical example of this effect is presented by the Purkinje cells of the cerebellum in which dendritic arborization is almost entirely absent in the hypothyroid brain and rearborizes with the administration of thyroid hormones (Legrand, 1971).

Biochemical changes at the synapse are associated with the morphologic changes. Cholinergic (Geel & Timiras, 1967b), adrenergic (Vaccari et al., 1977b), and serotonergic systems (Walker & Timiras, 1981) are all influenced by the thyroid state. Not only are the transmitters themselves and their metabolic enzymes dependent on thyroid hormones for optimal levels and activity but also for the number and affinity of some of their receptors (e.g., adrenergic). With respect to the adrenergic system, synergism between adrenergic stimulation and thyroid hormone on the heart is well known and accounts for the tachycardia of hyperthyroidism (Tse, Wrenn, & Kuo, 1980). Recent studies suggest that the dopaminergic receptors in the corpus striatum are also influenced by thyroid hormones (Vaccari & Timiras, 1981).

Current observations point to the membrane as a primary site of action of the thyroid hormones. This view, although still speculative, is supported by the effects of thyroid hormones on membrane-associated receptors, such as the adrenergic receptors mentioned above, as well as membrane-associated enzymes involved in ion transport, such as Na^+K^+ ATPase (Valcana & Timiras, 1969). In addition, thyroid hormones are necessary for myelin formation, a process which in the rat brain coincides with the critical period (i.e., 10 to 12 days), most vulnerable to the effects of thyroid hormones. In the absence of or in low levels of thyroid hormones at this critical age, both lipid and protein components of myelin are significantly reduced and the entire process of myelinogenesis is slowed down (Dalal, Valcana, Timiras, & Einstein, 1973; Valcana, Einstein, Csdjtey, Dalal, & Timiras, 1975). Finally, preliminary results show that in the hypothyroid animals the composition of the membrane, for example the ratio of unsaturated to saturated fatty acids and membrane fluidity of mitochondrial membranes, is altered in myocardial and neural tissues. Such changes in membrane fluidity could explain some thyroid hormone actions, such as the altered responsiveness of the hypothyroid animal to anesthesia (Skochko & Timiras, 1980).

Although the data that we have briefly summarized are important, per se, for providing a better understanding of the mechanisms of action of thyroid hormones on the brain, they have a broader significance for understanding and intervening in other types of mental deficiency (in humans) and behavioral deficits (in animals). Human and animal populations may be disadvantaged in their neural development and adult learning capacities by several factors besides hormonal abnormalities, such as genetic factors, undernutrition, drugs, etc. The hypothyroid animal can serve as one model, among several currently being explored, to test what environmental conditions or interventions (e.g., enriched or impoverished environments) might be beneficial to improve behavioral capacities, particularly those related to learning (Davenport, 1976; Pearson, Teicher, Shaywitz, Cohen, Young, & Anderson, 1980). In our complex society no route to ameliorate or prevent neurologic and intellectual dysfunctions should be left unexplored, and therefore, one must take advantage of the plasticity of the young brain to achieve the optimal potential in performance.

TIMING SIGNALS FOR REGULATION OF GROWTH, DEVELOPMENT, AND AGING

The emphasis in this article has been on the concept that events occurring during early development will produce long-term effects on the subsequent development of the whole individual and the psychophysiological competence of the adult. An extension of this concept suggests that events occurring at an early age might have repercussions also on aging and the duration of the life span. Herefrom have emerged several theories which may be grouped in those which encompass a programmed control of all age-related changes during the entire life span and those which limit the control of the program to the developmental period only. In the first group, aging would be viewed as a manifestation of an endogenous "clock" comparable to that which regulates growth and development; in the second group, growth and development would be regulated by a specific program (or clock) until optimal reproduction is achieved, but once the continuation of the species is guaranteed, the program would cease and its failure result in homeostatic 'disorganization' leading to aging and death. In both theories, a neuroendocrine signal would trigger the passage from one frame (age) of the lifespan to the other (Everitt, 1980). Pacemaker neurons in the brain, perhaps in the hypothalamus or in other integrative centers (e.g., limbic structures), would trigger, through the release of specific neurotransmitters, the neuroendocrine cells of the hypothalamus to release a hormone which would activate a specific pituitary-target endocrine system (Timiras, 1978). A number of neurotransmitters have been proposed, among which serotonin appears to be one of the best candidates; for the hormones, the thyroid hormones have been proposed   (Walker & Timiras, 1981). Thus, during development, thyroid hormones would determine at critical periods the maturation of neurotransmitter systems, particularly serotonergic, and these in turn would regulate the timetable of early development and maturation of the reproductive function as well as orchestrate the program necessary for homeostasis and survival.

ABSTRACT

Current data on the organizational and regulatory actions of sex and thyroid hormones on the brain are examined in the context of critical periods, periods of accelerated growth and differentiation as well as periods of maximal susceptibility to endogenous and exogenous stimuli of a nurturing or damaging nature. Thus sex hormones appear to be indispensable during early maturation for the differentiation of selected brain areas such as the hypothalamus and limbic structures, into a female or male type. Such differentiation extends not only to structural, biochemical, and hormonal organization but influences also the development of sex-related behaviors and brain functions. Similarly, the presence of thyroid hormones pre- or postnatally (depending on the mammalian species) is necessary for optimal brain maturation as manifested in optimal myelinogenesis, dendritic and synaptic growth, development of membrane structural characteristics, fluidity and associated enzymes, metabolic competence, etc. It is further suggested that neuroendocrine events occurring during early development produce long-term effects on the psychophysiologic competence of the adult and determine, in turn, the sequencing of the aging process and the duration of the life span. Thus neuroendocrine signals, either extending throughout the entire life or limited to the developmental period, would 'orchestrate' the timetable of growth, development, and aging.

REFERENCES

Andrews, W. W., & Ojeda, S. R. On the feedback actions of estrogens on gonadotropin and prolactin release in infantile female rats. *Endocrinology*, 1977, *101*, 1517–1523.

Child, C. M. *Patterns and problems of development*. Chicago: University of Chicago Press, 1941.

Dalal, K. B., Valcana, T., Timiras, P. S., & Einstein, E. R. Regulatory role of thyroxine on myelinogenesis in the developing rat. *Neurobiology*, 1971, *1*, 211–224.

Davenport, J. W. Environmental therapy in hypothyroid and other disadvantaged animal populations. In R. N. Walsh & W. T. Greenough (Eds.), *Environments as therapy for brain dysfunction*. New York: Plenum Press, 1976.

Dobbing, J. Prenatal nutrition and neurological development. In N. A. Buchwald & M. A. B. Brazier (Eds.), *Brain mechanisms in mental retardation*. New York: Academic Press, 1975.

Dörner, G., & Staudt, J. Structural changes in the hypothalamic ventromedial nucleus of the male rat, following neonatal castration and androgen treatment. *Neuroendocrinology*, 1969, *4*, 278–281.

Draves, D. J., & Timiras, P. S. Thyroid hormone effects in neural (tumor) cell culture: Differential effects on triiodothyronine nuclear receptors, Na^+, K^+ ATPase activity and intracellular electrolyte levels. In E. Giacobini, A. Vernadakis, & A. Shahar (Eds.), *Tissue culture in neurobiology*. New York: Raven Press, 1980.

Dussault, J. H., & Labrie, F. Development of the hypothalamic-pituitary-thyroid axis in the neonatal rat. *Endocrinology*, 1975, *97*, 1321–1324.

Eberhardt, N. L., Valcana, T., & Timiras, P. S. Hormone-receptor interactions in brain: Uptake and binding of thyroid hormone. *Psychoneuroendocrinology*, 1976, *1*, 399–409.

Eberhardt, N. L., Valcana, T., & Timiras, P. S. Triiodothyronine nuclear receptors: An *in vitro* comparison of the binding of triiodothyronine nuclei of adult rat liver, cerebral hemisphere and anterior pituitary. *Endocrinology*, 1978, *102*, 556–561.

Everitt, A. V. The neuroendocrine system and aging. *Gerontology*, 1980, *26*, 108–119.

Geel, S. E. Development-related changes of triiodothyronine binding to brain cystosol receptors. *Nature,* 1977, *269,* 428–430.

Geel, S. E., Gonzales, L., & Timiras, P. S. Properties of triiodothyronine binding sites in cerebral cortical cytosol. *Endocrine Research Communications,* 1981, *8,* 1–18.

Geel, S. E., & Timiras, P. S. The influence of neonatal hypothyroidism and of thyroxine on the ribonucleic acid and deoxyribonucleic acid concentrations of rat cerebral cortex. *Brain Research,* 1967a, *4,* 135–142.

Geel, S. E., & Timiras, P. S. Influence of neonatal hypothyroidism and of thyroxine on acetylcholinesterase and cholinesterase activities in the developing central nervous system of the rat. *Endocrinology,* 1967b, *80,* 1069–1074.

Geel, S. E., & Timiras, P. S. The role of hormones in cerebral protein metabolism. In A. Lajtha (Ed.), *Protein metabolism of the nervous system.* New York: Plenum Press, 1970.

Geel, S. E., Valcana, T. & Timiras, P. S. Effect of neonatal hypothyroidism and of thyroxine on L-(14C-)lysine incorporation in protein *in vivo* and the relationship to ionic levels in the developing brain of the rat. *Brain Research,* 1967, *4,* 143–150.

Gorski, R. A., & Barraclough, A. Effects of low dosages of androgen on the differentiation of hypothalamic regulatory control of ovulation in the rat. *Endocrinology,* 1963, *73,* 210–216.

Goy, R. W. Organizing effects of androgen on the behavior of rhesus monkeys. In R. P. Michael (Ed.), *Endocrinology and human behavior.* England: Oxford Press, 1968.

Goy, R. W. Early hormonal influence on the development of sexual and sex-related behavior. In G. C. Quarton, T. Melanchuk, & F. O. Schmitt (Eds.), *Neuro-sciences: A study program.* New York: Rockefeller University Press, 1970.

Grave, G. D. (Ed.), *Thyroid hormones and brain development.* New York: Raven Press, 1977.

Hamburger, V. Emergence of nervous coordination. In M. Locke (Ed.), *The emergence of order in developing systems. Developmental biology supplement* (Vol. 2). New York: Academic Press, 1968.

Harlan, R. E., Gordon, J. H., & Gorski, R. A. Sexual differentiation of the brain: Implications for neuroscience. In D. M. Schneider (Ed.), *Reviews of neuroscience* (Vol. 4). New York: Raven Press, 1979.

Harris, G. W. Electrical stimulation of the hypothalamus and the mechanism of neural control of the adenohyophysis. *Journal of Physiology (London),* 1948, *107,* 418–429.

Harris, G. W. Sex hormones, brain development and brain function. *Endocrinology,* 1964, *75,* 627–648.

Jost, A. Problems of fetal endocrinology: The gonadal and hypophyseal hormones. *Recent Progress in Hormone Research,* 1953, *8,* 379–418.

Kawakami, M., & Sawyer, C. H. Neuroendocrine correlates of changes in brain activity thresholds by sex steroids and pituitary hormones. *Endocrinology,* 1959, *65,* 652–668.

Legrand, J. Comparative effects of thyroid deficiency and undernutrition on maturation of the nervous system and particularly on myelination in the young rat. In M. Hamburgh & E. J. W. Barrington (Eds.), *Hormones in development.* New York: Appleton-Century-Croft, 1971.

Levine, S. (Ed.), *Hormones and behavior.* New York: Academic Press, 1972.

Lorenz, K. Der Kumpan in der Umwelt des Vogels. *Journal für Ornithologie,* 1935, *83,* 137–213.

Martin, L. Role of the metabolism of steriod hormones on the brain in sex differentiation and sexual maturation. In G. Dörner & M. Kawakami (Eds.), *Hormones and brain development.* Amsterdam: Elsevier/North-Holland Biomedical Press, 1978.

McEwen, B. S. Steroid hormone interactions with the brain: Cellular and molecular aspects. In D. M. Schneider (Ed.), *Reviews of neuroscience* (Vol. 4). New York: Raven Press, 1979.

Naftolin, F. Metabolism of steroids in the brain. In V. H. T. James (Ed.), *Endocrinology.* Amsterdam-Oxford: Excerpta Medica, 1977.

Naidoo, S., Valcana, T., & Timiras, P. S. Thyroid hormone receptors in the developing rat brain. *American Zoologist,* 1978, *18,* 522–545.

Pearson, D. E., Teicher, M. H., Shaywitz, B. A., Cohen, D. J., Young, J. G., & Anderson, G. M. Environmental influences on body weight and behavior in developing rats after neonatal 6-hydroxydopamine. *Science*, 1980, 209, 715–717.

Pfeiffer, C. A. Sexual differences of the hypophysis and their determination by the gonads. *American Journal of Anatomy*, 1936, 58, 195–226.

Phoenix, C. H., Goy, R. W., Gerall, A. A., & Young, W. C. Organizing action of prenatally administered testosterone propionate on the tissues mediating mating behavior in the female guinea pig. *Endocrinology*, 1959, 65, 369–382.

Phoenix, C. H., Goy, R. W., & Resko, J. A. Psychosexual differentiation as a function of androgenic stimulation. In M. Diamond (Ed.), *Perspectives in reproduction and sexual behavior*. Bloomington, Ind.: Indiana University Press, 1968.

Reinisch, J. M. Fetal hormones, the brain and human sex differences: A heuristic, integrative review of the recent literature. *Archives of Sexual Behavior*, 1974, 3, 51–90.

Sawyer, C. H., & Gorski, R. A. (Eds.), *Steroid hormones and brain function*. Berkeley: University of California Press, 1971.

Scott, J. P. *Early experience and organization of behavior*. Belmont, Calif.: Brooks/Cole, 1968.

Shapiro, B. H., Levine, D. C., & Adler, N. T. The testicular feminized rat: A naturally occurring model of androgen independent brain masculinization. *Science*, 1980, 209, 418–420.

Skochko, S., & Timiras, P. S. Effects of anesthetics on mitochondrial membrane fluidity in normal and hypothyroid myocardium. *Federation Proceedings*, 1980, 39, 719.

Spemann, H. *Embryonic development and induction*. New Haven: Yale University Press, 1938.

Sterling, K., Lazarus, J. H., Milch, P. O., Sakurada, T., & Brenner, M. A. Mitochondrial thyroid hormone receptor: Localization and physiological significance. *Science*, 1978, 201, 1126.

Stockard, C. R. Developmental rate and structural expression: An experimental study of twins, "double" monsters and single deformities, and the interaction among embryonic organs during their origin and development. *American Journal of Anatomy*, 1921, 28, 115–277.

Terasawa, E., & Timiras, P. S. Electrical activity during the estrous cycle of the rat: Cyclic changes in limbic structures. *Endocrinology*, 1968a, 83, 207–216.

Terasawa, E., & Timiras, P. S. Electrophysiological study of the limbic system in the rat at onset of puberty. *American Journal of Physiology*, 1968b, 215, 1462–1467.

Terasawa, E., & Timiras, P. S. Cyclic changes in electrical activity of the rat midbrain reticular formation during the estrous cycle. *Brain Research*, 1969, 14, 189–198.

Timiras, P. S. Estrogens as organizers of CNS function. In D. H. Ford (Ed.), *Influence of hormones on the nervous system*. Basel: S. Karger, 1971.

Timiras, P. S. *Developmental physiology and aging*. New York: Macmillan, 1972.

Timiras, P. S. Biological perspectives on aging: In search of a masterplan. *American Scientist*, 1978, 66, 605–613.

Tse, J., Wrenn, R. W., & Kuo, J. F. Thyroxine-induced changes in characteristics of β-adrenergic receptors and adenosine 3′, 5′- monophosphate and guanosine 3′, 5′- monophosphate systems in the heart may be related to reputed catecholamine supersensitivity in hyperthyroidism. *Endocrinology*, 1980, 107, 6–16.

Vaccari, A., Brotman, S., Cimino, J., & Timiras, P. S. Sex differences of neurotransmitter enzymes in central and peripheral nervous systems. *Brain Research*, 1977, 132, 176–185.

Vaccari, A., & Timiras, P. S. Alterations in brain dopaminergic receptors in developing hypo- and hyperthyroid rats. *Neurochemistry International*, 1981, 3, 149–153.

Vaccari, A., Valcana, T., & Timiras, P. S. Effects of hypothyroidism on the enzymes for biogenic amines in the developing rat brain. *Pharmacological Research Communications*, 1977, 9, 763–780.

Valcana, T. The role of triiodothyronine (T3) receptors in brain development. In E. Meisami & M. A. B. Brazier (Eds.), *Neural growth and differentiation*. New York: Raven Press, 1979.

Valcana, T., Einstein, E. R., Csdjtey, J., Dalal, K. B., & Timiras, P. S. Influence of thyroid hormones on myelin proteins in the developing rat brain. *Journal of the Neurological Sciences*, 1975, 25, 19–27.

Valcana, T., & Timiras, P. S. Effect of hypothyroidism on ionic metabolism and Na⁺K⁺ activated ATP phosphohydrolase activity in the developing rat brain. *Journal of Neurochemistry*, 1969, *16*, 935–943.

Valcana, T., & Timiras, P. S. Nuclear triiodothyronine receptors in the developing rat brain. *Molecular and Cellular Endocrinology*, 1978, *2*, 31–41.

Valcana, T., & Timiras, P. S. Changes in rat liver nuclear triiodothyronine receptors with age and thyroid activity. In L. Macho, & V. Strbak (Eds.), *Hormones and development*. Bratislava: VEDA, 1979.

Walker, R. F., & Timiras, P. S. Serotonin in development of cyclic reproductive function. In B. Haber, S. Gabay, M. R. Issidorides, & S. G. A. Alivisatos (Eds.), Serotonin: *Current aspects of neurochemistry and function. Advances in experimental biology and medicine* (Vol. 133). New York: Plenum Press, 1981.

Walker, R. F., & Timiras, P. S. Pacemaker insufficiency and the onset of aging. In D. Carpenter (Ed.), *Cellular pacemakers II*. New York: Wiley. 1982.

CHAPTER 6

Epigenetic Factors in Neuronal Differentiation

A REVIEW OF RECENT RESEARCH

Antonia Vernadakis

INTRODUCTION

In recent years evidence has been accumulating on the concept that neuronal differentiation and growth are under the influence of both genetic and epigenetic factors. A great portion of the information available has derived from studies using the autonomic nervous system and from *in vitro* neural model systems. In this chapter I will review some of the observations which have contributed to the view of a pluropotential neuron. Two basic observations have prompted the reevaluation of basic developmental phenomena. One example is that portions of neural crest that normally provide sympathetic neurons may, under certain experimental conditions, provide parasympathetic neurons instead. The other observation is that neurons from a predominantly adrenergic sympathetic ganglion grown under certain tissue culture conditions form cholinergic synapses among themselves and on several types of target tissue in coculture. Finally, studies both *in vivo* and *in vitro* have shown that neuronal growth and differentiation are regulated by various epigenetic intrinsic factors such as hormones and neurohumors or substances secreted by the glial cells, the "glial factors."

Antonia Vernadakis ● Departments of Psychiatry and Pharmacology University of Colorado School of Medicine, 4200 E. Ninth Avenue, Denver, Colorado 80262.

ROLE OF MICROENVIRONMENT ON NEURAL DIFFERENTIATION

Several examples lend support to the premise that humoral factors in the cellular microenvironment or cellular interactions may influence the direction of cell differentiation or, more importantly, influence a differentiated cell to transform into a cell with quite different characteristics. One of the more intriguing of the cellular interactions occurs between elements of the neural retina and the pigment epithelium. Although the cells of these two layers are derived embryologically from a single layer, they undergo considerable morphological divergence during development. It has been suggested that the pigment epithelium plays an important role in nourishing the neural retina or providing special cellular products for its use. In an elegant study, Keefe (1973a,b) demonstrated that epithelial cells can assume functions besides nourishment of neural retina. In the retina of the amphibian eye is destroyed, differentiated pigment-epithelial cells can lose most or all of their differentiated characteristics (e.g., pigment, phagocytic ability for photoreceptor outer segment) and transform into dividing cells which differentiate into all of the various cells of the retina (Keefe, 1973a,b). That cells programmed for a specific function can transform into another cell has also been suggested by the studies of Skoff, Price, and Stocks (1976a,b). They found that in the developing optic nerve of the rat, astroblasts and oligodendroblasts rather than undifferentiated glioblasts are the major sources for astrocytes and oligodendrocytes. Moreover, a population of poorly differentiated astrocytes divides and then transforms into oligodendrocytes. Thus two important findings derive from these studies: that proliferating glial cells can differentiate and also that differentiated glial cells can divide.

The use of neural culture has provided a useful tool to explore regulatory factors of neural growth and differentiation. Recent studies using cultures of dissociated neurons from autonomic ganglia of the perinatal rat have provided opportunities to study the functional expression of sympathetic neurons in culture (see review by Bunge, Johnson, & Ross, 1978). The neurons in these cultures are predominantly adrenergic (95%). However, after a period of some weeks in culture the number of adrenergic neurons decreases and neurons with cholinergic characteristics predominate. The authors propose on the basis of cytochemical studies that neurons in culture are undergoing a 'shift' from adrenergic function through an intermediate state to cholinergic function. Thus basic characteristics have been shown to change in cultures prepared from postmitotic neuronal populations during the period of early development. The up-to-now concept that the postmitotic neuron cannot make any changes in the state of its differentiation is challenged by the foregoing findings.

In a recent study using glioma cells (a rat astrocytoma) as a model for glial cells, we found that these glial cells 'transdifferentiate' with passage in culture (Parker, Norenberg, & Vernadakis, 1980). At early passages (20) glial cells express oligodendrocytic properties as assessed by cyclic nucleotide phosphohydrolase, an enzyme marker for oligodendrocytes; glial cells at late passages (80) express astrocytic properties as assessed by glutamine synthetase, an enzyme marker for astrocytes. These findings lend further support to the view that differentiated neural cells under appropriate conditions can transdifferentiate into cells with different characteristics.

Recently intraocular brain grafts have been used as a method for differentiating between intrinsic and extrinsic determinants of structural and functional development in the central nervous system (CNS). A group consisting primarily of Lars Olson, Robert Freedman, and Barry Hoffer have contributed greatly to the elucidation of neuronal differentiation or transdifferentiation using this methodology (see review by Olson, Seiger, Alund, Freedman, Hoffer, Taylor, & Woodward, 1979). In summary, they have found that grafts of developing rat locus coeruleus, an aggregation of 14,000 nonadrenergic cells in the floor of the fourth ventricle, will develop when transferred to the anterior eye chamber of adult recipients; also early developing cerebellar cortex, cerebral cortex, and hippocampal formation will survive grafting to the anterior eye chamber and continue their development using morphologic, histochemical, pharmacologic, and electrophysiological methods. These studies show that some CNS neurons can develop in an environment different from their original destination.

Studies using neural crest as a model system for the elucidation of mechanisms in cell differentiation have shown that the differentiation of autonomic neuroblasts is controlled by the environment in which crest cells are localized at the end of their migration. One of the striking properties of the neural crest is the extensive and well-defined migration that its cells achieve in the embryo. LeDouarin and Teillet (1974) have used the cell marking technique, which is based on structural differences of the interphase nucleus, in two species of birds closely related taxonomically, the Japanese quail and the chick, to explore some of the mechanisms of migration and differentiation of the neuroblasts of the autonomic nervous system. When the "adrenomedullary" level of the quail neural tube is grafted into the "vagal" region of a chick, the crest cells colonize the gut and differentiate into parasympathetic enteric ganglia of Auerbach's and Meissner's plexi. If quail cephalic neural crest is transplanted in the adrenomedullary level of a chick, quail cells migrate into the suprarenal glands and differentiate into adrenomedullary cells. Thus presumptive dorsal neuroblasts which in normal development would give rise to adrenergic sympathoblasts or adrenomedullary cells differentiate into nonadrenergic neurons when submitted to the splachnic mesoderm environment. In another study LeDouarin and associates (LeDouarin, Renaud, Teillet, & LeDouarin, 1975) further found that before the outset of neural crest cell migration the destination of autonomic sympathetic and parasympathetic neuroblasts is not determined with respect to cholinergic or adrenergic. The neurotransmitter synthesized by crest autonomic neuroblasts depends on the microenvironment in which crest cells become localized at the term of their migration. LeDouarin *et al.* (1975) showed that the splachnic mesoderm induces presumptive adrenergic cells to become fully differentiated cholinergic neurons. These studies demonstrate both the intrinsic inherited ability of a cell to differentiate into a specific functional cell and also the role of microenvironmental factors in cell differentiation.

HORMONES AS EPIGENETIC GROWTH FACTORS

Several studies have shown that both neuronal and glial growth and differentiation may be regulated by several intrinsic epigenetic factors present in the neural microenvironment, such as hormones and neurohumor substances. Both thyroid hormones and steroid hormones modulate neuronal growth as shown by the work of Timiras and associates (Timiras, 1972; Valcana & Eberhardt, 1977), Balazs and associates (see review by Balazs, 1977), and recently of Lauder and associates (Bohn & Lauder, 1978, 1980), and by our laboratory (Vernadakis, 1971; Vernadakis, Culver, & Nidess, 1978). Studies in the rat have shown that with the lack of thyroid hormone the number of cerebellar cells is decreased, nerve cells are smaller, dendrites are fewer, and synaptic spines on the dendrites are fewer. Thus thyroid hormone influences the number and the maturation of the neurons. Further evidence suggests that synaptic expression is also influenced by thryoid hormone (Hajos, Patel, & Balazs, 1973). Thus the lack of thyroid hormone results in a deficiency in the normal "wiring pattern" of nerve cells.

A number of studies which include the early work of Howard and associates (see review by Howard, 1974), Balazs and associates (Balazs, 1977), and more recently Lauder and associates (Bohn & Lauder, 1978) present evidence that excessive amounts of hormonal steroids such as glucocorticoids greatly affect the rate of nerve cell genesis and the differentiation and maturation of neurons, including synaptogenesis. Attention has been focused particularly on the role of the glucocorticoids on neurogenesis of the cerebellum. Normal cerebellar neurogenesis is well documented in the rodent. The external granular layer, a secondary germinal zone present on the surface of the developing cerebellum, gives rise to basket, stellate, and granule cells during the first three weeks postnatally in rats. The recent studies of Bohn and Lauder (1980) have shown marked effects of glucocorticoids on cell proliferation. Rats were treated neonatally (Days 1–4) with hydrocortisone, and the "birthdays" (time of origin) and numbers of various interneurons generated from the external granular layer were determined using autoradiography. During treatment, greater proportions of both granule cells and interneurons in the inner molecular layer (mainly basket cells) completed early final cell divisions. However, birthdays for the majority of granule cells were delayed, whereas stellate cell birthdays were unaffected. Thus hydrocorticose treatment has shifted the balance of the various cerebellar cell types during neurogenesis.

NEUROHUMOR SUBSTANCES AS GROWTH FACTORS

The possible role of neurohumor substances as growth factors for cell differentiation has attracted considerable attention, and several investigators are using various experimental approaches to further elucidate this intriguing phenomenon.

Early embryogenesis is described as the period between fertilization and the beginning of organogenesis, approximately the end of gastrulation. During this period the embryo consists of one cell or a complex of a few cells of different prospective significance that at this time have practically no morphological and functional differences and are often interchangeable. At this stage the presence of the neurohumor substances acetylcholine, serotonin (5-hydroxytryptamine), norepinephrine, dopamine, and other similar compounds cannot be functioning as neurotransmitters in the same manner as described in the mature nervous system. Buznikov and associates (Buznikov, Chudakova, & Znezdia, 1964; Buznikov, Chudakova, Berdysheva, & Vyazmina, 1968) were the first to advocate that these substances are involved in cell division, motility, and morphogenetic cell movements during cleavage and gastrulation. Later work by Burden and Lawrence (1973) suggested the role of monoamines in the closure of the neural tube.

We and others have used neural tissue and cell culture systems to explore the role of neurohumors in neural differentiation. Our findings show that monoaminergic substances, such as norepinephrine, enhance proliferation of glial cells (Vernadakis & Gibson, 1974; Vernadakis, Nidess, & Arnold, 1979). Again, since glial cells make up a large portion of the neuronal microenvironment, changes in their number or differentiation would be expected to affect neuronal differentiation.

Lauder and associates have addressed the question of the neurohumoral regulation of neuronal differentiation from a different point of view. Lauder and Bloom (1974) proposed that early forming monoamine neurons, which begin to differentiate (cease cell division) several days prior to those cells they will eventually innervate, might be important in regulating the time of differentiation of their target cells. This would mean that specific germinal cells influenced by monoamines to stop dividing are in some way 'marked' for later recognition and synaptogenesis, since these are the same cells innervated by monoaminergic afferents. Such a system could make these neurohumor substances direct participants in the construction of their own circuitry in the developing brain. Thus "monoamines" are proposed as "differentiating signals" in the neural tube. Recently Lauder and Krebs (1978) tested the hypothesis that 5-hydroxytryptamine influences the onset of differentiation of prospective 5-HT target neurons during embryogenesis. They administered the 5-hydroxytryptamine depleting drug p-chlorophenylalanine (pCPA) to pregnant rats from the 8th to 16th day of gestation and determined (using long survival ^{3}H-thymidine autoradiography) the time of the last cell division for fetal neurons. The onset of neuronal differentiation (cessation of germinal cell proliferation) in brain regions known to contain 5-HT terminals, or to have a high 5-HT content (5-HT target cells) in the adult was retarded with pCPA treatment. Such findings lend support to the hypothesis that monoamines acting as differentiation signals influence the onset of differentiation of those cells which will receive monoaminergic afferents.

GLIAL FACTORS IN NEURONAL GROWTH

The interrelations of neuronal-glial cells and the role of glial cells in neuronal growth are not understood and continue to be an active field of investigation. The regulatory role of glial cells that we and others are presently advocating is their role in the regulation of neurotransmission function. Evidence from other laboratories and ours (Vernadakis et al., 1978) has shown that glial cells accumulate putative neurotransmitter substances such as norepinephrine (NE), γ-aminobutyric acid (GABA), and glutamic acid. Therefore, the glial cells regulate the amount present in the synaptic cleft available to act on the respective neurons. Whether spongioblasts, as well as differentiated neuroglia cells, accumulate these neurohumor substances has not been elucidated. However, the effect in the neuronal microenvironment would be different. If spongioblasts can accumulate neurohumor substances, the amount available for the growing neuroblast would be affected and perhaps subsequently be reflected in the degree of growth of the neuron. On the other hand, if intrinsic or extrinsic conditions would produce excessive amounts of the neurotransmitter, then the glial cells can act as a "safety valve" by preventing excessive accumulation of the neurotransmitter substances and hence excessive neuronal stimulation. Using neural tissue culture we found that cortisol in high doses inhibits the low affinity uptake of norepinephrine in glial cells (Vernadakis, 1974). Thus under this condition excessive amounts of NE are available in the synaptic cleft to stimulate the neurons. This may partially explain the stimulatory effects of cortisol on neural function that we have observed in other studies using electrical stimulation (Vernadakis & Woodbury, 1963). These findings demonstrate two points which warrant further discussion: (1) there is a neuronal–glial interrelationship which regulates neuronal function, and (2) this neuronal–glial interaction is influenced by a homeostatic balance between various neurohumors such as norepinephrine and hormones.

Recent evidence has further supported the view that glial cells are vital for neuronal survival at least in culture condition. Patterson and associates (Patterson & Chun, 1977a,b) have shown that sympathetic neurons in the absence of nonneuronal cells in culture can develop the ability to synthesize and accumulate radioactive norepinephrine from ^{3}H-tyrosine but can synthesize little ^{3}H-acetylcholine from labeled choline. However, in the presence of certain types of nonneuronal cells or in medium conditioned by them, the neurons produced considerable acetylcholine from choline. Moreover, depending on the time in culture when a conditioned medium is added, the predominance of cholinergic or adrenergic neurons can be influenced. This adrenergic or cholinergic "decision" becomes less reversible as the phenotype becomes fully expressed. Such studies demonstrate the ability of the neuron to respond to both its genetic makeup and epigenetic environment.

CONCLUSIONS

The intrinsic epigenetic factors which modulate the microenvironment of neurons during early neurogenesis—neuronal and glial cell growth and differentiation, and finally, synaptic transmission—are only beginning to be understood. Understanding the regulation of these cellular events forms the basis of understanding behavioral expression as reflected in cell–cell interactions and at the organism level as reflected in human behavior. Our hypothesis is that there is a critical balance between genetic programming and the epigenetic influences for the final normal behavioral expression of the organism.

ABSTRACT

This chapter briefly reviews some of the recent research on epigenetic factors which influence neuronal growth and differentiation. Studies *in vivo* and in neural culture have shown that humoral substances in the cellular microenvironment influence the differentiation of both neurons and glial cells. In addition, hormones such as thyroxine and glucocorticoids and neurohumor substances such as norepinephrine, serotonin, and acetylcholine modulate neuronal growth either by acting directly on neurogenesis or by influencing glial cells which in turn modulate the neuronal environment. Finally, evidence shows that glial cells may regulate neuronal growth by producing substances vital for neuronal survival and differentiation.

REFERENCES

Balazs, R. Effect of thyroid hormone and undernutrition on cell acquisition in the rat brain. In D. Gilman-Grave (Ed.), *Thyroid hormone and brain development.* New York: Raven Press, 1977.

Bohn, M. C., & Lauder, J. M. The effects of neonatal hydrocortisone on rat cerebellar development: An autoradiographic and light-microscopic study. *Developmental Neuroscience,* 1978, *1,* 250–266.

Bohn, M. C., & Lauder, J. M. Cerebellar granule cell genesis in the hydrocortisone-treated rat. *Developmental Neuroscience,* 1980, *3,* 81–89.

Bunge, R., Johnson, M., & Ross, C. D. Nature and nurture in the development of the autonomic neuron. *Science,* 1978, *199,* 1409–1416.

Burden, H. W., & Lawrence, I. E. Presence of biogenic amines in early rat development. *American Journal of Anatomy,* 1973, *136,* 251–257.

Buznikov, G. A., Chudakova, I. V., & Znezdia, N. D. The role of neurohumors in early embryogenesis: I. Serotonin content of developing embryos of sea urchin and loach. *Journal of Embryology and Experimental Morphology,* 1964, *12,* 563–573.

Buznikov, G. A., Chudakova, I. V., Berdysheva, L. V., & Vyazmina, N. M. The role of neurohumors in early embryogenesis: I. Acetylcholine and catecholamine content in developing embryos of sea urchin. *Journal of Embryology and Experimental Morphology,* 1968, *20,* 119–128.

Hajos, F., Patel, A. J., & Balazs, R. Effect of thyroid deficiency on the synaptic organization of the rat cerebellar cortex. *Brain Research,* 1973, *50,* 387–401.

Howard, E. Hormonal effects on the growth and DNA content of the developing brain. In W. A. Himwich (Ed.), *Biochemistry of the developing brain* (Vol. 3). New York: Dekker, 1974.

Lauder, J. M., & Bloom, F. E. Ontogeny of monoamine neurons in the locus coeruleus, raphei nuclei and substantia nigra of the rat: I. Cell differentiation. *Journal of Comparative Neurology,* 1974, *155,* 459–482.

Lauder, J. M., & Krebs, H. Serotonin as a differentiation signal in early neurogenesis. *Developmental Neuroscience,* 1978, *1,* 15–30.

LeDouarin, N. M., & Teillet, M. A. Experimental analysis of the migration and differentiation of neuroblasts of the autonomic nervous system and neuroectodermal mesenchymal derivatives, using a biological cell marking technique. *Developmental Biology,* 1974, *41,* 162–184.

LeDouarin, N. M., Renaud, D., Teillet, M. A., & LeDouarin, G. H. Cholinergic differentiation of presumptive adrenergic neuroblasts in interspecific chimeras after heterotopic transplantations. *Proceedings of the National Academy of Sciences,* 1975, *72,* 728–732.

Keefe, J. R. An analysis of urodelian retinal regeneration: I. Studies of the cellular source of retinal regeneration in *Notophthalmus vividescens* ^{3}H-thymidine and colchicine. *Journal of Experimental Zoology,* 1973, *184,* 185–206. (a)

Keefe, J. R. An analysis of urodelian retinal regeneration: II. Ultrastructural features of retinal regeneration in *Notophthalmus vividescens. Journal of Experimental Zoology,* 1973, *184,* 207–232. (b)

Olson, L., Seiger, A., Alund, M., Freedman, R., Hoffer, B., Taylor, D., & Woodward, D. Intraocular brain crafts: A method for differentiating between intrinsic and extrinsic determinants of structural and functional development in the central nervous system. In E. Meisami & M. A. B. Brazier (Eds.), *Neural growth and differentiation* (Vol. 5). International Research Organization Monograph Series. New York: Raven Press, 1979.

Parker, K. K., Norenberg, M., & Vernadakis, A. "Transdifferentiation" of C-6 glial cells in culture. *Science,* 1980, *208,* 179–181.

Patterson, P. H., & Chun, L. Y. The induction of acetylcholine synthesis in primary cultures of dissociated rat sympathetic neurons: I. Effects of conditioned medium. *Developmental Biology,* 1977, *56,* 263–280. (a)

Patterson, P. H., & Chun, L. Y. The induction of acetylcholine synthesis in primary cultures of dissociated rat sympathetic neurons: II. Developmental aspects. *Developmental Biology,* 1977, *56,* 473–481. (b)

Skoff, R. P., Price, D. L., & Stocks, A. Electron microscopic autoradiographic studies of gliogenesis in rat optic nerve: I. Cell proliferation. *Journal of Comparative Neurology,* 1976, *169,* 291–311. (a)

Skoff, R. P., Price, D. L., & Stocks, A. Electron microscopic autoradiographic studies of gliogenesis in rat optic nerve: II. Time of origin. *Journal of Comparative Neurology,* 1976, *169,* 313–334. (b)

Timiras, P. S. *Developmental physiology and aging.* New York: MacMillan, 1972.

Valcana, T., & Eberhardt, N. L. Effects of neonatal hypothyroidism on protein synthesis in the developing rat brain: An open question. In D. Gillman-Grave (Ed.), *Thyroid hormones and brain development.* New York: Raven Press, 1977.

Vernadakis, A. Hormonal factors in the proliferation of glial cells in culture. In D. H. Ford (Ed.), *Influence of hormones on the nervous system. Proceedings of the International Society of Psychoneuroendocrinology.* Basel: S. Karger, 1971.

Vernadakis, A. Neurotransmission: A proposed mechanism of steroid hormones in the regulation of brain function. In N. Hatotani (Ed.), *Proceedings of the Mie Conference of the International Society of Psychoneuroendocrinology.* Basel: S. Karger, 1974.

Vernadakis, A., & Gibson, D. A. Role of neurotransmitter substances in neural growth. In J. Dancis & J. C. Hwang (Eds.), *Perinatal pharmacology: Problems and priorities.* New York: Raven Press, 1974.

Vernadakis, A., & Woodbury, S. M. Effect of cortisol on the electroshock seizure thresholds in developing rats. *Journal of Pharmacology and Experimental Therapeutics,* 1963, *139,* 110–113.

Vernadakis, A., Culver, B., & Nidess, R. Actions of steroid hormones on neural growth in culture: Role of glial cells. *Psychoneuroendocrinology,* 1978, *3,* 47–64.

Vernadakis, A., Nidess, R., & Arnold, E. B. Role of glial cells in neural growth. In E. Meisami & M. A. B. Brazier (Eds.), *Neural growth and differentiation* (Vol. 5). International Research Organization Monograph Series. New York: Raven Press, 1979.

CHAPTER 7

The Role of Hormones in Mother–Infant Transactions

Katherine Tennes

INTRODUCTION

Hormones have been implicated in the facilitation or maintenance of maternal–infant interactions in studies of animals (see Chapters 1, 3, & 6, this volume) and of humans (see Chapter 12, this volume). However, physiological studies of attachment behavior have been less concerned with the process of attachment than with disruptions in attachment; that is, separations between mothers and infants.

We utilized the response of one-year-old infants to brief separations from their mothers as a means of studying the effect of a psychological variable on the activity of the hypothalamic-pituitary-adrenocortical axis. Initially we were interested in determining whether the one-year-old infant was capable of responding with a rise in cortisol production to an age-appropriate psychological "stress." A second objective was to examine the effect of individual differences in the intensity of the infant's distress, when separated, on the level of corticosteroid response. As a result of finding significant correlations between expressions of distress and adrenocortical activity, we also attempted to assess the contribution of the quality of the mother–infant relationships to the level of arousal of the adrenocortical system.

ANIMAL MODELS

The importance of hormones in mediating maternal–infant behaviors has been investigated extensively in animal models. Studies of mater-

Katherine Tennes ● Department of Psychiatry, University of Colorado School of Medicine, Denver, Colorado 80262. Research reported in this paper was supported in part by USPHS Grant MH–23580 and by NIH General Research Support RR–05357.

nal–infant interactions in rats (Leon, 1979; Slotnick, 1975) suggest that pups are a necessary stimulus to changes in maternal hormone levels and that the hormones in turn facilitate maternal behaviors appropriate to the developmental stage of the pups. Separations between infants and mothers are regulated by these mechanisms. Thus the presence of the pups increases maternal prolactin which stimulates secretion of steroids and facilitates maternal behavior. Increased prolactin also is associated with emission of a maternal pheromone which attracts the infants to the mother. Rat pups are not distressed by being separated from the mother if they are provided with adequate physical care and with the specific maternal odor the lactating dam emits. Although these mechanisms for maintaining mother–infant contact appear to be efficient for the rat, this animal model may have limited applicability to the distress caused by separations between human mother–infant pairs.

Squirrel monkeys are regarded as a more useful model for study of the stress of brief separations (Coe, Mendoza, Smotherman, & Levine, 1978; Hennessy, Kaplan, Mendoza, Sally, Lowe, & Levine, 1979). If mother squirrel monkeys are removed from the home cage, the infants' plasma cortisol levels are elevated. If the infant is attended by an 'aunt' during the mother's absence, that is, carried by another adult female on her dorsal surface, the infant's cortisol level is also elevated, suggesting that the infant is experiencing stress in being separated from the mother, the specific object of its attachment. Furthermore, infants reared on a cloth surrogate do not respond to removal of the surrogate with an elevation of cortisol, even though they give behavioral evidence of missing the surrogate. Because qualitative aspects of the infants' attachment or the strength of the emotional bond may be attenuated in cloth-reared infants, the findings suggest that the quality of the mother–infant relationship may be a factor in arousal of the adrenocortical system to separations.

THE CORTICOSTEROID RESPONSE TO BRIEF SEPARATIONS

Cortisol and the Infant's Distress

We investigated the effects on excreted cortisol in response to brief separations between one-year-old children and their mothers (Tennes, Downey, & Vernadakis, 1977). We observed the infants at home during an hour-long separation from the mother. We were the baby-sitters. The mother collected the child's urine for cortisol assay on a control day, on the day of the separation, and on a third day when the researchers came to the home for the same length of time and at the same hour of the day as the separation had taken place; but the mother did not go away. We measured the cortisol excreted up to 120 min after the separations took place and compared values on the day of the experiment with the same time on the control days.

We rated the child's distress at the separation from the mother on a four-point scale. There was a consistent linear relationship between mean cortisol excretion levels and the four categories of separation distress (Table I). Infants who were not at all distressed by the mother's absence had lowest levels, infants who protested mildly but only briefly had moderate levels, and those who cried at the mother's departure and remained distressed during her absence excreted highest levels of cortisol.

When we examined the details of the behavior of the children in the highest group, we found there were two distinct types of distress response. All the infants in this category cried when the mother left the house. Some of them continued to be distressed and agitated throughout her absence. But a few of the infants behaved quite differently. After the initial distress when the mother left, they became very quiet, inactive, and refused social contact with the caretaker. When we compared the corticosteroid response of the distressed-agitated infants with the distressed-withdrawn infants, we found that the withdrawn infants had significantly lower levels of cortisol than the distressed-agitated. Thus there appeared to be a direct relationship between the behavioral expressions of distress and the adrenocortical response.

We found no statistically significant difference in the cortisol excretion levels on the day of the separation and on the control days for the group as a whole. The mean was higher on the day of the separation but the difference between the two days was not significant. Individual levels of excreted cortisol were significantly correlated across control and experimental conditions. The rank order correlation between experimental and control days was $+.69$, $p<.001$. This finding suggested there might be individual differences in chronic level of adrenocortical activity that were greater than the variability in response to the experimental stress. As an additional test of the stability of individual differences in chronic levels. we collected 8 hr of excreted cortisol from the same subjects when they were 3 years old. The correlation between

Table I. Cortisol Excretion Rates and Separation Distress $(N = 19)$

Separation distress rating	Cortisol excretion rate	
	Mean (ng/hr)	SD
1. Low	2.01	.36
2. Medium low	2.70	.43
3. Medium high	2.93	.51
4. High	3.85	.85
4A Agitated	4.74	.90
4W Withdrawn	2.05	.40

mean level of cortisol excreted for 8 hr 2 years apart in the same subjects was +.55, $p<.01$. This finding suggested relative stability in individual differences in chronic activity of the adrenocortical axis in infants or young children. Two alternative hypotheses were proposed: first, that genetic or constitutional differences determine individual differences in hormone production rates; and second, that transactions between mother and infant during the course of the first year are a primary determinant of the infant's adrenocortical responsivity. In either case the chronic level of adrenocortical activity in the infant predisposed him to respond to the stress of separations.

Cortisol and the Mother–Infant Relationship

The second hypothesis, the effect of mother–infant transactions, is of central importance to the topic of this volume. Unfortunately, we had no measures of variables in the mother–infant relationship aside from the separation situation. We had, however, recorded the response of the mother–infant reunions. Therefore, we adopted Ainsworth's method of categorizing reunion behaviors as a useful index of the quality of the mother–child relationship (Ainsworth, 1979). The written description of the mother–infant reunions as given by one observer were sorted into three categories. As might be expected from data limited to a single written record, three judges agreed on the assignment of the subjects to the categories.

As is shown in Figure 1, 14 of the infants were categorized as "responsive" (comparable to the group Ainsworth calls "secure"). They greeted the mother with eager pleasure, smiled, moved toward her, and were happy to see her. Three children, judged to be "ambivalent," reacted positively but then cried or hit her in anger or turned away. Four infants, categorized as "avoidant," ignored the mother's return and went on with whatever they were doing. Analysis of variance indicated significant differences in post-separation levels of excreted cortisol among the three groups of infants (F =

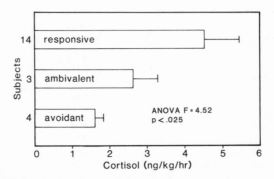

Figure 1. Reunion behavior and cortisol excreted 40–120 min post separation.

4.52, $p < .025$). Highest levels were excreted by the responsive infants, moderate by the ambivalent, and lowest by the avoidant. The four infants categorized as avoidant did not include the distressed-withdrawn infants. The withdrawn infants responded positively to the mother when she returned. The avoidant infants with low levels of adrenocortical activity were neither distressed by the mother's absence nor delighted with her return. Our data do not imply that these were poor or impoverished mother–child relationships. They indicate only that the emotional expression was low-keyed as compared with the distress and excitement of infants in the responsive category with high levels of corticosteroid.

CONCLUSION

In conclusion, the evidence suggests that hormones may play a *facilitative* role in behavioral interactions between mother and infants and that the level of the hormones may be related to the *intensity* of the behavior, or to the *form* of the behavior. That is, behavioral responses to mother–infant separations may determine adrenocortical activity. Alternatively, the causal relationship may be reversed. The level of adrenocortical activity with which the infant approaches the situation may be a determinant of the behavioral response. Furthermore, the differences in hormone responsivity may be, in part, a function of the quality of experiences the infant has had with the mother during the first year of life.

On the basis of these studies involving small numbers and preliminary results, the inclusion of hormone assay in studies of the development of mother–infant transactions in the early years of life is suggested as a fruitful area for further research.

ABSTRACT

Observations of one-year-old infants' responses to brief separations from their mothers suggest that adrenocortical activity associated with such stress may be either a precursor or a consequence of the level of distress. The child's emotional involvement with the mother, as judged by responses to reunion with her after a separation, may be related to chronic individual differences in corticosteroid levels.

REFERENCES

Ainsworth, M. *Attachment: Retrospect and prospect.* Presidential Address, Society for Research in Child Development, Biennial Meeting, San Francisco, March 1979.

Coe, C., Mendoza, S., Smotherman, W., & Levine, S. Mother–infant attachment in the squirrel monkey: Adrenal response to separation. *Behavioral Biology,* 1978, *22,* 256–263.

Hennessy, M., Kaplan, J., Mendoza, S., Sally, P., Lowe, E., & Levine, S. Separation distress and attachment in surrogate-reared squirrel monkeys. *Physiology and Behavior,* 1979, *23,* 1017–1023.

Leon, M. Mother–young reunions. In J. Sprague & A. Epstein (Eds.), *Progress in psychobiology and physiological psychology* (Vol. 8). New York: Academic Press, 1979.

Slotnick, B. M. Neural and hormonal basis of maternal behavior in the rat. In E. Eleftheriou and R. Sprott (Eds.), *Hormonal correlates of behavior* (Vol. 2). New York: Plenum Press, 1975.

Tennes, K., Downey, K., & Vernadakis, A. Urinary cortisol excretion rates in normal one-year-old infants. *Psychosomatic Medicine,* 1977, *39,* 178–187.

PART TWO

PERSPECTIVES FROM HUMAN STUDIES

CHAPTER 8

Parent-to-Infant Attachment

A CRITIQUE OF THE EARLY "BONDING" MODEL

Marilyn J. Svejda, Betty Jean Pannabecker, and Robert N. Emde

INTRODUCTION

Most research exploring attachment has been concerned with the development of the infant's attachment to his or her parents, especially to the mother Historically, much less attention has been devoted to the parental attachment systems—the parents' growth of love for the infant. A major step toward looking at the development of parental attachment came about through pioneering work of Klaus and Kennell and their associates (Klaus, Jerauld, Kreger, McAlpine, Steffa, & Kennell, 1972; Klaus & Kennell, 1976) who explored the manifestations of the mother's tie to her infant in the time shortly after the infant's birth. Subsequently, investigations have extended to the forgotten member of the triad—the father. Now, additional research has led to a need for reassessing the nature of the parent–infant attachment system.

Marilyn J. Svejda ● Parent–Child Nursing, School of Nursing, University of Michigan, Ann Arbor, Michigan 48109.   Betty Jean Pannabecker and Robert N. Emde ● University of Colorado, School of Medicine, 4200 E. Ninth Avenue, Denver, Colorado 80262. All authors were supported in part by funds from the Developmental Psychobiology Research Group of the Department of Psychiatry, University of Colorado School of Medicine. Additional support was provided by the following funding sources: Dr. Svejda is supported by a National Research Service Award for Nurse Predoctoral Fellowship 5F31–NU05059-02 and 3F1–NU05059-03S1 awarded by NIH. Dr. Pannabecker is supported by Nurse Scientist Predoctoral Fellowship, USPHS, Division of Nursing NU5008-05 and Postdoctoral Fellowship at the University of Washington School of Nursing 5–T32–NU07004-03. Dr. Emde is supported by Research Scientist Award 5–K05–MH 36808 and NIMH Project grant 2–R01–MH22803.

The goals of this chapter are twofold: (1) to briefly review the research concerning the importance of the time after birth for the development of maternal and paternal attachment systems, and (2) to suggest, on the basis of this, that the 'bonding' model of paternal attachment is misleading.

MOTHER-TO-INFANT ATTACHMENT

The original model for the importance of early contact for human mothers came from work with animals. In some animals, for example sheep and goats, separation of the young from the mother shortly after birth had a profound effect on subsequent maternal behavior. Ungulate mothers whose lambs or kids were removed soon after birth and returned one or more hours later butted their infants away when they approached, and withdrew from the young's attempts to nurse (Collias, 1956; Klopfer, Adams, & Klopfer, 1964). Those mothers that were not separated from their young, or separated following a 5–10 min period of contact immediately after birth, did not engage in these aberrant behaviors (Hersher, Moore, & Richmond, 1958). Thus the evidence was strong for the importance of the interval immediately after birth for the formation of the social bond between ungulate mothers and infants.

A Review of Maternal Bonding Research

The prototype for the several studies exploring the importance of the immediate postpartum period for maternal attachment in human mothers came from the Cleveland study of Klaus and associates (Klaus et al., 1972). In that study two groups of primiparous mothers of healthy fullterm infants had different amounts of contact with their infants immediately after delivery and during the next three postpartum days. The mothers of this study were from an inner-city disadvantaged poor population (most were unmarried teenagers who had not completed high school). Routine care mothers had the usual hospital contact: a glimpse of the infant shortly after birth, a 6–12 hr separation, and 20–30 min of contact every 4 hr for feeding. Extended contact mothers had their nude infants 1 hr within the first 3 hr after birth and 5 hr additional each day for the next 3 hospital days. At one month, extended contact mothers showed more soothing behavior when their infants became upset, engaged in more *en face* and fondling behavior during the feeding, and reported greater reluctance to leave their infants in the care of another person than did routine care mothers.

Since the original Cleveland study, there has been increasing interest in the possible influence of biological factors in the development of maternal attachment. Attachment, defined as a unique emotional relationship between two people which is specific and endures through time, is thought to be in-dexed by various behaviors including fondling, prolonged gazing, and cud-dling which serve to maintain proximity and express affection to the infant (Kennell, Trause, & Klaus, 1975). The biological basis of maternal attachment has been postulated as a result of findings from several studies which empha-size the importance of *contact* between mother and infant in the *time interval shortly after birth*—the maternal 'sensitive period.' Early contact is seen as the facilitator for a rapid process of mother to infant attachment more commonly known as bonding (Carlsson, Fagerberg, Horneman, Hwang, Larsson, Rodholm, Schaller, Danielsson, & Gundewall, 1978; de Chateau & Wiberg, 1977; Hales, Lozoff, Sosa, & Kennell, 1977; Klaus et al., 1972; Kontos, 1978). In these studies evidence for maternal bonding has been found in increased fre-quencies of affectionate behaviors (e.g., looking *en face*, holding, fondling, and rocking the infant) by those mothers who are given early contact with their infants as compared with those mothers who are given their infants for the first time several hours following birth. The effects of early contact on mater-nal behavior have been seen as soon as 36 hr (de Chateau & Wiberg, 1977; Hales et al., 1977) and have been seen as late as two and five years (Klaus & Kennell, 1976).

The notion that early contact between mother and infant may have posi-tive effects on their relationship has great theoretical and practical impor-tance. Nonetheless, although most of the research on mother–infant contact shortly after birth tends to support the importance of early contact, careful review of these studies indicates that the generalizable effects of early contact have not been convincingly demonstrated.

First, different effects have been reported even when similar dependent measures and paradigms were used. For instance, in one study primiparous mothers given skin-to-skin contact with their infants shortly after birth en-gaged in significantly more affectionate behaviors at 36 hr (looking *en face*, fondling) than did control mothers (Hales et al., 1977). Yet in a similar study (de Chateau & Wiberg, 1977) no significant differences were found in affec-tionate behaviors at 36 hr between control mothers and mothers given skin-to-skin contact with their infants.

Second, the effects of early contact have been subtle. Differences be-tween early contact and routine care (control) mothers often have been marginally significant (e.g., Klaus et al., 1972), and some behaviors, espe-cially those involved in caretaking (e.g., burping, cleansing) do not seem to be affected by early contact (de Chateau & Wiberg, 1977; Klaus et al., 1972).

Third, some behaviors which differentiated early contact (sits up more) from routine care mothers (leans on elbow) (de Chateau & Wiberg, 1977) are not in accord with behaviors that more typically characterize maternal attachment.

Finally, important methodological features (e.g., random assignment to contact conditions, blind scoring, control for demand characteristics) were not always evident in earlier studies.

Early Contact Fails to Generalize

In view of the practical importance of maternal attachment, the unclear findings to date, and the absence of important methodological features in earlier work, we were encouraged to design a study that included several methodological and procedural controls which would allow us to test the notion that early enhanced contact facilitates maternal attachment behavior (Svejda, Campos, & Emde, 1980).

Thirty lower-middle-class, healthy, primiparous mothers were randomly assigned to an extra contact (15 min of skin-to-skin contact in the delivery room, 45 min of contact in the recovery room, and $1\frac{1}{2}$ hr at each feeding for the next 7 feedings) or routine care group (5 min of contact while mother and infant were wheeled from the delivery room, no contact in the recovery room, and 20–30 min at each feeding for the next 7 feedings). Mothers were not informed about differences in contact conditions or the study's purpose until the study was completed. To avoid comparison about different contact conditions only one study mother was on the unit at a time. Nonstudy roommate mothers of extra contact mothers also had extra contact in order to reduce feelings of specialness in study mothers. Manipulation checks revealed that nurses spent an equal amount of time with all mothers. Mothers and infants were videotaped at 36 hr postpartum during an unstructured interaction and a breast feeding.

Results indicated that mothers in the two groups were very similar in their responses toward their infants. No significant differences were obtained on 28 discrete response measures or on categories of pooled response measures (i.e., affectionate, caretaking, or proximity-maintaining behaviors) as a function of early contact. We did, however, find a few sex differences related to contact condition. Early contact mothers talked more to their female infants and were more affectionate toward them during the unstructured interaction while routine care mothers touched their female infants more and looked *en face* more often at their male infants.

In general, we found little support for effects of early contact on maternal behavior. Further, the high frequency of attachment behaviors in routine care mothers suggested to us that these mothers were attached to their infants. While other studies did not state that mothers *not* having early contact were unattached, they do seem to imply that the quality of attachment was compromised in these mothers.

The results of our research are less surprising in view of other recent research reporting little support for meaningful effects of early contact on maternal behavior. One study (Leiderman & Seashore, 1975) compared mothers of fulterm infants and mothers of prematures who either had contact with their infants after delivery or who were separated from them. Differences observed in maternal behavior at one week and one month had largely disappeared at one year. Instead, parity, socioeconomic status, sex of infant, and play behavior of infant were significant predictors of maternal responsiveness (Leiderman & Seashore, 1975). At a two-year follow-up even these factors had disappeared as predictors of maternal behavior. In the words of Leiderman (1978), "it would appear that subsequent post-discharge events had major influence in reducing variations we found among groups in the first postpartum year" (p. 51). Interestingly, early separation may have had a more general effect on family stability since families in the separated group had a higher divorce rate (Leiderman, 1978).

Carlsson and associates obtained initial support for the effects of early contact on maternal behavior but effects did not persist on follow-up study. Primiparous mothers who were given early contact showed more affectionate behaviors (e.g., talks, smiles, touches, rocks) than did later contact mothers on the second and fourth day postpartum (Carlsson et al., 1978). However, a follow-up study at 6 weeks showed no statistically significant differences between groups of mothers on 18 discrete response measures or on pooled response categories (contact vs. noncontact behaviors) (Carlsson, Fagerberg, Horneman, Hwang, Larsson, Rodholm, Schaller, Danielsson, & Gundewall, 1979).

Finally, Taylor's research group (Taylor, Taylor, Campbell, Maloni, & Dickey, 1979) reported no differences between groups of mothers as a function of early contact on several measures: (a) time spent with their infants during the postpartum hospital stay, (b) responses to questions reflecting attachment, (c) responses on the Neonatal Perception Inventory at 2 days and at 1 month, and (d) the quality of the mother–infant interaction reflected during feeding at 2 days and 1 month. Some modest sex effects were obtained during feeding in favor of early contact mothers of males at the day 2 and at the 1 month observation.

What conclusions can be drawn about the effects of early contact on maternal attachment behavior?

Shortcomings of the Bonding Model

First, the general case for maternal bonding as currently conceptualized (i.e., as involving a sensitive period for infant contact immediately after birth) is weak. The diversity of findings in the several early contact studies suggests that the generality of the effect can be questioned.

Second, the evidence to date suggests a need to investigate other factors that may facilitate maternal responsiveness. One factor is the set of variables associated with a more economically advantaged population, for example, job, income, and education. A regular income provides the family with means to afford a private physician who can be consulted about matters related to pregnancy, delivery, and child care. Further, increased educational opportunities, including prenatal education, may enable the mother to identify many ways of relating to her infant and providing for his or her care. It is of interest that in studies reporting little or no effect of early contact, mothers were primarily middle-class, high school or college educated, married and living in stable families, and had husbands who were available during labor and/or delivery (Carlsson *et al.*, 1979; Leiderman, 1978; Svejda *et al.*, 1980; Taylor *et al.*, 1979).

Another factor which may play a significant role in facilitating the mother's responsiveness to her infant is the existence of support systems—family members, friends, physicians, and nurses. Especially important may be the father's presence at delivery. Wilson (1977) found that a significant predictor for the mother's responsiveness in the delivery room (e.g., talking to and touching the infant) was the father's general responsiveness, and that maternal responsiveness in the delivery room significantly predicted the mother's general responsiveness during a hospital feeding. Thus it seems quite possible that maternal behavior could be affected by the support provided by the father at delivery.

The characteristics of the infant and his or her ability to engage in interaction may also have important affects on maternal behavior. In early contact studies little attention has been given to the role of the infant as a participant in the first encounter with his or her parents.

Third, the bonding model proposed by the early contact work does not take into account the dynamic nature of the relationship between mother and infant. Maternal attachment appears to be an ongoing process and is probably not consolidated by any one experience or event (Harmon & Emde, in press). That events take place during a specified time interval, for example, immediately after birth, does not necessarily mean that they have a lasting impact on the development of the mother–infant relationship. In fact, long-term follow-up on infants of early contact mothers shows, in general, that these infants do not differ in any important way from infants of control mothers (de Chateau, 1979; Leiderman, 1978; Kennell, Jerauld, Wolfe, Chesler, Kreger, McAlpine, Steffa, & Klaus, 1974). To advocate the primacy of time-locked events tends to diminish the importance of subsequent interactions and events in the ongoing relationship between mother and infant. Further, such a position carries the potential for limiting or denying conceptualizing motherhood as a developmental process in its own right.

FATHER-TO-INFANT ATTACHMENT

Caregiving of the Father

Whereas it is true that mother-to-infant attachment has been a topic of relatively recent concern, father-to-infant attachment has been limited to even more recent interest. It was not long ago that fathers were thought to be unimportant for infant development; instead of becoming involved with their infants, the standard wisdom was that fathers were to become involved with their offspring in childhood when they became important influences for sex role, moral, and cognitive development. As Lamb (1977) has noted, recent studies of the father–infant relationship, with infants aged six months to two years, have indicated that the infant is clearly attached to the father by the second half of the first year. Thus, since we now know that father-to-infant attachment exists, it becomes relevant to ask about its beginnings. Is early contact important or facilitate this process? Is there anything analogous to maternal bonding in the immediate postpartum period?

Although childbearing used to be considered "women's work" with traditional attitudes keeping fathers away, there has been a dramatic historical change brought about by the childbirth education movement. Fathers have now become involved in prenatal classes and they assist their wives during labor and delivery. Hospital rules have been altered to allow husbands to attend deliveries, and fathers have been able to hold their infants in the delivery room and to participate in infant care during the postpartum hospital stay. It is now common for fathers to express pleasure and some confidence in the caring for their newborn infants.

A number of studies of early father–infant interaction documented these changes. Greenberg and Morris (1974) interviewed fathers within 48 hr of the delivery of their infants and noted a strong desire in the fathers to touch and hold their infants. Greenberg and Morris labelled this phenomenon "engrossment." Parke and O'Leary (1973) observed mother–infant, father–infant, and mother–father–infant interaction during the first 48 hr and found that fathers were very active participants in interactions with their infants whether or not the mothers were present. Only a few differences were found between mothers' and fathers' behavior with their infants. Mothers and fathers were found to be equally competent to meet their infants' needs during feeding.

Parke and Sawin (1977) observed father–infant and mother–infant interaction in a feeding situation and in a play situation at three times: during the postpartum hospital stay, at three weeks of age, and at three months of age. They concluded that fathers, again, were active participants in interaction with infants and that mutual regulation and adaptation between infant and parent begins in the newborn period. Both parents are seen to be active and sensitive figures in the early social development of their infants.

A Test of Father Bonding

The original Cleveland study (Klaus *et al.*, 1972) of early enhanced mother–infant contact served as a paradigm for our father–infant study. Experimental and hospital control groups were recruited prenatally (Pannabecker, Emde, & Austin, in press). Fathers in the experimental group were given extra contact with their infants during the postpartum hospitalization; however, the contact differed from the Klaus *et al.* (1972) study of mothers in several respects. Fathers had two periods of extra contact with their infants, one on each of the first two days postpartum. Although the amount of time added was only 50 min, this doubled the amount of infant contact fathers in the experimental group had compared to fathers in the control group. During extra contact, fathers were given information about selected physical and behavioral characteristics of their newborn infants. A hospital control group of fathers received the same information about physical and behavioral characteristics of newborn infants but without the contact with their own infant. (This group was introduced to control for the educational effect of learning about infants in general without added contact between fathers and their own particular infants.) An office control group was recruited on the last day of the postartum hospital stay to control for effects which may have been due to expectations related to being in the study up until that time (demand characteristics). All three groups of parents attended their infant's one-month pediatric checkup and observations were made of father's interactions with their infants.

Our results were striking. No differences were found between groups of fathers on 103 measures of father–infant interaction, either during the infant's physical examination or while father was dressing the infant and performing other unstructured activities. Our measures included *en face* behavior, and father-to-infant affectionate behaviors, as well as behaviors of other kinds. Thus enhancing early father-to-infant contact, under the conditions of this study, did not result in differences similar to those reported after enhancing mother-to-infant contact. How do we understand this?

The fact that all three groups of fathers attended childbirth education classes and the birth of their infant may have wiped out any differences related to other amounts of early contact. Peterson, Mehl, and Leiderman (1979) found that the father's participation in the birth and his attitude toward it were the most significant variables in predicting father attachment from 1 to 3 months postpartum. Alternatively, our lack of differences among groups may have been due to the fact that families were from a middle-class, educated, and childbirth-prepared population where early contact would have less of an impact than would be the case with families from a disadvantaged population. But perhaps the outstanding finding of our study concerned the large amount of involvement and participation of fathers with their infants at both the newborn and one-month age period. Like the previous studies of Parke and his collaborators, fathers were actively interested and demonstrated affection toward their infants. Obviously, not having the added early contact did *not* result in their not becoming attached. Certainly the case for the bonding model has been made more strongly for mothers where there has been a biological overtone. Since there is little or no evidence for an early contact or sensitive period phenomenon in the development of paternal attachment, it seems fortunate that the concept of bonding has been less frequently applied to fathers.

CONCLUSION

Bonding Model No Longer Useful

The pioneering work of Klaus and Kennell and their associates has facilitated important theoretical advances in emphasizing the parental side of the developing affiliative relationship between parents and infants. It has also led to important humanistic advances by encouraging hospitals to provide options for parents to be with their infants in the immediate postpartum period.

Still, we conclude that the bonding model, which grew out of this work, is no longer useful. In our view, it is misleading in the following ways:

1. The model carries the implication that parents who lack early contact do not love their babies or somehow are compromised. There is little or no research support for this position, especially for middle-class or advantaged populations.

2. The model carries the implications of a biologically-based sensitive period for attachment. This may further imply to some that attachment is primarily for mothers and is time-limited.

3. The model emphasizes newborn contact for attachment in such a way that it could lead to a relative neglect of the importance of interaction in infancy and early childhood.

4. The model is oversimplified. It tends to encourage a unidirectional view of the development of the attachment-interactive process. Current models of development are interactional and transactional and are more appreciative of factors in the family network.

5. There is a problem of reification. This was illustrated by a recent hospital nursing note which read "do not remove the baby to the nursery until bonding has taken place." As a metaphor, bonding reminds us of "getting stuck." Thus it can detract from the *process* aspects of a developing dynamic relationship between parent and infant.

6. Clinically, many parents cannot be with their infants; others may not choose to. Yet, because of some ideas fostered by the bonding model, they may feel disappointed and/or guilty for not having the opportunity to become "bonded."

In summary, the early work on maternal bonding has focused increased interest on mother and infant togetherness at the time of birth and made us more aware of parents' eagerness to participate more actively in the birth process. We have witnessed the great joy parents experience from this contact. Thus it seems important that parents have the opportunity for contact with their infants after delivery. However, they should not be led to believe that early contact is the direct route to maternal attachment, or that its absence confers difficulty. We recommend that the bonding model be discontinued as a misleading metaphor.

ABSTRACT

The importance of the time immediately after birth for the development of parental attachment to the infant has been proposed on the basis of findings from several studies. A review of this research, along with findings from recent studies, suggests that the generality of the effect of early contact can be questioned. Although the early work has led to important changes in hospital practice that allow parents more extensive contact with their infants, we conclude that the bonding model as an explanation for the development of parental attachment is misleading in several respects.

REFERENCES

Carlsson, S. G., Fagerberg, H., Horneman, G., Hwang, C.-P., Larsson, K., Rodholm, M., Schaller, J., Danielsson, B., & Gundewall, C. Effects of amount of contact between mother and child on the mother's nursing behavior. *Developmental Psychobiology, 1978, 11*, 143–150.

Carlsson, S. G., Fagerberg, H., Horneman, G., Hwang, C. P., Larsson, K., Rodholm, M., Schaller, J., Danielsson, B., & Gundewall, C. Effects of various amounts of contact between mother and child on the mother's nursing behavior: A follow-up study. *Infant Behavior and Development, 1979, 2*, 209–214.

Collias, N. E. The analysis of socialization in sheep and goats. *Ecology, 1956, 37*, 228–239.

de Chateau, P. *Long-term effects of early post-partum contact.* Research display discussion session, Society for Research in Child Development, San Francisco, March 1979.

de Chateau, P., & Wiberg, B. Long-term effect on mother–infant behavior of extra contact during the first hour post partum. I. First observation at 36 hours. *Acta Paediatrica Scandinavica*, 1977, *66*, 137–143.

Greenberg, M., & Morris, N. Engrossment: The newborn's impact upon the father. *American Journal of Orthopsychiatry*, 1974, *44*, 520–531.

Hales, D. J., Lozoff, B., Sosa, R., & Kennell, J. H. Defining the limits of the maternal sensitive period. *Developmental Medicine and Child Neurology*, 1977, *19*, 454–461.

Harmon, R. J., & Emde, R. N. Beyond maternal bonding: Clinical and research perspectives. *Journal of Nervous and Mental Disease* (in press).

Hersher, L., Moore, A. U., & Richmond, J. B. Effects of post-partum separation of mother and kid on maternal care in the domestic goat. *Science*, 1958, *128*, 1342–1343.

Kennell, J. H., Jerauld, R., Wolfe, H., Chesler, D., Kreger, N. C., McAlpine, W., Steffa, M., & Klaus, M. H. Maternal behavior one year after early and extended post-partum contact. *Developmental Medicine and Child Neurology*, 1974, *16*, 172–179.

Kennell, J. H., Trause, M. A., & Klaus, M. H. Evidence for a sensitive period in the human mother. In *Parent–infant interaction* (Ciba Foundation 33—new series). New York: Elsevier, 1975.

Klaus, M. H., Jerauld, R., Kreger, N. C., McAlpine, W., Steffa, M., & Kennell, J. H. Maternal attachment importance of the first post-partum days. *New England Journal of Medicine*, 1972, *286*, 460–463.

Klaus, M. H., & Kennell, J. H. *Maternal–infant bonding.* St. Louis: Mosby, 1976.

Klopfer, P. H., Adams, D. K., & Klopfer, M. S. Maternal "imprinting" in goats. *Proceedings, National Academy of Sciences*, 1964, *52*, 911–914.

Kontos, D. A study of the effects of extended mother–infant contact on maternal behavior at one and three months. *Birth and the Family Journal*, 1978, *5*, 133–140.

Lamb, M. E. Father–infant and mother–infant interaction in the first year of life. *Child Development*, 1977, *48*, 176–181.

Leiderman, P. H., & Seashore, M. J. Mother–infant neonatal separation: Some delayed consequences. In *Parent–infant interaction* (Ciba Foundation Symposium 33—new series). New York: Elsevier, 1975.

Leiderman, P. H. The critical period hypothesis revisited. Mother to infant social bonding in the neonatal period. In F. D. Horowitz (Ed.), *Early developmental hazards: Predictors and precautions.* American Academy for Advancement of Science, Selected Symposium 9, Boulder: Westview Press, 1978.

Pannabecker, B. J., Emde, R. N., & Austin, B. C. The effect of early extended contact on father–newborn interaction. *Journal of Genetic Psychology* (in press).

Parke, R. D., & O'Leary, S. *Family interaction in the newborn period: Some findings, some observations and some unresolved issues.* Paper presented at Biennial Meetings of the International Society for the Study of Behavior Development, Ann Arbor, August 1973.

Parke, R. D., & Sawin, D. B. *The family in early infancy: Social interactional and attitudinal analyses.* Paper presented at Society for Research in Child Development, New Orleans, March 1977.

Peterson, G. H., Mehl, L. E., Leiderman, P. H. The role of some birth-related variables in father attachment. *American Journal of Orthopsychiatry*, 1979, *49*(2), 330–338.

Svejda, M. J., Campos, J. J., & Emde, R. N. Mother–infant "bonding": Failure to generalize. *Child Development*, 1980, *56*, 775–779.

Taylor, P. M., Taylor, F. H., Campbell, S. B., Maloni, J., & Dickey, D. *Effects of extra contact on early maternal attitudes, perceptions and behaviors.* Paper read at the meetings of the Society for Research in Child Development, San Francisco, March 1979.

Wilson, L. *A predictive analysis of early parental attachment behavior.* Paper read at the meetings of the Society for Research in Child Development, New Orleans, March 1977.

CHAPTER 9

Silver Nitrate and the Eyes of the Newborn

EFFECTS ON PARENTAL RESPONSIVENESS DURING INITIAL SOCIAL INTERACTION

Perry M. Butterfield, Robert N. Emde, Marilyn Svejda, and Sandy Naiman

The emotional relationship which exists between parent and child is a unique and enduring affiliative system (Bowlby, 1958). From the parental side, the ontogeny of this system has presented some prominent issues in developmental research during the past decade. Two major themes have emerged. The first theme is the idea that the infant provides the stimulus which elicits and sustains parental love (Bell & Harper, 1977; Bowlby, 1958; Brazelton, 1973; Leiderman, 1980); the second, is the idea of rapid emotional bonding by the parents in the immediate postpartum period (for a critique of this concept see Chapter 8, this volume). This chapter will look more specifically at these themes by examining one major stimulus component, the eyes of the infant as they effect the parents' behavior during this postpartum period.

The eyes of the infant have been cited as central in maternal affiliation (Brazelton, 1966; Klaus & Kennell, 1976). Immediately after birth the newborn is usually wide-eyed and visually active. He quiets to visual stimulation (Wolff & White, 1965), orients to a face (Goren, 1976), follows a moving tar-

Perry M. Butterfield, Robert N. Emde, Marilyn Svejda, and Sandy Naiman • Department of Psychiatry, University of Colorado School of Medicine, Denver, Colorado 80262. All the authors were funded in part by the Developmental Psychobiology Research Group, Department of Psychiatry, University of Colorado Medical Center. Perry Butterfield was supported by MCH Research Grant RO–80398, and the Parent–Infant Project, University of Colorado School of Medicine. Robert N. Emde was supported by Research Scientist Award 5–K05–MH–36808 and NIMH Project Grant 2–R01–MH–22803. Marilyn Svejda was supported by NIMH Fellowships 5–F31–NU05059 and 3–F1–NU05059S.

get (Haith, 1976), and is characteristically more alert and active during the first two hours after birth than in the subsequent eight hours (Emde, Swedberg, & Suzuki, 1975).

In the past, mothers and infants were separated during this period. Mothers were thought to need rest, infants were taken to be cleaned and observed by nurses, and fathers were not permitted in birthing areas. However, the childbirth education movement, buttressed by research emphasizing the importance of this early period to the maternal attachment process (see Klaus & Kennell, 1976), led to changes in hospital practices (Korte & Scaer, 1977). Opportunity for parent–infant contact immediately following delivery is now commonplace. In addition, the reduced use of anesthesia has permitted mothers to be more awake during delivery, and most hospitals allow fathers to be present throughout labor and delivery. Thus both parents can now participate in the first social interactions with their infant.

In the midst of these changes, some hospital practices relating to the immediate care of the infant have changed relatively little. In most maternity units the eyes of the newborn are flushed with prophylactic medication for gonococcal infection within five minutes after birth (between the time of the standard APGAR ratings of cardiorespiratory status). The medication which is usually applied is silver nitrate, one which is known to cause swelling and redness of the tissue around the eyes (Holmes, 1976; Nishida & Risemberg, 1975; Yasunaga, 1977). Although routine eye prophylaxis is still believed to be needed, there is no evidence that it needs to be administered immediately after birth (Center for Disease Control, 1979: Shaw, 1973). Because of the importance placed upon early eye-to-eye contact (Robson, 1967) and because of the role attributed to the infant's visual behavior in maternal attachment process (Grossman, 1978), the effect of silver nitrate on the visual behavior of the baby becomes of interest. Does eye prophylaxis alter the appearance of the infant as he or she greets his or her parents? Does it effect the way in which the baby uses his eyes in his initial social interaction? Are such differences important to the parents and to the way in which they behave toward their new baby? The rest of this chapter will discuss two studies. One study examines the effects of routinely administered silver nitrate on eye openness and visual activity in the first postnatal hour and a second study examines such effects on parental interaction.

THE FIRST STUDY

Twenty infants from the University Hospital in Denver, Colorado were studied (Butterfield, Emde, & Platt, 1978). All met strict criteria for normal deliveries including APGAR scores above seven, gestational age of 38–42 weeks, temperature above 36° C, and birth weights between 2700 and 3600 g. Infants whose mothers had received sedation or general anesthesia were excluded. The infants were randomly assigned to receive silver nitrate (SN) in the delivery room between the one and five min APGAR scoring (the hospital routine), or to have silver nitrate delayed (No SN) until after the evaluation of visual behavior. All infants were taken to the nursery for assessment, where they were rated by the nursery personnel for behavioral state, then swaddled and placed in an infant seat for videotaping. The mean age of infants at testing was 47.5 min; $SD = 15$ min. In order to test for the effect of SN on the visual behavior of the infant we adapted the infrared corneal reflection used by Haith (1969) for video recording of eye movements. Stimulus conditions chosen for this study included complete darkness and a moderate light condition which was comparable to a dimly lit hospital room. In the moderate light condition, two moving stimuli were presented in random order. These stimuli were red wook at the end of a dowel and a standardized white bar on a black field. The latter was 6.7 cm wide and painted as a vertical bar on a black wire screen so that a camera could view through it. The infant sear was behind this screen approximately 36 cm Four infrared lights were used in order to produce separate corneal reflection images for assisting in later judgment of eye movements.* An infrared sensitive television camera (General Electric, 4TE, 33B) was mounted near the ceiling, perpendicular to the infant's line of sight, and was focused by remote control to record a close-up of the face and eyes on videotape (see Figure 1).

Each testing session took approximately 4 min The videotape recording for each subject included a 48-sec observation in the dark condition, a 5-sec period of increasing light intensity, a 15-sec period for visual adaptation, and a 48-sec observation in the moderate light condition. This latter 48-sec observation in moderate light was divided into eight presentations of 6 sec each, which allowed for each moving stimulus to be presented four times. The remaining 2 min were devoted to positioning the infant and focusing the camera.

Video tapes were reviewed separately by two independent observers who were naïve to the hypotheses of the study. These observers were trained to assess the extent of eye opening and the presence or absence of visual pursuit in the baby. Extent of eye opening was rated according to Haith's four point scale, in which (1) eyes appear closed, (2) one-fourth of the iris is visible, (3) three-fourths of the iris is visible, and (4) the total iris is visible (Figure 2). Eye openness was rated every two sec, with 24 scores rated in the soft light condition and 24 scores obtained in the dark condition. These 48 scores were then averaged for each subject. The interrater correlation for agreement of

---

* The light beam produced by these illuminators passed through a Wratten, 7–69 heat filter and 3 Polaroid HW7 filters which blocked wave lengths below 900 millimicrons of illumination to the infant's eye. The remaining infrared light energy was 1/2 of that used by Haith (1969) in his studies. He reported that 6 such illuminators produced a total of .17 mcal/second/cm² or approximately 1/200 of that produced by scattered light on a sunny day.

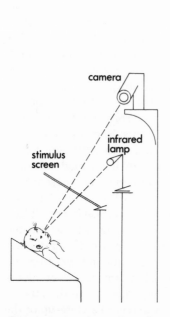

Figure 1. Apparatus for infrared videotaping of visual activity in the newborn during the first postnatal hour.

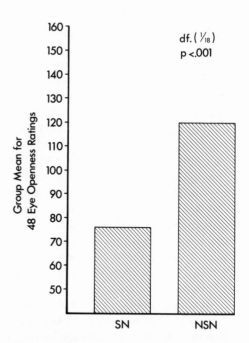

Figure 2. Rating scale for eye openness in the newborn infant.

total scores per baby by condition was high ($r = 0.96$). In addition to eye openness ratings, visual pursuit was recorded if the direction of eye movements corresponded to the direction of the stimulus motion two or more times in a given presentation. Raters agreed on 79 of 80 presentations ($r = .98$).

Results indicated dramatic differences between groups with respect to the degree of eye opening. Infants with SN were *not* observed to open their eyes beyond a squint (i.e., not far enough to show three-fourths of the iris above or below the pupil). Usually their eyes appeared as small slits even though there was vigorous activity, rooting, and other signs of alertness documented in both groups of infants (two nursery nurses judged 18 of the 20 babies to be alert). In contrast, babies without SN were usually observed to be open-eyed, sometimes even "wide-eyed" with the full circle of the iris exposed. The mean eye openness ratings for SN babies were 1.64 in the light and 1.70 in the dark; $SD = .30$. Corresponding means for the babies who did not receive treatment were 2.45 in light and 2.47 in dark; $SD = .38$ (*df* 1/18,

$p < .001$). The effect of light condition, darkness versus moderate light, was not a significant factor in the degree of eye openness.

Results with visual pursuit also showed striking differences. Visual pursuit to either moving stimulus was observed in only one of the 10 infants in the SN group, while pursuit was apparent in 9 out of 10 babies in the No SN group ($p < .01$; Fisher Exact Probability Test) (Siegel, 1956). Separate analyses showed that both the red wool and the white bar were effective in producing pursuit in the No SN group.

This study demonstrated that infants with SN were hampered in their ability to open their eyes and visually pursue a moving stimulus at one hour postpartum even though reddening and swelling of the conjunctiva were not apparent in the SN babies. Both the appearance and the visual behavior of the infant were altered.

The further investigation of early affiliative processes was therefore suggested. Are parents aware of differences in the infant's visual behavior? Do these differences change the way in which they respond to their infant? If indeed, the wide-eyed searching behavior of the newborn is central to eliciting parental responsiveness, a second study needed to be done. Accordingly, we designed a study in order to test the hypotheses that (1) SN would effect eye openness (replication of the first study) and (2) that lack of eye openness would effect infant-directed attention and affectionate behaviors of the parents.

THE SECOND STUDY

For this study a large maternity center (St. Joseph Hospital, Denver, Colorado) was chosen so that the subject population would include families from a broad economic range (Butterfield, Emde, & Svejda, 1981). One-fourth of the maternity patients were clinic patients from the core city, one-half were from a Kaiser group practice, and one-fourth were patients of private physicians, Eligible families were enrolled from prenatal classes or early admission to the delivery suite. Sixty families agreed to participate in a study which compared two different but accepted hospital procedures; one in which infants were weighed, measured, and given the standard medication in the delivery room, or one in which infants were not weighed or medicated until after they had been taken to the nursery. These 60 families were videotaped in a private recovery room after the birth of their baby. In all cases the father was present at delivery and during the taping.

The infants in this study were randomly assigned to one of two groups: the first group of infants received SN between the one and five minute APGAR scorings; the second group of infants had their eye prophylaxis delayed until after the family had been together. As in the First Study, all subjects had normal deliveries and were free from medical complications. Babies were shown to mother and father in delivery, then examined by a perinatal nurse, rated for state, swaddled, and taken to the recovery room where the taping would begin. The same infrared light-sensitive camera as in the First Study was mounted near the ceiling and operated by remote control from outside the room.

When the infants were brought to the recovery room, they were first placed in an infant seat for a one-minute full-faced filming in order to replicate the First Study procedure. Following this, they were placed next to their mothers in the recovery room and the family was left alone for ten minutes. No instructions were given to the parents except to enjoy their time together. Both mother and father had to adjust their position in order to look at or hold the infant. We found that in this situation parents very quickly forgot that video camera was running. They became involved with the infant and with one another. After taping, the mothers were interviewed about their impressions of the infant. They were then told the purpose of the study, about their infant's eye care, and they were given the opportunity to view the videotape. Videotaping and interviewing were done by two medical students from the University of Colorado School of Medicine.

Fifty-six of the 60 full-faced observations of the infants were ratable. In the other four tapes, shadows or squirming by the infant prevented adequate ratings. Two experienced observers who were naive to the aims and hypotheses of the study rated the tapes independently. Eye openness was scored every other second for one full minute of tape. A mean score for eye openness was obtained for each baby. Interrater reliability was high ($r = .95$).

The effects of SN on the appearance of the infant was replicated. As in the previous study, there was a significant difference in eye openness as a function of SN treatment. Mean eye openness for SN infants was 1.55, $SD = 24$, and for unmedicated infants 2.36, $SD = .43$ ($p < .005$; t-test). There was a broader range of scores for the nonmedicated babies. Ratings ranged from a mean score of 1.2, a virtually closed eye, to a mean score of 3.3 for an infant whose mother said "his eyes were as big as quarters." For the medicated babies mean scores clustered from 1.0 to 2.4. Ratings of the infant behavioral state showed 34 of the 56 infants to be in an alert state, 2 were drowsy, and 20 crying. Of the 20 crying infants, 14 had had immediate application of SN ($p < .02$; χ^2).

For the interaction part of our data analysis, 51 tapes were ratable. Seven mothers chose to nurse their babies during taping and were excluded from data analysis because we felt that the interaction between a mother, father, and baby was altered by maternal nursing behavior.

If the visual behavior of the newborn is a process variable in parental responsiveness, we would expect more attention to be focused on the babies who had their eyes wide open, and also we would expect more demonstrative affection to be shown by the parents toward those infants. Therefore, our raters viewed each tape twice in order to document behaviors in both parents which would define where they focused their attention. For example the direction of a mother's gaze, whom she talked to, touched, or smiled at were specifically scored. These behaviors were adapted for this study from those described by Klaus, Jerauld, Kreger, McAlpine, Steffa, and Kennell (1972). They included the existence of low-frequency behaviors such as rocking, stroking, kissing, nuzzling, and undressing the infant. When fathers were scored for close looking, this required that they bend down below the bed rail to regard the infant. Touching, holding, and talking to the infant were scored for fathers on the same criteria as for mothers; definitions for each of these behaviors are found in Table I.

The raters scored the existence or nonexistence of a behavior at 5-sec intervals throughout the 10-min period. Thus 120 intervals were scored for each behavior. Interrater reliability for each ranged from $r = .93$ to $r = .99$.

Although we initially randomized our sample into SN and No SN groups, to gain precision in our analysis of the effect of eye openness on the parents, we regrouped our sample according to the infant eye openness data. The mean eye openness for all infants was established to be 1.95, infants whose eye openness ratings fell above this mean formed the "wide-eyed" group, while infants whose eyes were rated below this mean formed a

Table I. Definitions of Behaviors Scored

1.	"Looks at baby"—head and eyes in direction of baby; for father, head in close below the bed rail.
2.	"*En face* looking"—mother positions baby or herself so that her face is directly in front of the baby's face.
3.	"Looks at F.O.C."—head and eyes in direction of father.
4.	"Looks away"—mother looking elsewhere in room.
5.	"Talks to baby"—any verbalization in the direction of the baby, including percussive sounds.
6.	"Talks away"—any verbalizations made looking away from the baby, except crooning, quieting songs.
7.	"Touching the baby"—affectionate touching of the baby's body, patting or stroking. Do not rate functional touches such as diapering or arraying the blankets.
8.	"Kissing and nuzzling"—any contact of mother's face and neck to any part of the infant.
9.	"Smiling at baby or at F.O.C."—any upturning of the lips in excess of mother's predominant appearance on the TV screen; a change of expression which denotes heightened pleasure.
10.	"Rocks baby"—any rhythmic soothing motion directed toward the baby with the mother's hand on body.
11.	"Undresses baby"—any effort to remove the blankets to view the baby beyond the head and face; straightening the blanket around the face or rearranging the baby are not included.

"closed-eyed" group. This regrouping of our independent variable affected 11 infants: in the wide-eyed group ($n = 28$), there were 7 infants who had been assigned SN, while in the closed-eyed group ($n = 23$), there were 4 infants who had been assigned No SN (delayed medication).

Results of this study showed that the eye openness of the infant did *not* significantly alter the attention of a mother toward her newborn. All mothers looked at their infants 70 to 80% of the time, and all mothers talked to and touched their infants about the same amount for each group. Beyond this, there were suggestions of group differences for some behaviors but they were difficult to interpret. Mothers of wide-eyed infants smiled at them more often (a mean of 21 vs. 10 intervals) and spent more time undressing them (a mean of 24 vs. 8 intervals) while kissing them less (3 vs. 8 intervals). They also talked less frequently with the father (42 vs. 53 intervals). Because these comparisons are based on less than a complete proportion of cases showing any given behavior, statistical tests of comparison are not practical. The above comparisons, as well as those for other maternal behaviors are presented in Table II.

Table II also presents a comparison of paternal behaviors. The overall participation of fathers was impressive: 86% of all fathers bent down below the bed rail to look closely at their infant, about one-half of the fathers talked to their infant, and 26% of both groups chose to take the infant from the mother to hold it. The reader will also note that, in contrast to mothers, the comparison of infant groups suggests an interpretable eye-openness effect on the affiliative behavior of fathers.

In the interviews following the taping, mothers seemed eager to express their feelings about their new infant. They were asked what they first noticed about the baby, that is, what features seemed most important or were of specific note. They were also asked if they had planned ahead for this time with the baby, and if the first meeting lived up to their expectations.

Most of the families had planned ahead for a "bonding period," which they had learned about through prenatal classes. Nineteen of the 56 interviewed said that they had worried about how to handle the situation, and two mothers said that they were too tired and found the time stressful.

Data from our postpartum interview are summarized in Table III. In answer to inquiries about important features of the babies, 17 specific features besides the eyes were mentioned. The most commonly mentioned characteristic was hair ($n = 35$), although eyes were the next most frequently remembered feature ($n = 32$). Thirty-four mothers made other spontaneous comments about their infants with "looks like" ($n = 28$) the most common statement.

A breakdown of what the 32 mothers noted about their infants' eyes is instructive. Thirteen mothers of the closed-eyed babies made 13 comments about the eyes, with 6 mentioning the color of the eyes and 7 mentioning the eyes being closed. Nineteen mothers of wide-eyed infants made 41 comments about their eyes, but there was no mention of eye color. Instead these

Table II. Behaviors Exhibited by Parents during the First 10 Minutes Alone with Their Newborn

Behavior definition	Number of subjects exhibiting the behavior		Mean Number of 5-sec intervals	
	$n = 28$ Wide-eyed	$n = 23$ Closed	Wide-eyed	Closed
Mother toward baby				
Looks at baby	100%	100%	96	88
	($n = 28$)	($n = 23$)		
Talks to baby	96%	96%	52	45
	($n = 27$)	($n = 22$)		
Touches baby	92%	100%	37	30
	($n = 25$)	($n = 23$)		
Smiles at baby	85%	95%	21	10
	($n = 23$)	($n = 21$)		
Rocks baby	75%	56%	23	32
	($n = 21$)	($n = 13$)		
En face looking	23%	39%	24	25
	($n = 7$)	($n = 10$)		
Undressing baby	21%	17%	24	08
	($n = 6$)	($n = 4$)		
Kisses baby	39%	30%	03	08
	($n = 11$)	($n = 9$)		
Mother away from baby				
Looks at father	96%	91%	47	52
	($n = 27$)	($n = 21$)		
Looks around room	96%	96%	37	47
	($n = 27$)	($n = 22$)		
Talks to father	96%	96%	42	53
	($n = 27$)	($n = 22$)		
Smiles at father	93%	100%	16	12
	($n = 26$)	($n = 23$)		
Father toward baby				
Looks at baby	89%	83%	59	34
	($n = 25$)	($n = 19$)		
Touches	96%	78%	21	13
	($n = 27$)	($n = 18$)		
Holds baby	29%	22%	36	18
	($n = 8$)	($n = 5$)		
Talks to baby	61%	52%	20	08
	($n = 17$)	($n = 12$)		

mothers expressed surprise at the appearance of the babies' eyes. Noting the "active searching," "looking around," eye size, and specific detail such as "sparkle," they did not seem to be anticipating such active visual behaviors in their infants but were enthusiastic about the babies' eyes and remembered them with pleasure.

It is also noteworthy that mothers in the closed-eyed group did not seem dismayed by the infants' appearance; they remarked instead on the baby being "too new" or "too tired" to open its eyes.

DISCUSSION

Both studies documented that the newborn is alert in the first postnatal hour. Typically, the eyes of most newborns are wide open and actively scanning. Our studies also documented a change in the appearance of the eyes and in visual activity following the administration of SN: early medication resulted in a dampening of wide-eyed activity. Still, the results of the second study did not support our hypothesis that such dampening would be associated with a lesser amount of maternal affectionate attention.

In light of this, we found the suggestion of father effects quite intriguing. For some fathers, the appearance of the infants' eyes seemed to influence their affectionate behavior. Perhaps the father, who has less acquaintance with the infant at the time of birth, is more sensitive to specific stimuli such as the baby's eyes. Aside from this speculation, early paternal attachment is an open issue and merits a good deal more study (see Chapter 10 and Chapter 8, this volume).

Are there broader implications of our findings? Our follow-up interviews indicated that the mothers of our study were excited by this initial encounter and experienced considerable pleasure and affection with their infants. Mothers of wide-eyed infants expressed surprise and pleasure about the size and the movement of their infants' eyes; however, eyes were only one of many features that impressed them. It seemed as though mothers were prepared to examine their infants in specific detail, to be sure they were "OK," and to note the infant's size, color, and whom he or she resembled. Many spoke of anticipating this experience for months and some used the word "beautiful" to describe it. Maternal affiliation seemed to be taking place in spite of the SN effect.

In generalizing our findings, the reader should bear in mind the constraints of our sample. Three-fourths of those in the second study were middle class and almost all experienced intensive prenatal education. It is with middle-class mothers that many of the effects of initial contact which were described by Klaus *et al.* (1972) have not been replicated (Carlsson, Fagerberg, Horneman, Hwang, Larsson, Rodholm, Schaller, Danielsson, & Gundewall, 1978; Svejda, Campos, & Emde, 1980). The use of other samples of mothers, such as those from a low socioeconomic status, teenagers, depressed women, and others deemed to be a parenting risk, might yield affiliation differences due to SN effects, whereas our investigation did not.

We would like to end on a practical note. Recently, the American Academy of Pediatrics suggested that ophthalmic SN might be delayed for one hour

Table III. Postpartum Interviews

A. Features mentioned				B. Spontaneous comments about the baby				C. Specific comments about baby's eyes		
18 Specific features mentioned	Total moms	Wide-eyed	Closed-eyed	Comment	Total moms	Wide-eyed	Closed-eyed	Comment	Wide-eyed $n=19$	Closed-eyed $n=13$
Eyes	37	19	18	"Looks like"	28	14	14	Eye color	0	6
Hair	30	12	18	He's OK	6	2	4	Closed or tried to open	0	7
Head shape	11	4	7	So alert	9	8	1	Eye movement following	14	0
Skin color	15	8	7	Beautiful, etc.	34	20	14	Eye size	8	0
Size	10	7	3					Detail about eyes "sparkle"	7	0
Sex	9	4	5					Surprise at eyes	9	0
Nose	13	5	8					Eyes "are like"	3	0
Fingers	10	2	8					Total comments	41	13
Ears	6	2	4							
Grip	5	1	4							
Cries	7	1	6							
Feet	5	1	4							
Toes	7	2	5							
Chin, knees tongue, skin	5	2	3							
"Nothing"	2	2	0							

after birth in order to facilitate maternal attachment, citing a brief report of our first study as one basis for this suggestion (American Academy of Pediatrics, Committee on Drugs, Fetus and Newborn, and Infectious Diseases, 1980). In view of the findings of our Second Study, we would now emphasize the adaptability of mothers who attend to their infants regardless of eye appearance. Our data do not give any direct scientific basis for suggesting a relationship between the delay of SN and maternal affiliation, rather they do document the enthusiasm which mothers felt about the eyes of their unmedicated babies. We applaud the humanistic basis for the Academy suggestion. Although it seems unlikely that any single stimulus alteration will impair the parents' desire and ability to fall in love with their infant, it also seems appropriate for parents to meet their infant without any alterations in his or her appearance and to be able to enjoy the beauty of the wide searching eyes of their newborn.

ABSTRACT

This chapter discusses two studies, one which examines the effects of routinely administered silver nitrate on the eye openness and visual activity of the newborn during the first postnatal hour, and a second study which examines such effects on parental interaction. These studies show that silver nitrate administered in the delivery room clearly alters the appearance of the infant's eyes and reduces visual activity in the newborn; however, this change in the eyes of the newborn did not alter the amount of maternal affection which was focused on the baby in the first postnatal hour. There were interpretable eye openness effects on the affiliative behavior of fathers.

Acknowledgments

Thanks is given to Lula Lubchenco, M.D., Watson Bowes, M.D., and their staffs for advice and encouragement, availability of patients, and use of equipment from the Maternity Suite and the Newborn Center of the University of Colorado School of Medicine. Thanks also to Marshall Haith, Ph.D., and Bruce B. Platt, Ph.D., University of Denver, for their help with the infrared video technology; and to C. Houston Alexander, M.D. and the staff of St. Josephs Hospital for the generous use of their maternity facilities. Special thanks to Donald Stilson, Ph.D., University of Colorado School of Medicine, for his statistical consultation.

REFERENCES

American Academy of Pediatrics, Committees on Drugs, Fetus and Newborn, and Infectious Diseases. Prophylaxis and treatment of neonatal gonococcal infection. *Pediatrics*, 1980, 65(5), 1047–1048.

Bell, R. Q., & Harper, L. V. *The effect of children on parents.* Hillside, N.J.: Lawrence Erlbaum, 1977.

Bowlby, John. The nature of a child's tie to his mother. *International Journal of Psycho-Analysis,* 1958, 39, 350–373.

Brazelton, T. B. *Neonatal behavior assessment scale.* Philadelphia: Spastics International Medical Publication, 1973.

Brazelton, T. B., School, M. L., & Robley, J. S. Visual responses in the newborn, *Pediatrics*, 1966, 37(2), 284–290.

Butterfield, P. M., Emde, R. N., & Platt, B. B. Effects of silver nitrate on initial visual behavior. *American Journal of Diseases in Children,* 1978, 132, 426.

Butterfield, P. M., Emde, R. N., & Svejda, M. J. Does the early application of silver nitrate impair maternal attachment? A commentary. *Pediatrics*, 1981, *67*, 5.

Carlsson, S. G., Fagerberg, H., Horneman, G., Hwang, C. P., Larsson, D., Rodholm, M., Schaller, J., Danielsson, B., & Gundewall, C. Affects of the amount of contact between mother and child on the mother's nursing behavior. *Developmental Psychology*, 1978, *11*, 143–150.

Center for Disease Control. Gonorrhea, CDC recommended treatment schedules. *Journal of Infectious Disease*, 1979, *139*, 496–501.

Emde, R. N., Swedberg, J., & Suzuki, B. Human wakefulness and biological rhythms after birth. *Archives of General Psychiatry*, 1975, *32*, 780–783.

Goren, C. *Form perception, innate form preference and visually-mediated head-turning in the human neonate*. Paper presented at the Society for Research in Child development. Denver, March 1975.

Grossman, K. Die Wirkung des Augenöffnens von Neugeborenen auf das Verhalten ihrer Mütter. *Geburtshilfe und Frauenheilkunde*, 1978, *38*, 629–635.

Haith, M. M. Infrared television recordings and measurements of ocular behavior in the human infant. *American Psychologist*, 1969, *24*(3), 279–283.

Haith, M. M. Visual competence in early infancy. In R. Held, H. Liebowitz, & H. L. Teuber (Eds.), *Handbook of sensory physiology* (Vol. 8) Berlin: Springer-Verlag, 1976.

Holmes, K. K. Gonococcal infections. In J. S. Remington & J. O. Klein (Eds.), *Infectious diseases of the fetus and newborn infant*. Philadelphia: Sanders, 1976.

Klaus, M. H., Jerauld R., Kreger, N. C., McAlpine, W., Steffa, M., & Kennell, J. H. Maternal attachment importance of the first post-partum days. *The New England Journal of Medicine*, 1972, *286*, 460–463.

Klaus, M., & Kennell, J. *Maternal–infant bonding*. St. Louis: C. V. Mosby, 1976.

Korte, D., & Scaer, R. *A survey of maternity care options*. Diana Korte, 564 Linden Park Court, Boulder, CO. 80302, 1977.

Leiderman, P. H. Human mother-to-infant social bonding: Is there a sensitive phase? In K. Immelmann & G. Barlow (Eds.), *Ethology and child development*. New York: Cambridge University Press, 1980.

Nishida, H., & Risemberg, H. M. Silver nitrate opthalmic solution and chemical conjunctivitis. *Pediatrics*, 1975, *56*, 368–373.

Robson, K. S. The role of eye-to-eye contact in maternal infant attachment. *Journal of Child Psychology and Psychiatry*, 1967, *8*, 13–25.

Shaw, E. B. Gonorrhea ophthalmia neonatorum. *Pediatrics*, 1973, *52*, 281–282.

Siegal, S. *Nonparametric statistics for behavioral sciences*. New York: McGraw-Hill, 1956.

Svejda, M. J., Campos, J. J., & Emde, R. N. mother–infant "bonding": Failure to generalize. *Child Development*, 1980, *51*, 775–779

Wolff, P. H., & White, L. Visual pursuit and attention in young infants. *American Academy of Child Psychiatry*, 1965, *4*, 473–484.

Yasunaga, S., & Kean, E. H. Effects of three ophthalmic solutions on chemical conjunctivitis in the neonate. *American Journal of Disease in Children*, 1977, *131*, 159–161.

Effect of Gender and Caretaking Role on Parent–Infant Interaction

Michael E. Lamb, Ann M. Frodi, Carl-Philip Hwang, Majt Frodi, and Jamie Steinberg

ATTITUDES AND BEHAVIOR OF TRADITIONAL AND NONTRADITIONAL PARENTS IN SWEDEN

Introduction

After decades in which developmental psychologists focused exclusively on mother–infant relationships, researchers have recently begun to study father–infant relationships as well (Lamb, 1978; Parke, 1979). These studies confirm that many fathers interact sensitively and responsively with their infants (Parke & Sawin, 1980) and that most infants form attachments to both their mothers and fathers at roughly the same age (Lamb, 1977b). Despite such similarities between mother– and father–infant relationships, some important differences between maternal and paternal styles have also been identified. Mothers' interactions tend to be centered around caretaking, whereas fathers' interactions are characterized by play—especially physically stimulating play (Clarke-Stewart, 1978; Lamb, 1976, 1977b; Yogman, Dixon, Tronick, Als, Adamson, Lester, & Brazelton, 1977). Lamb (1978) has speculated that the distinctive sex stereotyped patterns of parent–infant interaction occupy an important place in the development of gender identity.

Michael E. Lamb • Department of Psychology, University of Utah, Salt Lake City, Utah 84112.   Ann M. Frodi • Department of Psychology, University of Rochester, Rochester, New York 14627.   Carl-Philip Hwang and Majt Frodi • Department of Psychology, University of Göteborg, Göteborg, Sweden.   Jamie Steinberg • School of Public Health, University of Michigan, Ann Arbor, Michigan 48109. This research was supported by the Riksbankens Jubileumsfond of Stockholm, Sweden.

Several studies have involved naturalistic observations of parents and young infants (Parke & Sawin, 1980; Pedersen, Anderson, & Cain, 1980). Pedersen et al. reported that mothers verbalized, smiled, and fed liquids to their 5-month-old infants more frequently than fathers did. Parke, O'Leary, and West (1972) and Parke and O'Leary (1976) found few differences between maternal and paternal behavior toward newborns, although fathers held, rocked, and looked more than their wives did. When observed feeding their infants, mothers of 3-month-olds spent more time feeding and caretaking, but otherwise the behavior of mothers and fathers was similar (Parke & Sawin, 1980).

With one exception (Field, 1978) all previous studies have involved traditional families in which mothers were primary (if not sole) caretakers, while fathers had minimal caretaking responsibilities. This makes it impossible to determine whether the parental styles mentioned above are determined by the parents' gender or caretaking responsibility: these factors have usually been confounded. In her microanalytic study of face-to-face interaction with 4-month-olds, Field (1978) found that primary caretaking fathers resembled primary caretaking mothers in their tendency to smile, vocalize imitatively, and grimace in imitation, while resembling secondary caretaking fathers in their tendency to play games, poke at the infants, and avoid the limb-containing behaviors characteristic of primary caretaking mothers. Unfortunately, Field did not observe any secondary caretaking mothers. Her findings suggested that both gender and caretaking role account for the distinctive parental styles of mothers and fathers, although the brevity of the observations (3 mins) and the small sample size ($N = 12$ per group) make further study essential. The present research was designed to examine the influence of gender and caretaking role on the behavior of parents interacting in a naturalistic home setting with their 3-month-old infants.

In addition, we wished to determine whether the patterns of parent–infant interaction were affected by the sex and perceived temperament of the infants. Parke and Sawin (1980) reported that fathers interacted preferentially with infant sons and mothers with infant daughters; Lamb (1977a) and Rendina and Dickerscheid (1976) reported that fathers interacted preferentially with 1- to 2-year old sons and Hoffman (1977) concluded that both parents, expecially fathers, prefer sons. We wondered whether similar patterns would be evident in nontraditional families (i.e., families in which fathers assume some responsibility for caretaking) or whether nontraditional parents, committed as they are to nonsexist values, would avoid treating sons and daughters differently. As far as temperament is concerned, we were impressed by the suggestion that infant temperament may affect the quality and extent of parent–infant interaction. Feiring (1976), for example, reported that difficult infants elicited fewer and less sensitive bids from their mothers. In contrast, Pedersen (1975) reported that fathers played more with difficult infants while Rendina and Dickerscheid (1976) found that this occurred only among the fathers of first-born sons; difficult daughters received the least attention from their fathers.

Our study took place in Sweden, where we expected to find matched groups of traditional and nontraditional families more readily than in the United States. Since 1974 Swedish parents have been entitled to 9 months of paid parental leave following delivery, and the government has financed an extensive campaign designed to encourage both mothers and fathers to request parental leave. Immediately after birth, both parents take two weeks of leave; this leave is not transferable from one parent to the other whereas the remainder of the leave can be divided between the two parents at their discretion. In 1979, just under 10% of the fathers in Sweden took one month or more of paid parental leave, and it was from this group that we planned to draw our sample of nontraditional families.

Method

Subjects. The participants in this study were 51 couples who were interviewed during pregnancy and were later observed interacting with their 3-month-olds. The parents were recruited through childbirth- and parent-preparation classes in Göteborg, Sweden. Most of the families were middle class and moderately well educated: at the time of the babies' birth, the mothers ranged in age from 21 to 35 years ($\overline{X} = 27.2$ yrs), the fathers from 22 to 51 years ($X = 30.2$ yrs). The infants were all first born of the present union: two of the fathers had offspring from previous relationships. All the infants were healthy products of full-term pregnancies and all fathers were present during delivery.

When this study was conducted, Swedish parents were entitled to 9 months of paid leave that could be divided between the two parents in any way they chose. Parents were interviewed about their planned leaves during the last trimester of pregnancy. For the purpose of this study, we considered couples to be "nontraditional" when the fathers planned to spend 1 or more months alone with and as primary caretaker for the infant. The average nontraditional father chose to take 2.8 months (range, 1.0–6.5 months); the average "traditional" father chose to take 0.4 months (range, 0–0.9 months). On demographic variables, the nontraditional parents achieved slightly higher scores on the Hollinghead (1978) Four Factor Index ($\overline{X}_T = 42.2$, $\overline{X}_{NT} = 47.1$, $F = 5.96$, $p < .02$) than the traditional parents did. Fourteen of the 24 traditional couples had daughters (58%) as did 16 of the 27 nontraditional families (59%).

Interviews. The parents-to-be were separately interviewed in their homes during the last trimester of pregnancy. Each parent provided demographic information and information about the planned division of parental leave. (This information was highly reliable, suggesting that the parents had indeed discussed the issue thoroughly before the interview.) Thereafter, each parent was asked a series of questions concerning: the value of work to him or her, the value of parenthood to him or her, and the attitudes of friends and family regarding the couple's decision to have a baby and to divide childcare responsibilities in a particular way. The interviews were semistructured, in that the interviewers probed for revelant information if the initial questions were not answered in sufficient detail. The interviews were tape-recorded and were later rated independently by at least two individuals who had no other knowledge of the families. Value of parenthood, value of work, and social support were rated on 8-point scales that had been developed previously. When the raters assigned values within 1 scale point of one another, the mean value was used in analyses. In the rare instances when there was a greater discrepancy, the raters discussed their ratings, replayed the tape, and assigned a consensus rating. Interrater reliability in all cases exceeded .90.

On the value of parenthood scale, we attempted to rate whether the individual wished to become a parent and why he or she did so. Low scores were given when the individual did not particularly want to become a parent or could not articulate any rationale; high scores were given to individuals for whom parenthood was an integrally important aspect of self actualization and fulfillment. In an analogous fashion, the value of work scale quantified the extent to which work contributed to the individual's sense of fulfillment. The subjects, with few exceptions, reported a high degree of social support and consequently there was insufficient variance in the sample to permit analysis. English translations of the rating scales and interview protocols are available from the authors.

When the infants were 3 months old ($\pm$ 2 weeks) they were observed in their homes twice—once with their mothers and once with their fathers. Each observation lasted at least 45 min; if the baby fell asleep before then, the observation was rescheduled. All scores were adjusted (by proration) for variations in the length of observation before analyses were performed. During the observation, the observer recorded the infant's and parent's behavior using a portable keyboard system that automatically encoded the time of each entry (Stephenson, Smith, & Roberts, 1975). As suggested by Lamb (1977b), a second investigator (the "visitor") accompanied the observer in order to chat to the parent, relieving his or her anxieties about being observed and encouraging him or her to behave normally. All observations were conducted by two individuals (a male and a female) neither of whom had observed either parent in any family.

The observers noted each time the infant smiled, displayed excitement, vocalized, laughed, looked at the parent, coughed, or spluttered, cried, fussed, touched, reached in anticipation of being picked up, stiffened when held by, molded when held by, and attended to a toy proferred by the parent. They also recorded when the parent vocalized, smiled at (only when within 3 ft. of the infant in the infant's line of vision), made a "play face," went into *en face* position, offered a toy, touched, kissed or hugged, jiggled the limbs of, tended (e.g., wiped the baby's nose or burped it), tickled, picked up, changed the posture of, fed, bathed, or changed the infant, and when they were within 3 ft. ("proximity") of the infant. From these observational records, we computed two measures of parental responsiveness similar to those computed by Bakeman and Brown (1977). Our measure of "general responsiveness" represented the probability that any infant behavior was followed within 5 sec by any parental behavior. A measure of "responsiveness to distress" represented the probability that an infant's fuss or cry was followed within 5 sec by any parental behavior. Since the measure of general responsiveness was not reliable (interobserver agreement: $r = .46$), we did not include it in our analyses.

In addition to these two measures of dyadic integration, we also tabulated the frequencies with which each of the infant and adult behaviors occurred. Many of the behaviors were recorded rarely and/or unreliably, and so we did not include them in our analyses. In other instances, we created combined or composite measures on the basis of *a priori* considerations. Following this process, we had only two measures of infant behavior: distress (sum of fuss and cry), and social bids (sum of smile and vocalize). Our analyses of parental behavior involved four measures: functional behavior (sum of tend and change), contact (sum of touch, tickle, tend, and hug or kiss), play (sum of jiggle, play face, offer toy, and tickle), and vocalization.

Reliability. The two observers were trained on videotapes and pilot subjects until they were able to record the focal behaviors reliably. During the course of data-gathering, 14 of the 102 observations were conducted by the two observers simultaneously so that we could assess reliability. Pearson product–moment correlations between the two observers' records were computed to assess reliability. Coefficients of agreement were: responsiveness to distress, .85; distress, .97; social bids, .94; functional behavior, .86; contact, .94; play, .87; and vocalization, .96.

Infant Temperament. Each parent described his or her infant's temperament using a Swedish translation of Rothbart, Furby, Kelly, and Hamilton's (1977) Infant Behavior Questionaire (IBQ). The IBQ yields composite measures of the infant's perceived activity level, positive emotionality, fear, anger/frustration, soothability, and undisturbed persistence. Parents were asked not to discuss their responses with their spouses.

Results

Preliminary analyses of the interview data revealed no differences between pareents associated with the sex of the infant to whom they later gave birth.

Consequently, analyses of the interview data involved 2 (parental gender) $\times$ 2 (family type: traditional, nontraditional) analyses of variance. These analyses revealed predictable interactions between the two factors on both interview dimentions. In traditional families, mothers ($\overline{X}$ = 5.42) valued parenthood more than their spouses ($\overline{X}$ = 4.03) did, whereas the nontraditional mothers ($\overline{X}$ = 4.85) valued parenthood less than their spouses ($\overline{X}$ = 5.38) did (F 1,98 = 6.11, $p <$ .02). Furthermore, the traditional fathers ($\overline{X}$ = 5.74) valued work more than their wives did ($\overline{X}$ = 4.71), whereas the nontraditional fathers ($\overline{X}$ = 5.26) valued work less than their wives ($\overline{X}$ = 6.16) did (F 1,98 = 6.64, $p <$ .01). Given these values, it was not suprising that the nontraditional fathers planned to be more involved in caretaking that the traditional fathers did. Indeed, both types of families planned to divide caretaking responsibility in accordance with their attitudes and values. In the nontraditional families, fathers planned to take an average of 2.8 months leave, compared with 6.2 for their wives; in the traditional families the means were 0.4 and 8.5 months, respectively (parent gender by family type interaction, F 1,98 = 85.14, $p <$ .00001).

With the exception of the measure of responsiveness, all scores derived from the observations were converted into rates per hour in order to adjust for variations in the length of observation. Our primary analyses of the observational data involved computing 2 (parent gender) $\times$ 2 (infant sex) $\times$ 2 (family type) repeated measures univariate and multivariate analyses of variance. Of greatest interest to us were interactions between the factors, and the main effect for parent gender. We did not expect to find main effects of infant sex and family type.

The analyses revealed no significant main effects of family type or infant sex on any of the 7 measures of parent and infant behavior or on separate multivariate analyses of the parent and infant behavior measures. There was, however, a significant effect for parent gender on a multivariate analysis of vaiance of the parent behavior measures (F 4,95 = 4.99, $p <$ .001) and a trend on a multivariate analysis of the infant behavior measures (F 4,95 = 2.66, $p <$ .07). Univariate analysis showed significant effects only on the composite measure of contact behavior: mothers ($\overline{X}$ = 47.7) displayed more of these behaviors than fathers ($\overline{X}$ = 35.2) did (F 1,98 = 10.63, $p <$ .002). In addition, fathers ($\overline{X}$ = 0.75) tended to respond more than mothers ($\overline{X}$ = 0.68) did to infant distress signals (F 1,98 = 3.29, $p <$ .07). More distress occured when infants were with their fathers ($\overline{X}$ = 21.5) than with their mothers ($\overline{X}$ = 15.3; F 1,98 = 4.98, $p <$ .03).

There was only one near-significant interaction between parental gender and family type: traditional mothers ($\overline{X}$ = 89.8) vocalized to their infants more than their husbands did ($\overline{X}$ = 65.6), whereas in nontraditional families, the fathers ($\overline{X}$ = 73.8) vocalized more than the mothers ($\overline{X}$ = 69.8) did (F 1,98 = 3.18, $p <$ .07). Multivariate analyses of variance on the parent (p = .12) and infant ($p = .7$) behaviors did not reveal significant interactions between these two factors.

Two measures showed significant interactions between family type and infant sex. Traditional parents engaged in more functional behavior with sons ($\overline{X} = 16.6$) than with daughters ($\overline{X} = 13.8$), whereas the reverse was true in nontraditional families ($\overline{X}_{sons} = 12.3$, $\overline{X}_{daughters} = 17.2$; $F\,1,98 = 5.06, p < .03$). Similarly, boys ($\overline{X} = 63.1$) in traditional families directed more distal bids to parents than girls ($\overline{X} = 46.5$) did; the reverse was true in nontraditional families ($\overline{X}_{sons} = 38.7$, $\overline{X}_{daughters} = 45.6$; $F\,1,98 = 4.06, p < .05$).

Reanalysis. For the purpose of the analyses described above, family type was defined on the basis of the parents' desire that the fathers take or not take primary responsibility for infant care for one month or more sometime during the first year of the infants' life. Perhaps because all infants were breastfed, none of the fathers had taken extended parental leave prior to the observations. However, 29 of the fathers had been solely responsible for infant care for at least one whole day during the first three months of the infants' lives. These fathers were no more likely to have been nontraditional than traditional ($p < .13$) in their prenatal plans. We thus sought to examine effects of parental involvement in further 2 (parental gender) × 2 (parental involvement) × 2 (infant sex) repeated measures multivariate and univariate analyses of variance. When fathers had taken care of the infant for one full day or more, they were deemed to be involved; others were considered uninvolved for the purposes of these analyses.

As before, our primary interest was in interactions between parental involvement and the other factors. There were no significant interactions between paternal involvement and parental gender, or between parental gender and infant sex. There were, however, two significant interactions between paternal involvement and infant sex. When fathers were involved, parents engaged in more functional behaviors involving daughters ($\overline{X} = 16.0$) than sons ($\overline{X} = 10.3$), whereas the reverse was true when fathers were less involved ($\overline{X}_{daughters} = 15.0$, $\overline{X}_{sons} = 18.9$; $F\,1,98 = 8.63, p < .004$). When fathers were involved, girls made more distal bids to their parents ($\overline{X} = 45.6$) than boys did ($\overline{X} = 38.7$); the reverse was true when fathers were less involved ($\overline{X}_{daughters} = 46.5$, $\overline{X}_{sons} = 63.1$, $F\,1,98 = 4.07, p < .05$).

Other Results. Analyses of variance revealed no associations between any of the factors described and the parents' descriptions of their infants' temperament.

Discussion

It is clear from the responses obtained during the prenatal interviews that the traditional and nontraditional parents had very different attitudes and values. The nontraditional fathers valued parenthood more and work less than their wives did, whereas the opposite pattern occurred among the traditional parents. By definition the nontraditional fathers planned to spend more time than the traditional fathers as primary caretakers, and the attitude measures suggest that the plans of both traditional and nontraditional parents were in accordance with their values.

Despite these attitudinal differences, and contrary to our expectations, family type had little effect on the parents' behavior. Regardless of whether family type was assessed on the basis of a prenatal decision regarding paternal involvement or on the basis of the father's actual involvement during the first three months of the infant's life, there were no significant interactions between family type or paternal involvement and parental gender. There was, however, one significant effect and one trend involving main effects for parental gender. Thus the parents' behavior was predicted better by their gender than by their nontraditional attitudes and behaviors.

On the other hand, paternal involvement (anticipated or actual) was significantly related to the manner in which the parents differentiated between sons and daughters. Like traditional fathers and mothers studied in the United States (Hoffman, 1977; Lamb, 1977a; Parke & Sawin, 1980), the traditional Swedish parents interacted preferentially with sons. By contrast, the nontraditional Swedish parents interacted preferentially with their daughters. These findings suggest that the parents' nontraditional values did affect their parental behavior, even though the effects did not outweight the effects of parental gender. Perhaps because of their concern that daughters are traditionally accorded less attention than sons, the nontraditional parents not only eliminated but reversed this trend. Both mothers and fathers were responsible for this.

One reason for the small number of interactions between parental gender and family type may be that there were relatively few effects of parental gender. Our findings on this score are consistent with those of other researchers (e.g., Parke & Sawin, 1980; Pedersen et al., 1980) who have commented on the impressive similarities, rather than the differences, between mothers and fathers interacting with very young infants. Only microanalytic studies (e.g., Field, 1978; Yogman et al., 1977) have reported major effects of parental gender on parental behavior toward young infants; the other studies reporting substantial differences between traditional mothers and fathers have involved much older infants (e.g., Clarke-Stewart, 1978; Lamb, 1977b). Perhaps, therefore, we will find more statistical interactions between parental gender and family style in our observations of the families when the infants are older. In the course of this longitudinal study, we plan to observe the families again at home when the infants are 8 and 16 months old. By the time of the later observations, more of the fathers will have spent time as sole caretakers of their infants; as indicated earlier, the nontraditional fathers planned to take paternal leave later in the first year—after the infants had been weaned. In fact, our crude measure of paternal involvement revealed that during the first three months, the traditional and nontraditional families were distinguished by attitude or aspiration, not by actual involvement. In addition, differences between paternal and maternal behavior may have been harder to obtain than they are in the United States because even the traditional (uninvolved) fathers were markedly more involved than most American fathers. All the fathers in the study had regular responsibility for some caretaking chores: usually this involved taking the baby up and changing it in the morning and changing and putting it to bed at night.

Given these factors, it is notable that significant gender effects of any sort were obtained. The presence of these effects, and the absence of interactions between gender and family type, underscore the robustness and pervasiveness of gender differences in parental behavior. The data suggest that the differences between maternal and paternal behavior are more strongly related to either the parents' biological gender or sex roles than to either their degree of involvement in infant care or their attitudes regarding the desirability of paternal involvement in infant care.

ABSTRACT

Fifty-one Swedish couples and their first-born infants were involved in this study. The parents were separately interviewed during the last trimester of pregnancy and were each observed with their infants three months after delivery. Nontraditional families were those in which fathers planned to spend one or more months in the first year as primary caretaker ($N = 27$); on average, the traditional fathers planned to spend only the standard two-week period at home. Prenatal interviews revealed that nontraditional fathers valued parenthood more and work less than their wives did; the reverse was true in traditional couples. When observed with their 3-month-old infants, traditional and nontraditional parents behaved similarly; parental gender affected behavior more than planned (or actual) parental involvement. Several behavioral measures showed that mothers were more socially active than fathers were. Nontraditional parents interacted preferentially with daughters whereas the reverse was true in the traditional families.

Acknowledgments

We are grateful to Tom Corry and Britta Forsstrom for helping to rate the prenatal interviews and to Bob Wainwright for help with the analyses.

REFERENCES

Bakeman, R., & Brown, J. W. Behavioral dialogues: An approach to the assessment of mother–infant interaction. *Child Development*, 1977, 48, 195–203.

Clarke-Stewart, K. A. And daddy makes three: The father's impact on mother and child. *Child Development*, 1978, 49, 466–478.

Feiring, C. *The preliminary development of a social systems model of early infant–mother attachment.* Paper presented to the Eastern Psychological Association, New York, March 1976.

Field, T. Interaction behaviors of primary versus secondary caretaker fathers. *Developmental Psychology*, 1978, 14, 183–184.

Hoffman, L. W. Changes in family roles, socialization, and sex differences. *American Psychologist*, 1977, 32, 644–657.

Hollingshead, A. B. *The four factor index of social position.* Unpublished manuscript, 1978. Available from the author, Department of Sociology, Yale University, New Haven, CT 06520.

Lamb, M. E. Interaction between eight-month-old children and their fathers and mothers. In M. E. Lamb (Ed.), *The role of the father in child development.* New York: Wiley, 1976.

Lamb, M. E. The development of mother–infant and father–infant attachments in the second year of life. *Developmental Psychology*, 1977, 13, 637–648.(a)

Lamb, M. E. Father–infant and mother–infant interaction in the first year of life. *Child Development*, 1977, 48, 167–181.(b)

Lamb, M. E. The father's role in the infant's social world. In J. Stevens & M. Mathews (Eds.), *Mother/child, father/child relationships.* Washington, D.C.: National Association for the Education of Young Children, 1978.

Parke, R. D. Perspectives on father–infant interaction. In J. D. Osofsky (Ed.), *Handbook of infant development.* New York: Wiley, 1979.

Parke, R. D., & O'Leary, S. Father–mother–infant interaction in the newborn period: Some findings, some observations, and some unresolved issues. In K. F. Riegel & J. Meacham (Eds.), *The developing individual in a changing world* (Vol.2). *Social and environmental issues.* The Hague: Mouton, 1976.

Parke, R. D., & Sawin, D. B. The family in early infancy: Social interactional and attitudinal analyses. In F. A. Pedersen (Ed.), *The father–infant relationship: Observational studies in a family setting.* New York: Praeger, 1980.

Parke, R. D., O'Leary S., & West, S. *Mother–father–newborn interaction: Effects of maternal medication, labor, and sex of infant.* Paper presented to the American Psychological Association, Washington, D.C., September 1972.

Pedersen, F. A. *Mother, father, and infant as an interactive system.* Paper presented to the American Psychological Association, Chicago, September 1975.

Pedersen, F. A., Anderson, B., & Cain, R. Parent–infant and husband–wife interactions observed at age 5 months. In F. A. Pedersen (Ed.), *The father–infant relationship: Observational studies in a family setting.* New York: Praeger, 1980.

Rendina, I., & Dickerscheid, J. D. Father involvement with first-born infants. *Family Coordinator*, 1976, 25, 373–378.

Rothbart, M., Furby, L., Kelly, S. R., & Hamilton, J. S. *Development of a caretaker report temperament scale for use with 3-, 6-, 9-, and 12-month old infants.* Paper presented to the Society for Research in Child Development, New Orleans, March 1977.

Stephenson, G. R., Smith, D. P., & Roberts, T. W. The SSR system: An open format event recording system with computerized transcription. *Behavior Research Methods and Instrumentation*, 1975, 7, 497–515.

Yogman, M. W., Dixon, S., Tronick, E., Als, H., Adamson, L., Lester, B., & Brazelton, T. B. *The goals and structure of face-to-face interaction between infants and fathers.* Paper presented to the Society for Research in Child Development, New Orleans, March 1977.

An Investigation of Change in the Infant–Caregiver System over the First Week of Life

Louis W. Sander, Patricia F. Chappell, and Patricia A. Synder

CONCEPTUAL BACKGROUND

A combination of the two methods used in the investigation of postnatal adaptation between the infant and its caretaking environment will be described in this chapter: (1) continuous, around-the-clock bassinet monitoring of infant sleep and awake states, obtained while the infant is in the bassinet; and (2) continuous event-recording of an array of both infant and caretaker variables over the complete course of awake periods, including the entire caretaking intervention. In order to make meaningful our use of these methods, some explanation must be given for a study of the postnatal relationship between the infant and the caregiving environment within the concept of ad-

The data presented in this chapter was reported initially at the 1975 meeting of the Society for Research in Child Development held in Denver, Colorado.

Louis W. Sander ● Division of Child Psychiatry, University of Colorado Health Sciences Center, Denver, Colorado 80262. **Patricia F. Chappell** ● Division of Psychiatry, Boston University Medical Center, Boston,Massachusetts 02118. **Patricia A. Synder** ● Division of Psychiatry, Boston University Medical Center, Boston, Massachusetts 02118. This project has been supported primarily by the Grant Foundation, supplemented by Boston University Hospital General Research Support Funds and funds provided by NICHD contract N01–HD–3–2789. Dr. Sander was supported during the project by the NIMH Research Development Program 5–MH–20–505. Continuing work on the project has been made possible by the National Foundation, March of Dimes; the Developmental Psychobiology Research Group of the University of Colorado Health Sciences Center Department of Psychiatry, and the University of Colorado Faculty Research Support program.

aptation rather that as an investigation of their affiliative behaviors in terms of infant attachment or of parental bonding. The aim is to identify and document biological mechanisms in the interactions that constitute the adaptive process and that underlie these higher order functions.

Each infant can be regarded as arriving with a unique profile of self-regulatory characteristics, each then encountering a caretaking environment which also possesses a set of self-regulatory characteristics unique for it. Exchanges between these two dissimilar configurations are modified in the mutual regulation of the activities of each so that relatively stable coordinations are achieved as the adapted state is gained. The exchanges and the events related to them, which provide and maintain harmonious regulation, are organized in configurations which are idiosyncratic for each pair. Each infant caretaker pair can thus be regarded as representing a unique interactive-regulative system. It is the system, then, that becomes the essential unit of analysis, rather than the infant.

When viewed longitudinally, each system has a unique history of the course of modifications and their timing which have characterized the process of adaptation between partners. In this sense, the history and the later characteristics of the regulation of the system may be needed to identify the salience of initially selected variables to the idiosyncrasies of the system at outcome, and to trace the processes of change or transformation which these variables have undergone, that is, the system is open-ended, maintained by a lawful and essential linkage between regulation, adaptation, and organization.

The event of birth can be looked upon as a point of drastic change in the temporal organization of the fetus and its various functions. Birth necessitates change both in the intrinsic synchronization between subsystems within the infant and new synchronization between periodic functions of the infant as a whole and extrinsic periodicities of the caretaking environment. With birth, the entrainment provided by periodic cues from maternal sources impinging on the fetal environment is abruptly lost—including those related to the changing of a wide range of essential nutrients and regulatory substances in the maternal blood levels and of changing maternal states of activity and quiescence. Powerful new periodic functions begin within the infant such as hunger, feeding, and satiation or respiration; the infant begins to be exposed to sharp contrasts in light and dark, fluctuations in sound intensity, and caregiver contact. An instability in sleep cycling and sleep–awake periodicity can be observed over the first 3–4 postnatal days. These 3–4 days are associated with longer awake active states (Sander Julia, Stechler, & Burns, 1972) which are conceivably related to this loss of fetal entrainment and its associated loss of temporal organization. It appears essential now that the possibility be entertained that there is a postnatal reachievement, then a maintenance of coherence or phase-synchrony among the infant's physiological subsystems after birth, as their endogenous rhythmicity gradually entrains to exogenous periodicities (Hellbrugge, Lange, Rutenfranz & Stehr, 1964). This postnatal ontogeny is one that would depend on an interaction of endogenous infant rhythms with recurrent exogenous caretaker events. To the extent that this is true, one of the principal aims of caregiving in the neonatal period would be that of establishing a temporal organization that would facilitate synchrony between periodicities within the infant, such as those related to sleep and awake states and the larger periodicities of the caretaking environment, such as those of day and night, or the daytime interfeeding intervals. Research which would document the appearance of a relative regularity in daily onset times of naps and awake period would bear on these issues as would a regular recurrence in the events and interactions between infant and caretaker.

One of the difficulties in presenting a study of postnatal relationship between infant and caregiver in terms of the adaptive process lies in the unfamiliarity of the reader with the specific mechanisms underlying the adaptive process that biology and mathematics have formulated. Although it is well known that major contributions have been made to the understanding of early development by drawing on biology, and especially the concept of adaptation (Erikson, 1959; Hartman 1958; Piaget, 1936; Spitz, 1959), little effort is usually made to consider specific mechanisms suggested by the biologist as being documentable in human interaction, especially postnatally. It is not possible within the scope of this chapter to do more than briefly sketch two outstanding contributions with the hope that the reader may be stimulated to become better acquainted with the source literature. Such a sketch, however, is essential if the reader is to consider the extent to which empirical observations may be given order by these contributions.

Our conception of the initial adaptation between the newborn and the caretaking environment draws heavily on the interplay of two biological models for regulation of physiological and behavioral variables. The first is the model for adaptive behavior in living systems which has been proposed by Ross Ashby (1952/1970). This centers about his concept of "ultrastability," and formulates in terms of principles of cybernetic regulation many characteristics of adaptive behavior with which biologists are familiar. For the ultrastable system. Ashby essentially proposes the interaction of two levels of cybernetic regulation in the organism: one at the level of the state of the organism, represented by the values of an array of basic physiologic variables, which he terms *essential variables* and the other, at the level of the various sensorimotor functions which are in intimate exchange with the environment, and which he terms the *reacting parts.* These two levels represent two different time domains, one acting relatively slow and the other relatively more rapid. By means of "step functions," the first, more slowly changing feedback system sets parameters or biases on the feedback system of the reacting parts, thus changing the way they react to the environment. What is being specified here is the way foreground events in sensorimotor interactions between infant and caregiver become locked into a particular temporal locus in the background of more slowly changing oscillations of the infant's and caretaker's sleep and awake states. This is a mechanism of regulation that has relevance to the mechanism of entrainment of biorhythms.

The second biological model, underlying our conceptualization of the initial adaptation between infant and caretaking environment, derives from the phenomena of biorhythmicity itself. Although phenomena of biorhythmicity introduce a major additional dimension in the conceptualization of adaptive behavior, they fit beautifully with, and enhance, Ashby's model, especially as one realizes that the site of endogenous rhythmicity is to be found in Ashby's array of essential variables. Adaptation, from the point of view of biorhythmicity, is resolvable in terms of phase-sychronization between periodicities which characterize the organism's different functions and periodicities characterizing the environment (Halberg, 1960). Adaptation, as phase-synchronization of basic states in the participants, sets a context of mutual "readiness," providing conditions favoring co-occurrence of certain foreground activities of the partners. Co-occurrence in the timing of basic states of the partners provides a mutual appropriateness of context for those finer-grained exchanges of the reacting parts in which direct feedback regulation between partners can achieve a next, more differentiated, level of adapted precision.

This interaction of the two models has two immediate implications. The first implication relates to basic regulation. The stage is set for entrainment of endogenous biorhythmicity by the recurrence in the caregiving environment of specific extrinsic cues in relation to the endogenous rhythm. Entrainment is most effective when the exogenous cue approximates in time the point at which a shift in the endogenous cycle is occurring. With the establishment of a contingent relationship between times of change in the state of the infant and the occurrence of specific configurations of caretaking events, entrainment is favored. The second implication is, that in achieving a condition of regulatory balance or equilibrium in the system, based on mutual readiness in the basic states, the stage is set to facilitate initial cognitive development, inasmuch as a finer level of foreground discrepancy in recurrent interactions can then be appreciated by the partners. This would facilitate a finer tuned expectancy by each, favoring new operant schema formation because the foreground interactional behavior would not be preempted by the necessity to restore basic regulatory stability in the essential variables of either partner.

The combination of the two observational methods to be described is intended, then, to permit investigation in the immediate postnatal period of the interaction of events at Ashby's two levels, namely, that of essential variables (states), and that of the reacting parts, the senisorimotor modalities involved in the actual infant–caretaker interaction.

METHODS OF DATA COLLECTION

For the investigation of change in infant and caretaker variables over the first week of life, we were fortunate to be able to collaborate with one of the hospitals affiliated with Boston University Medical Center, namely the Chelsea Naval Hospital. This hospital provided a maternity service in which normal primiparous mothers could elect to room-in with their newborn infants and remain in-hospital over the first 7 days of life. The subjects for investigation were normal mother–infant pairs drawn from a population of wives of enlisted service personnel who wished to bottle-feed their infants. The newborn infants were placed in the nursery for the first 12 hours following birth, during which time observation and examination established the presence of criteria for their normality. They then were placed in the bassinet monitor and transferred to the room-in situation with the mother, who provided sole care around-the-clock until discharge from the hospital late in the morning of the 8th day of life. Visiting privileges were flexible, with visits primarily occurring in an afternoon and evening period.

The Bassinet Monitor

The bassinet monitor is a standard nursery bassinet, which has been modified by the addition of a thin, rectangular air chamber on top of the regular Kapok mattress. Movement of the infant produces a signal through activation of a pressure transducer. The signal can be recorded in analogue form or filtered, digitalized, and recorded as eleven channels on a 20 pen Esterline Angus event-recorder, running at 12 inches per hr of real time. Four days of continuous recording can be stored on one roll, allowing unattended operation. The record gives information in real time on infant respiration, crying, motility, presence in the bassinet, and presence of caregiver, that is, intervention.

Pattern in the eleven channels of digital output has allowed the development of rules for scoring infant states—those of awake–crying, awake–active, major shift from awake to sleep and vice versa, and four sleep states; active, quiet, transitional, indeterminant. In a previous study to validate the method of sleep monitoring, a correlation of active and quiet sleep states obtained by the monitor with those obtained by a concurrent 5 channel standard sleep polygraphy was carried out for 15 interfeed intervals on 15 newborns. A mean of 37 quiet sleep durations for the monitor was 13.6 min $(SD = 7.9)$ and for standard sleep polygraphy 13.4 $(SD = 7.9)$, $r = .94$, $p < .001$. A mean of 45 active sleep durations was 20.5 min $(SD = 17.1)$ by monitor and 20.4 $(SD = 17.2)$ by polygraphy, $r = .98$, $p < .001$. Sleep polygraphy was based on the 5 parameters of electrooculogram (EOG), electromyogram (EMG), electroencephalogram (EEG), heart rate (HR), and respiratory rate (RR). Sleep was scored as active or quiet if 4 out of 5 parameters met the criteria defining these two sleep states. The monitor output, therefore, provides not only real time distributions of major sleep and awake periods around-the-clock, and the corresponding substages, but also the state context in which each intervention takes place (see Table I).

Observation and Recording of Caregiver–Infant Interaction

The first two full awake periods after 7:30 A.M. were observed on Days 2, 5, 6, and 7. On Day 7, we provided a nurse to substitute for the mother during the early awakening to test the effect of a strange caretaker on infant latency to attain a state of quiet sleep. The data reported cover the entire week with the exception of the observation of this one interaction of the nurse and infant on Day 7. The mother summoned the observer when she judged her infant was waking. The observer stood in the room at a minimal distance of 4 ft. from the mother–infant pair, and recorded events and interaction occurring during the entire awake period until the infant fell asleep

Table I. Comparison of Scoring by Two Methods for 24-Hour Records of Two Subjects

	Intervention	Awake in crib	Active sleep	Quiet sleep	Indeterminant sleep
1. Total minutes = 1108					
Observed sleep	150 (13.5%)	223 (20.1%)	478 (43.1%)	173 (15.6%)	79 (7 .1%)
Digital monitor record	151 (13.6%)	199 (17.9%)	474 (42.7%)	154 (13.8%)	125 (11.2%)
2. Total minutes = 1416					
Observed sleep	305 (21.5%)	130 (9.1%)	647 (45.6%)	224 (15.8%)	110 (7.7%)
Digital monitor record	312 (22%)	106 (7.4%)	663 (46.8%)	191 (13.4%)	142 (10%)

and reached the first episode of quiet sleep. A transistorized tone generator sounded a tone every 15 sec, transmitted to the ear of the observer by an ear plug, at which time the behaviors that occurred during the 15 sec were recorded. The behaviors recorded include categories of infant state, mother–infant proximity, infant posture, visual-facial signs, feeding behaviors, manipulations, and vocalizations. The definitions of behavioral variables reported here are listed in Table II; also given are the results of interobserver agreements for each category as assessed during 9 reliability sessions between two observers. The second author was the formal observer of mother–infant interactions and responsible for the design and analysis of the observational and interactional data.

RESULTS

Bassinet Monitor

The data obtained by the bassinet monitor illustrate the ways two methods of observation and recording can be combined to study change in both infant and caretaking variables over the first week of life. The monitor data represent an initial report of continuous sleep and awake state observation over 7 days for a single male infant. Although over the 7-day course, there were individual differences in the day of maximum disorganization, the same general pattern of disorganization and reorganization was encountered in the monitoring of the other subjects. The purpose here of using the single case illustration is to report the quantitative documentation over days of sleep, awake, and caregiving variables with the two methods and the ways the relationships between these multiple sets of variables can be arranged in terms of the mechanisms of adaptation described above.

The following set of figures represent the results for the illustrative subject and for the several categories of variables measured by the bassinet monitor.

Figure 1 is a phase-plot of each major awake–sleep cycle as it occurred, in sequence, over the first 7 days of life. The beginning of each subsequent awake period is placed on the abscissa in terms of its duration in minutes, with the sleep period immediately following, joined to it for the duration over which it occurred. In this infant, the sleep periods in the first day or two after birth are relatively long, but over Days 3–5 sleep periods become much briefer and more numerous, finally becoming longer again by Days 6 and 7.

It is quite striking that although the average sleep period length follows the overall pattern illustrated in Figure 1, the average awake period length

Table II. Definitions of Behaviors Recorded in Observations of Caretaker-Infant Interaction during Full Awakening[a]

I. Proximity (.89)
   1. The infant is against the mother's ventrum; no space can be seen between the mother's ventral surface and the infant.
   2. The infant is in the mother's lap area but space can be seen between the pair; usually the mother's arms are flexed at the elbows with forearms extended for feeding or burping manipulations.
II. Infant Posture (.98)
   1. The infant is in an upright position, perpendicular to the plane of the floor.
   2. The infant is seated, or semi-reclining; the angle of recline can vary from 45° to 90° as measured from the plane of the mother's lap or from the bed.
   3. The infant is in a supine or prone position, parallel to the bed or to the mother's lap. The infant may be propped slightly, but less than a 45° angle.
III. Infant states (.90)[b]
   1. Quiet Sleep: Regular respiration, eyes closed, face quiet, no activity except startles, no vocalization.
   2. Active sleep: Irregular respiration, eyes closed and/or REM activity, facial movements, vocalizations can occur, and peripheral movements or mild limb movements.
   3. Transitional sleep: Irregular respiration, eyes closed, facial movements, vocaliations can occur, and trunk and gross limb movements.
   4. Drowiness: Regular or irregular respiration, eyes slowly open or close, facial movement can occur, generally no vocalization or movement, though a startle or mild limb movement can occur.
   5. Alert inactivity: Regular or semi-regular respiration, eyes open and shiny, facial movements, no vocalizations, no movements except mild limb or peripheral movements.
   6. Wakeful activity: Irregular respiration, eyes open, facial movements, no vocalization, gross limb activity.
   7. Fussiness: Irregular respiration, eyes closed, facial movements, fussy vocalizations, gross movements.
   8. Crying: Irregular respiration, eyes closed, facial movements, crying vocalization, gross limb activity.
IV. Vocalizations (scored on the basis of occurrence at any time within the 15 second epoch)
   1. Mother verbalizes to infant (.89).

[a] All measures were judged independent of all other measures and judgments were made on the basis of which category best represented the behavior occurring for the majority of the 15 sec epoch. Percentage agreement between two observers is given in parentheses.
[b] This state scale, Chappell Infant State Scale (CISS), is modified from Chappell, Boismier & Meier 1973.

shows a remarkable stability (Figure 2). Awake period here is defined from the monitor record to include the span from the end of one major shift from sleep to awake to the beginning of the next major shift from awake to sleep. It, therefore, includes awake crying, awake active, removal from and return to bassinet plus brief sleep spans from which the infant awakens spontaneously and which occur between removals from the bassinet that are less than 30 min apart. The "major shift" is the motility pattern produced by the moni-

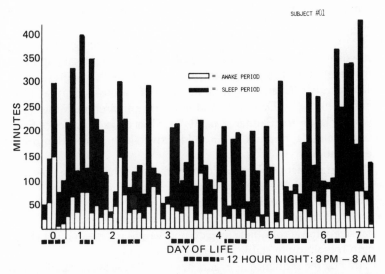

Figure 1. An awake–asleep phase plot showing sequential awake–asleep cycles over first 7 days. Occurance in night or day 12 is indicated by dark seqment at bottom; each cycle begins with onset of awake period, depicted by solid line rectangle.

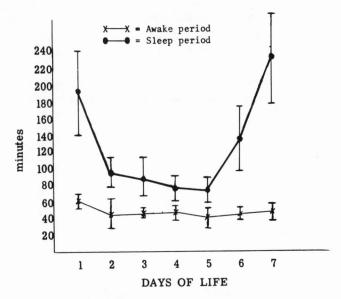

Figure 2. Change in sleep period and awake period durations over the first 7 days of life in one normal male infant (mean and standard error of mean are given).

tor during a major transition from or to a sleep period longer than 30 min in duration.

The twenty-four hr sleep total, usually a very stable figure, also shows a decrease during Days 3–5, as does the 24-hr active sleep total (Figure 3). The findings here for a 24-hr sleep total are consistent with our previous finding of a significantly greater 24-hr total duration of awake–active states (activity segment time) during Days 2, 3, and 4 when compared with the rest of the first two weeks of life (Sander *et al.*, 1972). Thus there is evidence for both a mild total sleep deprivation and a mild active sleep deprivation during the days of instability.

The average active sleep period length for each day provides a picture consistent both with the increase in state transitions during Days 3–5 and the decrease in total sleep and total active sleep per 24 hr (Figure 4). One relationship that is apparent is that while the values for active sleep follow the values for total sleep, those for quiet sleep do not. Values for mean quiet sleep period length remain quite stable over the 7 days.

In tracing the sequence of events over the 7 days as the bassinet monitor appears to portray them in the case of this infant, there is a breakdown in the number of active–quiet sleep cycles by the second day of life (Figure 5). This seems to be the first striking event. The number of good active–quiet sleep cycles then gradually returns over Days 5, 6, and 7, reaching the level found during the first day. We have operationally defined the number of "good active–quiet cycles" during naps as the number of complete active–quiet sleep cycles that are not interrupted by indeterminate sleep in either the active or the quiet phase, and which do not begin or terminate in a major shift to or from awake.

In the hours associated with the breakdown in active–quiet sleep cycling, crying of the infant begins to increase, reaching its peak by the third day of

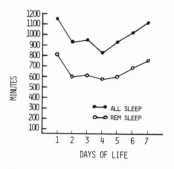

Figure 3. Change over first 7 days of life in daily total sleep and daily total REM sleep (for same infant)

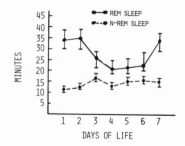

Figure 4. Change in duration of mean REM and mean quiet sleep stages over first 7 days of life.

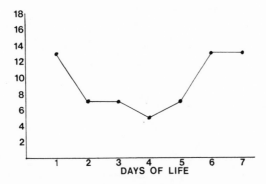

Figure 5. Change in number of intact REM-non REM cycles per day over first 7 days; showing initial drop on Day 2.

life (Figure 6). The increase in crying during the days of instability 3–4 can be found not only in the number of 15-min intervals having at least one crying blip (crying extensity), but also in the number of cumulated crying blips per day, each representing 15 sec of crying (crying intensity).

During the days of instability, Days 3–5, there is a qualitative change in intervention also. Single interventions are replaced by multiple interventions (Figure 7). A single intervention we have defined as one which is successful, so that the baby returns to sleep and does not have to be picked up again within 30 min. A multiple intervention is one in which the baby does not

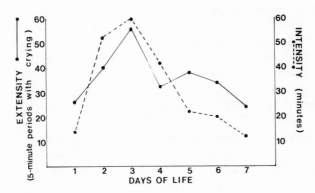

Figure 6. Increase in two measures of crying on day 2 with a peak on Day 3 of life.

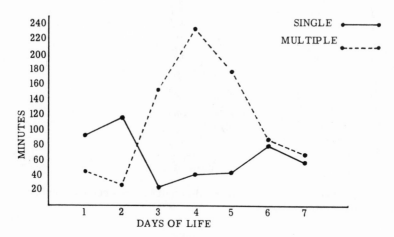

Figure 7. Change in daily duration of caretaking interventions over first 7 days of life, depicted separately in terms of single and multiple interventions.

return to sleep or returns to sleep only briefly, wakes up again, begins crying, and is picked up again within 30 min. We look on multiple interventions as central to the adaptive process. It is through the repeated trials that specificity in critical relationships between infant and caregiver events becomes established. The figures suggest that as sleep cycling regains its coherence, crying diminishes; multiple interventions also diminish and single interventions again begin to predominate.

Observation and Recording of Caregiver–Infant Interaction

We examined first the population of events occurring within single variables, then the intersection of selected separate populations of events in both infant and caregiver to provide a measure of co-occurrence of caregiver–infant behaviors, and last we examined contingent relationships between infant state changes and caregiver manipulations of the infant. The interactional data reported are for the same infant whose monitor data have been presented. Definition of behavioral variables used in interactional observations is given in Table II.

Proximity 1. Time during the interaction that caregivers held the infant in close proximity increased across days with the major increase seen on Day 7. Beginning with 6% of interaction time in Proximity 1 (the closest measured degree of proximity) on Day 2, an increase was seen over all days until Day 7, when during 75% of the interaction span, the infant was held in close proximity to the caregiver. This increase in proportion of interaction time in which the infants are held in close proximity is to be viewed in relation to total interaction time which decreased between Days 6–8 (Figure 8).

Infant Alertness. Only a slight increase occurred in the proportion of interaction time the infant spent in a state of alertness (state 5) across days. The infant began on Day 2 with 57% interaction time in an alert state, and increased only slightly until Day 6 when the time spent in alertness was 65% of the interaction between the mother and infant, this was followed by a slight decrease on Day 7 at 61%. This stability of alertness is to be viewed in relation to the fact that total duration of observed interaction time, as well as the 24-hr interaction time, decreases between Days 6 and 8—in other words, a tighter co-occurrence between the time spent in an alert state and the time spent in the intervention.

Co-occurrences of Caregiver–Infant Behavior. *Alertness and Proximity 1.* There was an increase in the co-occurrence of times when the infant was alert and held by the caregiver in the closest proximity. Beginning with 24% co-occurrence on Day 2, an increase occurred over all days, until Day 7 when a 49% co-occurrence was observed.

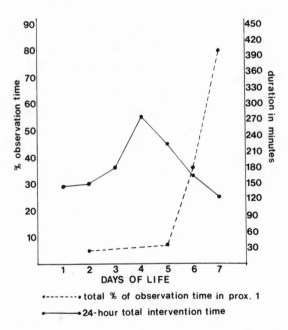

Figure 8. Change in co-occurance of awake-alert state state and proximity 1 over the first 7 days of life.

Alertness and Caregiver Verbalizations. Since auditory cues may play a role in entraining biorhythms, we examined the relation between the state of the infant and the occurrence of maternal verbalization. The importance of each modality in establishing a pattern of multimodal input is determined in part by the mother. Some prefer visual, some verbal, some kinaesthetic, and some tactile means of contacting their infants. For this particular infant no increase in co-occurrence of alertness and maternal verbalization occurred. In fact, this particular mother verbalized only 14 times to the infant during the observations in the first week of the infant's life. This was far less than we have found for other mothers for whom the co-occurrence of verbalization by the mother to the infant and alertness in the infant showed a significant increase over the 7 days. Multimodal patterning of maternal stimulation may characterize the more even regulatory interactions.

Contingent Caregiver–Infant Behaviors. We wanted to determine whether infant state change cued the mother to initiate a change in position of the infant or whether the position change of the infant was followed by a state change in the infant. We scored the records of observations for contingent relationships obtaining between two events, a posture change which occurred contiguous to a change in infant state. At each posture change we noted the state of the infant before the time of the posture change and whether a change in state occurred either in the same or next 15 sec epoch. When we examined the occurrence of an infant state change in the 15 sec *prior* to the mother's change of the infant's posture (as a cue, let us say, for her next caregiving maneuver), this contingency, almost without exception, did *not* occur. On the other hand, when we looked at state change in the 15 sec *following* a posture change, there was a high probability of state change. This was true of all states, except for the "alert–inactive states," state 5. We combined data across all states, excepting state of alert–inactivity, producing a 2 × 2 contingency table of state change—no state change on one dimension and alert-or-not-alert state on the other. When we compared the frequency of co-occurrence of state change following a posture change, the results are very clear: infant state changes are contingent on environmental events if consideration is given to the state of the infant when the event occurred (the chi-square value for this contrast is 17.78, $p < .001$).

DISCUSSION

We have reported the methods that we have developed to study change in an array of infant and caregiver variables, over the first 7 days of life, illustrating with one mother–infant pair the combination of methods used to chart the course of change. We conceptualize the process, underlying change in the array of variables, in terms of a combination of biologic models of adaptive behavior—a conceptualization essentially cybernetic and biorhythmic. Our methodology provides us with empirical data with which we can begin to consider the relation of the context for behavior to the content of behavior, in terms of the temporal organization of states in a 24-hr framework and over the full awake period.

In the introduction it was proposed that from the perspective of biorhythms, the event of birth can be looked upon as a point of drastic change in the temporal organization of the fetus and its various functions. Birth necessitates change both in the *intrinsic* synchronization between subsystems within the infant and new synchronization between periodic functions of the infant as a whole and extrinsic periodicities of the caregiving environment. In the data presented, the organization of events at the macroscopic level of sleep–awake periods within each 24-hr period shows such a relatedness to the organization of associated events at the microscopic level of state substages within the awake-sleep periods.

In the interactional observations over the awake period, there is a tightening co-occurrence between the duration of the awake–inactive state and the duration of close proximity to caretaker over the first week of life. In the subject illustrated, this increasing co-occurrence coincides with returning active–quiet sleep cycling and 24-hr sleep organization. One can only speculate at this point the way new entrainment may be affected by the increasing co-occurrence of specific caretaking events with appropriate awake states and the contingency between specific caretaking events and state change at points of transition.

Further perspective on the relation of these findings to possible initial mechanisms of organization in the infant–caregiver system is gained when one considers the question of coherence between multiple infant physiological subsystems as the infant cycles from one state to another over time. The semi-independence of physiological subsystems has been shown in investigations of neonatal sleep physiology. The coherence or temporal synchrony displayed by subsystems governing heart rate, respiratory rate, eye movement, brain waves, etc., as the infant cycles through active and quiet sleep has been identified as an important indicator of neurophysiologic intactness (Prechtl, 1968). Furthermore, the semi-independence of other infant functions and physiologic subsystems, for example, galvanic skin reflex, body temperature, and urinary excretion, has been evidenced by the finding that circadian rhythmicity is gained for each in a sequence of chronological points over the first months of life and not for all the component functions of the infant at the same chronological point (Hellbrugge *et al.*, 1964). Desynchronization of physiological subsystems at later points in the life span with jet travel, illness, exposure to environments free of times cues, etc., indicates the necessity for the continuous maintenance of the complex components of our physiology in temporal organization or phase relationships (Luce, 1970). It appears essential now that the possibility be entertained that achievement and maintenance of this coherence involves a postnatal ontogeny, the outcome of an interaction of endogenous infant and exogenous caregiver determinants.

One of the principal aims of caretaking in the neonatal period then becomes that of facilitating the achievement of phase synchrony at both the intrinsic and extrinsic levels. The effect is to bring the multiple semi-independent subsystems of the infant into intrinsic coherence in relation to recurrent states on the sleep–awake continuum. The latter can then be brought into proper phase relations with the larger periodicities characterizing the caretaking environment, such as those of day and night, or the daytime intermeal intervals. From work we have previously carried out (Sander, 1969; Sander *et al.*, 1972) in regard of 24-hr distributions of infant sleep and awake states over the first months of life, it is the interaction between these infant and caregiver determinants, in the course of the postnatal temporal reorganization, that influences the time of appearance of a predominance of awake states occurring in the day 12 hr and a predominance of sleep behavior occurring in the night 12 hr.

The interactional analysis of events over the awake period begins to spell out the mechanisms involved in the organizing process. Phase-shifting by entrainment of biorhythms is most effective when the entraining cues are given within a certain temporal ·proximity to the natural time of phase-change. If the cue falls outside this proximity there is no effect of the cue to entrain by shifting the phase and the rhythm is said to be "free-running." In a previous study we have observed how the experienced natural mother over the first weeks of life is using many maneuvers to shift the onset and duration of sleep or awake states, aiming at a more optimal synchronization of the baby's temporal organization with that of the household (Sander, Stechler, Burns, & Lee, 1979).

The stability of the alert-inactive state occurring during the first week of life while the mother and infant are interacting, indexes self-regulatory capacity, and, as an indicator of stability in the infant, may also provide a measure which will differentiate among infants who vary in intactness, as reflected in differing degrees of self-regulation. The appropirate mobilization of a focus of attention in the neonate, which meets and synchronizes with attentive organization in the caretaker over optimal spans of the intervention, can be suggested also as a mechanism facilitating systems coherence. Such a proposal has been put forth by Parmalee (1973) who has suggested that coherence and stability in regulation of physiological subsystems will be found related to the capacity for attentive behavior during awake periods.

The strategy of charting the course of multiple variables related both to infant and caretaker by a combination of quantitative methods is being applied now at the University of Colorado Health Sciences Center in an effort to identify and understand basic mechanisms of regulation in a range of infant–caregiver systems, some in which infant endowment is compromised and some in which caregiving is less than optimal—such as in the intensive care nursery. How can regulation be defined and then facilitated in these different systems? A long-term question that has first been addressed by these methods (Sander et al., 1979) is the way that higher level perception, cognition, and social functions are deployed in later adaptation depends on the particular course by which they have become employed in the establishing of initial regulation. it is our impression that it will only be when sufficient quantitative data collected concurrently for multiple variables in a number of interaction subsystems become available that the lawful relationships between regulation, adaptation, integration, and organization of the infant–caregiver system will be identified, documented, and conceptualized.

Acknowledgments

Grateful acknowledgment is made to the staff of the Chelsea Naval Hospital for their generous assistance in data collection and the nursing staff of the Department of Pediatrics of the University of Colorado Health Sciences Center. Particular appreciation is expressed to Dr. Jeffrey Gould, Director of the Department of Newborn Medicine at Boston City Hospital, for his suggestions and help in the treatment of the monitor state data.

ABSTRACT

The combination of two methods of observing and recording infant and caretaker variables is described as a means of investigating change over days in the postnatal organization of the infant environment system. The methods are the continuous 24-hr nonintrusive bassinet monitoring of infant states, and the continuous observation of both infant and caretaker behavioral variables over the total span of the infant's awake period. A single case illustrates the distribution of continuous around-the-clock sleep and awake data over the first week postnatally. The project has been undertaken to investigate the hypothesis that because the maternal factors that have entrained foetal biorhythms are lost at birth, disorganization of infant states over the first few days results. Reorganization of circadian and ultradian rhythms takes place as new entraining cues are established by specificity in the infant–caregiver interactions over the first week of postnatal life.

REFERENCES

Ashby, W. R. *Design for a brain* (2nd ed)., Science Paperback, New York: Barnes & Noble, 1970. (Originally published, 1952).

Chappell, P. F., Boismier, J. D. & Meier, G. W. *The infant's entering repertoire.* Paper presented at the meeting of the Society for Research in Child Development, Philadelphia, March 1973.

Erikson, E. H. Identify and the life cycle. *Psychological Issues,* 1959, *1,* 50–101.

Halberg, F. Temporal coordination of physiologic functions. *Symposia on Quantitative Biology,* 1960, *25,* 189–310.

Hartman, H. *Ego psychology and the problem of adaptation.* New York: International Universities Press, 1958. (Originally published, 1939.)

Hellbrugge, T., Lange, J. F., Rutenfranz, F & Stehr, K. Circadian periodicity of physiological functions in different stages of infancy and childhood. *Annals of the New York Academy of Sciences,* 1964, *117,* 361–373.

Luce, G. G. *Biological Rhythms in Psychiatry and Medicine.* National Clearinghouse for Mental Health Information, PHS Publication #2088, 1970.

Parmalee, A. H. The ontogeny of sleep patterns and associated periodicities in infants. In *Prenatal and postnatal development of the human brain.* Basel: S. Karger, 1973.

Piaget, J., *The origins of intelligence in children.* Translated by M. Cook, New York: International Universities Press, 1952. (Originally published, 1936).

Prechtl, H. F. R. Polygraphic studies of the full term newborn II. Computer analysis and recorded data. In M. Bax & R.C. MacKeith (Eds.), *Studies in infancy clinic in developmental medicine.* SIMP, London: Heineman, 1968.

Sander, L. W. Regulation and organization in the early infant-caretaker system. In R. Robinson (Ed.), *Brain and early behavior,* London: Academic Press, 1969.

Sander, L. W., Julia, H., Stechler, G. & Burns, P. Continuous 24 hour interactional monitoring in infants reared in two caretaking environments. *Psychosomatic Medicine,* 1972, *34,* 270–282.

Sander, L. W., Stechler, G., Burns, P. & Lee, A. Change in infant and caregiving variables over the first two months of life: Integration of action in early development. In E. Thoman (Ed.), *Origins of the infant's social responsiveness,* Hillsdale N.J.: Lawrence Erlbaum, 1979.

Spitz, R. A. *A genetic field theory of ego formation.* New York: International Universities Press, 1959.

CHAPTER 12

Biological Aspects of the Mother–Infant Bond

Melvin Konner

The use of the word *bond* to describe the mother–infant relationship—long out of fashion and still viewed negatively by most psychologists—has been resumed of late, in reference to what some investigators presume to be happening when mother and infant are brought into contact during the first few postnatal days (Klaus & Kennell, 1976).

Such "maternal–infant bonding," which certainly occurs in various ungulates (it has been best studied in goats), is still very much a hypothetical phenomenon in our own species, and it is at most only a small part of what I refer to in the title of this chapter. I have formerly shared the skepticism of psychologists about the term, but there is something about what happens between parent and child that is not denoted by terms such as *interaction, communication relations, relationship,* or even Harlow's excellent term *affectional system.* Attachment is perhaps what I mean, but this term has become so controversial in recent psychological discussions that when I use it I am not sure what the hearer or reader understands me to mean. The term *bond,* then, is what I have settled on. It is a perfectly good English word with a great tradition of use in the description of social ties. The *Oxford English Dictionary* (OED) has among its definitions, "a force which enslaves the mind through the affections or passions." But it also includes some less intense ties, as indicated by John Locke's phrase, "Speech being the great bond that holds society together." It is the full range of intensity of such ties as they gradually grow an change on both sides of the dyad, as long as its exists, to which I refer.

As for the word *aspect* in the title of this chapter, that too is a carefully chosen word, and I hope that potential critics of my biological approach will

Melvin Konner • 80 Hammond Street, Cambridge, Massachusetts 02138. The author acknowledges the financial assistance of the Social Science Research Council.

take it seriously. I use it because (again according to the *OED*) it means not cause, determinant, basis, foundation, or even explanation, but rather a view, a side, a vantage point, a way of looking. I consider here three such biological aspects: a neuroendocrine aspect of the nursing mother; a neural developmental aspect of the growing infant during the first year; and an evolutionary or phylogenetic aspect of the bond that is implicit throughout these discussions. The latter is a consequence of the fact that most of the research which gave rise to the following observations was conducted among the !Kung San, hunter-gatherers of the Kalahari Desert in Botswaana, who represent in some respects the social and ecological circumstances during which the mother–infant bond evolved. It is, in Bowlby's fine phrase, one of the "environments of human evolutionary adaptedness," and as such can tell us something about what the mother–infant bond may be for. I should hasten to add that, although I do not discuss the father–infant bond, I know from personal experience that it too can be "a force which enslaves the mind through the affections or passions," even on the mature, parental side—and this despite the absence of neuroendocrine turmoil associated with pregnancy, delivery, and nursing. This should give us pause as we explore the more immediately obvious biological aspect of maternal affection.

CONSEQUENCES OF FREQUENT INFANT NURSING: A VIEW OF THE MATERNAL SIDE OF BOND

In the course of a two-year study of infant growth and development among the !Kung, which I conducted in 1969–71 (Blurton Jones & Konner, 1973; Konner, 1972a, b, 1973, 1975, 1976, 1977, 1979, 1981; Konner & Worthman, 1980; West & Konner, 1976), I observed a pattern of nursing that was striking in several respects. First, age at weaning was typically later than three years. All infants under a year of age in the population were nursing, as were 90% of these in the second year, and 75% of those in the third year (Konner, 1976). Second virtually all mothers of children younger than three years of age reported that there children awoke to nurse one or (usually) more times during the night (of the overall sample of nursing mother–child pairs). Third, and most striking to me, was the frequency of daytime nursing. Nursing sessions were brief—a few seconds to a few minutes—and frequent. For all ages under two years (older children were not studied by this method), fewer than 25% of 15-min observations of the mother–infant pair elapsed without a nursing session.

From ecological studies by Richard Lee (1979) and demographic studies by Nancy Howell (1976, 1979), it was also known that the !Kung population had unusually long birth spacing—as high as 44 months in traditional bands. For a noncontracepting, nonabstinent population, this was a noteworthy interval between live births, and it resulted in an overall low natural fertility of 4.7 live births per woman. The nutritional hypothesis of infertility seemed one possible explanation of this long interbirth interval, but not a sufficient one; studies of !Kung diet and nutritional status by Lee, Trusswell, Hansen, and others (see their chapters in Lee & DeVore, 1976; but also see Wilmsen, 1978; Howell, 1979; and Gaulin & Konner, 1977) suggested that mild seasonal caloric undernutrition was the only form of malnutrition endemic in this population.

It seemed reasonable to hypothesize that the unusual temporal pattern of nursing throughout early childhood might help to account for the long interbirth interval. An extensive experimental and clinical literature shows that prolactin is promptly secreted in response to nipple stimulation in human females, increasing 2 to 20-fold in plasma during 5 to 15 min of mechanical stimulation, with a half-life in plasma of 10 to 30 min. Prolactin suppresses gonadal function, either directly at the ovary or indirectly through gonadotropin antagonism at the anterior pituitary. There has even been an *in vitro* demonstration of prolactin suppression of progesterone secretion from cultured ovarian granulosa cells. (See Konner & Worthman, 1980 for references and for further details on the study described below.)

This and other evidence suggested the possibility that temporal patterning of nursing was a key variable mediating the influence of nursing on fertility. Briefly, in populations such as our own, where the interval between nursing sessions is an order of magnitude higher than the half-life of prolactin in plasma, there is little reason to expect effective suppression of ovarian secretion; but in a population such as the !Kung, with intervals between nursing sessions shorter than the half-life of prolactin in plasma, effective suppression might occur.

We tested this hypothesis among the !Kung in a return field study in which nursing behavior and the gonadal hormones progesterone and estradiol-17β were measured in 17 mother–infant pairs, with infants ranging in age from 12 to 139 weeks (mean, 64 weeks). For each mother–infant pair, six hr of nursing observations (at standard times on three separate days) and two maternal blood samples (at 10 A.M. on different days) were collected. In a related study, the monthly ovarian cycle was followed in eight women with normal cycles. Both estradiol-17β and progesterone were significantly lower in the 12 noncycling nursing women than in the 8 cycling women during follicular phase, when both hormones were at their usual low ebb. For the former group, the mean hormone values (E_2, 24.7 pg/ml; P, 186 pg/ml) were comparable to those found in the hyperprolactinemic subgroup of amenorrheic Western women.

More interesting, a product–moment correlation matrix for the nursing sample showed that levels of the two hormones were significantly related to infant's age, and more highly related to the mean interval between nursing sessions (for E_2, $r = .67$, $p < .01$; for P, $r = .71$, $p < .01$; two-tail), but not to total nursing time or mean length of nursing session. That is, even within this frequently nursing sample, interval between nursing sessions predicts levels of ovarian hormones in plasma, giving confirmation to the hypothesis beyond that provided by the overall profound suppression seen in the sample. Of the many variables of the nursing pattern that might be involved in suppression, this study points to the interval between nursing sessions as a crucial one.

Causal inferences cannot be finally made from correlations but our present working model holds that the key change as the infant grows is the lengthening of the interval between nursing sessions. Late in the child's second year, its play occasions longer separations from the mother. When the child is between two and three years of age, the level of prolactin, which presumably has been tonically high previously, is allowed to fall sufficiently low for a long enough time so that its antigonadal or antigonadotrophic effects are impaired, and ovarian cycling is reinstated. Subsequent pregnancy could be further postponed by other effects of suckling such as erratic or anovulatory cycles, with short luteal phases or otherwise imparied luteal competence and, conceivably, interference with implantation, either by prolactin or by suckling-induced oxytocin release. After the end of lactation amenorrhea, such effects, together with some nutritional infertility and some fetal wastage (estimated to be quite low in this population), could lengthen the birth interval to more than three years. We believe that this solves the puzzle of !Kung birth spacing.

However, there are other possible implications of this nursing pattern apart from those evident for fertility. For example, Marjorie Shostak (1981) has interviewed !Kung women extensively and finds that almost all assert that they experience this suckling pattern as physically pleasant, in spite of its obvious freedom-limiting effects. It is not beyond the realm of possibility that the pleasant subjective experience of the women is linked to altered levels of hormones in plasma such as those described above—they may, in some sense, be "drugged" by the nursing pattern—in addition to the reinforcing effects of pain reduction produced by breast emptying.

There are, of course, many potential implications for the infant as well. For example, Blurton Jones (1972) has noted that all higher primates have frequent nursing, and that human milk has a similar distribution of chemical constituents to that of these, and other, frequent feeders, while the makeup of milk of spaced feeders is different. Judith Wurtman (1977) has shown that spacing of feeding influences the composition of laboratory rats' milk on a short-terms basis. She has also analyzed !Kung milk and found it high in fat and low in the amino acid tryptophan, although higher in tryptophan than is the milk of Guatemalan women on a corn diet. Richard Wurtman and John

Fernstorm (1974a,b; 1975) showed that the amount of dietary tryptophan alters the levels of a neurotransmitter, serotonin, which is made by the brain from tryptophan. Lytle (Lytle, Messing, Fisher, & Phebus, 1975) subsequently showed that dietary tryptophan affects pain sensitivity by changing brain serotonin—the first demonstration of an immediate effect of diet on behavior mediated by known dimensions of brain function. It was also shown that any large carbohydrate-containing meal elevates brain serotonin by an indirect metabolic effect (Fernstrom & Wurtman, 1972). Spaced feedings of long duration in American infants might fall into this latter category.

Brain serotonin level has known relations not only to pain sensitivity, but to sleep and waking, depression, and other behavioral dimensions. Because of the different pattern of meal size and trypotophan content for !Kung infants, the Whiting and Whiting model (1975) in different societies now seemed incomplete in at least one important respect (see Konner, 1981 for further critique of the model). It seemed possible that some of the features of !Kung infant behavior and development that I observed differed from the American pattern because of dietary causes. It did not seem likely, but it seemed possible. In addition, the infant is, of course, growing. This does not mean merely "getting larger" or even "changing shape" but also changing and increasing in behavioral competence. It now seems undeniable that the transformation of competence in early infancy is largely driven by the process of brain growth—again, not mere growth in size but differential maturation of the functional characteristics of specialized neural systems. Much about mother–infant relations may now be understood by reference to such maturation. To take a trivial example, it is only because of the complex state of organization of the oral reflexes at the time of birth—rooting, sucking, stripping with the tongue, and swallowing, all while continuing to breathe—that the !Kung can choose to make nursing such a central feature of mother–infant relations. In the middle of the first year, the regulation of the timing of nursing will gradually shift the mother to the infant, due to the maturational emergence of the visually directed grasp. The breast is always exposed, and it is now the infant who will initiate nursing, simply and literally by reaching out for it. Finally, maturation of the infant's social, cognitive, and motor capacity in the second and third years will draw the infant away from the mother often enough and long enough so that the infant's control of the mother's neuroendocrine balance will pass away, and she will become fertile again. The latter process will, by the end of the fourth year, produce an end to the first child's infancy in the form of a younger sibling. It is now possible to relate some of these developing capacities to specific and universal maturational changes in the human infant's brain, given no more than current knowledge of neural structure and function, as will be shown in some detail below.

FOUNDATIONS OF INFANT SOCIAL BEHAVIOR IN
NEUROBEHAVIORAL GROWTH

In the first year of life the brain more than doubles in volume, fully reaching 60% of its adult size (Yakovlev, 1962). During this epoch there are profound structural changes, but generally we are at a loss to interpret them, and the temptation to ignore them is great. Some basic processes are almost complete by birth; few neurons will still be dividing, and cell bodies have already migrated to their destined places. But other processes proceed almost as if birth had never happened: proliferation of synapses, branching of dendrites, changes in the density of dendritic spines, changes in connectivity, proliferation of glial support cells through cell division, and the formation of myelin sheaths around axons in the white matter of the central nervous system. All these processes involve attendant and/or underlying neurochemical changes.

For the sake of simplicity only, this discussion will focus on myelination. It is certainly not the only change, and probably not the most important one, but it is one change we have some understanding of.

When an axon becomes myelinated, its conduction velocity increases dramatically. It is not functionless before this event, but its function is imperfect (Angulo y Gonzalez, 1929; Windle, Fish, & O'Donell, 1934; Martinez & Friede, 1970). The longer the axon, the more the cell has to gain by becoming myelinated. Thus the myelination of the very long neurons of the pyramidal tracts which control the motor neurons predict quite well the dramatic gains in neuromuscular function during the first year of life. Fortunately, the process of myelination is easy to see, thanks to several variations of the Weigert stain, which stains myelin black. A section through the spinal cord of a human newborn has white patches on both sides at the location of the pyramidal tracts, resembling what one might see on one side in a stroke patient experiencing degeneration of the pyramidal tract unilaterally. The reflexes of the human newborn resemble some of those seen in a patient with spinal transection, with the crucial difference that the normal newborn is in the process of developing a normal adult spinal cord (Rorke & Riggs, 1969).

Similar development is taking place in many parts of the nervous system. Here it is worth giving serious consideration to the classic work of Yakovlev and LeCours (1967) on the cycles of myelin formation in all the major subsystems of the human central nervous system. This is not done with the intention of suggesting that myelination sequences are the central feature of brain development; others already mentioned are equally or more important. But they are much more difficult to study in the developing human brain. Myelination, then, is taken only as a convenient index of general and regional brain growth (Conel, 1947; Martinez & Friede, 1970; Matthews, 1968). Furthermore, as mentioned earlier, the use of myelination as an index is not meant to suggest that the nerve fibers in question are functionless before they are myelinated; merely that the precision, speed, timing, and efficiency of their function is greatly enhanced after myelin is formed. Finally, reference to myelination as an index of brain growth should not be taken to suggest that experience has no influence on the process of myelin deposition. There is reason to believe that it does (Kingsley, Collins, & Converse, 1970); but in fact that influence is relatively minor, with experimental studies suggesting an upper limit for effects of exercise at about 10–12% of total myelin, as in the developing optic nerve of a completely occluded eye (Wendell-Smith, 1964).

Therefore, myelination must be considered to be a process largely intrinsic to the growth of the brain. Its influence on developing behavior is likely to be large compared with the reciprocal influence of experience on myelination—although mutual interaction of biology and experience must always be considered to be the rule. Among the events and sequences of myelination are several with suggested behavioral consequences that are familiar. The system subserving detection of postural orientation and vestibular stimulation is myelinated before birth. As Korner (1972) has noted, this may explain the unique effectiveness of rocking stimulation in quieting the newborn. The major tracts of the visual system begin to show evidence of myelin staining just before birth and complete myelination rapidly in the first few months of life. This corresponds to the rapid attainment of visual maturity in the same epoch. It contrasts with the cycle of myelination of the auditory projection to the cortex, requiring several years, and corresponding to the pace of growth of the major function of the human auditory analyzer, namely language comprehension. Lecours (1975) mentioned that cycles of the pyramidal tracts, along with those of cerebellar and other motor structures, correspond to the course of motor maturation. The cortical association areas, the crowning glory of brain evolution, may continue to gain myelin up to the age 30 years (Figure 1).

Consider now some less well-noted changes. Some of the major tracts of the limbic system, which mediate the emotions, do not begin to stain until weeks or months after birth. The cingulum, linking the frontal lobes to the limbic system (Nauta, 1971), myelinates rapidly between two and ten months. The fornix, a massive fiber bundle leaving the hippocampus, myelinates in the second half of the first year and later. Other major connecting tracts of the limbic system myelinate in the first, second, third and later years. The cerebral commissures connecting the two hemispheres, which have been studied a great deal lately, continue to gain myelin throughout the first decade. Finally, the corpus striatum and globus pallidus myelinate in the first and second years. These structures, long thought of as mere modulators of movement, are now known to participate intimately in the initiation of movement (Evarts, 1975). But more interesting for present purposes, stimulation of sites within them has been shown to produce highly ritualized species-specific fixed action patterns which serve as social displays in squirrel monkeys

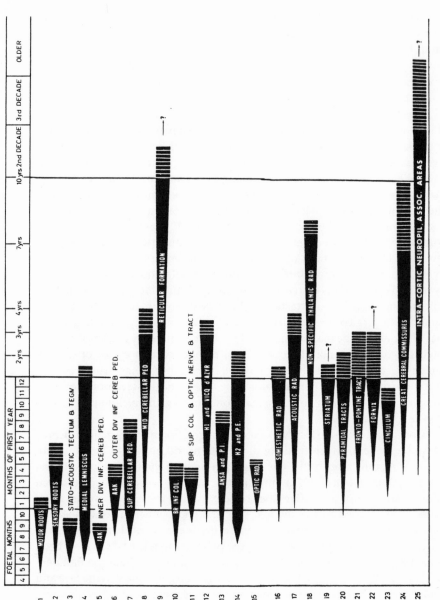

Figure 1. Cycles of myelination, from Yakovlev and LeCours (1967) (their Figure 1). The width and lengthen of graphs indicates the progression in the intensity of staining and density of myelinated fibers. The vertical stripes at the end of the graphs indicate approximate age-range of termination of myelination.

MacLean, 1978). This raises the possibility that if there are any fixed action patterns in human social behavior, they may be controlled in part from homologus sites. None of these various tracts and structures are principally concerned with human information processing and problem solving, with the possible exception of the fornix. All are possibly crucial to human social behavior, and all undergo dramatic, preprogrammed changes during infancy.

THE GROWTH OF SOCIAL SMILING

An early developmental event that is clearly maturational and also specifically social is the smile in response to a human face. To the human adults, smiling in greeting is universal, or at least exists as an option. It has been filmed and measured in the same form and context in societies on all continents, primitive and modern, some remote from the influence of the others (Eibl-Eibesfeldt, 1971a,b). Adults in societies similarly widely distributed universally interpret pictures of smiles as signalling friendliness or happiness (Ekman, 1973). Young children exhibit the social smile in typical form and context and make the usual interpretation (Izard, 1977).

There is undoubtedly quantitative variation in form and function which reflects the influence of learning, but such variation does not bear on the fundamental qualitative constancy of the behavior. It is as close as we are likely to come to a human fixed action pattern, or to a human species-specific social display. It is evidently related to the "playface," an open-mouthed smile occurring during social play, and to the submissive closed-mouth grin shown in greeting a dominant animal, both of which are displays characteristic of catarrhines (Old World monkeys, apes, and humans) (van Hooff, 1972, Andrew, 1963). But the relaxed friendly smile in social greeting is evidently characteristically human.

For practical purposes this behavior is absent at birth and emerges during the first few months of postnatal life. Incidence of smiling in naturalistic social contexts (Figure 2A) or in experimental settings in which the infant is presented with a face (Figure 2B) is two orders of magnitude higher at four months of age than at term, and the response cannot be indisputably identified until some time in the second month (Ambrose, 1959; Emde, Gaensbauer, & Harmon, 1976; Emde & Harmon, 1972; Spitz & Wolf, 1946; Sroufe & Waters, 1976). Considerable quantitative variation attributable to learning occurs after four months of age, but variation in early incidence and in rate of emergence among samples in different environments, although statistically significant, is quantitatively minor (Gewirtz, 1965). This growth process produces a marked change in parent–offspring relations, and mothers may report that they did not subjectively sense the existence of a relationship, or even that they did not love the infant, before the emergence of gaze fixation and competent social smiling (Robson, 1967; Robson & Moss, 1970). The absence of this care-eliciting behavior at birth is an evolutionary puzzle, the solution of which probably lies in the phylogenetic constraint on gestation length imposed by a narrowing birth canal on a slowing rate of growth (Konner, 1979, 1981).

A convincing developmental explanation of the emergence of social smiling has also eluded investigators. Well-formed nonsocial smiles occur regularly in neonates during rapid eye movement (REM) sleep and may be observed for 30 weeks of gestational age(Emde & Harmon, 1972; Emde *et al.*, 1976, Wolff, 1963). Anencephalic infants with a mesencephalic level of functioning exhibit such smiles (Monnier, 1956), making telencephalic or diencephalic involvement in their regulation unlikely. Thus, at birth, with only lower brain functions mature, intricately timed facial muscle action patterns are already under complex central control (Oster, 1978).

Also at birth, gaze fixation and even visual following of a face by the infant can be elicited, suggesting the existence of some underlying perceptual-cognitive capacity (Als, 1977; Brazelton, 1973). Since blind infants develop reliable social smiling only a month or two later than sighted infants (Fraiberg, 1977; Freedman, 1974), a crucial role for visual perception in the growth of the behavior can be ruled out. Since the mean age of the onset of social smiling in samples of low-risk mature infants can be better predicted from their postmenstrual than from their postnatal ages (Brachfeld,

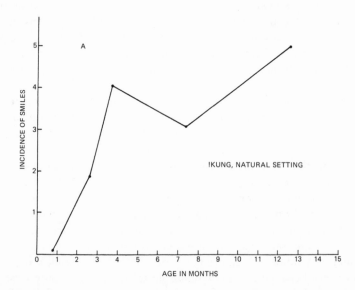

Figure 2 A. Number of smiles seen in infants of !Kung sample in naturalistic observations with the mother present, distributed over the daylight hrs; cross-sectional sample, *N* = 43.

Goldberg, & Sloman, 1980), a key role for associative or operant condition-ing, both readily demonstrated later in infancy (Ahrens, 1954; Ambrose, 1959; Brackbill, 1958), also seems unlikely. Finally, since monozygotic twins are significantly more concordant in the rate of emergence of social smiling than are dizogotic twins (Freedman, 1974), some genetic contribution to the individual variation seems quite plausible.

What is evidently happening, then, is that some central connection be-tween the perceptual mechanism and the already well-formed motor output is maturing during the growth of this behavior. Some of the change may be purely perceptual and cognitive, rather than social or emotional. For exam-ple, by four months of age there is evidence of visual pattern memory unlike-ly earlier in life (Super, Kagan, Morrison, Haith, & Weiffenbach, 1972) and by two months, of substantially improved visual following of eyes and faces (Haith, Bergman, & Moore, 1977). By three months there is evidence that an infant is most attracted to stimuli whose changes it can control ("contingently responsive stimuli," Watson, 1972; Watson & Ramey, 1972) or at least to stimuli (such as are provided by an indulgent caretaker) that change at a pace ideally suited to challenge infant attention (Stern, 1974; Stern & Gibbon,

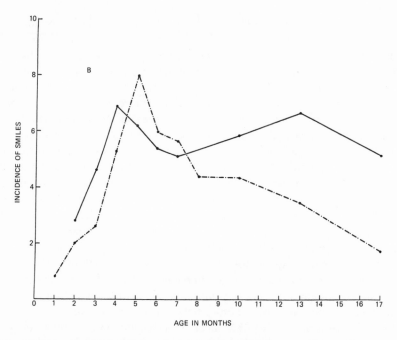

Figure 2 B. Number of smiles seen in response to presentation of the experimenter's face, in two of four samples in Israel studied by Gewirtz (1965); solid line, town fami-lies; dotted line, residential institution. The experimenter's face was unresponsive.

1977) faculties that are largely absent earlier. These are essentially cognitive changes, and general ones at that; but it is also quite likely that some aspects of the maturing competence are specifically social, perhaps even in the ethological sense of the word.

Initial approaches to a developmental neurology of the pattern must be indirect, and the following facts are noteworthy. Myelination of the motor roots of the fifth and seventh cranial nerves is completed prenatally (Langworthy, 1933; Rorke & Riggs, 1969), consistent with the mature form of nonsocial smiling even in premature neonates. It is perhaps worth noting in this connection that the motor nuclei of these nerves are in close proximity to the pontine neurons believed to control REM sleep (McCarley & Hobson, 1975).

Voluntary and emotional control of the smile can each be lost separately as the result of regionally localized brain damage. In facial paralysis due to a corticospinal lesion above the level of the motor nuclei, voluntary retraction of the corners of the mouth is weak or absent, while smiling in appropriate emotional contexts is preserved. "Mimic" paralysis (the emotional form) is less clear in origin, but is believed to result from lesions of the anterior part of the frontal lobe or from "lesions in the neighborhood of the thalamus" (Brain & Walton, 1969). These findings seem to tentatively clear the way for ignoring the growth of the corticospinal path in interpreting the emergence of social smiling.

If it is accepted that smiling is a species-typical social display, then certain neuroethological findings that would otherwise seem remote become relevant. Maclean and his colleagues have long maintained that the striatopallidal complex plays a key role in the control of fixed social displays (Maclean, 1978). They note the prominence of these structures (or their homologues) in birds and reptiles, taxa which (more exclusively than mammals) utilize fixed displays in their social behavior. More important, they have found and repeatedly confirmed that electrocoagulative lesions of the pars interna of the globus pallidus specifically abolish a species-typical fixed action pattern (genital presentation) that serves as a social display in the squirrel monkey, *Saimiri sciureus* (Maclean, 1978). No other deficits are observable in these monkeys, although these were assiduously sought, particularly in the realm of motor function which is traditionally associated with striatopallidal circuits. This has led them to redefine the striatopallidal complex as a regulator of species-specific displays.

From these findings the following model of the growth of social smiling may be tentatively advanced. In late prenatal life the smile appears in mature form, due to the high level of development of the fifth (trigeminal) and seventh (facial) nerves and their motor nuclei, but it does not appear in mature context. Its association with REM sleep is perhaps due to the relatively easy access of the pontine reticular formation to these motor nuclei. In the course of the first few postnatal months the response is brought into the realm of social control. Regional brain growth changes likely to be involved in this change are: (1) sensory changes, perhaps especially tectal (Fig. 1, lines 10, 11, and 15); (2) motor changes, especially cerebellar (lines 5 and 6); and (3) changes in the striatopallidal complex, especially the globus pallidus and its efferents, and ansa lenticularis and the fields of Forel (lines 12–14), with the ansa and pars interna showing the most rapid change at this age (line 13).

THE GROWTH OF THE SOCIAL FEARS

At the end of the phase transition just described, social smiling is well established but relatively undiscriminating. It appears to the observer to be associated with positive emotion, but the emotion seems impersonal; almost anyone can elicit it and, despite subtle signs of discrimination of primary caretakers, strong emotional bonds do not appear to exist. This situation changes markedly in the second half-year. Strangers begin to be discriminated in social responding, often negatively, and increasingly so through the course of the second six months; (Morgan & Ricciuti, 1969; Tennes & Lampl, 1964; Lewis & Rosenblum, 1974); crying when left by the mother in a strange situation, with or without a strange person, becomes common, although it is certainly not universal; (Ainsworth, Blehar, Waters, & Wall, 1978; Bretherton & Ainsworth, 1974); vulnerability to the adverse effects of separations of substantial duration from primary caretakers become demonstrably more marked (Bowlby, 1973); and "attachment behaviors" such as following, clinging, and cuddling become frequent in distinctive relation to the primary caretaker(s), especially in strange situations or in the presence of strange persons (Ainsworth et al., 1978).

Such changes are, to be sure, not all functions of the growth of fear. But they can be summarized as changes in the emotional valence of the interpersonal space of the infant so as to make certain key individuals very attractive while rendering the rest of the species less so, if not actually repelling. The changes are often characterized by primary caretakers as indicative of a deepening of the emotional bond they feel they share with the infant, and by theorists of affective development such as Bowlby (1969, 1980) and Ainsworth (1978) as signalling the onset of the capacity for attachment, a major event in the growth of emotional and social competence.

All the above measures have been made in at least some non-Western cultures, with the result that the underlying concepts now have considerable cross-cultural validity (Kagan, 1976; Super, 1981). The growth of the social fears and the concomitant growth of attachment, as defined by these and related measures, is a putative universal of the second half-year of human life (with much individual variation in the degree of overt expression) and is, at least in its ontogenetic timing, a species-specific feature of human behavioral organization. The percentage of infants who withdraw, fret, or cry when a stranger appears (Figure 3A); who cry when left by the mother either alone or with a stranger (Figure 3B); or who go to the mother rather than a stranger or a secondary caretaker when mildly apprehensive (Kagan, Kearsley, & Zelazo, 1978), rises steadily from the middle of the first to the middle of the second year, whether the sample is drawn from the !Kung San of Botswana (who have 24-hr mother–infant physical contact in a dense social context), a remote Guatemalan Indian village (who have high mother–infant contact in relative isolation), a large Guatemalan town (less mother–infant contact with more social stimulation), an Israeli kibbutz (mother–infant contact on afternoons and weekends), or various subcultures of the United States (Kagan, 1976). Among Chinese-American and Caucasian-American subcultures in Boston, infants who have eight hr a day of day-care separating them from the mother do not differ significantly from control infants with no such separation on measures of social fear and attachment at any age, despite the fact that the day-care regime began before four months of age (Kagan et al., 1978). This latter finding is confirmed by similar studies conducted by other investigators of the effects of day-care on social behavior in other cities (Blanchard & Main, 1979; Brookhart & Hock, 1976; Caldwell, Wright, Honig, & Tannenbaum, 1970; Ricciuiti, 1974).

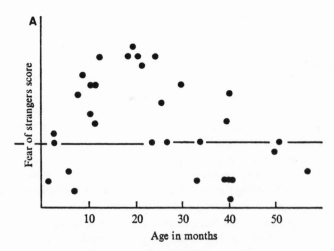

Figure 3 A. Responses to strangers. The ordinal ranking of subjects by fear of strangers scores (y-axis, increasing fearfulness) is shown in relation to age in calendar months. The broken line indicates the rank of individuals whose algebraically summed responses were equal to zero (neither fearful nor positive). Each dot represents a child.

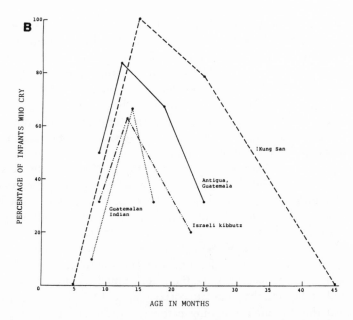

Figure 3B. Percentage of infants who cry in episode 6 of the Ainsworth separation experiment (mother leaves infant alone) in four different cultural settings, by age in months (after Kagan, 1976).

Similarly organized behaviorial patterns, with species-typical motor components and ontogenetic timing, may be seen in the early postnatal development of higher primates (Rosenblum & Alpert, 1974) and other mammals (Scott, 1962), and analogous, although probably not homologous, events may be seen in the very early posthatching development of precocial birds (Sluckin, 1970). Observation in the environments of evolutionary adaptedness (Rheingold, 1963; Altman, 1979), including one such environment for humans (Konner, works cited), clearly suggests an adaptive role for such behaviors in two ways; prevention of predation, and intergenerational transfer of adaptively relevant acquired information. The ontogenetic association of independent locomotion and active imitation with the growth of social fear and attachment behavior (in several species) supports, respectively, the two putative adaptive significances postulated for these heady infant emotions. The concatenation of fixed-action-pattern-like components with one another, and with apparently innate releasing mechanisms, in an organized, goal-corrected, predictable, "driven" fashion resembles, in important respects, some other patterns that are usually called instincts.

There is some evidence that individual variation in the precise ontogenetic timing and the degree of expression of the social fears is under genetic influence. In at least two studies fear of strangers in infancy has been shown to have significantly higher concordance in identical than in fraternal twins pairs, with one study focusing on specific behaviors toward the stranger (Plomin & Rowe, 1978) and the other on the longitudinal pattern of growth of fear (Freedman, 1974). There is no evidence for similar heritability of positive behavior toward caretakers, but little work has been done on this question. It may be, however, that only the negative aspects of the fear/attachment complex have their individual variation under significant genetic influence.

In any case, for present purposes, it is the control not of individual variation but of universal features of maturation that is of interest. In view of the known facts relating fear and other strong emotions to the nuclei and pathways of the limbic system (see Isaacson, 1974, for review), these would seem an appropriate place to look for developmental events that might help to dispel the mystery of the rise of the social fears. In Papez's original formulation, the burden of the "stream of feeling" was laid for the first time on a core of circuitry, including especially the hippocampus, the fornix, the mammillary body, the mammillothalamic tract, the anterior nucleus of the thalamus, the cingulum bundle, and the cingulate cortex (Papez, 1937). It subsequently became clear that the main outgoing pathways of the amygdala—the ventral amygdalofugal path and the stria terminalis, various parts of the hypothalamus, and the septal area—also belong in the proposed emotional circuitry. In addition, Nauta has formulated or discovered three major extensions of the system beyond these primarily diencephalic and older cortical nuclei and circuits: (1) a two-way communication with the frontal granular cortex, leading to a proposed redefinition of the frontal lobes as "the neocortex of the limbic system" (Nauta, 1971); (2) direct fiber connections with the striatopallidal circuitry, via the ansa lenticularis and fields of Forel (Nauta & Mehler, 1966), perhaps providing a basis for species-specific displays of the emotions as proposed by MacLean (1978); and (3) various connections with the "limbic midbrain," over the mammillary peduncle, the dorsal longitudinal fasciculus, the habenulointerpeduncular tract, and other pathways (Nauta, 1958; Nauta & Domesick, 1978), which probably constitute an important part of the nonendocrine effector output of the system, especially, but not only, in the visceral realm. The limbic system and its relations have recently been authoritatively reviewed (Nauta & Domesick, 1980).

Turning to Figure 1, we note that at four months of age there is little or no myelin in the striatum, the fornix, and the cingulum (lines 19, 22, and 23), but that these have achieved almost the adult level of staining by the end of the first year (Yakovlev & Lecours, 1967). The mammillothalamic tract (bundle of Vicq d'Azyr, line 12) also gains heavily in staining density during this period. Although there are other dramatic changes during the second half-year of life, they have mainly to do with the neocortical and cerebellar control of movement; as such they are likely to be less relevant to the growth of the emotions than are the structures mentioned previously. With the absence of myelin on the fornix, the cingulum, and to a lesser extent the mammillothalamic tract, it is probable that the level of functioning in the Papez circuit is very poor at four months compared to its level of functioning at the end of the first year. Thus it is not surprising to find that the emotional competence of the older infant is much greater, and it seems likely that more than an increase in information processing ability is involved. Furthermore, the gains in myelin staining in the striatum, and in the fiber fields of Forel (H1 and H2, lines 12 and 14) suggest the possibility that not only emotional competence but the ability to express emotion in motor action are maturing at this age. However, it would be preferable to refer to data that link some of these structures directly to fear rather than merely to emotional competence in general. In fact, there are data from stimulation studies, lesion studies, and to a lesser extent psychosurgical practice (for reviews see Isaacson, 1974; Gray, 1971; Valenstein, 1973) to support the involvement of portions of the amygdala, the cingulum, the hypothalamus, and the limbic midbrain in the mediation of fear and anxiety. In the original classic experiments on the consequences of temporal lobe lesions, Klüver and Bucy found that removal of large portions of the temporal lobe in monkeys resulted in a syndrome including fearlessness, tameness, tendency to approach objects indiscriminately, mouthing of objects indiscriminately, and hypersexuality (Klüver & Bucy, 1939). With the exception of hypersexuality, which may require previously mature reproductive competence, the syndrome is in some respects reminiscent of the behavior of normal human infants in the four-to-five-month age range. It is possible that the absence of myelin in the limbic circuitry gives them a partial temporal lobe disconnection syndrome that mimics physiologically as well as phenomenologically the Klüver-Bucy syndrome in postoperative adult monkeys, although of course other explanations of the resemblance are possible.

CONCLUSION

The mother–infant bond, a universal characteristic of the higher primates of the Old World (the Catarrhines), evolved under severe selection pressure that acted by culling through predation and, later, by impairment of normal subsistence and reproductive behaviors in those young that failed to experience that bond. With such pressure it would be surprising indeed if there were not genetically coded physiological adaptations that have evolved in the service of bond maintenance. These include adaptations of maternal as well as of infant physiology.

Human infants are not capable of attachment at birth. They are also not universally appealing creatures at this time. The burden is thus on the mother or other caretaker to provide the greatest share of the bond for the first few months. Although it is clear that she is aided in this by cultural training and social expectations, it is also possible that the hormonal changes of pregnancy, delivery, and lactation play some role in facilitating the maternal emotions. It is possible that frequent nursing of the !Kung, with its special hormonal effects, is uniquely effective in producing such facilitation. What seems clear is that it helps to postpone the birth of a subsequent offspring to give ample time for the full cycle of the current offspring's mother–infant bond. In the case of the !Kung, that period is about four years.

Meanwhile, in consequence of phylogenetically programmed brain development sequences, interacting with normal social experience, the infant is developing social competence. Within three or four months of birth this process provides a powerful supporter of the maternal side of the bond, namely, social smiling and the associated eye-to-eye gaze, which before this have been absent or erratic. These intensify the attachment to the infant of the mother and other caretakers. Attachment of the infant to them, on the other hand, develops only subsequently. One of its many hallmarks is the appearance of wary or fearful behavior when left by them, especially in a strange situation or with strange persons.

A neurological accounting for these maturational events in behavior has been proposed. It is tentative. It is not an attempt to rule out a major role for experience, only to assign a major role for neurological development. Given the normal expectable social environment of a newborn of our species, it will develop a bond with a mother or with one or more other caretakers during the course of the first year. After that time, the gradual emergence of cognitive competence, especially in the realm of linguistic communication, will both complicate the already existing bond and deliver the child into a wider human social and cultural world.

ABSTRACT

There is no doubt that learning plays a major, perhaps the central role in the development and maintenance of the mother–infant bond. However, there are biological substrates for this learning on both sides of the unit. This chapter considers the role of nursing frequency on the maternal side, making special reference to an African hunting-gathering population in which infants are nursed four times an hour. It goes on to consider some features of the growth of infant social competence, particularly smiling and the infant social fears, which show considerable constancy across human cultures, despite individual variation. A preliminary attempt is made to correlate these relatively constant features with known characteristics of human brain growth. Throughout, these biological features of the two sides of the bond are viewed, in so far as possible, in relation to their phylogenetic background and adaptive context. These approaches, far from attempting to constrain future interventions for change, are seen as facilitating such interventions by placing them on a more secure foundation.

Acknowledgments

The author thanks J. Kagan, W. Nauta, and P. Yakolev for valuable discussions.

REFERENCES

Ahrens, R. Beitrag zur Entwicklung des Physiognomie and Mimmerkennens. *Zeitschrift für experimentelle und angewandte Psychologie* 1954 *II*, 3 412–454 and *II*, 4,599–633.

Ainsworth, M. D. S., Blehar, M. C., Waters, E., & Wall, S. *Patterns of attachment: A psychological study of the strange situation.* Hillsdale N. J.: Lawrence Erlbaum, 1978.

Als, H. The newborn communicates. *Journal of Communication,* 1977, 27(2), 66–73.

Altman, J. *Baboon mothers and infants.* Cambridge: Harvard University Press, 1979.

Ambrose, J. A., The development of the smiling response in early infancy. In B. M. Foss (Ed.), *Determinants of infant behavior I.* London: Methuen, 1959.

Andrew, R. J. Evolution of facial expressions. *Science,* 1963, *142,* 3595, 1034–1041.

Angulo Y Gonzalez, A. W. Is myelinogeny an absolute index of behavioral capability? *Journal of Comparative Neurology,* 1929, *48,* 459–464.

Blanchard, M., & Main, M. Avoidance of the attachment figure and socio-emotional adjustment in day-care infants. *Developmental Psychology,* 1979, *4,* 445–446.

Blurton Jones, N. G. Criteria for use in describing facial expressions. *Human Biology,* 1971, *43*(3), 365–413.

Blurton Jones, N. G. Comparative aspects of mother–child contact. In N. G. Blurton Jones (Ed.), *Ethological studies of child behavior,* New York: Cambridge University Press, 1972.

Blurton Jones, N. G., & Konner, M. Sex differences in behavior of two to five year olds in London and among the Kalahari Desert Bushmen. In R. P. Michael & J. H. Crook (Eds.), *Comparative ecology and behavior of primates,* London: Academic Press, 1973.

Bowlby, J. *Attachment.* New York: Basic Books, 1969.

Bowlby, J. *Separation:* Anxiety and anger. New York: Basic Books, 1973.

Bowlby, J. *Loss: Sadness and depression.* New York: Basic Books, 1980.

Brackbill, Y. Extinction of the smiling response in infants as a function of reinforcement schedule. *Child Development,* 1958, *39,* 114–124.

Brachfeld, S., Goldberg, S., & Sloman, J. Parent infant interaction in free play at eight and twelve months: Effects of prematurity and immaturity. *Infant Behavior and Development,* 1980, *3,* 289–305.

Brain, L., & Walton, J. N. *Brain's diseases of the nervous system.* Oxford: Oxford University Press, 1969.

Brazelton, T. B. *Neonatal behavioral assessment scale.* London: Heinemann, 1973.

Bretherton, I., & Ainsworth, M. Response of one-year-olds to a stranger in a strange situation. In M. Lewis & L. Rosenblum (Eds.), *The origins of fear.* New York: Wiley, 1974.

Brookhart, J., & Hock, E. The effects of experimental context and experiential background on infants' behavior toward the mother and a stranger. *Child Development,* 1976, *47,* 333–340.

Caldwell, B. M., Wright, C., Honig, A., & Tannenbaum, J. Infant day-care and attachment. *American Journal of Orthopsychiatry*, 1970, *40*, 397–412.

Conel, J. *The postnatal development of the human cerebral cortex* (Vol. 3). Cambridge: Harvard University Press, 1947.

Eibl-Eibesfeldt, I Vorprogrammierung in menschlichen Sozialverhalten. *Mitteilungen an die Max-Planck-Gesellschaft*, 1971, *5*, 307–338. (a)

Eibl-Eibesfeldt, I. Zur Ethologie menschlichen Grussverhaltens: II. Das Gruss verhalten and einige andere Muster freundlicher Kontaktaufnahme der Waika-Indianer (*Yanoama*). *Zeitschrift für Tierpsychologie*, 1971, *29*, 196–213. (b)

Ekman, P. Cross-cultural studies of facial expression. In P. Ekman (Ed.), *Darwin and facial expression*. New York: Academic Press, 1973.

Emde, R. N., & Harmon, R. J. Endogenous and exogenous smiling systems in early infancy, *Journal of the American Academy of Child Psychiatry*, 1972 *11*,(2), 177–200.

Emde, R. N., Gaensbauer, T. J., & Harmon, R. J. Emotional expression in infancy: A biobehavioral study. *Psychological Issues Monograph*, 1976, *37*.

Evarts, E. B. The third Stevenson lecture. Changing concepts of central control of movement. *Canadian Journal of Physiology*, 1975, *53*, 191–201.

Fernstrom, J., & Wurtman, R. J. Brain serotonin content: Physiological regulation by plasma neutral amino acids. *Science*, 1972, *178*, 414–416.

Fraiberg, S. *Insights from the blind: Developmental studies of blind children*. New York: Basic Books, 1977.

Freedman, D. G. *Human infancy; An evolutionary perspective* New York: Wiley, 1974.

Gaulin, S., & Konner, M. J. On the natural diet of primates, including humans. In R. J. & J. J. Wurtman (Eds.), *Nutrition and the brain*. New York: Raven Press, 1977.

Gewirtz, J. L. The course of infant smiling in four child-rearing environments in Israel. In B. M. Foss (Ed.), *Determinants of infant behavior III*. London: Methuen (New York: Wiley), 1965.

Gray, J. A. *The psychology of fear and stress*. New York: McGraw-Hill, 1971.

Haith, M. M., Bergman, T., & Moore, M. J. Eye contact and face scanning in early infancy. *Science*, 1977, *198*, 853–855.

Howell, N. The population of the Dobe area !Kung. In R. Lee & I. DeVore (Eds.), *Kalahari hunter-gatherers*. Cambridge: Harvard University Press, 1976.

Howell, N. *Demography of the Dobe !Kung*. New York: Academic Press, 1979.

Isaacson, R. L. *The limbic system*. New York: Plenum Press, 1974.

Izard, C. E. *Human emotions*. New York: Plenum Press, 1977.

Kagan, J. Emergent themes in human development. *American Scientist*, 1976, *64*(2), 186–196.

Kagan, J., Kearsley, R., & Zelazo, P. *Infancy: Its place in human development*. Cambridge: Harvard University Press, 1978.

Kingsley, J. R., Collins, G. H., & Converse, W. K. Effect of sciatic neurectomy on myelinogenesis in the rat spinal cord. *Experimental Neurology*, 1970, *26*, 498–508.

Klaus, M., & Kennell, J. *Maternal–infant bonding*. St. Louis: Mosby, 1976.

Klüver, H., & Bucy, P. C. Preliminary analysis of the temporal lobes in monkeys. *Archives of Neurological Psychiatry*, 1939, *42*, 979–1000.

Konner, M. J. Aspects of the developmental ethology of a foraging people. In N. G. Blurton Jones (Ed.), *Ethological studies of child behavior*. Cambridge: Cambridge University Press, 1972. (a)

Konner M. J. Review of Baby and Child Care. (Review of *Baby and Child Care* by B. Spock). *Mulch*, 1972, *2* (1), 70–78. (b)

Konner, M. J. Newborn walking: Additional data. *Science*, 1973, *179*, 307.

Konner, M. J. Relations among infants and juveniles in comparative perspective. In M. Lewis & L. Rosenblum (Eds.), *Friendship and peer relations*. New York: Wiley, 1974. (Reprinted in *Social Science Information*, 1976, *15*(2), 371–402.

Konner, M. J. Maternal care, infant behavior and development among the !Kung. In R. B. Lee & I. DeVor (Eds.), *Kalahari hunter-gatherers*. Cambridge: Harvard University Press, 1975.

Konner, M. J. Infancy among the Kalahari Desert San. In H. Liederman, S. Tulkin, & A. Rosenfeld (Eds.), *Culture and infancy*. New York: Academic Press, 1977.

Konner, M. J. Biological bases of social development. In M. W. Kent & J. E. Rolf (Eds.), *Primary prevention of psychopathology. Vol. II: Social competence in children*. Hanover: New England Universities Press, 1979.

Konner, M. J. Evolution of human behavior development. In R. H. Munroe, R. Munroe & B. B. Whiting (Eds.), *Handbook of cross-cultural development*, New York: Garland, 1981.

Konner, M. J., & Worthman, C. Nursing frequency, gonadal function and birth spacing among !Kung hunter-gatherers. *Science*, 1980, *207*, 788–791.

Korner, A. State as variable, as obstacle and as mediator of stimulation in infant research. *Merrill-Palmer Quarterly*, 1972, *18*, 77–94.

Langworthy, O. Development of behavior patterns and myelination of the nervous system in the human fetus and infant *Contributions to Embryology*, 1933, *139*, 1–57.

Lecours, A. R. Myelogenetic correlates of the development of speech and language. In *Foundations of language development* (Vol. 2). New York: Academic Press, 1975.

Lee, R. *The !Kung San: Men, women and work in a foraging society*. New York: Cambridge University Press, 1979.

Lee, R., & DeVore, I. (Eds.). *Kalahari hunter-gatherers*. Cambridge: Harvard University Press, 1976.

Lewis, M., & Rosenblum, L. A. (Eds.). *The origins of fear*. New York: Wiley, 1974.

Lytle, L. D., Messing, R. B., Fisher, L., & Phebus, L. Effects of long-term corn consumption on brain serotonin and the response to electric shock. *Science*, 1975, *190*, 692–694.

MacLean, P. D. *A triune concept of brain and behavior. The Hincks Memorial Lectures*. Toronto: University of Toronto, 1973.

MacLean, P. D. Effects of lesions of globus pallidus on species-typical display behavior of squirrel monkeys. *Brain Research*, 1978, *149*, 175–196.

Martinez, A. J., & Friede, R. L. Changes in nerve cell bodies during the myelination of their axons. *Journal of Comparative Neurology*, 1970, *138*, 329–338.

Matthews, M. A. An electron microscopic study of the relationship between axon diameter and the initiation of myelin production in the peripheral nervous system. *Anatomical Record*, 1968, *161*, 337–352.

McCarley, R. W., & Hobson, J. A. Discharge patterns of cat brain stem neurons during desynchronized sleep. *Journal of Neurophysiology*, 1975, *38*, 751–766.

Monnier, M. The behaviour of newborn anencephalics with varying degrees of anencephaly. In J. M. Tanner & B. Inhelder (Eds.), *Discussions on child development* (Vol. 1). London: World Health Organization/Tavistock, 1956.

Morgan, G. A. & Ricciuti, H. N. Infants responses to strangers during the first year. In B. M. Foss (Ed.), *Determinants of infant behavior*, (Vol. 4). London: Methuen, 1969.

Nauta, W. J. H. Hippocampal projections and related neural pathways to the midbrain in the cat. *Brain*, 1958, *81*, 319–340.

Nauta, W. J. H. The problem of the frontal lobe: A reinterpretation. *Journal of Psychiatric Research*, 1971, *8*, 167–187.

Nauta, W. J. H., & Domesick, V. B. Crossroads of limbic and striatal circuitry: Hypothalamo-nigral connections. In K. E. Livingston & O. Hornykiewicz (Eds.), *Limbic mechanisms*. New York: Plenum Press, 1978.

Nauta, W. J. H., & Domesick, V. B. Neural associations of the limbic system. In A. Beckman (Ed.), *Neural substrates of behavior*. New York: Spectrum, 1980.

Nauta, W. J. H., & Mehler, W. R. Projections of the lentiform nucleus in the monkey. *Brain Research*, 1966, *1*, 3–42.

Oster, H. Facial expression and affect development. In M. Lewis & L. A. Rosenblum (Eds.), *The development of affect*. New York: Plenum Press, 1978.

Papez, J. W. A proposed mechanism of emotion. *Archives of Neurological Psychiatry*, 1937, *38*, 725–743.

Plomin, R., & Rowe, D. C. Genes, environment and development of temperament in young human twins. In G. M. Burghardt & M. Bekoff (Eds.)., *The development of behavior: Comparative and evolutionary aspects*. New York: Garland, 1978.

Rheingold, H. (Ed.). *Maternal behavior in mammals*. New York: Wiley, 1963.

Ricciuti, H. N. Fear and the development of social attachments in the first year of life. In M. Lewis & L. A. Rosenblum (Eds.), *The origins of fear*. New York: Wiley, 1974.

Robson, K. S. The role of eye-to-eye contact in maternal–infant attachment. *Journal Child Psychology and Psychiatry*, 1967, *8*, 13–25.

Robson, K. S., & Moss, H. A. Patterns and determinants of maternal attachment. *Journal of Pediatrics*, 1970, *77*(6), 976–985.

Rorke, L. B., & Riggs, H. E., *Myelination of the brain in the newborn*. Philadelphia: Lippincott, 1969.

Rosenblum, L. A., & Alpert, S. Fear of strangers and attachment in Monkeys. In M. Lewis & L. A. Rosenblum, (Eds.), *The origins of fear*. New York: Wiley, 1974.

Scott, J. P. Critical periods in behavioral development. *Science*, 1962, *138*, 949–958.

Shostak, M. Personal communication, 1981.

Sluckin, W. *Early learning in man and animal*. Cambridge: Schenkman, 1970.

Spitz, R. A., & Wolf, K. M. The smiling response: A contribution to the ontogenesis of social relations. *Genetic Psychology Monographs*, 1946, *34*, 57–125.

Sroufe, L. A., & Waters, E. The ontogenesis of smiling and laughter: A perspective on the organization of development in infancy. *Psychological Review*, 1976, *83*(3), 173–189.

Stern, D. Mother and infant at play: The dyadic interaction involving facial, vocal, and gaze behaviors. In M. Lewis & L. A. Rosenblum (Eds.), *The effect of the infant on its caregiver*. New York: Wiley, 1974.

Stern, D. & Gibbon, J. Temporal expectancies of social behaviors in mother–infant play. In E. Thomas (Ed.), *The origins of the infant's responsiveness*. New York: Lawrence Erlbaum, 1977.

Super, Charles S. Behavioral development in infancy. In R. H. Munroe, R. L. Munroe, & B. B. Whiting (Eds.), *Handbook of cross-cultural human development*. New York: Garland, 1981.

Super, C., Kagan, J., Morrison, F., Haith, M., & Weiffenbach, J. Discrepancy and attention in the five-month infant. *Genetic Psychology Monographs*, 1972, *85*, 305–331.

Tennes, K. H., & Lampl, E. E. Stranger and separation anxiety in infancy. *Journal of Nervous and Mental Disorders*, 1964, *139*, 247–254.

Valenstein, E. S. *Brain control*. New York: Wiley, 1973.

Van Hooff, J.A.R.A.M. A comparative approach to the phylogeny of laughter and smiling. In R. A. Hinde (Ed.), *Non-verbal communications* Cambridge: Cambridge University Press, 1972.

Watson, J. S. Smiling, cooing and "the game." *Merrill-Palmer Quarterly*, 1972, *4*, 323–339.

Watson, J. S., & Ramey, C. P. Reactions to response contingent stimulation in early infancy. *Merrill-Palmer Quarterly*, 1972, *18*, 219–228.

Wendell-Smith, C. P. Effects of light deprivation on the postnatal development of the optic nerve. *Nature*, 1964, *204*, 707.

West, M., & Konner, M. The role of the father: An anthropological perspective. In M. Lamb (Ed.), *The role of the father in child development*. New York: Wiley, 1976.

Whiting, B., & Whiting, J. *Children of six cultures*. Cambridge: Harvard University Press, 1975.

Wilmsen, E. Seasonal effects of dietary intake on Kalahari San. *Federation Proceedings*, 1978, *37*, 65–72.

Windle, W. F., Fish, M. W., & O'Donell, J. E. Myelogeny of the cat as related to development of fiber tracts and prenatal behavior patterns. *Journal of Comparative Neurology*, 1934, *59*, 139–165.

Wolff, P. H. Observations of the early development of smiling. In B. M. Foss (Ed.), *Determinants of infant behavior II.* London: Methuen, 1963.

Wurtman, J. Personal communication, 1977.

Wurtman, R. J., & Fernstrom, J. Control of brain serotonin by the diet. *Advances in Neurology,* 1974, *5,* 19–29. (a)

Wurtman, R. J., & Fernstrom, J. Effects of the diet on neurotransmitters. *Nutrition Reviews,* 1974, *32,* 193–200. (b)

Wurtman, R. J., & Fernstrom, J. Control of brain monamine synthesis by diet and plasma amino acids. *American Journal of Clinical Nutrition.* 1975, *28,* 638–647.

Yakovlev, P. I. Morphological criteria of growth and maturation of the nervous system in man. *Mental Retardation,* 1962, *39,* 3–46.

Yakovlev, P. I., & Lecours, A. R. The myelogenetic cycles of regional maturation of the brain. In A. Minkowski (Ed.), *Regional development of the brain in early life.* Oxford: Blackwell Scientific, 1967.

CHAPTER 13

Toward a Theory of Infant Temperament

H. Hill Goldsmith and Joseph J. Campos

RELEVANCE OF TEMPERAMENT TO ATTACHMENT

Why do we have a chapter on temperament in a volume primarily devoted to the concepts of attachment and affiliation? Years ago, such a chapter would have been unthinkable because attachment and temperament appeared to refer to different phenomena. Classic theories of mother–infant relations such as those of Spitz (1965) and Bowlby (1951) leaned in the direction of a "tabula rasa" model of the human infant by proposing that emotional and drive-regulating experiences provided by the mother were crucial for the formation and maintenance of ego functions. The individual differences these theorists were interested in were those resulting from successes and failures of maternal interaction, although on occasion they did invoke genetic and constitutional factors to account for unusual tolerances or susceptibilities to the ill effects of maternal separation. Individual differences in temperament, then, were relegated to a shorthand description of the susceptibility of the "tabula rasa" to experience—how hard or soft the tablet was, so to speak. Little speculation took place about how such differences in the infant could be assessed or whether they played a role in attachment.

Portions of this chapter were initially prepared for a chapter by Campos, Goldsmith, Lamb, Svejda, and Stenberg on emotional development during infancy for *Carmichael's Manual of Child Psychology*, Volume 4 (P. H. Mussen, Ed.).

H. Hill Goldsmith • Department of Psychology, 330 Mezes Hall, University of Texas, Austin, Texas 78712. **Joseph J. Campos** • Department of Psychology, 2040 South York Street, University of Denver, Denver, Colorado 80208. H. Goldsmith was supported during the preparation of this chapter by an NIMH Individual Postdoctoral Fellowship MH–08239 and J. Campos was supported in part by an NIMH grant MH–23556. The research based on the conceptualizations presented in this chapter is supported by grants from the Developmental Psychobiology Research Group Endowment Fund, NIMH MH–35270, and the Spencer Foundation.

Today, a more dynamic view of temperament prevails. Rather than referring merely to differences in the infant's *susceptibility* to experiences, temperament is now generally considered to include processes which help to regulate the child's social relationships (e.g., Lewis & Rosenblum, 1974). Differences in temperament can elicit, modify, and prevent many social behaviors of the primary caregiver. Numerous factors have contributed to this change in the *zeitgeist* about temperament. Bell's (1968) seminal paper on the infant's contribution to the development of social relations was one. The transactional model of development described bby Sameroff and Chandler (1975) was another, and the New York Longitudinal Study of Thomas, Chess, Birch, Hertzig, and Korn (1963) was a third. These latter researchers have recently adopted explicitly the notion that early temperament predicts subsequent behavior only when considered in the context of the parent's reactions (Thomas & Chess, 1977; 1980). Notions such as this one imply that a full understanding of the development of attachment relationships will not be possible in the absence of an understanding of infant temperament.

As a result of its newly recognized implications for the development of social relations, as well as for entirely unrelated reasons, research on infant temperament is burgeoning. The following is a sampling of the topics under active investigation: (1) the construction of parental-report measures infant temperament and investigation of the determinants of these parental perceptions (e.g., Bates, Freeland, & Lounsbury, 1979; Carey & McDevitt, 1978; Goldsmith, Campos, Benson, Henderson, & East, 1980; Pederson, Anderson, & Cain, 1976; Rothbart 1981); (2) the development of laboratory and home observation measures of temperament (e.g., Goldsmith *et al.*, 1980; Lytton, Martin, & Eaves, 1977; Plomin & Foch, 1980; Plomin & Rowe, 1979; Rothbart, 1981; Wilson, 1979); (3) the degree of genetic and environmental influences on variation in infant temperament (see review on page 168); (4) the predictive power of measures of temperament for later (a) temperament assessments (e.g., Carey & McDevitt, 1978; Rothbart, 1981; Thomas & Chess, 1977; Vaughn, Deinard, & Egeland, 1980), (b) quality of attachment (Waters, Vaughn, & Egeland, 1980), (c) childhood behavioral disturbance (e.g., Thomas & Chess, 1977), and (d) later educational adjustment (e.g., Holden, 1980; Keogh, 1979; Korn, unpublished, cited in Thomas & Chess, 1977; Scholom & Schiff, 1980; Sobesky, Holden, & Rossman, 1979). In sum, the broadest claims imply a substantial contribution of infant temperament to adaptive functioning, both during infancy and later.

Unfortunately, much research in this field seems to be proceeding without the benefit of precise and delimited definitions of the temperament concept. Perhaps one of the reasons for this is that the concept of temperament has accumulated considerable surplus meaning over the years. Among the outmoded connotations are immutability, lack of any environmental influence, presence at birth, and direct and intimate connections with body type (e.g., Kretschmer, 1925; Sheldon, 1942). Our primary purpose in this chapter is to provide a precise definition of temperament for infant behavioral research. This definition will suggest that individual differences in temperament are very closely related to, yet dissociable from, emotion systems. Before proposing our definition, we shall review some of the major approaches to infant temperament. After describing our conceptualization, we shall explain why, despite formidable obstacles to investigating the relationship empirically, temperament has a plausible role as a determinant of individual differences in the quality of attachment, and, in addition, as a confound in the assessment of attachment in Ainsworth and Wittig's (1969) strange situation.

SOME PREVIOUS EFFORTS TO DEFINE TEMPERAMENT

Temperament in Adult Personality Theories

Antedating the current interest in infant temperament, adult personality theories addressed the importance of temperament and attempted to differentiate temperament from other aspects of personality. For example, according to Allport (1937):

> Temperament refers to the characteristic phenomena of an individual's emotional nature, including his susceptibility to emotional stimulation, his customary strength and speed of response, the quality of his prevailing mood, and all peculiarities of fluctuation and intensity in mood; these phenomena being regarded as dependent upon constitutional make-up, and therefore largely hereditary in nature. (p.54)

Within another system of the structure of personality, Cattell (1946) postulates three "modalities" of traits: the dynamic modality (including for example, needs, drives, and attitudes), the ability modality (including, for example, intelligence and memory), and the temperament modality (including, for example, excitability, sensitivity, perseveration, and impulsiveness). Cattell defines temperament traits primarily by exclusion. Dynamic traits are those which change in response to change of incentive in a situation; abilities change most in response to changes in the complexity of the path to a goal; and temperament traits are those which change least in response to any change in the field.

Four Theories of Temperament with Developmental Orientations

There were notable contributions to the study of temperament in infants and children in the 1930's (Gesell & Ames, 1937; Shirley, 1933), but with a few exceptions (e.g., Escalona, 1968), little developmental theorizing about temperament occurred until recently.

We shall focus on four contemporary and rather different theoretical approaches to the study of temperament which have explicit developmental orientations. Our intention is to describe and evaluate the theoretical formulations and assessment strategies of each approach rather than to review the pertinent empirical literature. In particular, we will note the position of each theory with regard to four issues which will be central to our own conceptualization of temperament:

1. Can temperament traits motivate the infant?
2. Is temperament related to affect?
3. Does temperament play a role in the regulation of social interaction?
4. Can temperament traits serve initiaing as well as reactive functions?

To anticipate our own definition in section III, we think that there is an affirmative answer to each of these questions.

A Style Approach (Thomas and Chess). Certainly the best-known developmentally oriented theory in this field is that proposed by Thomas and Chess (1977); Thomas, Chess and Birch (l968); Thomas et al. (1963). In the New York Longitudinal Study (NYLS), Thomas and Chess conceptualized temperament as early-appearing behavioral style. For example, a child might be characteristically slow to adapt to any new situation. Thus temperament is meant to be conceptually distinct from the content and motivation of behavior, it refers to the how, not the what or why of behavior. By adhering to the "style" definition, this research group succeeds, in much the same way many adult personality theories do, in differentiating temperament from other behavioral domains. However, a conception of temperament as purely style carries some rather stringent empirical implications. For instance, Sroufe and Waters (1977) regard temperament characteristics as sets of behaviors which are "constantly and uniformly operative" (p. 1185). Rothbart and Derryberry (1981) point out that a strict style definition of temperament can be interpreted to imply that an infant characteristic such as intensity should be consistent across all expressive modalities; for example, the extremely active infant would, at different times be intensely negative in mood or extremely happy. Such strictures are unduly constraining for a workable definition of infant temperament.

The NYLS conception of temperament as style (i.e., as nonmotivational) would seem to preclude a role for temperament in the initiation of the individual's behavior. However, Thomas and Chess (1977) do describe ways in which an infant's temperament can motivate parental behavior.

Thomas and Chess emphasize the importance of interactive processes (both between infant temperament and parental caregiving style and between temperament, motives, and abilities within the individual) for later development and mental health. They have endorsed the notion of goodness-of-fit between an individual's temperament characteristics and the environment (primarily the rearing environment) as a central feature of their "interactive" viewpoint. This interactive orientation, while open to challenge as being so general that it offers few guidelines for contemporary research (Lamb, 1980) does redress the imbalance of earlier theories of temperament which were heavily imbued with biological determinism.

In general, Thomas and Chess do not conceptualize temperament in terms of affect (with the exception of their "mood" category; however, several of their temperament categories can be recast in affective terms (see Table I).

Besides these four issues, Thomas and Chess attend to other questions including origins, stability, clinical implications, and assessment of temperament. With regards to the origins of temperament, no clear stand is taken. Thomas and Chess (1977) use *temperament* as a "phenomenologic" term with no implications as to etiology or immutability. They consider that "temperament is influenced by environmental factors in its expression and even in its nature as development proceeds" (p. 9).

A major focus of theorizing has been on continuity/discontinuity of temperament traits, with the conclusion seeming to be that, in the face of apparent discontinuity, underlying continuity can be uncovered by recognizing the role of intervening factors such as the aforementioned goodness-of-fit between infant temperament and parental caregiving style. In some cases, the continuity of temperament may be evident only when an individual faces novel or stressful situations.

An even more pervasive focus of attention for this research group has been on the relationship between temperament and domains of clinical importance—parent–infant interaction, mental retardation, childhood behavioral disturbance, and educational adjustment. However, some of the empirical findings of the NYLS and related projects regarding the predictive power of temperament are subject to alternative interpretations (cf. McNeil, 1976; Persson-Blennow & McNeil, 1979).

Although Thomas, Chess, and coworkers admit the possibility of other dimensions of temperament, in practice they have paid exclusive attention to nine putative dimensions (called "categories") of temperament (activity level, approach/withdrawal, regularity, adaptability, threshold, intensity, mood, distractability, and attention span/persistence). From these were derived three typological characterizations of infants: "easy," "difficult," and "slow-to-warm-up." In the NYLS, parental interviews were utilized to assess the nine categories of temperament. More recently, parent- or teacher-report questionaires have sometimes been used.

The derivation process for the nine categories mentioned above has important theoretical ramifications. According to Thomas and Chess (1977),

"Nine categories of temperament were established by an inductive content analysis of the parent interview protocols for the infancy periods of the first 22 children studied" (p. 20). This procedure has resulted in several problems: (1) There are no guidelines for independent replication of the derivation procedure just described. (2) Whether the same categories would be uncovered (even supposing the original derivation procedure could be replicated) at later ages is not known. (3) The nine categories refer to seemingly disparate levels of analysis; for example, activity level and mood are broad constructs with many possible behavioral manifestations while approach/avoidance describes a behavioral tendency which could apply to many constructs (e.g., fear or attachment), and adaptability seems to be a supraordinate construct of some type (see Table I for elaboration of these ideas). (4) There are problems of overlap among the proposed categories, both in the NYLS measures and in Carey's (1970; 1972) and Thomas and Chess's (1977) questionnaire measures of the NYLS dimensions (see Martin & Pfeffer, 1980; Rowe & Plomin, 1977; Taraldson, Brunnquell, Deinard, & Egeland, 1977; Vaughn et al, 1980). This fourth problem is only partially due to flaws in the original Carey questionnaire, some of which have been corrected (Carey & McDevitt, 1978). (5) Independent attempts to operationalize some of the nine dimensions using caretaker-report questionnaires have not been successful (Pederson et al., 1976; Rothbart, 1981). For these reasons and others, investigators recently have derived, usually via factor analysis, smaller sets of scales from NYLS-derived items (e.g., Rowe & Plomin, 1977; Scholom, Zucker, & Stollack, 1979). Such efforts are likely to be psychometrically more satisfactory than the original scales; however, the rationale for selection of the initial item pool places important constraints on the dimensions which can be uncovered.

Another set of problems concerns the "typological thinking" (Dobzhansky, 1970) inherent in the value-laden characterization of infants as temperamentally "difficult," "easy," or "slow-to-warm-up." These problems have been discussed by Bates (1980). To some extent, the problems of typological thinking parallel the problems of typological classifications in the attachment realm. The latter are treated by Connell and Goldsmith in this volume.

A Criterial Approach (Buss and Plomin) Buss and Plomin's (1975) approach (which was updated by Plomin & Rowe, 1978) includes an endorsement of Allport's (1937) definition. The key feature of their temperament theory is the postulation of five inclusion criteria which are biological or developmental in nature. These criteria require that valid dimensions of temperament be (1) heritable, (2) stable, (3) predictive of adult personality, (4) adaptive (in the evolutionary sense), and (5) perhaps present in other animals. (This last criterion has been emphasized by Diamond, 1957). Consideration of the evidence relevant to these criteria led Buss and Plomin to postulate four broad dimensions of temperament: emotionality (E), activity (A), sociability (S), and impulsiveness (I). A positive aspect of this approach is that a parental-report questionnaire, the EASI, was constructed to operationalize these four temperaments.

The elaboration of Buss and Plomin's theory is, of course, guided by their own criteria, but their position regarding some of the four issues of direct concern to us can be inferred. Some, if not all, of their broad temperament dimensions are clearly related to emotion systems. Although Buss and Plomin refer to temperament as involving the style of behavior, we would infer from their explication of the theory that the EASI dimensions are imbued with the same motivational and behavior-initiating properties of personality traits in that they consider temperaments to be the heritable subset of personality dimensions.

Buss and Plomin's theory of temperament has had a heuristic effect on the field; each of their biological or developmental criteria addresses an issue which a complete theory of temperament must address. However, there are practical problems in the application of these criteria, and some investigators prefer to consider these criteria as hypotheses rather than as the defining characteristics of temperament. Chief among the problems is the unobservable nature of the criterion of evolutionary adaptedness. It is not a difficult task to fashion a plausible case for the selective advantage of almost any putative temperament dimension in a hunter–gatherer society. A second problem is that there is a potential conflict between the "heritabiality" and the "evolutionary adaptedness" criteria if directional rather than balancing selection has occurred for the trait in question (Dobzhansky, 1970; Thiessen, 1972).* Recognizing this problem, Plomin and Row (1978) have modified the heritability criterion so that it applies only to those temperament dimensions for which intermediate levels of trait expression would be expected to have been adaptive. This modification of criteria is logically necessary, but it makes the heritability criterion dependent on an untestable evolutionary assumption. This issue aside, accurate estimation of heritability faces a number of practical obstacles, including the need for very large samples, for accurate point estimates of heritability (Klein, 1974; Martin, Eaves, Kearsey, & Davies, 1978), the specificity of heritability estimates to the population sampled with its particular joint distribution of environments and genotypes, and the possible specificity of heritability estimates to developmental stages of the lifespan.

The criteria dealing with stability and predictive power for adult personality are more likely to yield to empirical investigation, but the problems are

---

* Directional selection, which favors extreme values of a trait, has the effect of depleting genetic variance as unfavored alleles are eliminated from the gene pool while favored alleles approach a frequency of 1.0. Thus, heritability can tend toward zero for a trait largely influenced (in a developmental, but not an individual differences, sense) by genotype provided that directional selection has occurred. Balancing selection favors intermediate values of a trait at the expense of extreme values.

thorny (Lewis & Starr, 1979) and the relevant literature is too wide-ranging for treatment here. We will concentrate only on recent results bearing on the most central criterion, heritability, as applied to the four EASI dimensions, however assessed.* Goldsmith and Gottesman's (1981) tabulation of published twin studies (which met certain criteria of sample size and sample selection) of preadolescent personality and temperament contains twenty such studies, nine of which were published since Buss and Plomin's (1975) review. Of these nine, Matheny's (1980) and Goldsmith's (1978; Goldsmith & Gottesman, 1981) were both longitudinal and large in size, and each employed a version of Bayley's (1969) Infant Behavior Record. Goldsmith and Gottesman (1981) found evidence for significant, but moderate, levels of genetic variance for an infant (eight month) "activity level" factor, but not for an "interest in persons" factor. However, the authors expressed reservations regarding the generalizability of the "interest in persons" factor to the broader domain of infant sociability. Matheny (1980), analyzing data from the Louisville twin study, uncovered little evidence for the heritability of an activity factor before 18 months but did demonstrate significant, though longitudinally inconsistent, genetic variance for a "test affect/extraversion" factor which seems similar to Buss and Plomin's emotionality dimension. A large nonlongitudinal study utilizing parental ratings of twins ranging in age from 1 to 6 years (Cohen, Dibble, & Grawe, 1977) included two of the Buss and Plomin dimensions among the five personality factors assessed. Strong evidence for genetic variance on the behavior modulation (activity) and sociability scales emerged.

Using factor-analytic techniques, Rowe and Plomin (1977) constructed the Colorado Childhood Temperament Inventory, a six-scale questionnaire which combined the EASI with items derived from the NYLS dimensions. From the same sample, Plomin and Rowe (1977) reported significantly greater identical than fraternal co-twin similarity for sociability, emotionality, activity, attention span, persistence, and soothability. However, with the exception of the emotionality scale, the fraternal co-twin similarity was lower than genetic theory would originally predict. This has been a common finding for the EASI dimensions (cf. Harris & Rose, 1977).

Despite this caution, one must conclude that evidence for the heritability of various dimensions of temperament has continued to accumulate when questionnaire measures are utilized.

In their efforts to assess temperament, Buss and Plomin opted for measuring broad, but distinct, behavioral constructs which imply that more than

---

* For reviews of the empirical findings relevant to the other criteria see Buss and Plomin (1975), as well as Beckwith (1979) for discussion of the predictive value of early behavioral assessment for later personality, and Fuller and Thompson (1978) for review of temperament-related studies of nonhuman animals.

style is implicated in temperament. The best validity evidence which has accumulated for the EASI takes the form of factorial validity and some evidence of heritability. Typical items from the activity scale of the EASI inventory are given by Buss and Plomin (1975):

> Child is always on the go.
> Child cannot sit still long.

The items on a given scale are quite similar in content, and each calls for a global judgment of the child's behavior on the part of the respondent—circumstances likely to enhance the probability of attaining the factorial validity referred to above.

Plomin and Foch (1980), among others (Goldsmith, 1978; Lytton *et al.*, 1977; Wilson, 1979) have called attention to the possible limitations of "paper and pencil" assessment of temperament and have expanded twin studies to include objective laboratory and home-based assessments of the four EASI dimensions (Plomin & Foch, 1980; Plomin & Rowe, 1979).

A Psychobiological Approach (Rothbart and Derryberry). This wide-range, multilevel theory of temperament seeks to integrate the views of adult temperament represented by Gray (1973), Eysenck (1967), and Zuckerman (1979), and related Eastern European concepts of the reactivity of the nervous system (Nebylitsyn, 1972; Pavlov, 1935; Strelau, 1975; Teplov, 1964), with research on social and emotional development during infancy. The key concepts in Rothbart and Derryberry's (1981; in press) theory are reactivity of the nervous system and self-regulation of reactivity. According to Rothbart and Derryberry (in press):

> In our model, temperament refers to individual differences in reactivity and self-regulation assumed to have a constitutional basis. "Consititutional" is defined here [somewhat vaguely] as the relatively enduring biological make-up of the organism influenced over time by heredity, maturation, and experience. "Reactivity" refers to the excitability, responsivity, or arousability of the behavioral and physiological systems of the organism, while "self-regulation" refers to neural and behavioral processes functioning to modulate this underlying reactivity.

Examples of self-regulation include approach and avoidance behavior and channeling of attention. In discussing reactivity and self-regulation, these authors emphasize that the two constructs can be utilized to describe temperament at the neural level, the level of interacting physiological systems, and at the behavioral level. Rothbart and Derryberry (1981) specify the somatic, endocrine, and autonomic response systems (including motor activity, facial expressions, vocal activity, and emotional reactions) through which reactivity and self-regulation are expressed. They also discuss the intensive and temporal response characteristics of these response systems: intensity (the peak level of excitement), threshold (sensitivity to low-intensity stimulation), latency of response, rise time of response (the interval from onset to peak intensity), and recovery time. Individual differences in these five elements of the phasic nature are *not* necessarily expected to be consistent across the various response systems.

With regard to the four issues of prime importance in this review, Rothbart and Derryberry (1981) clearly reject the notion of temperament as merely style and place "affective-motivational systems at the center of the developing personality." These authors also postulate a connection between temperament and affect in that the emotion systems constitute one of the response systems for reactivity. Thus one aspect of temperament would be "threshold of reactivity in the fear response system." However, the emotion systems are not the only behavioral components of temperament; variability in the cognitive systems, such as the alerting, orienting, and detecting components of attention are postulated to be components of temperament. Indeed, the explication of the theory is so wide-ranging (i.e., the theory refers to cognition, social interaction, motivation, and emotional development at neural, physiological, and behavioral levels) that it is difficult to determine just which individual differences in the infant's behavioral repertoire are *not* temperament-related.

Rothbart and Derryberry stress the importance of temperament for understanding social development. For example, in discussing the implications of individual differences in rise times for negative affect, they explain that more gradual rise times will allow the caregiver more time to administer soothing ministrations, thereby averting the distress and any sequelae.

At first glance, it might seem that any theory with reactivity as the pivotal concept would not postulate a role for temperament in the initiation of behavior. However, the notion of self-regulation of reactivity has implications for the initiation of behavior since the regulatory mechanisms can function in an anticipatory manner. For example, individual differences in the direction of attention determine which objects become the reactivity-eliciting stimuli.

This psychobiological approach has several other positive features. First, the commonalities of this approach with neo-Pavlovian traditions provide the potential to integrate a large body of research on "strength of the nervous system" with contemporary investigations of caretaker–infant interaction. Second, although Rothbart and Derryberry (1981) only sketch in putative relationships between temperament and cognitive development, they do begin to integrate these two fields in which research has proceeded largely independently. Third, this approach provides guidance for laboratory-based research—it seems to imply that an infant's temperamental qualities can be determined by measuring the temporal and intensive aspects of reactivity in well-controlled laboratory settings. Indeed, this is the approach these investigators are currently pursuing (Rothbart, 1980).

Additional questions also arise regarding the Rothbart and Derryberry approach as a comprehensive theoretical statement on temperament. One may question the analogies of temperament phenomena with sensory and perceptual phenomena. At the present state of our knowledge of causal relations between neurophysiology and behavior, it is difficult to understand how response characteristics (e.g., threshold) at the behavioral level may be related to the same-named response characteristic at, say, the neural level. This theory would seem to imply strong functional relationships between individual differences in, say, threshold for fearfulness at the various levels of analysis.

A second criticism common to many systematic, interactive theories of behavior is that a host of variables—emotional, cognitive, and social—must be examined before clear predictions for behavior at the more molar level can be generated.

Since this particular theoretical approach has only recently been put forth, no research based directly on the theory has yet appeared. However, Rothbart and Derryberry (1981) have provided a current review of research which supports the plausibility of many elements of theory, taken singly or in various combinations.

A Neonatal Approach (Brazelton). Although there have been several attempts to assess temperament in later infancy, and there have been numerous assessments of individual differences in neonates (e.g., Lipton, Steinschneider, & Richmond, 1966); by far the most comprehensive attempt to investigate temperament-related behaviors in neonates has utilized the framework of the Brazelton Neonatal Behavioral Assessment Scale, or NBAS (Brazelton, 1973).

This theoretical approach is somewhat different from the previous three in that the conceptualization of temperament is intimately tied to the NBAS. Thus our focus must be on the adequacy of the NBAS as a measure of temperament. Before examining this topic, however, we will discuss the positions of Brazelton and his collegues with regard to the four issues set forth above.

The main objective of the NBAS is the identification of individual differences in the quality of the neonate's adaptation to its physical and social extrauterine environment. In the design of the scale, the neonate was conceptualized as an active organism, capable of surprisingly competent activities. These include self-initiated behaviors such as self-quieting following distress and defense against noxious procedures. The scale also assesses the neonate's competence in response to stimulation, such as the capacity to shut out unwanted forms of stimulation through response decrement and state changes, as well as to direct attention to interesting and socially significant stimuli in the environment. The neonate's biological preparedness for social interaction is assessed through ratings of its cuddliness, soothability, irritability, activity level, peak of excitement, and by changes in states of sleep and wakefulness.

The NBAS is not exclusively, or even primarily, a temperament scale. It assesses medically relevant neurophysiological reflexes and physiological reactions. However, the NBAS manual states, "We would hope that this scale would lend itself to an appraisal or [sic] individual behaviors in the neonatal period which might predict to the future outcome of the baby's personality." (p. 53). Thus one of the purposes of the NBAS would seem to be the measurement of temperament, an idea supported by the observation that the NBAS assesses many processes conceptualized as temperament-related by the theories described above. For instance, like Rothbart, Brazelton includes assessment of temporal and intensive response characteristics. Like Buss and Plomin, he attempts to index levels of sociability, emotionality, and activity level. Like Thomas and Chess, Brazelton endorses the importance of goodness of fit between infant and caregiver, and includes in the NBAS items relevant to some of the nine NYLS categories. With regard to the issues raised at the outset of this section, it would appear that the NBAS implies that neonatal temperament is motivational, related to parameters of affect, and clearly important for the regulation of social interaction.

The NBAS has an impressive history of utilization: as a means of differentiating high-risk infants from controls, as an assessment of neurological problems and of the effects of perinatal medication, as a predictor of cognitive functioning both in the immediate neonatal period and at much later ages, as a tool for training parents in the behavioral competencies of their infants, and as a differentiator of cultural, ethnic, or racial subgroups.

The scale has had some success in measuring the infant's preparedness for the social interaction (e.g., Horowitz, Sullivan, & Linn, 1978) and it has been reported to correlate with the distractibility and intensity dimensions of the Carey (1972) Infant Temperament Questionnaire in the first month of life (Sostek & Anders, 1977). However, with the exception of an occasional significant correlation, the findings generally support neither short-term stability of the NBAS nor predictive relationships between neonatal and subsequent assessments (Sameroff, 1978)

The failure to observe stability of neonatal assessments could be seen by some as a challenge to the assumption in most theories that temperament consists of a pattern of constitutionally based and relatively stable individual differences. Of course, not all theories would predict high stability, but with NBAS assessment, it may be that much of the instability rests in the testing procedure and the measurement properties of the instrument rather than in the infant. In some cases, potential sources of error variance are built into the administration of the NBAS items. Consider, for example, the four response decrement items, which constitute nearly 20% of the item pool, and which are subject to a regression to the mean artifact and are potentially confounded with fluctuations of background sleep states. The regression to the mean problem results from the instruction to the examiner to wait until the infant shows an aversive reaction to a stimulus before beginning to administer a train of up to nine subsequent stimuli in rapid succession. Since the examiner begins the response decrement series only after a stimulus application has been associated with an aversive reaction, the response decrement which appears to ensure may well be a return to prior levels of low reponsiveness rather than an active "shutting out of stimulation." The state confounds result from the response decrement series being administered in any one of three states (REM or non-REM sleep or drowsy wakefulness), with no provisions for correcting scores for state shifts during the series. Prechtl (e.g., Hutt, Lenard, & Prechtl, 1969) has argued that response decrement in neonates may be attributable to changes of state, and that it may be difficult to observe response decrement within a stable state. For instance, startles can be readily elicited from neonates during quiet sleep and less so during active sleep. Therefore, an infant who happens to shift from quiet to active sleep during a train of repeated stimulations will thus appear to show response decrement. The reverse pattern of state transitions would not be expected to show such decrement. If an infant shows different patterns of state changes on, say, two different testing occasions, the apparent differences in response decrement patterns may be artifactual.

Also problematic are the five "orientation" items which require that the neonate shift his eyes and head to the source of stimulation (an inanimate object, a sound, the examiner's face, his voice, and his face and voice together) and track it in order to obtain a high score. One of these orientation items seems to be a literal transcription of the Wertheimer (1962) study on neonatal auditory localization, a study with an N of 1. When one considers the great difficulty of showing directionally appropriate eye movements to the location of sounds by newborns, even with the use of extremely sophisticated eye tracking apparatus (Mendelson & Haith, 1977), one has reason to wonder whether the scoring of this item may be subject to bias, such as the interpretation of occasional random eye or head movements toward the source of a sound as a directionally appropriate reaction.

The foregoing potential problems pertain to any application of the NBAS. When we focus on other items which seem particularly relevant to temperament—peak of excitement, rapidity of buildup, irritability, activity, consolability, self-quieting activity, cuddliness, and activity—we find that all are assessed by single item rating scales, most of which are fairly objective. We will argue later (p. 182) that single item assessment is inappropriate for the measurement of temperament; therefore, in the temperament domain we support Brazelton's (1978) call for multiple NBAS assessment of individual infants.

Overall summary scores for the NBAS may be useful for purposes such as determining the level of behavioral maturation of the newborn, but they have little meaning as far as the newborn's temperament is concerned. Similarly, previous *a priori* clusters and factorial dimensions derived from one-time administrations of the NBAS show characteristics (see Sameroff, 1978) which argue against their adequacy for temperament research (with the possible exception of an arousal dimension). The crucial point is that the NBAS has a number of peculiar psychometric properties which have been recognized by its authors (see Sameroff, 1978) but whose implications for the measurement of temperament seem to have been overlooked by its users.

This discussion should clarify why low observed stability and predictive validity of NBAS assessments may have methodological sources (both in item administration procedures and in lack of psychometrically adequate measurement of temperament) and do not necessarily have negative implications for stability and predictive potential of early temperament. Whether stability and predictive power should be *expected* if an adequate temperament instrument could be derived from the foundation provided by the NBAS is another question.

A BEHAVIORALLY BASED DEFINITION OF INFANT TEMPERAMENT

Before proposing our definition of infant temperament, we should explain why the definition is limited to the infancy period and why it is elaborated at the behavioral level.

Why Confine Our Definition to the Infancy Period?

Each of the four approaches discussed in the preceding section, with the exception of the Brazelton approach, is explicitly intended to apply both to infancy and to later developmental periods. Although we may be unduly cautious, we think that the study of infancy can be best served at the present time by a conceptualization of temperament specifically tailored to that developmental period.

Advantages of studying temperament during infancy are fairly obvious. Compared to the older child or adult, the infant is less susceptible to a number of socialization influences which can later mask underlying temperament, his or her behavioral expressions may be less strongly mediated by cognitive processes, and confounding phenomena such as response sets are less problematic.

Certain other considerations, not necessarily disadvantageous, are more salient in the study of infant temperament than at later developmental periods. The first such consideration stems from two facts: (1) temperament is an individual differences concept rather than a notion derived from the study of normative development, and (2) the infant shows a relatively rapid pace of behavioral development. Given individual differences in the *rate* of developmental change, assessments at any specific time during infancy are likely to reflect variations in the onset, maturation, and, in some cases, the decline of temperament-related behaviors rather than being a direct measure of the characteristic level of the fully developed behavior. For example, since infants differ in both the onset time of the emergence of smiling and in the characteristic intensity of smiling shown, individual differences in social smiling measured at eight weeks of age will reflect both "timing" and "level" of positive emotionality directed toward others. In contrast, assessment of adult temperament is usually understood to refer only to characteristic level of temperament-related behavior.

The second issue involves the widespread expectation that individual differences in temperament should be stable across time. This expectation of stability needs to be qualified in two ways to make it applicable to the infancy period. First, it is unnecessary to require that the various aspects of temperament be stable from the neonatal period onward. The stability may be confined to the intervals between periods of behavioral reorganization such as those suggested by Piaget (1937), Kagan (1971), and McCall (1979). The second qualification, suggested by Bell (1980) is that the stability of temperament should be expected to be high, not necessarily in an absolute sense, but only relative to some other aspects of behavior.

We might also note that a "strong" version of the trait concept of temperament would require that the stability of behavior reside primarily in the individual rather than in the stability of the environment. For example, if soothability is considered to be a temperament characteristic, the source of stability in the rank ordering of infants' soothability ratings would be assumed to inhere within the infant rather than to be a function of stability of caretaker soothing style.

A third consideration involves another widespread expectation—that the various aspects of temperament should be, at least to some extent, cross-situationally consistent. One lesson to be learned from recent research in social psychology is that one cannot expect to demonstrate cross-situational consistency unless the situations involved are assimilated similarly in the minds of the individuals being tested. This means that we must understand the coherence of situations from the individual's point of view. From either Kagan's (1971) or Piaget's (1960) theoretical perspectives, the infant's cognitive development can be expected to modulate his or her understanding of the relationship between situations and this must somehow be taken into account when investigating cross-situational consistency. To illustrate the point, consider the cross-situational consistency, or lack thereof, of the infant smile. An infant may smile broadly on the first effortful assimilation of the schemes of vision and hearing. However, at the same, he or she may show no smiling at all at the same age when he or she happens, by chance, to assimilate vision and prehension to one another. The later assimilation begins to take place at a somewhat later age than the former in most infants. Hence,

when a child is successfully but effortfully assimilating one intercoordination, he may just be initiating the other type of intercoordination. The consequence is that smiling will be much more readily observed in one situation
than in the other, and cross-situational consistencies in smiling will therefore
not be demonstrable unless developmental constraints, such as the cognitive/
maturational one just described, are taken into account.

We can summarize a key issue, and a potential measurement problem,
in studying temperament from a developmental perspective as follows:
There may be differences between individuals which are secondary to some
infants being advanced or slow in the ontogeny of a developmental process;
and, there may be differences within individuals in cross-situational consistency of behavior that may reflect differential assimilability of the various
situations.

Most theories of temperament postulate a biological basis of some type,
and the study of infant temperament might facilitate identification of biological substrates. The presumption would be that genetic and other biological
influences would be more evident during infancy than (1) after environmental factors have operated on the individual for a longer period, and/or (2)
after exposure to certain elements of the social environment (e.g., peer interaction) not salient for infants. However, the foregoing presumption may be in
error because the relative influence of environmental factors on individual
differences in behavior depends on their degree of impact, which may be
independent of the duration of time for which they have acted on the
individual.

Why a Behaviorally Based Definition of Infant Temperament?

For two reasons we have chosen to pursue a behaviorally based definition of temperament rather than one which emphasizes biological criteria (cf.,
Buss & Plomin, 1975) or postulates underlying central nervous system constructs (cf., Rothbart & Derryberry, 1981); the first is theoretical and the second practical. From our perspective, the temperament phenomena of prime
importance during infancy are those which have socially communicative
functions. Neurophysiological and biochemical factors are significant as substrates (or, in geneticists' terminology, as endophenotypes) of temperament
and, in rare cases (e.g., blushing) may have social communicative value, but
initial analysis must be at a level reliably detectable by, and meaningful to,
social others (caregivers, siblings, and even experimenters). From the practical standpoint, behavioral signs of underlying temperament dimensions are
easier to detect and quantify than physiological indicators. If one begins with
physiological indicators, the question "indicator of what" must then be faced,
and the answer to this question will, we submit, involve the same type of
behavioral analysis we propose as the initial step in the investigation of temperament. We expect that an ultimate definition of temperament will be

framed in both biological and behavioral terms. However, we hope that a carefully drawn behavioral definition will focus biologically oriented research (such as our own) in fruitful behavioral domains.

Infant Temperament Defined

Definition of Terms. A *parameter of temperament* refers to the intensive or temporal characteristics of expression (e.g., *latency* to smile). An *expressive system for temperament* refers to any element of the behavioral repertoire which can function in the service of temperament (e.g., the facial expression system, the motor system, or the vocal system). *Dimensions of temperament* refer to the content domains of individual differences which comprise temperament (e.g., fearfulness or irritability).

At this point, we can state a comprehensive series of inclusion and exclusion criteria for a behavioral definition of temperament.

Inclusion criteria:

1. *Temperament is an individual differences construct.*

2. *Temperament is a dispositional construct.* One implication of this criterion is that dimensions of temperament are stable, although the degree and nature of stability may vary.

3. *In infancy, the dimensions of temperament are affect-related (i.e., they are emotional in nature).* These inclusion criteria are basically an endorsement of one element of Allport's definition (see p. 163). Affect-related phenomena include both the discrete emotions and generalized arousal. At this point, it is important to specify our definition of emotions (see Campos, Goldsmith, Lamb, Svejda, & Stenberg, 1983): Essentially, we define emotions as feeling states with their associated central nervous system states which serve both to *motivate* the individual, and, unless blocked from behavioral expression, to *communicate* socially significant information to others in the environment. Emotions can be distinguished from most motivational and drive states in that drives such as hunger and thirst are not ordinarily associated with communicative social signals. They can be distinguished from conventional social signals (such as learned gestures and language) in that they appear to be universal and may require no social learning (Ekman, 1980; Izard, 1977).

According to some classical personality theories, personality traits have motivational properties while temperament traits do not. However, individual differences in characteristic expression of affect motivate significant social others in the infant's environment, and affect certainly influences the infant's own drive states. Thus there is no clear distinction between stylistic and motivational components in the infant's emerging temperament.

4. *Variation in temperament refers to individual differences in the intensive and temporal parameters of expression of dimensions of temperament.* We would endorse Rothbart and Derryberry's (1981) list of the relevant temporal (latency, rise time, and recovery time) and intensive (threshold and intensity) parameters.

In our definition, these parameters are understood to apply to *behavioral* expression; their correspondence with neurophysiological parameters is not treated in the present definition. Thus individual differences in "threshold for anger" (i.e., frustration tolerance) and "recovery time from distress" (i.e., self-soothing) would exemplify temperament characteristics.

This criterion also implies that variation in temperament includes individual differences in the regulation of arousal and its associated motoric activity—differences which also communicate socially significant information. Thus characteristic individual differences in the speed, vigor, and patterning of fine and gross motor actions, for example, cuddliness (Schaffer & Emerson, 1964), tempo (Kagan, 1971), and other phenomena sometimes subsumed under the broad rubric of activity level, are characteristics of temperament.

In summary, the inclusion criteria define infant temperament as the set of characteristic individual differences in the intensive and temporal parameters of behavioral expression of affect-related states. Temperament has a role in individual differences in both susceptibility to stimuli and initiation of behavior.

Exclusion criteria:

1. *Temperament dimensions are not cognitive or perceptual in nature.* It should be clear that cognition and perception do interact with temperament to produce behavior. For example, high levels of task persistence probably involves both an extended duration of interest (an element of temperament) in an object and cognitive processing directed toward that object. As another example, most discrete instances of fearful behavior involve a cognitive evaluation of the fear-eliciting situation; however, observed differences in the parameters of fear expression, as well as the frequency of observed instances of fear, would exist if it were possible to hold the cognitive evaluation component constant across individuals. According to the present view, these remaining individual differences would be due to differences in temperament.

Indeed, a full explanation of any complex behavior is likely to require multiple explanatory constructs such as temperament, cognition, perception, learning, and situational context. This fact does not imply, however, that conceptual distinctions among these constructs are unimportant.

2. *Temperament dispositions are not affective states.* However, individual differences in the parameters of expression of an affective state can be a function of temperament.

IMPLICATIONS OF THE PRESENT DEFINITION OF TEMPERAMENT

The Relationship between Temperament and Manifest Behavior

A crucial implication of our definition is that *there are no behaviors which are unique to a given dimension of temperament.* For example, the frequency of crying may be indicative of the degree to which an infant is prone to distress (a temperament characteristic), but specific instances of crying may be indicative of hunger (which, not being affect-related by our definition of emotion, is not a temperament characteristic). Temperament dispositions are manifest through expressive systems. During infancy, there are three primary expressive systems for temperament: motoric, facial, and vocalic, all of which can serve the affective systems. The state of maturation of an expressive system places limitations on what we can observe of temperament. For example, the tendency to react in an angry manner when encountering a frustrating situation is not observable until the observable anger response begins to develop, presumably at about 3–4 months of age. Whether a tendency to be angry exists before anger can be behaviorally expressed is a moot point when only behavioral indicators of temperament exist. However, the development of temperament as a dispositional characteristic is not synonymous with the development of an expressive system. For example, we can conceive of the physiological substrate for individual differences in fearfulness being present before the infant ever exhibits the facial expressions indicative of fear.

Temperament and Personality

It is also important to address the relationship of temperament to personality. Temperament dimensions are like personality traits in that they may be considered to have a causal (in some sense) role in producing behavior or that they may serve as rubrics for organizing our perception of the patterning of individual differences in behavior. We would suggest that there is no clear-cut distinction between the infant's temperament and his or her emerging personality. However, personality is distinguished from temperament in degree by the increased salience of two influences: social relations with others besides the primary caretaker(s) and the emerging concept of self.

Contemporary Function of Temperament

Another issue which deserves comment is the function of infant temperament. We are concerned with the contemporary role of temperament, which may or may not correspond to its evolutionary function. With regard to the infant, we would propose that temperament dispositions serve to organize behavior into coherent patterns. That is, the development of consistent, temperamentally based response patterns leads to increased organization of emotional expression.

With regard to other persons in the infant's environment, temperament dispositions should increase the predictability of the infant's behavior and accordingly modify caretaker behavior. This latter function is an example of the socially communicative role of temperament. For example, the caretaker who is sensitive to the signals of a characteristically very irritable (i.e., low threshold for distress) infant will, in all likelihood, attempt to avoid exposing the infant to irritating stimuli.

Cross-situational Generality of Temperament

It might be noted that our definition does not address the issue of the cross-situational generality of temperament (however, see the discussion on p. 175). There is little *a priori* reason to expect a uniform answer to the question of how "broad" temperament dimensions might be. Cross-situational consistency is an issue to be investigated separately for each dimension. Investigations of this subject within the infancy period have just begun (Goldsmith, 1978; Goldsmith *et al.*, 1980; Matheny & Dolan, 1975).*

Origins of Temperament

Our behavioral definition does not deal with the issue of the origins of temperament. We would follow Buss and Plomin in expecting appreciable genetic influences on the development of many temperament dimensions, but we would also agree with Goldsmith and Gottesman (1981) that the range of heritabilities for temperament characteristics, if they could be accurately measured, may be from near zero to near 1.0. Recent advances in developmental genetics imply that heritability of a characteristic may change during different developmental periods and that genetic influences may emerge after birth. Thus the current dynamic conceptualization of the nature of gene action cautions us to avoid not only postulation of a heritability criterion which would apply across temperament dimensions but also postulation of constant intraindividual genetic influences across times of biological change for any given temperament trait.

Temperament and Affect

The relationship between temperament and affect is the final substantive issue which is in need of elaboration. We have already pointed out that the emotion systems constitute the dimensions of temperament. Indeed, as Table I illustrates, it is possible to conceptualize most of the temperament di-

---

* This issue is central to the controversy concerning of the usefulness of the "trait" concept—a debate which has dominated much of the activity in the fields of personality and social psychology since the late 1960's. We cannot review the complicated issues involved at this point (see Mischel, 1968; 1973; Bowers, 1973; Block, 1968; Allport, 1966; and Endler & Magnuson, 1976).

Table I. Mapping of Selected Dimensions of Temperament onto Affects

Temperament Dimension	Affects
Activity Level[a]	General arousal expressed via the motoric system
Smiling and Laughter	Happiness or pleasure
Fear	Fear
Distress to Limitations	Anger
Soothability	Recovery time of negative affect, given appropriate stimulation by caretaker
Undisturbed Persistence	Duration of interest
Emotionality[b]	Fear, anger, and distress
Activity	General arousal expressed via the motor system
Sociability	Interest and positive affects expressed toward people
Impulsiveness	Latency of expression of affect or activity
Activity Level[c]	General arousal expressed via the motor system
Approach/Withdrawal	The initial balance of positive and negative affect (plus associated motor activity) given a novel stimulus
Regularity	No clear relationship
Adaptability	Higher order construct involving, in part, the degree to which initial affective reactions to novel stimuli can be modified
Threshold	A parameter of affect (as well as of other phenomena)
Intensity	A parameter of affect
Mood	Characteristic balance of positive and negative affect
Distractability	Latency of response to a new stimulus, given ongoing activity
Attention Span/Persistence	Duration of interest/duration of interest given a new stimulus

[a] Rothbart, 1981.
[b] Buss and Plomin, 1975.
[c] Thomas and Chess, 1977.

sions which have been suggested by other investigators by combining a dimension of affect expression with one or more of the parameters of temperament. The temperament dimensions listed in Table (are those suggested by Rothbart (1981), Buss and Plomin (1975), and Thomas *et al.* (1963); the discrete affects used are those described by Ekman (1971) and Izard (1977) plus a category of general arousal (Duffy, 1962; Lindsley, 1951); and the parameters of temperament are those used by Rothbart and Derryberry (1981).

It might be noted that the three groups of temperament dimensions in Table I differ in the level of the specificity of their relationship to discrete affects: Rothbart's dimensions are quite congruent with a discrete affect approach; Buss and Plomin's dimensions are affect-related, but much broader than Rothbart's; and Thomas and Chess's categories are more difficult to categorize, although they are, as a group, more related to the parameters of temperament than to the dimensions of temperament.

It is possible to conceptualize dimensions of temperament other than those in Table I into an affective framework. For example, irritability can be thought of as a temperament disposition which is a function of the threshold or intensity of negative emotions such as anger, fear, or generalized distress. Rothbart and Derrberry's concept of reactivity can be interpreted as a higher order construct which explains relations among the temporal and intensive parameters of temperament. To the extent that an overarching construct of reactivity is viable, we would expect a positive manifold for short latency and rise time, low threshold, and high intensity within the domain of individual differences in any affective dimension.

It should be noted that activity level, perhaps the most studied temperament dimension, cannot be related to a single discrete affect. Instead, we assume that an infant's basic activity level reflects generalized arousal expressed via the motoric system.

Measurement Implications of the Present Conceptualization of Temperament

The current surge of interest in temperament has not been without its pitfalls. There is danger that easy-to-administer but unvalidated caretaker-report temperament questionnaires will be included in studies without sufficient theoretical justification, giving rise to an uninterpretable body of positive and negative results (some serendipitous). At times, there has also been a failure to appreciate the distinctions between parental report and direct observational measures of temperament. Attention to measurement issues should aid in avoiding these and other pitfalls.

The conceptualization presented in this chapter has a number of important implications for the measurement of temperament, both by questionnaire and in the laboratory. First, it should be quite clear that single instance assessment of temperament is not advisable; neither single questionnaire items nor single occurrences of behavior in the laboratory are likely to capture significant individual differences in temperament. Rather, temperament is to be discovered in the *commonality* among items or occurrences of behavior.

Second, in both questionnaire and laboratory assessment, it is important to attend to the situational context. As mentioned above, a given behavior which is expressive of temperament can also serve other functions not related to temperament; therefore, in the laboratory, the aim of temperament assessment should be to focus both the stimulus situation and the behavioral coding in such a way as to lessen the probability of the elicited behavior being nontemperament-related. For example, if the researcher wishes to use crying as a measure of fearfulness, he or she should ensure that the infant is not in a tired state which could produce fussiness. A slightly more complex precaution related to situational context involves discrimination among various dimensions of temperament. For example, in attempting to assess anger during a frustrating situation, it is important to avoid novel elements in the situation which might elicit fear. There are two ways to deal with situational context in questionnaire assessment, one represented by the Rothbart approach on the Infant Behavior Questionnaire and the other, for example, by Buss and Plomin's strategy in constructing the EASI. The former approach specifies the situational context for every item on a scale while the latter approach implicitly asks the respondent to generalize across all situations. Of course, an assumption of the former approach is that the test designer has sampled adequately the situations relevant to the expression of the targeted temperament dimension, and an assumption of the latter approach is that the respondent attends to the relevant situations and weighs each appropriately in formulating his or her answers. On *a priori* grounds, the specification of situational context in each item might be preferred since it would seem to be more objective; however, the final arbiter of the relative value of the two approaches should be evidence of superior external validity of one or the other.

A related caveat is that the researcher must be aware of the constraints of the assessment situation which cannot be controlled and attempt to assess the effects of these constraints directly or in related studies. Examples of such constraints are the effects of parental perception independent of actual infant behavior in the questionnaire measures and the effects of the unaccustomed surroundings in laboratory studies.

There are dangers in attempting to assess temperament across too broad an age range with a single instrument, whether the instrument is a questionnaire or a battery of laboratory tests. These dangers arise from the changes in expression of temperament due to such factors as cognitive and motoric development. The desirability of incorporating measures of stability and cross-situational generality into the assessment process should also be clear.

There is an additional problem of disentangling measures of the infant from measures of caretaker interaction. In the parental report questionnaire approach, one must accept that the parents' possibly biased perception is what is actually being assessed and then proceed to evaluate (according to one's hypotheses) the degree of distortion introduced by this perception (e.g., see Goldsmith *et al.*, 1980). This evaluation may take the form of validity scales on the questionnaire, comparison with converging measures of temperament contaminated by fewer, less powerful, or different sources of bias, or direct attempts to measure biasing factors in the parents. In the laboratory, one can, of course, minimize the parents' role in temperament assessment, but this factor must be balanced against concerns about ecological validity.

Of several problems specific to the questionnaire approach, we would emphasize three psychometric concerns. First, selection of the initial item pool, always a rational decision, largely determines the characteristics of scales derived from the pool. Second, various scale construction approaches contain different assumptions about the independence of temperament dimensions "in nature," the correlation of individual differences in parameters of expression across dimensions, and the "breadth" of temperament dispositions. Third, some attempt should be made either to minimize or to assess parental response sets, especially when the poles of the dimensions being measured differ in social desirability.

The laboratory approach has its own set of unique problems; here we will emphasize psychometric considerations. To assess temperament, laboratory paradigms should be modified to maximize individual differences. This can be accomplished by devising graded measuring scales which show high variance for dependent variables and by adjusting the difficulty levels of dichotomous dependent variables. In addition, both internal consistency reliability, and stability should be computed for laboratory measures, just as one would do for questionnaire scales. To achieve satisfactory internal consistency and an adequate sampling for situations, a fairly extensive series of laboratory paradigms are necessary.

Unresolved Issues

As the title of this chapter indicates, our expanded definition of temperament does not qualify as a true theory of temperament. The reason, briefly stated, is that the nomological network is not adequately elaborated. Our definition offers no framework for conceptualizing the intraindividual patterning of temperament dimensions; it offers no explicit guidance for investigating the biological processes which are involved in the development of temperament; and it only hints at the complex processes which signal the emergence of personality from early temperament.

Perhaps the most restrictive aspect of our definition is its limitation to the infancy period. Although this feature makes our task more manageable and allows us to deal with specific developmental phenomena rather than generalities, the definition will require elaboration and may require modification before it is applicable past infancy. For example, it may be difficult to handle language-related expressions of temperament at later ages with the present conceptualization. However, the definition is promising because it does not preclude elaboration along the lines indicated.

TEMPERAMENT AND ATTACHMENT

Temperament and Social Interaction: An Overview

Empirical research on temperament in infancy is moving in many directions, several of which we have discussed above. However, for developmentalists, the most crucial field within which temperament is being discussed is perhaps that of parent–infant attachment. Before venturing into a discussion of the relationship between temperament and attachment, we should entertain the more general question of the nature of the relationship between dyadic interaction and the development of infant temperament. We would argue that temperament is not an interactional phenomenon in that it does exist apart from the interactional process. However, (1) caretaker–infant interaction presumeably influences the normative development of temperament and it may influence individual differences in temperament; and (2) some dimensions of temperament are typically observed in the context of social interaction, for example, the assessment of temperament often involves interactional processes.

Possible Relationships between the Development of Temperament and Attachment

Temperament is closely related to affect, and attachment between mother and infant refers to the presence of an affective bond. Affect is closely linked to social interaction, and the quality of mother–infant social interaction is thought to influence greatly the attachment process. This nexus of relationships suggests the plausibility of functional relationships between temperament and attachment, which might take several forms. For instance, individual differences in temperament at birth and afterward might influence the mother's social responsiveness to her infant, with consequences for the type of relationship that the child develops with the mother. Alternatively, individual differences in maternal social responsiveness to the infant may affect both the quality of attachment and some of the parameters of expression of temperament. As an example of the latter alternative, an infant might learn from observing his or her mother that there are a number of features of the environment to be fearful of, and if the learning is of sufficient breadth, the child may show cross-situationally stable thresholds for fearfulness (Campos & Stenberg, 1980). Still another way in which temperament may be related to attachment is as one of the factors that determine the classification of infants' individual differences in "security of attachment." That is, temperament may affect the assessment of attachment. Kagan (1981) makes the point that the differences among "avoidant," "ambivalent," and "securely attached" infants in the Ainsworth and Wittig (1969) strange situation may not reflect a history of mother–infant interaction, but rather individual differences in susceptibility to stress—any stress, not just temporary loss of the mother. "Avoidantly attached" infants (i.e., "A" babies, in the Ainsworth scheme) may be those who are not very distressed by repeated maternal separations, and hence appear nonchalant at reunion. "Ambivalently attached," or "resistant," infants ("C" babies) may be those who are very easily upset. Hence, when mother returns, these infants may cry intensely and appear to cling and resist contact simultaneously. "Securely attached" infants ("B" babies) are those with intermediate, modal levels of susceptibility to stress. Kagan's point then, is that any infant could be made to appear to be an A, B, or C infant simply by titration of the stress of the environment into which the infant is placed, and that patterns of mother–infant interaction which appear to characterize the A, B, and C infants actually only reflect the temperamental susceptibility of the infants to stress, rather than determining it.

It is very difficult to choose from among these alternatives, given our current data base on the relationship between temperament and attachment. Nevertheless, what data exist suggest intriguing continuities between individual differences in infants' temperament-related behaviors and eventual strange situation classification. This is particularly evident in individual differences in crying. Ainsworth, Blehar, Waters, and Wall (1978) review evidence that C babies already differ from securely attached infants at 3 months of age on various parameters of crying. Specifically, in the first quarter year of life, C babies were observed to cry nearly twice as much as B babies. That C babies appear to be, characteristically, "cry babies" is clearly shown in their performance in the strange situation, where in each of the seven episodes, C infants cry much more than B babies, who in turn cry more than A babies.* Since by the first quarter year of life, an extensive history of mother–infant interaction can account for individual differences in crying, we cannot conclude that temperament-related factors in C infants determine both the reported differences in the maternal treatment of such infants and the strange situation classification. However, Waters, Vaughn, and Egeland (1980), studying economically disadvantaged mother–infant pairs, recently presented suggestive evidence of the operation of early-appearing individual difference in parameters of crying for subsequent attachment classification. In this study, Waters *et al.*, assessed NBAS performance at 7 and 10 days of age, and strange situation performance at 12 months. Infants later classified as C babies were significantly higher in irritability (i.e., tendency to cry) on the Day 7 assessments. These infants were also significantly less alert, and showed lower attentiveness scores than did babies later classified as B infants, possibly reflecting the greater proneness of these infants to be crying during the Bra-

---

* This pattern of differentiation which, of course, is not in itself sufficient to actually make the A, B, C classification, was first brought to our attention by J. Connell.

zelton assessment. Infants later classified into the C2 subgroup, who are characterized by their passivity, also showed some evidence of continuity with early Brazelton assessments: as neonates, these infants scored lower on motoric maturity measures such as muscle tonus and pull-to-sit facility, factors which may underlie their subsequent lethargy and inactivity in the strange situation. Complicating any easy interpretation of these data is the fact that Waters *et al.* (1980) did not uncover any relationship between Day 10 Brazelton scores and strange situation classification 12 months later. Why one assessment should show continuity and a second one three days later should not would be puzzling were it not for the reservations regarding the NBAS expressed on p. 172 (cf. Waters *et al.*, 1980, for a possible explaination). Nevertheless, the overall pattern of consistent crying and irritability in infants later characterized as C infants and the proneness of C infants to cry much more than A or B infants in the strange situation suggests that the role of temperament in attachment cannot readily be dismissed.

In arguing that the strange situation does not measure temperament, Sroufe (1982) suggests that the variables entering into patterns of attachment appear to be quite different from those proposed as dimensions of infant temperament. However, Sroufe discusses temperament from a perspective which does not recognize the complexities pointed out in this chapter and elsewhere. Sroufe also argues that patterns of attachment are subject to change with change in life circumstances, and by way of contrast, he proposes stability to be one of the hallmarks of temperament. However, we have already noted how the definition of temperament need not be constrained by expectations of rigid stability. Finally, he argues that attachment predicts different adaptations to school situations and to problem-solving situations at later ages (see Sroufe, 1979, for a review of this evidence), and that these predictions are much more robust than any stemming from temperament. On the other hand, although certain important methodological problems exist, a number of workers have linked individual differences in temperament to individual differences in school performance (e.g., Carey, Fox, & McDevitt, 1977; Holden, 1980; Scholom & Schiff, 1980; Thomas & Chess, 1977). It is not immediately clear that attachment classifications provide better or more integrative predictions than individual differences in the various dimensions of temperament; at this point, there is simply too little evidence on the question.

It is important to remember that the suggestion that individual differences in one or more aspects of infant temperament influence attachment classifications in the strange situation (either as a confound of the strange situation paradigm or as a real developmental contributor to attachment formation) is not tantamount to dismissing other influences on the development of attachment.

Waters and Deane (1982) have taken a somewhat different approach from Sroufe (1982) to attachment/temperament interrelationships. In their view, individual differences in infant temperament can produce individual differences in maternal behavior, particularly in the case of C infants. However, although continuity can be shown between the neonatal infant temperament and later strange situation assessment, the continuity is believed by them to be mediated through the maternal reactions to the infant's temperament. Their prediction seems to be that two groups of infants with equivalent neonatal temperaments would eventually be assigned to different strange situation subgroups if the maternal behavior in the two groups differed in sensitivity, accessibility, cooperation, and other maternal variables presumed to be related to strange situation classification.

Future Directions for the Study of Temperament

Given the recent upsurge of interest in attachment, our brief discussion of some of the ways in which temperament and attachment may be interrelated should suffice to point out one important direction of future research on infant temperament. However, our definition of temperament suggests other important areas of study of this construct. For example, how does the infant's temperament affect other social relationships in infancy besides that with its caregivers? Do siblings, mother-substitutes, and day-care workers react differently to infants who differ temperamentally, and do these differences influence the child's later social and emotional growth? Does infant temperament produce differences in engagement in cognitively challenging situations, with consequences for subsequent intellectual growth? Is there a significant genetic influence on parameters of temperament, or on their cross-situational consistency, or on their stability? What are the long-term stabilities of temperament-related phenomena in the infant and young child?

We believe that these and many other questions one can pose regarding infant temperament are best studied only after one has laid out a conceptual framework for their delineation. This chapter represents the beginnings of such an attempt. In summary, our major points are as follows:

1. Contrary to widespread belief in this field, not all individual differences in infancy are temperament-related. Rather, we propose that investigators focus on those individual differences that are affect-related and sociallly communicative.

2. Although two appropriate expectations of temperament dimensions are relative stability over time and consistency across situations, it is a mistake to assume that temperament is not susceptible to environmental modification.

3. Temperament requires assessment through multiple means: parental report, home observation, laboratory elicitation, etc. In addition, the assessment must tap multiple situations in which temperament may be manifested.

4. The manifestation of temperament involves both the quality of the affect-related dimensions being expressed (e.g., anger, fear, and joy) and the parameters of the affective and motoric expression itself (e.g., characteristic threshold, rise time, duration, and peak intensity).

5. Given the complexity of influences on personality development, a broader empirical base is needed before a coherent and complete theory of temperament can be generated.

ABSTRACT

After reviewing current developmentally oriented theories of temperament, we propose a new behaviorally based definition of infant temperament. In brief, we define temperament as the set of characteristic individual differences in the intensive and temporal response parameters of behavioral expression of affect-related states. Temperament has a role in both susceptibility to stimuli and initiation of behavior; in addition, it possesses social communicative value. We explain the implications of this definition for a number of issues in temperament research and examine the nature of relationships which may exist between temperament and attachment.

Acknowledgments

We appreciate the comments of M. K. Rothbart on earlier drafts of this chapter.

REFERENCES

Ainsworth, M., Blehar, M., Waters, E., & Walls, S. *Patterns of attachment.* Hillsdale, N. J.: Lawrence Erlbaum, 1978.

Ainsworth, M., & Wittig, B. Attachment and exploratory behavior of one-year-olds in a strange situation. In B. Foss (Ed.), *Determinants of infant behavior* (Vol. 4). New York: Barnes & Nobel, 1969.

Allport, G. W. *Personality: A psychological interpretation.* New York: Holt, 1937.

Allport, G. W. Traits revisited. *American Psychologist,* 1966, *21,* 1–10.

Bates, J. E. The concept of difficult temperament. *Merrill-Palmer Quarterly,* 1980, *26,* 299–319.

Bates, J. E., Freeland, C. A., & Lounsbury, M. L. Measurement of infant difficultness. *Child Development,* 1979, *50,* 794–803.

Bayley, N. *Manual for the Bayley Scales of Infant Development.* New York: Psychological Corporation, 1969.

Beckwith, L. Prediction of emotional and social behavior. In J. D. Osofsky (Ed.), *Handbook of infant development.* New York: Wiley, 1979.

Bell, R. Q. A reinterpretation of the direction of effects in studies of socialization. *Psychological Review,* 1968, *75,* 81–95.

Block, J. Some reasons for the apparent inconsistency of personality. *Psychological Bulletin*, 1968, 70, 210–212.

Bowlby, J. *Maternal care and mental health*. World Health Organization Monograph, No. 2. London: Her Majesty's Stationery Office, 1951.

Bowers, K. Situationism in psychology: Analysis and critique. *Psychological Review*, 1973, 80, 307–336.

Brazelton, T. B. *Neonatal Behavioral Assessment Scale*. National Spastics Society Monograph. Philadelphia: Lippincott, 1973.

Brazelton, T. B. Introduction. In A. J. Sameroff (Ed.), Organization and stability of newborn behavior: A commentary on the Brazelton Neonatal Behavioral Assessment Scale. *Monographs of the Society for Research in Child Development*, 1978.

Buss, A. H., & Plomin, R. *A temperament theory of personality development*. New York: Wiley, 1975.

Campos, J. J., & Stenberg, C. R. Perception, appraisal, and emotion: The onset of social referencing. In M. Lamb & L. Sherrod (Eds.), *Infant social cognition*. Hillsdale, N. J.: Lawrence Erlbaum, 1980.

Campos, J. J., Goldsmith, H. H., Lamb, M. E., Svejda, M. J., & Stenberg, C. R. Socioemotional development in infancy. In P. Mussen (Ed.) *Carmichael's manual of child psychology*. New York: Wiley, 1983.

Carey, W. B. A simplified method of measuring infant temperament. *Journal of Pediatrics*, 1970, 77, 188–194.

Carey, W. B. Measuring infant temperament. *Journal of Pediatrics*, 1972, 81, 414.

Carey, W. B., & McDevitt, S. C. Revision of the Infant Temperament Questionnaire. *Pediatrics*, 1978, 61, 735–739.

Carey, W. B., Fox, M., & Devitt, S. C. Temperament as a factor in early school adjustment. *Pediatrics*, 1977, 60, 621–624.

Cattell, R. B. *Description and measurement of personality*. New York: World Book, 1946.

Cohen, D. J., Dibble, E., & Grawe, J. M. Father's and mother's perceptions of children's personality. *Archives of General Psychiatry*, 1977, 34, 480–487.

Diamond, S. *Personality and temperament*. New York: Harper, 1957.

Dobzhansky, T. *Genetics of the evolutionary process*. New York: Columbia University Press, 1970.

Duffy, E. *Activation and behavior*. New York: Wiley, 1962.

Ekman, P. Universals and cultural differences in facial expressions of emotions. In J. B. Cole, (Ed.), *Nebraska symposium on motivation, 1971*. Lincoln: University of Nebraska Press, 1972.

Ekman, P. Biological and cultural contributions to body and facial movement in the expression of emotions. In A. Rorty (Ed.), *Explaining emotions*. Berkeley: University of California Press, 1980.

Endler, N. S., & Magnusson, D. *Interactional psychology and personality*. New York: Wiley, 1976.

Escalona, S. K. *The roots of individuality: Normal patterns of development in infancy*. Chicago: Aldine, 1968.

Eysenck, H. J. *The biological basis of personality*. Springfield, Ill. Charles C Thomas, 1967.

Fuller, J. L., & Thompson, W. R. *Foundations of behavior genetics*. St. Louis: Mosby, 1978.

Gesell, A., & Ames, L. B. Early evidences of individuality. *Human Infant Scientific Monthly*, 1937, 45, 217–225.

Goldsmith, H. H. *Behavior-genetic analyses of early personality (temperament): Developmental perspectives from the longitudinal study of twins during infancy and early childhood*. Unpublished doctoral dissertation, University of Minnesota, 1978.

Goldsmith, H. H., Campos, J. J., Benson, N., Henderson, C., & East, P. *Genetics of infant temperament: Parental report and laboratory observations*. Paper presented at the International Conference on Infant Studies, New Haven, Connecticut, April 1980.

Goldsmith, H. H., & Gottesman, I. I Origins of variation in behavioral style: A longitudinal study of temperament in young twins. *Child Development*, 1981, *52*, 91–103.

Gray, J. A. The psychophysiological nature of introversion–extraversion: A modification of Eysenck's Theory. In V. D. Nebylitsyn & J. A. Gray (Eds.), *Biological bases of individual behavior*. New York: Academic Press, 1973.

Harris, E. L., & Rose, R. H. *Personality resemblance in twin children: Comparison of self-description with mother's ratings*. Paper presented at the Second International Congress on Twin Studies, Washington, D. C., August 1977.

Holden, D. *Child temperament and teacher expectation: Their interactive effect on children's school achievement*. Unpublished doctoral dissertation, Department of Psychology, University of Denver, 1980.

Horowitz, F. D., Sullivan, J. W., & Linn, P. L. Stability and instability of newborn behavior: The quest for elusive threads. In A. J. Sameroff (Ed.), Organization and Stability of Newborn Behavior: A commentary on the Brazelton Neonatal Behvioral Assessment Scale. *Monographs of the society for research in child development*, 1978.

Hutt, S. J., Lenard, H. G., & Prechtl, H. F. R. Psychophysiological studies in newborn infants. In L. P. Lipsitt & H. W. Reese (Eds.), *Advances in child development and behavior* (Vol. 4). New York: Academic Press, 1969.

Izard, C. E. *Human emotions*. New York: Plenum Press, 1977.

Kagan, J. *Change and continuity in infancy*. New York: Wiley, 1971.

Kagan, J. Discrepancy, temperament and infant distress. In M. Lewis & L. Rosenblum (Eds.), *The origins of fear*. New York: Wiley, 1974.

Kagan, J. *Review of Research in Infancy*. New York: Grant Foundation Publication, April 1982.

Keogh, B. *Project REACH progress report, Academic Year 1978–79*. Unpublished manuscript, Moore Hall, University of California, Los Angeles, 1979.

Klein, T. W. Heritability and sample size: Statistical power, population comparisons, and sample size. *Behavior Genetics*, 1974, *4*, 171–189.

Kretschmer, E. *Physique and character*. New York: Harcourt, 1925.

Korn, S. Temperament and academic achievement. Cited in A. Thomas & S. Chess (Eds.), *Temperament and development*. New York: Brunner/Mazel, 1977.

Lamb, M. E. Unfulfilled promises: A review of *The dynamics of psychological development* by Alexander Thomas & Stella Chess. *Contemporary Psychology*, 1980, *25*, 906–907.

Lewis, M., & Rosenblum, L. A. *The effect of the infant on its caregiver*. New York: Wiley, 1974.

Lewis, M., & Starr, M. D. Developmental continuity. In J. D. Osofsky (Ed.), *Handbook of infant development*. New York: Wiley, 1979.

Lindsley, D. B. Emotion. In S. S. Stevens (Ed.), *Handbook of experimental psychology*. New York: Wiley, 1951.

Lipton, E. L., Steinschneider, A., & Richmond, J. B. Autonomic function in the neonate: VII. Maturational changes in cardiac control. *Child Development*, 1966, *37*, 1–16.

Lytton, H., Martin N. G., & Eaves, L. Environmental and genetical causes of variation in ethological aspects of behavior in two-year-old boys. *Social Biology*, 1977, *24*, 200–211.

Martin, N. G., Eaves, L. H., Kearsey, M. J., & Davies, P. The power of the classical twin study. *Heredity*, 1978, *40*, 97–116.

Martin, R., & Pfeffer, J. *A report on an item analysis, reliability, and validity study of the Thomas, Chess, and Korn Temperament Questionnaire—Parent Form—for children age 3 to 7, Report #2*. Unpublished manuscript, University of Georgia, 1980.

Matheny, A. P. Bayley's Infant Behavior Record: Behavioral components and twin analyses. *Child Development*, 1980, *51*, 1157–1167.

Matheny, A. P., & Dolan, A. M. Persons, situations, and time: A genetic view view of behavioral change in children. *Journal of Personality and Social Psychology*, 1975, *32*, 1106–1110.

McCall, R. B. Qualitative transitions in behavioral development in the first two years of life. In M. H. Bornstein & W. Kessen (Eds.), *Psychological development for infancy: Image to intention.* New York: Wiley, 1979.

McNeil, T. F. *Temperament revisited: A research-oriented critique of the New York Longitudinal Study of Temperament.* Unpublished manuscript, December, 1976.

Mendelson, M. J., & Haith, M. M. The relation between audition and vision in the human newborn. *Monographs of the Society for Research in Child Development,* 1977.

Mischel, W. *Personality and assessment.* New York: Wiley, 1968.

Mischel, W. Toward a cognitive social learning reconceptualization of personality. *Psychology Review,* 1973, *80,* 252–283.

Nebylitsyn, V. D. *Fundamental properties of the human nervous system.* New York: Plenum Press, 1972.

Pavlov, I. P. General types of animal and human nervous activity. *Selected works.* Moscow: Foreign Language Publishing House, 1955 (Originally published, 1935).

Pedersen, F. A., Anderson, B. J., & Cain, R. L. *A methodology for assessing parental perception of infant temperament.* Paper presented at Fourth Biennial Southeastern Conference on Human Development, April 1976.

Persson-Blennow, I., & McNeil, T. F. A questionnaire for measurement of temperament in six-month-old infants: Development and standardization. *Journal of Child Psychology and Psychiatry,* 1979, *20,* 1–13.

Piaget, J. *The construction of reality in the child.* New York: Basic Books, 1937.

Piaget, J. *Psychology of intelligence.* Paterson, N.J.: Littlefield, Adams, 1960.

Plomin, R. & Foch, T. A twin study of objectively assessed personality in childhood. *Journal of Personality and Social Psychology,* 1980, *39,* 680–688.

Plomin, R., & Rowe, D. C. Genes, environment, and development of temperament in young human twins. In G. M. Gurghardt & M. Bekoff (Eds.), *The development of behavior: Comparative and evolutionary aspects.* New York: Garland STPM Press, 1978.

Plomin, R., & Rowe, D. C. Genetic and environmental etiology of social behavior in infancy. *Developmental Psycholgy,* 1979, *15,* 62–72.

Plomin, R., & Rowe, D. A twin study of temperament in young children. *The Journal of Psychology,* 1977, *97,* 107–113.

Rothbart, M. K. Measurement of temperament in infancy. *Child Development,* 1981, *52,* 569–578.

Rothbart, M. K., & Derryberry, D. Development of individual differences in temperament. In M. E. Lamb & A. L. Brown (Eds.), *Advances in Developmental Psychology* (Vol. 1). Hillsdale, N.J.: Lawrence Earlbaum, 1981.

Rothbart, M. K., & Derryberry, D. Theoretical issues in temperament. In M. Lewis & L. Taft (Eds.), *Developmental disabilities: Theory, assessment and intervention.* New York: S. P. Medical and Scientific Books, in press.

Rowe, D. C., & Plomin, R. Temperament in early childhood. *Journal of Personality Assessment,* 1977, *41,* 150–156.

Sameroff, A. J. (Ed.). Organization and stability of newborn behavior: A commentary on the Brazelton Neonatal Behavioral Scale. *Monographs of the Society for Research in Child Development,* 1978.

Sameroff, A. J., & Chandler, M. J. Reproductive risk and the continuum of care-taking casuality. In F. D. Horowitz (Ed.), *Review of child development research* (Vol. 4). Chicago: University of Chicago Press, 1975.

Schaffer, H., & Emerson, P. E. Patterns of response to physical contact in early human development. *Journal of Child Psychology and Psychiatry,* 1964, *5,* 1–13.

Scholom, A., & Schiff, G. Relating infant temperament to learning disabilities. *Journal of Abnormal Child Psychology,* 1980, *8,* 127–132.

Scholom, A., Zucker, R. A., & Stollack, G. E. Relating early child adjustment to infant and parent temperament. *Journal of Abnormal Psychology,* 1979, *7,* 297–308.

Sheldon, W. H. *The varieties of temperament: A psychology of constitution differences.* New York: Harper, 1942.

Shirley, M. M. *The first two years: A study of twenty-five babies.* Minneapolis: University of Minnesota Press, 1933.

Sobesky, W., Holden, D., & Rossman, B. *An empirical test of the temperamental goodness-of-fit hypothesis.* Unpublished manuscript, University of Denver, 1979.

Sostek, A. M., & Anders, T. F. Relationships among the Brazelton Neonatal Scale, Bayley Infant Scales, and early temperament. *Child Development,* 1977, *48,* 320–323.

Spitz, R. *The first year of life.* New York: International Universities Press, 1965.

Sroufe, L. A. The coherence of individual development: Early care, attachment, and subsequent developmental issues. *American Psychologist,* 1979, *34,* 834–841.

Sroufe, L. A. *Emotional development.* In preparation, 1982.

Sroufe, L. A., & Waters, E. Attachment as an organizational construct. *Child Development,* 1977, *48,* 1184–1199.

Strelau, J. Reactivity and activity style in selected occupations. *Polish Psychological Bulletin,* 1975, *6,* 199–206.

Taraldson, B., Brunnquell, D., Deinard, A., & Egeland, B. *Psychometric and theoretical credibility of three measures of infant temperament.* Paper presented at the Biennial Meeting of the Society for Research in Child Development. New Orleans, March 1977.

Teplov, B. V. Problems in the study of general types of higher nervous activity in man and animals. In J. A. Gray (Ed.), *Pavolov's typology.* New York: Macmillan, 1964.

Thiessen, D. D. A move toward species-specific analyses in behavior genetics. *Behavior Genetics,* 1972, *2,* 115–126.

Thomas, A., & Chess, S. *Temperament and development.* New York: Brunner/Mazel, 1977.

Thomas, A., & Chess, S. *The dynamics of psychological development.* New York: Brunner/Mazel, 1980.

Thomas, A., Chess, S., & Birch, H. G. *Temperament and behavioral disorders in children.* New York: New York University Press, 1968.

Thomas, A., Chess, S., Birch, H. G., Hertzig, M, & Korn, S. *Behavioral individuality in early childhood.* New York: New York University Press, 1963.

Vaughn, B., Deinard, A., & Egeland, B. Measuring temperament in pediatric practice. *Pediatrics,* 1980, *96,* 510–514.

Waters, E., & Deane, K. Infant-mother attachment: Theories, models, recent data, and some tasks for comparative developmental analysis. In L. Hoffman & R. Gandelman, (Eds.), *Parental behavior: Causes and consequences.* Hillsdale, N.J.: Lawrence Erlbaum, 1982.

Waters, E. Vaughn, B. E., & Egeland, B. R. Individual differences in infant–mother attachment relationships at age one: Antecedents in neonatal behavior in an urban economically disadvantaged sample. *Child Development,* 1980, *51,* 208–216.

Wertheimer, M. Psycho-motor coordination of auditory-visual space at birth. *Science,* 1961, *134,* 1692.

Wilson, R. Personal communication, 1979.

Zuckerman, M. *Sensation seeking: Beyond the optimal level of arousal.* Hillsdale, N. J.: Lawrence Erlbaum, 1979.

Parent–Infant Interaction, Attachment, and Socioemotional Development in Infancy

Michael E. Lamb

INTRODUCTION

Perhaps the most dramatic and significant event occurring during the first year of life is the formation of social attachments. Infantile attachments constitute the first social relationships, crown a rapid phase of emergent social understanding, and appear to have long-term implications for the individual's personality development. In this chapter, I review recent evidence concerning the development of parent–infant attachments in the first year of life. Then I present a perspective on the manner in which the formation of attachments and individual differences can be interpreted. Finally, I discuss evidence concerning the long-term implications of individual differences in the quality of infant–parent attachments.

Since this chapter is designed to be a position paper, my goal is to provide a heuristic framework for future research. Instead of dwelling upon factors that seem well established, I focus upon issues that are less clearly understood, yet need to be addressed if we are to advance in our understanding of social development. Consequently, my literature review is necessarily imbalanced and selective, concerned largely with those issues that, in my view, define the cutting edge of significant work in this area.

I should also emphasize at the outset that I am interested primarily in the infant's developing emotions and concepts of others rather than in the development of the parent's emotions, the development of relationships, or the

Michael E. Lamb • Departments of Psychology, Psychiatry, and Pediatrics, University of Utah, Salt Lake City, Utah 84112.

determinants of interactional patterning. This introduces a significant and intentional bias toward focusing on the effects of others on the infant, but does not reflect an assumption on my part that all significant influences are unidirectional. On the contrary, I am fairly confident that influences are multidirectional, but in the present context I am more interested in the effect of the adult's behvior (however determined) on the infant rather than in the reverse. *Caveat lector.*

THE DEVELOPMENT OF PARENT–INFANT ATTACHMENTS

Like the young of most species, human infants are born with a repertoire of behaviors and characteristics that are effective in influencing the behavior of those around them. Among newborns, the most important signal is the cry, which has a remarkable ability to elicit intervention by adults who wish to terminate the infant's cry. The adults' motivation appears to involve an altruistic or empathic desire to relieve the infant's distress and a more selfish desire to terminate a signal which they find unpleasant (Frodi, Lamb, Levitt, & Donovan, 1978; Murray, 1979). The cry elicits responses from adults more reliably than any other infant behavior or characteristic. In addition, adults regard neonates, especially their own, as particularly attractive by virtue of their characteristic "cute" features, and so provide them with substantial amounts of social stimulation. Most of this stimulation involves presenting the face while holding or rocking the infant. Vestibular stimulation reliably elicits alertness in infants, who also find faces (by virtue of their multiple characteristics) the most interesting and "attention-grabbing" stimuli to look at (Sherrod, 1980). Repeated and frequent exposures to the caretaker's face at times when infants are most attentive facilitate the infants' ability to recognize specific people. Whereas newborns are indiscriminately sociable, infants develop the capacity to recognize their parents by the second or third month of life at the latest (Lamb, 1981a) and start to behave preferentially toward them (Bowlby, 1969). These preferences for familiar over unfamiliar persons sharpen over the succeeding months until, around 6–8 months, another transition takes place (Bowlby, 1969). Only now do infants begin to protest discriminatively when one of the preferred people leaves; if they are separated from their families for an extended period, infants characteristically respond with protest and despair (cf. Bowlby, 1980), whereas formerly such separations were accepted. This transition roughly coincides with the development of more advanced conceptions of the permanence of people and things and of means–end relationships (Emde, Gaensbauer, & Harmon, 1976; Piaget, 1954; Spitz, 1959) but it is not clear whether these developments are causally related to the apparent change in the nature of attachment relationships (Campos & Stenberg, 1980). The third quarter-year of life is also noted for the emergence of some degree of locomotor ability. Instead of being reliant upon adults to respond to their signals (e.g., cries) infants can now take the initiative in approaching adults and seeking contact with them. They can thus emit social behaviors, directed at specific individuals, in order to elicit certain responses. According to most theorists (Ainsworth, 1973; Bowlby, 1969; Freud, 1965) we can only speak of "true" attachments after the 6–8 month transitions have occurred. Of course, further developments take place after this stage is reached, but I will be concerned in this chapter mostly with the factors determining to whom infants become attached and the factors determining individual differences in the nature and security of parent–infant attachments.

To Whom Do Attachments Form?

The most important factor determining to whom infants will attach appears to be time: infants form attachments to those people who have been available to them extensively and consistently during the first 6–8 preattachment months (Ainsworth, 1973; Rajecki, Lamb, & Obmascher, 1978). Presumably, it is also important that the adult interact with the infant, responding to its signals appropriately and providing for some of its needs (e.g., for contact comfort) but unfortunately this has not been established (Lamb, 1978a). As a recent debate in The Behavioral and Brain Sciences (see Rajecki et al., 1978) indicates, this is a theoretically important issue for future research to address.

As for the ability to perceive infant signals accurately and respond to them promptly and appropriately, there is evidence that mothers and fathers respond similarly to prepotent infant signals (Frodi et al., 1978a, b) and that while they may respond somewhat differently, they are equally likely to respond in some way (Parke & Sawin, 1980). However, traditional fathers tend to defer to their wives, even when they are present and are quite capable of responding sensitively to the infants' needs (Parke & Sawin, 1980).

In most societies, the mother assumes primary, if not sole, responsibility for the infant's care. It is her face that the infant is most likely to see when it is alert; she is likely to pick up and comfort it when it is distressed and feed it when it is hungry. By virtue of the mother's consistent availability and responsiveness, one would expect the infant to form a primary attachment to her, as indeed most infants seem to do (Lamb, 1980a). From around 6–8 months, infants begin to respond differentially to separations from their mothers (Stayton, Ainsworth, & Main, 1973) and they begin to retreat to their mothers when alarmed by the appearance of strangers or by other stressful circumstances. Mothers are better able to soothe their infants than other women are (Ainsworth, 1973). Less evident, perhaps, is the fact that most infants form attachments to other figures—fathers in traditional western cultures (Lamb, 1977b) or consistent substitute caretakers in others (Fox, 1977) —at about the same time as they form attachments to their mothers, even though the amount of time infants spend interacting with their fathers is significantly lower than the amount of time they spend with their mothers (Lamb & Stevenson, 1978). At least within those families willing to participate in research projects (a somewhat selected sample, one suspects), infants discriminate both mothers and fathers from strangers (Lamb, 1977a,b, 1980a). They seek proximity, contact, and comfort from their fathers with the same intensity and frequency as from their mothers, without apparent preference (Lamb, 1976b, 1977a). By the end of the first year, however, the situation changes somewhat. Although infants continue to show no preference for either parent in familiar or stress-free situations, they turn to their mothers preferentially when distressed (Lamb, 1976e). This tendency is still evident at 18 months of age (Lamb, 1976a), but appears to have disappeared by 24 months (Lamb, 1976c).

Sex Differences

A rather different shift in preference occurs in the stress-free home environment during the second year of life. Although there are no major sex differences in the behavior of either parents or infants in the latter part of the first year, the situation changes during the second year. Starting around the first birthday, fathers begin to pay greater attention to sons than to daughters, and apparently as a result, boys start to focus their attention and proximity/contact-seeking behaviors on their fathers preferentially (Lamb, 1977a,b). By the end of the second year, all but one of the boys in one small longitudinal study were showing marked and consistent preferences for their fathers on a number of attachment behavior measures (Lamb, 1977b). Girls were much less consistent: by age two, some preferred their mothers, some their fathers, and some neither parent. This is consistent with other evidence suggesting that parents are initially more concerned about establishing sex-appropriate behaviors in daughters than in sons (cf. Lamb, 1976d, 1981c).

Because attachment figures are defined by Bowlby (1969) as sources of protection and comfort, the preferences for mothers when distressed, alarmed, or frightened are especially pertinent in defining mothers as the primary attachment figures for most infants. However, this does not mean that mothers are preferred in all circumstances and for all types of interaction. Rather, mothers and fathers engage in different types of interaction with their infants, and thus come to represent different types of experiences. Mothers, as primary caretakers, are much more likely to engage in caretaking routines than fathers are; for their part, fathers are relatively more likely than mothers to play with their infants, and the play itself is likely to be more unpredictable and physically stimulating than mothers' play is (Belsky, 1979;

Lamb, 1976b, 1977c). Infants respond more positively to play bids from their fathers (Lamb, 1977b), and through 30 months, prefer to play with their fathers when they have a choice (Clarke-Stewart, 1978). Boys continue to show this preference through 4 years of age, whereas girls switch to a preference for play with their mothers between 2 and 4 years of age (Lynn & Cross, 1974).

One key issue for researchers interested in early social development and experience is to determine the origin of these differences in maternal and paternal behavior. As my colleagues and I note in Chapter 10, these differences may reflect the social roles assumed by males and females in traditional families, or they may reflect underlying biologically based sex differences in behavioral propensities, or they may derive from a combination of biological and social influences (see also Lamb, 1980b, and Lamb & Goldberg, 1982). As reported in our other chapter, early results from an ongoing longitudinal study suggest that gender is a more important influence on the style of parental behavior than the caretaking role is, but our most crucial data have yet to be analyzed. Regardless of their caretaking role, unfortunately (for researchers), all western parents have been subjected to many years of socialization into gender-appropriate sex roles that govern many aspects of behavior, not simply caretaking. Consequently, any observed sex differences that transcend reversals in caretaking roles cannot be attributed to biological sources, although the absence of sex differences in parental behavior would indeed suggest that biological influences are modest and are readily amenable to experimental modification. In another effort to elucidate the origins of gender differences in parental behavior, I have undertaken, with Avi Sagi, a study of the behavior of mothers and fathers on Israeli kibbutzim where neither parent has responsibility for childcare.

Regardless of the origins of the distinctive interactional styles that characterize mothers and fathers, their formative significance remains to be established. I have suggested that they may permit infants to learn about the pervasive sex differences in human behavior and may also facilitate the establishment of a sense of gender identity, especially in boys (Lamb, 1977b; Lamb & Lamb, 1976). However, my suggestions are largely speculative as the evidence is wholly circumstantial. There have yet to be longitudinal studies in which outcome measures are used to determine whether variations in maternal and paternal roles have long-term developmental implications. We hope to gather relevant information in our current longitudinal project in Sweden.

Individual Differences in Parent–Infant Attachments

Whether or not the responsiveness or unresponsiveness of adults determines whether infants form attachments to them (see above), the adults' sensitivity does appear to influence the quality or security of attachment relationships (Ainsworth, Blehar, Water, & Wall, 1978). Ainsworth and her colleagues have reported that when mothers were sensitively responsive to their infants during the first year of life, their infants formed secure attachments to them. When the mothers were insensitive, insecure relationships resulted. As yet, no one has determined whether the same factors account for individual differences in the security of infant–father attachments, but my colleagues and I are currently investigating this issue by means of longitudinal studies in which both parents are observed interacting with their infants in the preattachment months, and are later observed as parent–infant dyads in the "strange situation."

In order to assess individual differences in the quality of infant–adult attachments, Ainsworth devised a laboratory procedure, the strange situation, which permitted one to determine how infants organized their attachment behaviors around attachment figures when they are distressed. This procedure is outlined in Table I. The primary focus in the strange situation is on the infant's responses to reunion with the attachment figure following two brief separations. Securely attached infants behave in the manner predicted

Table I. Summary of Strange Situation Procedure[a]

Episode Number	Duration	Description
1	3 min	Parent and child alone
2	3 min	Stranger, parent and child
3	3 min (or less)	Stranger and child
4	3 min (or more)	Parent returns to room; stranger leaves room
5	3 min (or less)	Parent leaves child is alone
6	3 min (or less)	Child and stranger
7	3 min	Parent returns; stranger leaves

[a]After Ainsworth and Wittig (1969) and Ainsworth et al., (1978). The duration of episodes 3, 4, 5, and 6 may vary depending on the degree of distress shown by the infant. Note that Ainsworth and her colleagues refer to an initial introduction as episode 1, thus calling my episode 1 their episode 2, etc.

by ethological attachment theory: they use their parents as secure bases from which to explore, especially in the preseparation episodes, and they attempt to reestablish interaction (often by seeking proximity or contact) when reunited with their parents following brief separations. Some insecurely attached infants are labelled "avoidant" because they actively avoid their parents when reunited; others are called "resistant" because they respond to reunion with angry ambivalence, seeking contact/interaction and rejecting it when it is offered. Further details about the scoring and classification of infant behavior in the strange situation are provided by Ainsworth *et al.*, (1978).

Ainsworth's reports concerning the consistent relationship between early parental behavior and infant behavior in the strange situation has elicited a great deal of attention, particularly in light of evidence that the patterns of behavior observed in the strange situation are characteristic of the relationship rather than the infant (i.e., the same infants may behave differently with their mothers and fathers: Grossman & Grossman, 1980; Lamb, 1978b; Main & Weston, 1981), and that the patterns of behavior are remarkably stable over time (Connell, 1976; Waters, 1978). The theoretical interpretations offered in the next section reflect my own confidence in the reliability and validity of the behavior observed in the strange situation. Some caveats are in order, however. First, the relationship between parental behavior and behavior in the strange situation was established in only one small longitudinal study—the very study from which the hypotheses grew. There is thus a clear need for replication in a larger, hypothesis-testing study and for more serious consideration of the role played by initial differences among infants in determining security of infant–parent attachment. Second, the stability of strange situation behavior over time is not always as high as Waters and Connell reported: Vaughn, Egeland, Sroufe, and Waters (1979) and Thompson, Lamb, and Estes (1982) reported substantially lower stability (62% and 53%, respectively) over a comparable period of time. In both cases, temporal instability was systematically related to stress and major changes in family circumstances and caretaking arrangements. This suggests that the security of attachment, as assessed in the strange situation, reflects the current status of the infant–adult relationship. When patterns of interaction change for any reason, the quality of the relationship may change also, and thus we observe changes in the organization of the infant's attachment behavior. Like Gaensbauer and Harmon (Chapter 17), I perceive infant behavior in the strange situation as a correlate of the current circumstances and relationship. Only in especially stable circumstances are we likely to find long-term stability or consistency. This conclusion has obvious and optimistic implications for clinicians. For example, when an insecure parent–infant attachment results from the adverse influence of severe emotional stress on the parent's behavior, one could promote the formation of a more secure bond by appropriate intervention—whether this involves financial support or professional counseling. There does not appear to be a sensitive period during which infants establish unchangeable patterns of behavior with respect to their parents, but the degree of flexibility and the consequences (if any) of individual or repeated changes in the security of attachment remain to be established. Here, too, there is a clear need for further research.

INTERPRETING STRANGE SITUATION BEHAVIOR

In recent publications, I have speculated about the meaning of the behavior observed in the strange situation (Lamb, 1981a, 1981b). In this section, I briefly review the notions advanced in these chapters, emphasizing those aspects that are most amenable to test and have greatest heuristic significance.

As noted earlier, ethological attachment theorists define attachment as specific, enduring relationships characterized by (and growing out of) the infants' use of proximity to adults as a means of assuring protection and care. Proximity and contact-seeking should be, and are, accentuated when infants are uncertain, distressed, alarmed, fatigued, or unwell (Bowlby, 1969). The preferential desire for proximity to and contact with specific persons rather than others indicates that the infants have come to realize that they can count on certain people to respond to their needs for comfort and security. Attachments thus involve a tendency to rely upon or *trust* certain people more than others. Following Erikson (1950), it would seem that one of the principal tasks of the infancy period is to establish trusting relationships with others. The evidence reviewed in the previous section suggested that such relationships are commonly established by the third quarter-year of life.

In order for infants to rely upon or trust specific adults, those adults must have been responsible in early months for predictable and consistent behavior in relation to the infants. As defined here, trust would develop when the adults concerned had demonstrated a propensity for prompt, consistent, and appropriate responses to the infants' signals. The infants' expectations regarding adult responsiveness are most likely to arise from repetitive distress–relief sequences in the first few months of life. The reasons for the special importance of these interactions are multiple (Lamb, 1981a); only the most important will be mentioned here. First, adults are more likely to respond to infant cries than to any other infant behaviors, the nature of their response is more predictable (picking the baby up) than in other contexts, and the consequence (quieting the infant) is quite reliable. Thus the predictability of the sequence is unexcelled. Second, the events to be associated in the infant's mind are extremely salient since they involve the aroused states of distress and quiet alertness, and this enhances associability. Third, the sequence concludes with vestibular stimulation (as the infant is picked up) which brings the infant to a state of quiet alertness. In this state, the infant is most readily able to perceive and to learn the characteristics of the adult responsible for the relief of distress.

Expectations regarding adult responses to infant distress are evident by the third month of life, if not before (Gekoski, 1974). Thus the ability to recognize specific individuals develops alongside the capacity to associate those individuals with behavioral propensities—most notably, the propensity to respond promptly and consistently to signals of infant distress. These expectations regarding the adults' reliability form the core of discriminating attachments around 6—8 months of age.

Individual Differences in Strange Situation Behavior

Adults, of course, differ in their responsiveness to infant signals (e.g., signals of distress) as everyday observation and Ainsworth's longitudinal study confirm. I believe that these individual differences among parents result in individual differences in infants' expectations regarding their parents' behavior, which in turn account for individual differences in the way infants behave in the strange situation in the following way (Lamb, 1981a, 1981b). Adults may differ along two dimensions—predictability and appropriateness—with deviation along either dimension constituting insensitivity as defined by Ainsworth (Ainsworth, Bell, & Stayton, 1974) and myself (Lamb & Easterbrooks, 1981). Adults who respond predictably and appropriately should have infants who turn to them unhesitatingly when alarmed or in need of comfort, and who are able to use the adults as secure bases from which to explore. This is the secure pattern of behavior described earlier. Adults who are fairly consistent but often behave inappropriately or aversively should have infants who expect inappropriate responses from their parents, and who thus turn away from, rather than toward, them when distressed. Such avoidant patterns of behavior are also observed in the strange situation. Adults who are unpredictable and who sometimes respond aversively should produce uncertainty and ambivalence in their infants, and this is in fact the third major pattern of behavior ("resistant") observed in the strange situation. From the limited data currently available (Ainsworth et al., 1972, 1974), it appears that the major patterns of behavior observed in the strange situation are reliably associated with the styles of parental behavior described here. Of course, we still need to see this replicated in an independent sample.

Although it is assumed by most researchers that the infant's behavior in the strange situation is determined by the adult's prior behavior, there is some evidence that the adult's behavior in the immediate situation may provide cues for the infant. Observing mothers and infants eight months after a strange situation assessment, Main, Tomasini, and Tolan (1979) found that the mothers of insecurely attached infants were less emotionally expressive, more angry, and more averse to contact/proximity than the mothers of securely attached infants. It seems likely that the mothers had behaved similarly during the strange situation assessment, although this issue was not addressed. David Estes and I are currently attempting to investigate this, using videotape segments of the mothers' behavior both inside and outside strange situation assessments at both 12 and 19 months. If the mothers' behavior in the strange situation is systematically correlated with the infants' behavior in the strange situation, we must then determine whether the mothers' immediate behavior in the strange situation: (a) directly causes the infants' behavior; (b) simply reminds the infants of their mothers' typical mode of behavior; (c) is causally unrelated to the infants' behavior.

For the present, however, let us assume that infants develop expectations regarding the appropriateness and predictability of their parents' behavior from their interactions during the first year, and that these experiences influence the infants' behavior in the strange situation. As noted earlier, these expectations are specific to the individual attachment figure, since many infants have different expectations of their mothers and fathers (Grossman & Grossman, 1980; Lamb, 1978b; Main & Weston, 1981). At the same time that they are learning about the behavioral propensities of other people, infants are also learning about themselves—specifically, about their ability to elicit responses from others, and thus to control, or at least influence, their own experiences. Recognition of one's own efficacy, which I call "perceived effectance," is as important developmentally as a sense of trust in others. Once again, I expect individual differences among infants in perceived effectance to be correlated with variations in their parents' behavioral propensities. When adults repond promptly and consistently to their infants' signals, the infants should develop high perceived effectance. When the adults responses are less predictable, lower perceived effectance should result. Variations in the appropriateness of the adults' behavior probably have little effect on the development of perceived effectance: contingent predictability is the crucial, formative, variable. This contrasts with the significance of both contingent predictability and appropriateness in the development of interpersonal trust. Consequently, one could have cases where infants have little trust in the parents (whose responses were predictably inappropriate), yet still develop high perceived personal effectance (because the adults were contingently predictable). In fact, avoidant infants have parents who behave in roughly this fashion, and so I would expect them to have higher perceived effectance than resistant infants, even though both are insecurely attached (i.e., lack trust).

The degree to which any infant develops interpersonal trust and perceived effectance should of course depend on the combined sensitivity of the various individuals with whom it interacts frequently; the formative importance of each adult's behavior should vary in accordance with the amount of time he or she spends interacting with the infant. Thus the behavioral propensities of the primary caretaker (mother) are likely to be especially important in traditional western cultures. This prediction has received support in a recent study (Main & Weston, 1981) which unfortunately lacked certain methodological controls.

A Research Agenda

The above paragraphs constitute an attempt to explain why the various patterns of behavior observed in the strange situation occur, and how they are related to antecedent patterns of parental behavior. In the next section, I review evidence on the predictive validity of strange situation behavior—evidence which appears consistent with my interpretation. Before doing so, I briefly mention some of the researchable questions raised by this approach to the study of social development.

First, there is my claim that expectations regarding the adult's behavior develop first in distress–relief interactions. This emphasis contrasts with the view, adopted by several theorists recently (e.g., Brazelton, Yogman, Als, & Tronick, 1979; Bruner, 1977; Stern, 1977), that an appreciation of social rules, reciprocity, and others' behavior develops from face-to-face interactions. I am currently planning research designed to determine when infants first demonstrate expectations in the two social contexts (distress–relief and face-to-face play) in order to resolve this contradiction empirically. Even if I have mistakenly exaggerated the importance of distress–relief sequences, we should at least pay more attention to them than we have since the demise of drive reduction theory.

Second, we need to investigate the relationship between antecedent parental behavior and subsequent security of attachment in a new, large longitudinal study in which distinctions are made between the two dimensions of sensitivity (predictability and appropriateness) and where the affective quality of interaction is taken into account. This would permit a test of my proposal that these dimensions are differentially related to the two major patterns of insecurity, the avoidant and the resistant. At the same time, one could test the prediction that while both avoidant and resistant infants lack trust in their attachment figures, resistant infants have low, and avoidant infants fairly high, degrees of perceived personal effectance.

Third, we need to determine whether individual differences in infant temperament are causally related (directly or indirectly) to later patterns of behavior in the strange situation. I have suggested elsewhere (Lamb & Easterbrooks, 1981) that the infant's temperament may affect the adult's sensitivity or responsiveness, and thus affect the security of attachment indirectly. Waters, Vaughn, and Egeland (1980) have presented some rather equivocal evidence of a direct relationship between neonatal temperament and later behavior in the strange situation. Infants who were scored lower on the Brazelton Neonatal Assessment Scale's measures of orientation, motor maturity, and orientation at day 7 (but not day 10) were more likely to be resistant in the strange situation at one year of age. Direct relationships between constitutionally based differences and later security of attachment are unlikely to be very strong, however, given that infants may form distinctly different relationships with their two parents. The unreliability of the Brazelton Scale also poses problems for researchers (Sameroff, 1978). Rothbart and Derryberry (1981) have suggested an alternative way in which to view the relationship between infant temperament and security of attachment. These authors suggest that differences in temperament may lead some infants to need less proximity or contact than others do in order to become soothed or to feel secure. This results in different patterns of attachment behavior. In addition, what constitutes an appropriate response may differ depending upon the infants' temperament, and infants may differ in their ability to recognize the predictability of adult responses. All these possibilities should become testable as we improve our ability to measure infant temperament (Rothbart & Derryberry, 1981; see also Chapter 13).

PREDICTIVE VALIDITY OF SECURITY OF ATTACHMENT

Security of attachment is a developmentally interesting construct in large part because it has predictive validity. Several studies have shown that that way infants behave in the strange situation predicts how they behave in a variety of situations months and even years later. In the relevant studies, researchers have not distinguished between indices of trust and perceived effectance, but it is possible to make post hoc decisions about the nature of the effects reported.

In an early study, Main (1973) reported that infants who were securely attached to their mothers at one year of age were more cooperative with and friendly toward an unfamiliar woman 8 months later than were insecurely attached infants. Waters, Wippman, and Sroufe (1979) showed that securely attached infants were later more socially competent in interaction with peers than insecurely attached infants were. Arend, Gove, and Sroufe (1979) reported that securely attached infants later demonstrated more ego control and ego resiliency than insecurely attached infants did. Securely attached 18-month-olds later displayed greater persistence and enthusiasm in problem-solving situations than insecurely attached infants did (Matas, Arend, & Sroufe, 1978). Unfortunately, most of these effects seem related—and then not unambiguously—to the perceived effectance dimension. Only Main's (1973) findings seem to be more closely related to trust than perceived effectance; social competence, as assessed by Waters et al. (1979), contains elements of both dimensions. It is also unfortunate that the performance of avoidant and resistant infants has not been distinguished consistently.

Main and Weston (1981) sought to determine what would happen when infants were securely attached to one parent and were insecurely attached to the other. They found that the nature of the attachment to the mother (primary caretaker) had the greatest impact on the infants' responses to a strange adult, although the quality of the infant–father attachment also had an independent influence. (Unfortunately, the assessments of sociability all took place in the mothers' presence, six months before the father–infant attachment was assessed.) My colleagues and I are investigating similar issues in two ongoing longitudinal studies. In one of these studies (an early phase of which is described in Chapter 10), we are studying some families in which parental responsibilities are essentially shared by the parents. We expect to find that the predictive importance of the relationship with each parent varies in accordance with the parents' relative involvement with the child and its care. Further, by systematically varying the sex of the stranger with whom the child interacts in the measure of sociability, we hope to determine whether the nature of the father–child relationship better predicts sociability with male than with female strangers and the reverse.

Future Research Issues

Three major problems await clarification in future research. First, investigators have yet to show that the avoidant and resistant patterns of insecure attachment in the strange situation have different long-term implications, as they should if my interpretation of these patterns is correct. Indeed, even if my notions are incorrect, the patterns of behavior are so different that one would expect them to yield different outcomes. Second, we need research in which the nature of the dimensions showing continuity is clearly defined. I have suggested that perceived effectance and interpersonal trust be distinguished as central developmental constructs, and that there may be other important dimensions. Yarrow and his colleagues (Jennings, Harmon, Morgan, Gailer, & Yarrow, 1979; Morgan, Harmon, Gaiter, Jennings, Gist, & Yarrow, 1977) have developed several measures that might be useful indices of perceived effectance. In one recent study, Harmon, Suwalsky and Klein (1979) used one of these to show that avoidant infants were as persistent as securely attached infants, whereas anxious infants performed more poorly.

Finally, since attachments are defined as enduring affective bonds or relationships (Ainsworth, 1973; Bowlby, 1969; Lamb, 1974), it is surprising that no attempts have been made to relate security of attachment to indices of affective organization and expressiveness. Ross Thompson and I are currently investigating this issue, using as dependent indices fine-grained measures of facial expression, vocalizations, and toy play. We are studying stability over time (7 months), not only in security of attachment but also in these measures of affect. This study, we hope, will elucidate not simply the predictive validity of strange situation behavior, but also the underlying meaning of these dramatic differences among infants.

CONCLUSION

We need many more studies like this if we are to understand the formative significance of individual differences in attachment. I am optimistic that the behavior observed in the strange situation will prove to have replicable predictive validity, but I doubt that the significance will be a great as some now seem to believe (e.g., Sroufe, 1978, 1979). As discussed elsewhere (Lamb & Campos, 1982), I believe that infant experiences are formatively significant, but so too are the other experiences that children encounter as they mature. An infant who has established insecure relationships with both of its parents is more likely to develop in a suboptimal way than is one who is securely attached to both parents, particularly if the parents' behavior and circumstances remain reasonably consistent over the years. Parents do change, however, either because their circumstances change, because they find it easier/harder to relate to infants than to preschoolers, or because they have adjusted to their child's temperament. As their behavior changes, so too may the security of the infant–parent attachments. Furthermore, a variety of people other than parents affect the socialization process, and this makes it highly unlikely that one will find strong linear continuity from infancy. However, we need to determine what children do learn in infancy so that we will know where to look for long-term implications of early experiences. This is why I have urged that we focus on the fundamental social conceptions established in infancy.

ABSTRACT

This chapter reviews the issues of major importance to advances in current understanding of early socioemotional development. Contemporary theorists believe that humans (both infants and adults) are biologically predisposed to respond to one another's signals. Infants form attachments to those who consistently and predictably respond to their signals. Individual differences in infant–adult interaction lead infants to develop distinctive expectations of the adults and of themselves, and these expectations influence behavior in both social and nonsocial contexts. Infants' expectations change as the quality of interaction change: there is apparently no sensitive period.

REFERENCES

Ainsworth, M. D. S. The development of mother–infant attachment. In B. M. Caldwell & H. N. Ricciuti (Eds.), *Review of child development research* (Vol. 3). Chicago: University of Chicago Press, 1973.

Ainsworth, M. D. S., Bell, S. M., & Stayton, D. J. Individual differences in the development of some attachment behaviors. *Merrill-Palmer Quarterly, 1972, 18,* 123–143.

Ainsworth, M. D. S., Bell, S. M., & Stayton, D. J. Infant–mother attachment and social development: "Socialization" as a product of reciprocal responsiveness to signals. In M. P. M. Richards (Ed.), *The integration of a child into a social world.* Cambridge: Cambridge University Press, 1974.

Ainsworth, M. D. S., Blehar, M., Waters, E., & Wall, S. *Patterns of attachment.* Hillsdale N.J.: Lawrence Erlbaum, 1978.

Ainsworth, M. D. S., & Wittig, B. A. Attachment and exploratory behavior of one-year-olds in a strange situation. In B. M Foss (Ed.), *Determinants of infant behavior,* (Vol. 4). London: Methuen, 1969.

Arend, R., Gove, F. L., & Sroufe, L. A. Continuity of individual adaptation from infancy to kindergarten: A predictive study of ego-resiliency and curiosity in preschoolers. *Child Development, 1979, 50,* 950–959.

Belsky, J. Mother–father–infant interaction: A naturalistic observational study. *Developmental Psychology, 1979, 15,* 601–607.

Bowlby, J. *Attachment.* New York: Basic Books, 1969.

Bowlby, J. *Loss: Sadness and depression.* New York: Basic Books, 1980.

Brazelton, T. B., Yogman, M. W., Als, H., & Tronick, E. The infant as a focus for family reciprocity. In M. Lewis & L. A. Rosenblum (Eds.), *The child and its family.* New York: Plenum Press, 1979.

Bruner, J. S. Early social interaction and language acquisition. In H. R. Schaffer (Ed.), *Studies in mother-infant interaction.* London: Academic Press, 1977.

Campos, J., & Stenberg, C. R. Perception, appraisal and emotion: The onset of social referencing. In M. E. Lamb & L. R. Sherrod (Eds.), *Infant social cognition: Empirical and theoretical considerations.* Hillsdale N.J.: Lawrence Erlbaum, 1980.

Clarke-Stewart, K. A. And daddy makes three: The father's impact on mother and young child. *Child Development, 1978, 49,* 466–478.

Connell, D. B. *Individual differences in attachment behavior.* Unpublished doctoral dissertation, Syracuse University, 1976.

Emde, R. N., Gaensbauer, T. J., & Harmon, R. J. *Emotional expression in infancy: A biobehavioral study.* New York: International Universities Press, 1976.

Erikson, E. G. *Childhood and society.* New York: Norton, 1950.

Fox, N. Attachment of kibbutz infants to mother and metapelet. *Child Development, 1977, 48,* 1228–1239.

Freud, A. *Normality and pathology in childhood: Assessments of development.* New York: International Universities Press, 1965.

Frodi, A. M., Lamb, M. E., Leavitt, L. A., & Donovan, W. L. Fathers' and mothers' responses to infant smiles and cries. *Infant Behavior and Development, 1978, 1,* 181–198. (a)

Frodi, A. M., Lamb, M. E., Leavitt, L. A., Donovan, W. L., Neff, C., & Sherry, D. Fathers' and mothers' responses to the faces and cries of normal and premature infants. *Developmental Psychology, 1978, 14,* 490–498. (b)

Gekoski, M. *Changes in infant quieting to mother or stranger over the first six months.* Unpublished masters thesis, Rutgers University, 1974.

Grossman, K. & Grossman, K. *The development of relationship patterns during the first two years of life.* Paper presented to the International Congress of Psychology, Leipzig, East German Democratic Republic, July, 1980.

Harmon, R. J., Suwalsky, J. D., & Klein, R. P. Infants' preferential response for mother versus an unfamiliar adult. *Journal American Academy of Child Psychiatry*, 1979, *18*, 437–449.

Jennings, K. D., Harmon, R. J., Morgan, G. A., Gaiter, J. L., & Yarrow, L. J. Exploratory play as an index of mastery motivation: Relationships to persistence, cognitive functioning, and environmental measures. *Developmental Psychology*, 1979, *15*, 386–394.

Lamb, M. E. A defense of the concept of attachment. *Human Development*, 1974, *17*, 376–385.

Lamb, M. E. Effects of stress and cohort on mother– and father–infant interaction. *Developmental Psychology*, 1976, *12*, 435–443. (a)

Lamb, M. E. Interactions between eight-month-old children and their fathers and mothers. In M. E. Lamb (Ed.), *The role of the father in child development*. New York: Wiley, 1976. (b)

Lamb, M. E. Interactions between two-year-olds and their mothers and fathers. *Psychological Reports*, 1976, *38*, 447–450. (c)

Lamb, M. E. The role of the father: An overview. In M. E. Lamb (Ed.), *The role of the father in child development*. New York: Wiley, 1976. (d)

Lamb, M. E. Twelve-month-olds and their parents: Interaction in a laboratory playroom. *Developmental Psychology*, 1976, *12*, 237–244. (e)

Lamb, M. E. The development of parental preferences in the first two years of life. *Sex Roles,—* 1977, *3*, 495–497. (a)

Lamb, M. E. Father–infant and mother–infant interaction in the first year of life. *Child Development*, 1977, *48*, 167–181. (b)

Lamb, M. E. Social interaction in infancy and the development of personality. In M. E. Lamb (Ed.), *Social and personality development*. New York: Holt, Rinehart and Winston, 1978. (a)

Lamb, M. E. Qualitative aspects of mother– and father–infant attachments. *Infant Behavior and Development*, 1978, *1*, 265–275. (b)

Lamb, M. E. The development of parent–infant attachments in the first two years of life. In F. A. Pedersen (Ed.), *The father–infant relationship: Observational studies in the family setting*. New York: Praeger Special Studies, 1980. (a)

Lamb, M. E. On the origins of sex differences in human sexuality. *Behavioral and Brain Sciences*, 1980, *3*, 192–193. (b)

Lamb, M. E. Developing trust and perceived effectance in infancy. In L. P. Lipsitt (Ed.), *Advances in infancy research*. Norwood N.J.: Ablex, 1981. (a)

Lamb, M. E. The development of social expectations in the first year of life. In M. E. Lamb & L. R. Sherrod (Eds.), *Infant social cognition: Empirical and theoretical considerations*. Hillsdale N.J.: Lawrence Erlbaum, 1981. (b)

Lamb, M. E. Paternal influences on child development: An overview. In M. E. Lamb (Ed.), *The father's role in child development*. New York: Wiley, 1981. (c)

Lamb, M. E., & Campos, J. J. *Development in infancy: A integrative perspective*. New York: Random House, 1982.

Lamb, M. E., & Easterbrooks, M. A. Individual differences in parental sensitivity: Origins, components, and consequences. In M. E. Lamb & L. R. Sherrod (Eds.), *Infant social cognition: Empirical and theoretical considerations*. Hillsdale N.J.: Lawrence Erlbaum, 1981.

Lamb, M. E., & Goldberg, W. A. The father–child relationship: A synthesis of biological, evolutionary, and social perspectives. In L. W. Hoffman, R. Gandelman & H. W. Schiffman (Eds.), *Parenting: Its causes and consequences*. Hillsdale N.J.: Lawrence Erlbaum, 1982.

Lamb, M. E., & Lamb, J. E. The nature and importance of the father–infant relationship. *The Family Coordinator*, 1976, *25*, 379–385.

Lamb, M. E., & Stevenson, M. B. Father–infant relationships: Their nature and importance. *Youth and Society*, 1978, *9*, 277–298.

Lynn, D. B., & Cross, A. R. Parent preferences of preschool children. *Journal of Marriage and the Family*, 1974, *36*, 555–559.

Main, M. B. *Exploration, play and cognitive functioning as related to child–mother attachment*. Unpublished doctoral dissertation, Johns Hopkins University, 1973.

Main, M. B., Tomasini, L., & Tolan, W. Differences among mothers of infants judged to differ in security. *Developmental Psychology*, 1979, *15*, 472–473.

Main, M. B., & Weston, D. R. Security of attachment to mother and father: Related to conflict behavior and the readiness to establish new relationships. *Child Development*, 1981, *52*, 932–940.

Matas, L., Arend, R. A., & Sroufe, L. A. Continuity of adaptation in the second year: The relationship between quality of attachment and later competence. *Child Development*, 1978, *49*, 547–556.

Morgan, G. A. Harmon, R. J., Gaiter, J. L., Jennings, K. D., Gist, N. S., & Yarrow, L. J. A method for assessing mastery in one-year-old infants. *JSAS Catalog of Selected Documents in Psychology*, 1977, *7*, 68.

Murray, A. D. Infant crying as an elicitor of parental behavior: An examination of two models. *Psychological Bulletin*, 1979, *86*, 191–215.

Parke, R. D., & Sawin, D. B. The family in early infancy: Social interactional and attitudinal analyses. In F. A. Pedersen (Ed.), *The father–infant relationship: Observational studies in the family setting.* New York: Praeger Special Studies, 1980.

Piaget, J. *The construction of reality in the child.* New York: Basic Books, 1954. (Originally published 1937.)

Rajecki, D. W., Lamb, M. E., & Obmascher, P. Toward a general theory of infantile attachment: A comparative review of aspects of the social bond. *Behavioral and Brain Sciences*, 1978, *1*, 417–463.

Rothbart, M. K., & Derryberry, D. The development of individual differences in temperament. In M. E. Lamb & A. L. Brown (Eds.), *Advances in developmental psychology* (Vol. 1). Hillsdale N.J.: Lawrence Erlbaum, 1981.

Sameroff, A. J. (Ed.). Organization and stability of newborn behavior: A commentary on the Brazelton Neonatal Behavior Assessment Scale. *Monograph of the Society for Research in Child Development*, 1978, *43* (Whole No. 177).

Sherrod, L. R. Issues in cognitive and perceptual development: The special case of social stimuli. In M. E. Lamb & L. R. Sherrod (Eds.), *Infant social cognition: Empirical and theoretical considerations.* Hillsdale N.J.: Lawrence Erlbaum, 1981.

Spitz, R. A. *A genetic field theory of ego formation.* New York: International Universities Press, 1959.

Sroufe, L. A. Attachment and the roots of competence. *Human Nature*, 1978, *1* (10), 50–57.

Sroufe, L. A. *The problem of continuity in development.* Presentation to the Society for Research in Child Development, San Francisco, March 1979.

Stayton, D. J., Ainsworth, M. D. S., & Main, M. The development of separation behavior in the first year of life: Protest, following, and greeting. *Developmental Psychology*, 1973, *9*, 213–225.

Stern, D. *The first relationship.* Cambridge: Harvard University Press, 1977.

Thompson, R. A., Lamb, M. E., & Estes, D. Stability of infant–mother attachment and its relationship to changing life circumstances in an unselected middle class sample. *Child Development*, 1982, *53*, 144–148.

Vaughn, B., Egeland, B., Sroufe, L. A., & Waters, E. Individual differences in infant–mother attachment at twelve and eighteen months: Stability and change in families under stress. *Child Development*, 1979, *50*, 971–975.

Waters, E. The reliability and stability of individual differences in infant–mother attachment. *Child Development*, 1978, *49*, 483–494.

Waters, E., Wippman, J., & Sroufe, L. A. Attachment, positive affect, and competence in the peer group: Two studies in construct validation. *Child Development*, 1979, *50*, 821–829.

Waters, E. Vaughn B., & Egeland, B. The reliability of individual differences in infant–mother attachment relationships at age one: Antecedents in neonatal behavior in an urban, economically disadvantaged sample. *Child Development*, 1980, *51*, 204–216.

A Structural Modeling Approach to the Study of Attachment and Strange Situation Behaviors

J. P. Connell and H. Hill Goldsmith

OVERVIEW

The purpose of this chapter is to present a new methodological strategy for examining the organization of behaviors thought to reflect the attachment system. The structural modeling approach offers great promise for precise specification and evaluation of hypotheses concerning the organization and development of the parent–infant attachment bond. This approach is presented as an alternative to traditional methods of analyzing attachment behaviors, as represented by the ABC classification system (Ainsworth, Blehar, Waters, & Wall, 1978).

The chapter begins with a description of these traditional methods and a discussion of some concerns raised by these methods. Next, we describe and illustrate the structural modeling approach by specifying and testing models of attachment behaviors assessed in the strange situation. The results from these analyses highlight the importance of the infant's affective reactions to separation in predicting reunion behavior in the strange situation.

Ideally, the reader will come to understand the types of questions which can be asked of a set of data by using the structural modeling approach. In order to achieve this goal, we have sacrificed, to some extent, technical dis-

J. P. Connell ● Graduate School of Education and Human Development and Department of Psychology, University of Rochester, New York 14627.   H. Hill Goldsmith ● Department of Psychology, 330 Mezes Street, University of Texas, Austin, Texas 78712. Dr. Goldsmith was supported by an NIMH Individual Postdoctoral Fellowship MH–08239-01 and a grant from the Developmental Psychobiology Research Group Endowment Fund.

cussion of complex issues involved in the analyses themselves. However, to compensate partially for this oversimplification, we have included an appendix which attempts to explain structural equation modeling (Jöreskog & Sörbom, 1978) and its relationship to traditional data-analytic procedures such as factor analysis, path analysis, and analysis of variance.

It should be emphasized that the chapter is directed toward the non-statistician and is primarily intended to elucidate a promising statistical methodology for the study of attachment behaviors rather than to provide definitive empirical results. However, we hope the reader will be intrigued by the substantive implications of our analyses.

PREVIOUS ATTACHMENT RESEARCH: CONCEPTS AND METHODOLOGY

Overview

The concept of attachment has recently been accorded a central explanatory role in infancy, both in accounting for behavior during infancy (Ainsworth, *et al.*, 1978) and in predicting post-infancy competence (Arend, Gove & Sroufe, 1979; Matas, Arend & Sroufe, 1978; Sroufe, 1979; Waters, Wippman, & Sroufe, 1979). All these studies share two important features, one theoretical and one methodological. The theoretical commonality is their view of attachment as an "organizational construct." The methodological commonality is their use of the ABC typology as the primary assessment of individual differences in the quality of attachment as it is expressed in the strange situation paradigm. Even though these two features have been associated historically, they can be evaluated independently. Our alternative approach to the study of attachment is a methodological alternative to the ABC typology which is nevertheless compatible with the view of attachment as an organizational construct.

Before indicating the deficiencies in the traditional approach and how they may be resolved using the structural modeling approach, we will first describe briefly three important aspects of previous attachment research.

Attachment as an Organizational Construct

Although a number of researchers have presented theoretical statements on attachment (e.g., Bischof, 1975; Cairns, 1972; Gewirtz, 1972; Maccoby & Masters, 1970) we will focus exclusively on the nature of attachment as elaborated by Bowlby (1969, 1973, 1980); Ainsworth (1969, 1979); Ainsworth *et al.*, (1978), and Sroufe and Waters (1977). As theoreticians, these individuals have developed an internally coherent view of the attachment system as an "organizational construct":

> attachment is not viewed as a static trait; rather, it has the status of an intervening variable or an organizational construct, to be evaluated in terms of its integrative power. It is not a set of behaviors that are constantly and uniformly operative (in the manner of a temperamental characteristic) or even operative with a fixed probability of occurrence. Neither is it reducible to the interaction between infant and caregiver, though it is a product of that interaction (as it is shaped by species general characteristics, cognitive development, and characteristics of the individual baby and caregiver). Rather, attachment refers to an affective tie between infant and caregiver and to a behavioral system, flexibly operating in terms of set goals ["proximity" according to Bowlby, 1969, and "felt security" according to Sroufe and Waters, 1977], mediated by feeling, and in interaction with other behavioral systems. In this view, behavior is predictably influenced by context rather than constant across situations. (Sroufe & Waters, 1977, p. 1185)

In pursuing our alternative approach to the study of attachment we accept, as a theoretical foundation, the concept of attachment as an organizational construct. In fact, our approach shares some important common ground with this conceptualization. First, both approaches consider the behavioral patterns observed in the strange situation to serve important, self-regulatory functions for infants as they attempt to cope with shifting stressors imposed by the strange situation paradigm. Second, both perspectives assume that the same overt behavior observed in different contexts may serve different functions. Third, both approaches examine relationships between patterns of behavior in different contexts in order to glean insights into the organization of the infant–caretaker relationship.

The Strange Situation Paradigm

Perhaps as influential as the theoretical position outlined above has been Ainsworth and Wittig's (1969) design of the strange situation to assess individual differences in the quality of the attachment bond. Seldom has the influence of a single laboratory procedure and its associated data-analytic technique been so pervasive in an important theoretical area. The strange situation is a twenty-minute laboratory procedure designed to engage the attachment system and to highlight individual differences in the quality of the infant–mother attachment bond. The procedure consists of eight standardized episodes (description taken from Ainsworth *et al.*, 1978):

(1) A brief introductory episode during which mother (M) and baby (B) are introduced to the experimental room.
(2) M and B alone. M is nonparticipant while B explores.
(3) Strange (S) enters, converses with M, then approaches B. M leaves unobtrusively at end of episode.
(4) First separation episode. S's behavior geared to that of B.

(5) First reunion episode. M greets and comforts B. M leaves again at end of episode.
(6) Second separation episode. B alone.
(7) Continuation of second separation. S enters and gears behavior to that of B.
(8) Second reunion episode. M enters, greets B, picks up B. Meanwhile, S leaves unobtrusively.

The ABC Typology

The vast majority of infants (100% of the infants in the four samples reported by Ainsworth *et al.*, 1978) can be classified by judges into one of three categories based on their pattern of behavior in the strange situation. The categories reflect secure attachment (Group B) and two varieties of insecure attachment: avoidant (Group A) and resistant (Group C). Currently, infants are classified into the three groups (or their eight associated subgroups) largely on the basis of their scores on several interactive behavior dimensions. A full description of the interactive behaviors and details of the ABC classification system can be found in Ainsworth *et al.*, (1978).

PROBLEMS IN ATTACHMENT RESEARCH USING THE ABC TYPOLOGY

Our initial motivation for pursuing an alternative approach to the study of attachment was our concern that the ABC typology had become prematurely reified as the sole indicator of individual differences in the quality of attachment (Connell, Goldsmith, & Buhrmester, 1980). We believe this methodological feture of previous attachment research has led to both empirical and conceptual problems.

How Well Does the ABC System Account for Individual Differences in Strange Situation Behaviors?

The strange situation was originally designed to capture several theoretically and clinically derived indicators of attachment: use of the mother as a "secure base" for exploration, differential preference for mother versus a stranger, and use of the mother as a "haven of safety." The interactive categories were designed to assess these theoretical indicators within contexts (the strange situation episodes) appropriate to each. However, the notion of secure versus insecure groups antedated the design of the strange situation (Ainsworth, 1964). Since measures in the reunion episodes best differentiated these groups, theoretically important behaviors in the nonreunion episodes are relegated to secondary importance. (However, Waters *et al.*, 1979, have reported that pre-separation indices of the A, B, and C groups can be derived.)

In our opinion, it is always appropriate to ask how well a summary measure accounts for the observed variation in the theoretically related, primary observations. Two attempts have been made to evaluate empirically the extent to which the ABC typology captures individual differences in patterns of strange situation behaviors (Ainsworth et al., 1978; Connell, 1976). These efforts have involved applying multiple discriminant functions* to a small subset of attachment behaviors assessed in the strange situation paradigm (approximately 30% of the interactive categories). The two analyses cited are flawed in that only those behaviors that had already shown the ability to discriminate between the groups were included in the multiple discriminant function analyses. Thus any claims that distinctions between the A, B, and C groups account for individual differences in strange situation behaviors are limited to individual differences in behaviors which had already shown mean differences between the groups.

A more appropriate procedure for addressing this issue would have entailed selection of subsets of strange situation behaviors which were *theoretically* implicated as being important indices of the quality of attachment followed by application of the multiple discriminant function procedure or other appropriate techniques.

The Issue of Stability of Patterns of Attachment Behaviors

The argument has been made that the ABC classifications are more stable than other, alternative levels of assessment of attachment behaviors emerging from the strange situation paradigm, that is discrete behaviors and interactive categories (Ainswroth et al., 1978; Waters, 1978). In fact, one major argument for the validity of the ABC typology as a measure of the quality of attachment is the stability of the ABC classifications over time. Initial studies of the effects of reassessment over a two-week period (Ainsworth et al., 1978) yielded results indicating little stability in the classifications. Fifty-eight percent of the infants were correctly reclassified. Given the marginal distributions of the ABC classifications at the two time periods, the percentage of correct reclassifications expected by chance is 54%. This instability was interpreted as being due to the greater separation distress aroused in the second assessment due to the short time span between the sessions. Subsequent studies have examined stability over the first half of the second year of life.

---

* Mutliple discriminant function analysis is a data-analytic procedure designed to find patterns of behaviors which maximally discriminate between pre defined groups of subjects. The percentage of the variance in the set of predictor variables accounted for by each discriminant function may also be computed.

One study (Waters, 1978) demonstrated remarkable stability during this period (96% of infants receiving the same classification at 12 and 18 months, chance level equals 39%). Two more recent studies have reported considerably less stability over approximately this same period. Vaughn, Waters, Egeland, and Sroufe (1979) report 62% stability in a lower-class sample, (chance level equals 43%). Thompson, Lamb, and Estes (in press,) report 53% stability in a middle-class sample (chance level equals 52%).* When these percentages of correct reclassifications are compared to the percentages expected, the pooled results argue for exploring alternative approaches to the ABC typology in the search for stable patterns of strange situation behaviors.

One alternative strategy for identifying sources of stability in attachment behaviors would be to empirically derive patterns of attachment behaviors which will maximize the correlation between two repeated strange situation assessments (canonical correlation analysis). The measures to be included in this analysis could be discrete (e.g., frequency of smiling during the pre-separation episode), broad (e.g., clinical ratings of the infant's mood during pre-separation), or a combination of these two levels of assessment. Another, more theoretically oriented approach would be to specify alternative patterns of behaviors hypothesized by different theoretical perspectives to show stability over time (e.g., the pattern of interactive categories used to make the ABC classifications versus ratings of the infant's affective reactions to separation and reunion) and then to compute and test the relative stability of these alternative patterns.

The Issue of the Predictive Validity of Patterns of Attachment Behaviors

Several studies have examined the relationships between the ABC typology and behaviors outside of the strange situation. The purpose of this section is to emphasize potential problems of this set of studies.

First, many of the analyses in these studies combine the A (avoidant) and C (resistant) groups and contrast these "insecurely" or "anxiously" attached groups with Group B ("securely" attached) in order to demonstrate external validity. Thus these studies (e.g., Arend et al., 1979; Matas et al., 1978; Waters et al., 1979), imply that the "secure versus insecure" categorization carries more differential predictive power than the A, B, and C groups. Our concern here is that the predictive validity of a complex construct is becoming wed to the ability of a single, global categorization to predict a wide array of dependent measures (e.g., peer competence, problem-solving skills, and ego resili-

---

* In this review of the studies examining the 6 month stability of the ABC classification system we excluded studies which did not use the classification criteria as described in Ainsworth *et al.*, 1978. We also excluded studies in which more than two times of assessment were involved in the stability estimates.

ency). The more entrenched this strategy becomes, the more researchers run the risk of merely confirming that atypical behavior in one context predicts atypical behavior elsewhere.

Our second concern is more methodological in nature. A series of findings have been reported which relate the ABC classifications to behavioral observations of mother–infant interaction in the home at 12 months and to earlier mother and infant behaviors, for example maternal responsiveness to crying, face-to-face interaction (Ainsworth et al., 1978; Blehar, Lieberman, & Ainsworth, 1977). These findings must remain tentative, at best, since the ABC classifications were derived, in part, on the basis of some of these same home observations. A recent project at the University of Minnesota promises to help clarify the question of antecedents of quality of attachment (Vaughn, Egeland, & Sroufe, 1980; Waters, Vaughn, & Egeland, 1980).

A feature common to the vast majority of studies examining external correlates of strange situation behaviors is that, while many putative antecedents, and/or consequences, are typically examined, the ABC classification system stands alone as the focus of the prospective and retrospective hypotheses. We refer to designs which attempt to identify large numbers of antecedents and consequences of a particular measure of a single construct as "hour glass designs." The use of the hour glass design in attachment research, with the ABC system as the narrow waist, precludes any conclusions that other constructs are as central in infant behavioral development as the aspects of attachment captured in the ABC classification.

The Limitations of Typologies as Related to the ABC System

The problems, real and potential, referred to in the preceeding sections may have a common root—the limitations inherent in using an overly simplified, value-laden typology to represent complex patterns of individual differences in strange situation behaviors.

Bolz (1977) makes several general points about typological approaches which are of relevance in evaluating the ABC system: (1) most previous typologies, especially in areas related to personality research, have been flawed by attempts for global coverage and oversimplified in an effort to encompass behavioral diversity within a few categories; (2) unless typologies are derived by appropriate empirical means (e.g, cluster analytic techniques), they are unlikely to exhibit the same predictive capacity and internal structure in subsequent applications; and (3) the most useful typologies are those which are intended to be valid in samples other than the one on which they were derived and to yield the same homogeneous and distinct groupings when additional relevant attributes are measured.

We will now elaborate each of Bolz's points as they pertain to the ABC typology.

1. The ABC typology is clearly intended to capture a rather global construct, that is, the quality of the caretaker–infant affective bond. These broad, typological characterizations are imbued with long-term positive and negative implications for antecedent mother–infant interactions and for later adaptive functioning. The typology also encompasses a wide range of behavioral diversity within each of the three groups. Ainsworth and her colleagues address this issue by including classifications. However, these finer-grained typological characterizations are rarely used in studies of external validity or stability.

2. In contrast to the empirical derivation of typologies suggested by Bolz, the ABC classifications were initially derived from clinical observations of 23 infants in the home and in the laboratory. The subjective quality which marked the original group classifications still exists in the current system. For example, Ainsworth et al. (1978) state,

> the classificatory specifications in many cases can be only guidelines; and under these circumstances judges build on the experience they have gained with previous cases, as though they had to see several infants in each classificatory group (and subgroup) before they 'get the feel' for the range of variation covered by each. (P.64)

This subjective element in judging infants as A, B, or C may lead to problems of replication by independent laboratories. The subjectivity also opens the possibility that single instances, or "signs," of behavior (in context, of course) may be used as unambiguous indicants of one of the varieties of attachment and may override other evidence, such as scores on interactive behaviors. It is possible that such clear-cut signs of attachment may exist; however, the prevalence, reliability, and validity of such signs should be established before they are given full credence.

3. The ABC classification is clearly intended to be a typology of the kind described in Bolz's final point. There is little doubt that the ABC system is generalizable across samples, but whether infants would be classified into the same categories given alternative, valid measures of attachment is an important question. This issue becomes increasingly salient when one recognizes that a very small subset of the theoretically implicated behaviors elicited in the strange situation are being used to place infants into the ABC groups (i.e., primarily a subset of those in the second reunion episode).* We will argue that utilization of more of the behaviors observed in the strange situation will contribute to a fuller understanding of the attachment construct.

---

* This choice can be defended on theoretical grounds (i.e., the attachment system is not maximally engaged until the second reunion episode) as well as on (potentially) empirical grounds. (The behaviors actually used to derive the classification could be superior to other possible sets in predicting behavior outside the strange situation.)

THE STRUCTURAL MODELING APPROACH TO THE STUDY OF STRANGE SITUATION BEHAVIORS

Differences between the Structural Modeling Approach and the Traditional Approach

The methods and conceptual underpinnings of the structural modeling apporach diverge from the traditional ABC classification system in at least three important ways—each of which attempts to address one or more of our concerns with the traditional method of organizing patterns of strange situation behaviors.

Dimensional versus Typological Approach to Analyzing Attachment Behaviors. The structural modeling approach is based on a multidimensional conceptualization of the nature of attachment. It yields a set of empirically verifiable and theoretically related dimensions as its description of what transpires in the strange situation. The traditional approach, of course, results in a single typological characterization of the quality of the caretaker–infant attachment bond.

Greater Potential for Uncovering Important Constructs Other Than Quality of Attachment. Our approach emphasizes the possibility that important individual difference dimensions other than attachment may underlie patterns of behaviors over the course of the entire strange situation assessment (a position not totally at odds with the traditional perspective). These other dimensions may have their ontogenetic roots in the complex interplay of infant characteristics (e.g., individual differences in dimensions of temperament such as frustration tolerance) and the child's previous affective experiences (e.g., fear, sadness, or anger) with situations similar to those created in the strange situation paradigm (e.g., being left with a stranger).

Thus a broader interpretive framework is being employed in the structural modeling approach—one in which the contributions of factors such as temperament and contextual influences on strange situation behaviors are recognized and made explicit. This framework remains sensitive to the significant role of the quality of the affective bond between the caretaker and the infant. In addition, explicit attention is focused on the infant's affective reactions to the various episodes of the strange situation. Furthermore, the motivational qualities of these affective reactions are considered to be important factors in producing the patterns of behaviors observed in the strange situation (Gaensbauer, Schultz, & Connell, 1981; see also Chapter 17, this volume).

Inductive versus Deductive Approach to Evaluating Hypotheses Concerning the Organization of Strange Situation Behaviors. In the present approach, hypotheses concerning the organization of the infant's behaviors within and across the strange situation episodes are tested directly. In the traditional approach, assumptions concerning the organization of the infant's behavior in the strange situation are built into the ABC classification system and are not directly tested.

These three distinctions between the two approaches will become clearer as we describe in detail two substantive applications of the structural modeling approach.

Substantive Applications of the Structural Modeling Approach

A Factor-Analytic Model of Infant Behaviors During Separation. The purpose of this example is to show how the structural modeling approach may be used to test a model which includes theoretical dimensions thought to account for individual differences in a set of observed behaviors. In this example, the observed (manifest) variables are the six interactive categories assessed in the first separation episode of the strange situation paradigm—proximity seeking toward stranger, contact maintaining toward stranger, resistance toward stranger, avoidance of stranger, search for mother, and positive distance interaction with stranger. The correlations among these six interactive categories are presented in Table I.* In specifying a structural model, we are, in effect, attempting to explain this pattern of observed correlations. In testing a model, we are statistically evaluating how well our explanation fits these observed data. (A fuller explanation of the rationale behind the factor-analytic component of the structural modeling approach is included in the Appendix.)

The model to be presented is only one of many possible models that could be specified. This particular model emerged from our multidimensional conceptualization of what transpires in the separation episode and from previous exploratory analyses of data emerging from this episode. The labeling of the latent variables reflects our theoretical focus on the affectively motivated reactions of the infant to the stresses imposed by separation from the mother and/or the presence of the stranger (Connell, Goldsmith, & Gaensbauer, 1980).

Notation. Figure 1 presents the notation used in specifying the model-shown in Figure 2. The six manifest (observed) variables are indicated by boxes. The latent variables (circles) in the model are three theoretically derived constructs which are hypothesized to be underlying observed individual differences in the six observed behaviors. The relationships among the latent variables, that is the correlations between the theoretical constructs, are indicated by the curved lines connecting the circles in Figure 2. The

---

* The data for these analyses were provided by Michael Lamb, Margaret Owen and Lindsey Chase-Lansdale.

Table I. Correlations among Six Interactive Categories Assessed during the First Separation Episode of the Strange Situation[a]

	Ps	Cs	Rs	As	Ds
Proximity seeking toward stanger (Ps)					
Contact maintaining with stranger (Cs)	59				
Resistance toward stranger (Rs)	−23	−09			
Avoidance of stranger (As)	−03	01	48		
Positive distance interaction with stranger (Ds)	−04	−14	−42	−25	
Search for mother (Sm)	−05	−16	21	45	−04

[a] Data taken from 55 mother-infant pairs participating in an ongoing study of mother– and father–infant attachment by Michael Lamb, Margaret Owen and Lindsey Chase-Lansdale.

arrows from the three latent variables to the manifest variables reflect the hypothesized directed relationship between these three latent variables and the six interactive category scores. The curved lines on the boxes represent the variance in the manifest variables which is unaccounted for by the latent variable.

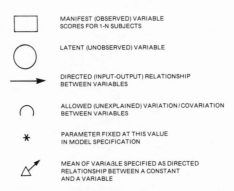

Figure 1. Notation used in specifying structural models. Taken from Horn and McArdle (1980).

Specification. Since the directed relationships between the latent and manifest variables comprise the substantive core of the model, we will elaborate them more fully in the form of specific hypotheses:

1. The type of affective reaction children have toward a stranger (the middle circle) will be manifest negatively in the degree to which they resist contact with the stranger and positively in the degree to which they engage in positive distance interaction with the stranger.
2. The extent to which the child is distressed by the mother's departure (the bottom circle) will manifest itself in a search for the mother and concomitant avoidance of the stranger.
3. The extent to which the child seeks out the stranger for comfort on the mother's departure (the top circle) will be manifest in the infant's seeking proximity to and maintaining contact with the stranger.

The absence of an arrow connecting a latent and an observed variable indicates that this relationship is hypothesized to be zero. Starred [*] parameters indicate these values have been fixed for reasons of model identification or model fitting.

The model also reflects the hypothesis (represented by the curved line connecting the middle and bottom circles) that positive affect toward the stranger relates negatively to separation distress upon the mother's departure, that is, the greater the positive affective reaction to the stranger the less

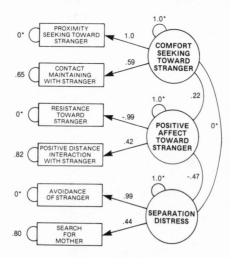

Figure 2. A 3 common factor structural model of behaviors during the first separation episode of the strange situation paradigm. ($x^2 = 7.59$; $df = 10$ and $N = 55$. All nonfixed parameter values significant at $p < .05$.)

separation distress on mother's departure and vice versa. Since neither of these latent variables can be assumed to have temporal priority in this analysis, the model does not include a directed relationship between these two latent variables. Similarly, the positive relationship between positive affective reaction to the stranger and comfort seeking toward the stranger is not specified as a directed relationship.

In the more general case, the structural modeling approach allows the researcher to specify a model in which a number of unobserved theoretical constructs (latent variables) are hypothesized to be functionally related to a larger number of observed behaviors (manifest variables). (See Section A of the Appendix for a more detailed description of the factor-analytic component of structural equation modeling.) To specify such a model the researcher must draw on a theory and/or previous empirical results to address the following questions:

1. How many latent variables are necessary to account for the covariation/correlation among the manifest variables?
2. What is the pattern of the directed relationships (the structure) from the latent variables to the manifest variables?
3. What is the structure of the relationships, both directed and undirected, among the latent variables?

Estimation. Once the model is specified, values for the hypothesized relationships in the model are estimated using maximum likelihood procedures. The numerical values in Figure 2 indicate the magnitude of these relationships. Values are estimated for the directed relationships between the latent variables and the manifest variables (the numbers associated with the arrows connecting the circles and the boxes). These values may be interpreted as standardized regression weights. Values are simultaneously estimated for the specified relationships among the latent variables (the numbers associated with the curved lines connecting the circles). These values may be interpreted as correlations. Values are also estimated for the unexplained variance in the manifest variables (the numbers associated with the curved lines on the boxes). These latter values represent the variance that is not accounted for by the relationships between the latent variables and the manifest variables; they may be interpreted as proportions of observed variance not accounted for by latent variables in the model. The statistical significance of each of the nonfixed parameters can be estimated from their standard errors. All the nonzero values in Figure 2 are at least twice as large as their standard errors.

Evaluation. The statistical evaluation of the overall fit of the model to the observed data is an important element of this approach. The goodness of fit, given in the form of a chi-square statistic, is presented at the bottom of Figure

2. This statistic (and its associated degrees of freedom) indicates the likelihood that the correlations among the six interactive categories could have emerged if the model specified in Figure 2 was "true." The degrees of freedom of the statistic are a function of the number of manifest variables and the number of parameters (relationships) being estimated. The larger the chisquare is relative to the degrees of freedom the poorer is the fit of the model (see Appendix). In this case, the model specified in Figure 2 appears to fit the data quite well. (Since this model was partially derived from exploratory data-analytic procedures, and since the sample size is relatively small, stronger confirmatory evidence for this model awaits cross-validation of these results in a larger sample and with additional measures specifically designed to tap the underlying constructs of interest.)

A Longitudinal Model of Separation and Reunion Behaviors. In order to demonstrate how the structural modeling approach may be used to elucidate longitudinal aspects of the attachment construct, we treat the strange situation assessment as a type of "mini-longitudinal" study. In the following example, the analyses are restricted to the interactive categories assessed in the first separation and the first reunion episodes, that is, the six interactive categories discussed in the previous section and the following five interactive categories assessed in the reunion episode—proximity seeking toward the mother, initial distance interaction with mother, contact maintaining with mother, resistance toward mother, and avoidance of mother. The purpose of this example is to illustrate how the approach may be used more generally to track the stability and predictive capacity of theoretical constructs (latent variables) such as those specified in the previous model of separation behaviors.

Specification. Specification of this longitudinal model involves two steps. First, a model must be specified for each of the two episodes. The model for the separation episode has already been discussed. The model for the reunion behaviors is presented in the right-hand portion of Figure 3.

This model attempts to explain the correlations among the five reunion behaviors represented as boxes in the model. The first latent variable, initial proximity seeking (the top circle), represents individual differences in the extent to which children immediately go to the mother upon her return, rather than staying at a distance. Resistance/ambivalence (the middle circle) represents individual differences in the extent to which infants alternate between maintaining and resisting contact with the mother. The third latent variable, avoidance, represents individual differences in the extent to which infants turn away and actively avoid the mother.

The interpretation of the three latent variables specified in the reunion episode captures essential components of the interpretations of the A, B, and C classifications. However, the structural modeling approach implicitly places each infant at some position on each of these three dimensions rather than classifying the infant as belonging to only one of the three types.

The second step in specifying this model is to hypothesize directed relationships from the latent variables in the separation episode to the latent variables in the reunion episode. These directed relationships between the two episodes represent a "path model" of the carry-over between separation and reunion. Essentially, this path model is attempting to account for the pattern of correlations between the three latent variables during separation and the three latent variables during reunion. (For more detail on the path-analytic component of the structural modeling approach see p. 237).

Results Involving Relationships between Separation and Reunion Behaviors. The middle path indicates that the infant's affective reaction to the stranger significantly predicts the level of resistance/ambivalence toward the mother. Positive affect toward the stranger decreases the likelihood of a resistant/ ambivalent reaction to contact upon reunion. A negative affective reaction to the stranger increase the likelihood of the resistant/ambivalent reaction to the mother. Resistance/ambivalence is also predicted, although less strongly, by the level of separation distress during separation (the bottom path). The top path indicates that infants who seek comfort from the stranger during separation tend to immediately go to the mother upon her return.

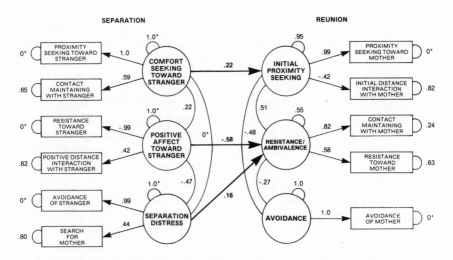

Figure 3. A "longitudinal" structural model of the relationships between behavior during the first separation and the first reunion episodes of the strange situation paradigm. ($\chi^2 = 67.48$; $df = 42$; and, $N = 55$. All non-fixed parameter values significant at $p < .05$.)

Evaluation of Goodness of Fit. The chi-square estimate of the goodness of fit of this longitudinal model of separation and reunion behaviors is given at the bottom of Figure 3. The fact that the chi-square and degrees of freedom are relatively close indicates that a reasonable fit to the data has been achieved. (The observed data in this case are the correlations among the interactive categories within and between the separation and reunion episodes.) Again, these results should be viewed as preliminary in nature.* Before firm conclusions are drawn, this model must be subjected to cross-validation.

Discussion. Taken as a whole, this model indicates that the latent constructs in the separation episode clearly influence those in the reunion episode. It would appear that infants' affective reactions to the absence of their mothers and/or to the presence of a stranger motivate, to a certain extent, their subsequent reunion behavior. To be sure, the underlying causes of the affective reactions are at this point unspecified, as are the processes underlying the translation of affect to subsequent behavior. However, we believe these intial results offer some support for a theoretical framework which incorporates affective and motivational constructs beyond the quality of attachment. More importantly, given the purposes of this chapter, these results demonstrate how the structural modeling approach may be used profitably in conjunction with a theoretical framework which incorporates multidimensional and temporal aspects of underlying constructs.

Comparison of Models in Different Contents and in Different Groups of Subjects

Rationale. Perhaps the greatest potential of the structural modeling approach lies in testing hypotheses concerning developmental change in the nature of attachment and hypotheses concerning the organization of attachment behaviors in different populations. Previous empirical research using the typological approach typically compares infants' classifications (either A, B, and C, or secure vs. insecure) in different contexts or in different groups. For instance, Lamb (1978) demonstrates that while the majority of infants retain the same classification when tested separately with the mother or the father present, there is a tendency for infants classified as insecurely attached with one parent to be classified as securely attached with the other parent.

---

* Since the goodness of fit estimate is a large sample statistic, the estimates of overall fit of these "small sample" models have to be viewed as approximations. A general "rule of thumb" (Jöreskog, personal communication) for evaluating the adequacy of the overall goodness of fit is that the ratio of the chi square to its degrees of freedom should be no greater than 2-3 to 1.

Another example is the study of Vaughn *et al.* (1979) in which the ABC classifications were shown to be less stable for lower-class families who experienced more stressful environments than for Water's (1978) middle-class sample.

The structural modeling approach is well suited for drawing comprehensive, theoretically specified comparisons between groups or between contexts. Three general types of hypotheses may be tested using the structural modeling approach. Each of these types of hypotheses may be tested with regard to each of the latent variables specified. We will illustrate each of these three types of hypotheses by comparing models of the separation and reunion behavior (Figure 3) in two hypothetical groups of infants—Group 1 and Group 2. (With only minor alterations, the procedures for comparing models between different groups vs. comparing models with the same group in different contexts are very similar*.)

Types of Hypothses Which Can Be Tested Using the Structural Modeling Approach. (A) We can compare the structure of the relationships among the latent variables and the manifest variables. That is, we may ask whether the same constructs are being measured by the interactive categories in the two groups: Do both groups show three latent variables in the separation episode, and do these latent variables have the same pattern of functional relationships to the interactive categories in both groups? (Structure hypotheses are tested by restricting the number of factors and the pattern of directed relationships between the latent and manifest variables to be equivalent in the two groups. This structure equivalent model is then compared, using differences between the goodness of fit statistics, to an alternative model where the structure is allowed to differ in the two groups).

(B) Given comparability of structure, hypotheses concerning group differences in the level of the latent variables may be tested. For example, we may ask whether there are differences between Groups 1 and 2 in the amount of positive affect toward the stranger in the separation episode. (Level hypotheses are tested by restricting the mean of the latent variable, positive affect toward the stranger, to be the same in the two groups and then examining the goodness of fit of this model compared to a model where the group means are allowed to differ.)

(C) Again given comparability of structure, we can compare the "centrality" of each latent variable in the two groups. Centrality is defined in two

---

* The major difference between these two procedures is that in the between group analysis two separate sets of covariances and means are the observed data. In the between context analysis, covariances and means representing both within- and between- context information on one group of subjects are the observed data.

conceptually independent ways: (1) the extent to which a latent variable accounts for the variance of the manifest variables to which it has directed relationships (structural centrality); and (2) the extent to which a latent variable predicts other latent variables to which it has directed relationships (predictive centrality).

An example of a question involving structural centrality is the following: Is the underlying dimension of separation distress as central in accounting for observed search behavior in Group 1 as in Group 2? In more statistical terms, does the latent variable separation distress account for equal proportions of the variance in the manifest variable search in Group 1 and Group 2? (This hypothesis may be tested by restricting the allowed [residual] variation in search, once standardized, to be the same in the two groups and comparing this model to a model in which the allowed variation in search is not thus restricted.)

A predictive centrality hypothesis would be that separation distress is a more potent motivating influence toward resistant/ambivalent reactions to the mother in Group 1 than in Group 2. (In order to test this hypothesis, the directed path from separation distress during the separation episode to resistance/ambivalence in the reunion episode is fixed to be equivalent in the two groups. This model would then be compared to a model in which the strength of this path is allowed to vary between groups.)

Summary. Figure 4 depicts the sets of parameters involved in the structure, level, and centrality comparisons. Each of these types of comparisons forces the researcher to specify two or more alternative models for the same set of data, for example, for level hypotheses, a model in which the level of given latent construct is the same in two groups and an alternative model in which the group levels are different. (For a more detailed description of the substantive and statistical rationale behind each of the hypothesis-testing capacities of the structural modeling approach, see Appendix.) By restricting sets or subsets, of these parameters to be equivalent in different groups or at different times of assessment, a broad range range of substantive questions can be asked of a given set of data. For the researcher studying the ontogeny of attachment, this approach allows testing of models which specify theoretical reasons for stability and change in the organization of attachment behaviors. Similarly, theories which postulate constancy or change in the level and predictive power of theoretical constructs can be tested. For the researcher interested in the impact of situational and/or historical factors on the assessment of attachment, the structural modeling approach offers similar potential through its capability for group comparisons. It is important to note that, in order to effectively tap the potential of the structural modeling approach for evaluating different models, an hypothesis testing "plan of attack" is essential.

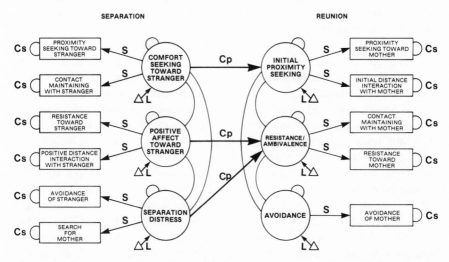

Figure 4. Sets of parameters involved in between-group and between-context structural model comparisons. (Parameters labelled S are involved in "structure" comparisons. Parameters labelled L are involved in "level" (mean) comparisons. Parameters labelled C_s are involved in "structural centrality" comparisons. Parameters labelled C_p are involved in "predictive centrality" comparisons.)

SUMMARY AND EVALUATION OF THE STRUCTURAL MODELING APPROACH

Suggested Applications

The purpose of the previous sections of this chapter was to provide the researcher interested in caretaker–infant attachment with a description of an alternative methodological approach to the study of the construct. In this initial presentation, we applied this approach to the interactive categories rated in two episodes of the standard strange situation paradigm. We agree with Ainsworth *et al.* (1978) that

> [it would be] foolish to believe that the dimensions [the interactive categories] that we have so far subjected to quantification take into account all of the behaviors that are important components of the patterning of individual differences in strange situation behaviors. (p. 57)

We fully recognize that more direct measures of caretaker/stranger–infant interaction and of infant affective variables are needed before the relative centrality of the quality of attachment versus other dimensions of individual differences such as those discussed in this chapter may be evaluated. We also recognize that the predictive centrality of these other dimensions vis à vis variables assessed outside the strange situation must be evaluated as well.

Hypotheses concerning the role of attachment as the central mediating variable in early social development have been primarily tested in a "one at a time" fashion, that is, looking for mean differences between the A, B, and C (or secure vs. insecure) groups on individual dependent variables. Using the present approach, these bivariate relationships can be integrated into multivariate models. Alternative explanatory constructs can also be included in such models to enable evaluation of the relative predictive centrality of the different constructs. Also, the total predictive power of the model could be evaluated when quality of attachment and these other dimensions are included. Finally, structural models of the organization among the variables thought to be antecedents or consequences of strange situation behavior patterns may be included in such a model. (The complexity of the models being specified, i.e., the number of variables and relationships included, will, of course, depend on the complexity of the questions being asked of the data.)

Disadvantages of the Approach

Along with the elegance and comprehensiveness of this approach come certain disadvantages as well. These disadvantages are best stated in the form of cautions to the potential user. Obviously, these cautions should be kept in mind in using any data analytic strategy.*

1. Theory is needed to guide the use of this approach at every turn—from the initial selection of the manifest variables, to the specification of the number and composition of the factors, to the selection of directed relationships among the latent variables, to the setting of model constraints between models. In the two substantive examples presented in this chapter, we felt acutely the lack of theory in making certain decisions.

2. Even with a theory in hand we cannot expect to obtain *confirmatory* evidence using this approach. The accumulation of evidence for a particular theoretical position depends on the ability to replicate models emerging from the position in different samples of subjects and using different sets of theoretically implicated measures.†

---

* See Horn and McArdle (1980) for a more complete evaluation of the structural modeling approach as applied to adult abilities data, and Goldberger (1973), Bentler (1978) and Kenny (1979) for introductory and material on structural equation modeling.

† As in simultaneous multiple regression analysis, the problem of suppression effects among the variables can lead to sample-specific results using these procedures.

3. Since this approach relies heavily on a relatively new data-analytic procedure (Horn & McArdle, 1980; Jöreskog & Sorbom, 1978), the robustness of the significance testing component of the approach to violation of statistical assumptions is relatively unclear—for example, with distributions other than multivariate normal, with nonlinear relationships in the "true" model, and with use of small samples to obtain population parameter estimates.

4. The possibility of "overfitting" a model is present with this approach. It is possible to find ways (some subtle, some not) to increase the degrees of freedom without increasing the chi-square estimate significantly. (For a not so subtle example, one could fix a parameter at the exact value obtained in a previous model estimation in which the parameter was allowed to be free.) The less theoretically based these model adjustments are, the less likely that the model will cross-validate in a new sample.

CONCLUSION

As with any new methodological approach, structural equation modeling must be evaluated in terms of its potential for advancing the level of substantive thinking in a research area. The ABC typology has served as an effective vehicle for communicating a major theoretical viewpoint to a large audience. However, many of the more recent theoretical arguments emerging from this viewpoint are quite complex and far-reaching, both in terms of the number of constructs involved and the developmental time span being implicated. The inherent limitations of the typological ABC classification system restrict the ways in which empirical evidence can be marshalled for or against these arguments. Using the structural modeling approach, the possibility now exists for simultaneously testing hypotheses concerning the structure, level, and centrality of theoretically derived and empirically verifiable dimensions (including the quality of attachment) over time and in different groups and contexts. It is the flexibility and integrative capacity of this approach which potentiates a more rigorous and elegant comparison of alternative theoretical models of attachment.

Acknowledgments

The authors would like to thank the following people for their helpful comments on previous versions of this manuscript: Joseph Campos, Duane Buhrmester, Don Stilson, and Ted Gaensbauer.

APPENDIX

A Brief Introduction to Structural Equation Modeling

Structural equation modeling is an important first step toward a comprehensive data-analytic strategy which integrates the hypothesis-testing capacities of three previously separate data-analytic traditions—factor analysis, path analysis, and analysis of variance. One unique property of structural equation modeling (and one which makes the technical aspects of the technique so difficult to understand) is that this integration is accomplished in a *simultaneous* fashion. Put differently, the algorithm which underlies structural equation modeling is capable of estimating factor pattern weights, regression coefficients between latent factors, and the mean of latent factors in the same analysis. We will now discuss each of these subcapacities of structural equation modeling using idealized examples. We will not discuss the actual computational procedures. We hope this introduction will aid the reader in gaining an intuitive grasp of this data analytic strategy.

Confirmatory Factor Analysis

The factor analytic component of the approach (also known as "confirmatory factor analysis" [Jöreskog, 1969]) is based on the "common factor model" proposed by Spearman (1927) and further elaborated by Thurstone (1947). There are two major meta-theoretical assumptions underlying this component:

1. The observed variation in a given behavior is due to influences shared in common with other measures (common factors) and influences unique to that particular measure, including measurement error (unique factors).
2. The influences of these common and unique factors on the observed variables produce the pattern of observed correlations among a given set of variables. (In the idealized, bivariate case, two variables are correlated because they are both influenced by the same, common factor[s]. The lack of perfect correlation between these variables is a result of each variable having its unique set of underlying influences [including its lack of reliability].) The role of theory in this approach is to generate hypotheses concerning the ways in which theoretical (unobserved) constructs influence observed (manifest) variables.

Suppose we have four mesures of 18-month-olds' reactions to an approaching stranger—gaze avoidance, facial expression of fear, withdrawing

Table A-I. Hypothetical Correlations among Four Measures of Fear of Stranger

	GAZE	FACE	POST	VOC
GAZE	1.0			
FACE	r_{fg}	1.0		
POST	r_{pg}	r_{pf}	1.0	
VOC	r_{vg}	r_{vf}	r_{vp}	1.0

posture, and distress vocalization. The hypothetical correlations among these four manifest variables are presented in Table A-I. The hypothesis is that the common influence shared among these observed behaviors is fear of the stranger. This hypothesis is stated in the form of a structural model, that is, a model of the underlying causal structure which produces a given set of correlations. A model may be specified as a set of linear equations such as the single common factor model specified in Table A-II.

Each of the manifest variables (GAZE, FACE, POST, VOC) is thought to be a weighted function of a single common factor (FEAR) and a set of influences unique to each particular behavior (e.g., U-GAZE). U-GAZE represents factors which influence gaze avoidance but are independent of fear of the stranger. One of these unique influences is the extent to which the measure of gaze avoidance is unreliable, that is, measured with error. The relationships between the common factor and the manifest variables are represented by the factor pattern, that is, fc_1, fc_2, fc_3, and fc_4. These weights represent the extent to which the common factor (fear of the stranger) influences the observed behavior.

The same model may be specified graphically as a set of directed and undirected relationships between latent and manifest variables using the notation described in Figure 1 (see text). Figure A-1 presents the graphic specification of the model which translates directly into the set of equations in Table A-II. The manifest variable GAZE is hypothesized to be a function

Table A-II. Structural Equations Emerging from a Single Common Factor Model

Observed variables	=	Common factor	+	Unique factors
GAZE	=	fc_1 FEAR	+	U-GAZE
FACE	=	fc_2 FEAR	+	U-FACE
POST	=	fc_3 FEAR	+	U-POST
VOC	=	fc_4 FEAR	+	U-VOC

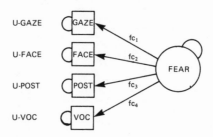

Figure A-1. Graphic representation of a single common factor model.

of the common factor FEAR as indicated by the directed relationship from the circle labeled FEAR to the box labled GAZE. GAZE is also influenced by sources of variation which are unaccounted for by the common factor and which are unique to GAZE, that is, U-GAZE. This allowed, or unaccounted for, variation is represented graphically by the curved line on the box labeled GAZE. The nature of the relationship between GAZE and U-GAZE is considered undirected. (One major advantage of the graphic representation of structural equation models is that the distinction between directed [hypothesized] relationships and undirected [allowed] relationships is made explicit.)

Once this single common factor model is specified, maximum likelihood estimates of the values of the unknown parameters (e.g., fc_1, U-GAZE, fc_2, U-FACE) are computed along with the standard errors associated with each of the estimates. This solution is then evaluated statistically as to the likelihood of the observed correlations among the variables having emerged from this particular model of the common and unique influences on the set of manifest variables. This likelihood function can be converted into a chi-square statistic with degrees of freedom (df = the number of independent correlations and variances in the observed data [10 in this example], minus the number of free parameters which must be estimated). The statistical probability associated with the chi-square and degrees of freedom indicates the probability that if a given model was "true" (in this case a single common factor model), the observed correlations among the manifest variables would have emerged.

In sum, the factor-analytic component of the structural modeling approach allows the researcher to specify, estimate, and statistically evaluate a model which reflects a set of hypotheses about the underlying factors thought to account for the variation and covariation among a set of manifest (observed) variables.

Path Analysis of Functional Relationships Among Latent Variables

The path-analytic component of structural equation modeling allows the researcher to test hypotheses regarding patterns of functional (directed) relationships among a set of theoretical constructs (latent variables). In most cases these directed relationships will be evaluated using a research design which includes longitudinal assessment of the sets of manifest variables.

We can expand upon our first hypothetical example to show how the path-analytic component of this approach can be used to test alternative hypotheses about longitudinal relationships among theoretical constructs. Suppose that, in addition to our four measures of fear of stranger, we have also assessed, at 18 months, four measures of a latent variable which our theory terms *dependency on the mother* during an episode of free play—physical prox-

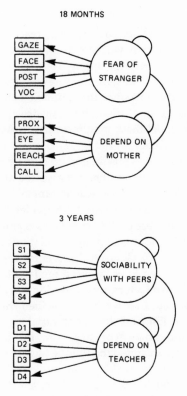

Figure A-2. Common factor models of latent constructs on two occasions of measurement.

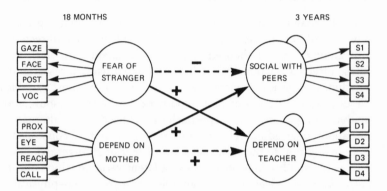

Figure A-3. Two hypothetical models of longitudinal functional relationships among four latent variables.

imity to the mother, eye contact with mother, reaching out to be held, and calling for attention. In addition, we have followed up these infants at 3 years of age and assessed, in a preschool setting, four measures which we believe reflect sociability with peers and four measures of dependency on the teacher. For the sake of brevity, and since the rationale behind the factor analytic approach to the specification of theoretical constructs has already been discussed, we will simply label these manifest measures S1, S2, S3, and S4 for the latent construct sociability and D1, D2, D3, and D4 for the latent construct dependency on teacher. Thus we end up with four latent variables. Fear of stranger and dependency on mother are assessed at 18 months and sociability with peers and dependency on teacher are assessed at 3 years.

The first step is to specify the two-factor model at each time period and test these models for goodness of fit to correlations among the eight manifest variables measured at 18 months and the correlations among eight manifest variables measured at 3 years. Figure A-2 presents the graphic representation of these models. (The curved lines between the latent variables at each time period indicate that the two factors are allowed to correlate. The absence of a curved line would indicate that we have specified that the two factors are orthogonal. The curved lines on the latent variables [circles] represent the allowed variation [factor variance] of each. Also, for the sake of simplicity of presentation, we have not included the unique factors associated with each of the manifest variables.)

Once the factor model is specified (as discussed above) at each time period and an acceptable fit to the data is achieved, the relationships between the latent variables over time become the focus of interest. (This approach im-

Table A-III. Hypothetical Cross-Time Correlations among Four Latent Constructs

		3 Years	
		Social with peers	Depend on teacher
18 Months	Fear of stranger	r str/peer	r str/teach
	Depend on mother	r moth/peer	r moth/teach

plies that longitudinal stability, if it exists, will be found primarily at the latent variable level since the latent variables reflect theoretical dimensions of individual differences thought to be organizing the observed patterns of behavior.) The longitudinal relationships among these four latent variables are given in the 2 × 2 correlation matrix shown in Table A-III. The role of the theory is to generate a model which can explain these cross-time correlations among this set of constructs.

In this hypothetical example, a number of alternative models come to mind. Again, thse models may be specified in the form of a set of equations or as a diagram of the directed and undirected relationships among, in this case, the latent variables. We will use the graphic form to present two possible models. Figure A-3 presents the two alternative models. The first model, indicated by dashed paths, postulates that the only stability among these constructs lies in the relationships between early fear of strangers and later sociability with peers (presumably a negative relationship) and early dependency on mother and later dependency on teachers. The second model, indicated by solid paths, reflects a different theoretical orientation. These two paths represent the hypothesis that early dependency on mother provides a positive basis for the child's later ability to relate competently with peers and that early anxiety (fear) of adult strangers will be manifested later in dependency on adult authority figures.

These are only two of the possible models that may be specified. Each of these models has different substantive implications and each may be tested as to its ability to reproduce the cross-time patterns of correlations among these latent variables. (The structural modeling approach is capable of testing cross-lag panel type models as well, Kenny, 1979.)

The path-analytic component of structural equation modeling is most useful when two or more theoretically derived models of directed relationships among latent variables can be pitted against each other and the goodness of fit of each is evaluated. The differences between the two alternative models should represent hypotheses generated from the different theoretical positions. Although no single model can ever be absolutely confirmed or disconfirmed using this approach (or any other approach for that matter), the relative goodness of fit of two theoretically competing models to the same set of data can help lead the researcher in more fruitful directions. In combination with the factor-analytic strategy, this feature offers a powerful and elegant data-analytic strategy for longitudinal research on a wide spectrum of developmental phenomena.

Analysis of Latent Variable Means

The analysis of variance component of structural equation modeling allows the researcher to test hypotheses regarding the means or levels of theoretical constructs. The mean of a latent variable is estimated using the information provided by the means of the manifest variables to which it has directed relationships. The logic behind using the means of latent variables (vs. means of the observed variables) is an extension of the previously developed rationale for the father analytic model of observed correlations. The idea is that the means of the manifest variables reflect to varying degrees the level of the common (unobserved) factor which influences them. And, in that the common factor represents the variance shared by the observed measures, its mean is a more reliable and valid index of the level of the theoretical construct of interest than the mean of any individual manifest variable.

Testing hypotheses concerning the means of common factors is most appropriate in cases where the same latent variables are being specified in more than one group of subjects or on more than one occasion of measurement. For example, the eight manifest variables used to measure fear of stranger and dependency on mother could be assessed in groups of abused and nonabused infants. In this case, the researcher's focus of interest is the two groups' levels of fear of strangers and dependency on mother. Using the structural modeling approach, the researcher can test level hypotheses. An example of a level hypothesis might be the following: the abused infants will show less dependency on the mother and less fear of the stranger than the non-abused infants. (In order to test this hypothesis, the researcher must first determine that the same latent variable is being measured in the two groups. Briefly, this test of factor invariance is accomplished by restricting the factor patterns in the two groups to be equivalent and testing the goodness of fit of this factor model to each group's pattern of observed correlations.)

The statistical procedure involved is conceptually equivalent to evaluating the null hypothesis that the means of the two groups on the two latent variables are equal. The means of fear of strangers and dependency on mother are restricted to be equivalent in the abused and non-abused groups. This model is tested for goodness of fit (to the patterns of observed covariances and means). Then, this chi-square statistic is compared to the chi-square obtained when the mean of fear of stranger and the mean of dependency on mother is not restricted. If the lack of restriction of the mean of a latent variable significantly improves the fit of the model (i.e., a significant chi-square difference is obtained) the null hypothesis of no mean difference is rejected at the level of significance of the chi-square difference. (The direction of the effects of abuse vs. non-abuse on the latent constructs may be determined from the obtained estimates of both groups' latent variable means.)

This subcapacity of structural equation modeling encompasses the full range of analyses possible using either between-groups or repeated measures analysis of variance.

ABSTRACT

In this chapter we present a new methodological strategy for examining the organization of behaviors thought to reflect the operation of the caregiver-infant attachment system. The structural modeling approach is presented as an alternative to traditional methods of analyzing data emerging from the strange situation paradigm as represented by the ABC classification system (Ainsworth, Blehar, Waters, & Wall, 1978). The chapter begins with a description of these traditional methods. We then discuss three specific areas of concern with the use of the ABC typology—internal validity, stability, and predictive validity. Differences between the traditional approach and the structural modeling approach are discussed in light of these concerns. Next, the structural modeling approach is applied to data emerging from the strange situation assessment. The substantive focus of these analyses is the organization of attachment behaviors within and across the separation and reunion episodes of the strange situation. We present the rationale for each analysis and describe how the structural models are specified and statistically evaluated for goodness of fit to the observed data. We also show how structural equation modeling can be used to examine how the attachment system operates in different contexts and in different groups of infants. Finally, limitations of the approach are discussed along with cautions to be considered when using the approach. Also included with the chapter is a technical appendix which gives the reader a more detailed discussion and further examples of the data analytic capacities of structural equation modeling.

REFERENCES

Ainsworth, M. D. Patterns of attachment behaviors shown by the infant in interaction with his mother. *Merrill-Palmer Quarterly, 1964, 10,* 51–58.

Ainsworth, M. D. S. Object relations, dependency and attachment: A theoretical review of the infant–mother relationship. *Child Development, 1969, 40,* 969–1025.

Ainsworth, M. D. S. Infant–mother attachment. *American Psychologist, 1979, 34,* 932–937.

Ainsworth, M. D. S., & Wittig, B. A. Attachment and exploratory behavior of one year olds in a strange situation. In B. M. Foss (Ed.), *Determinants of infant behavior IV.* London: Methuen, 1969.

Ainsworth, M. D. S., Bell, S. M., & Stayton, D. J. Individual differences in the development of some attachment behaviors. *Merrill-Palmer Quarterly, 1972, 18,* 123–143.

Ainsworth, M. D. S., Blehar, M. C., Waters, E., & Wall, S. *Patterns of attachment: A psychological study of the strange situation.* Hillsdale, N. J.: Lawrence Erlbaum, 1978.

Arend, R., Gove, F. L., & Sroufe, L. A. Continuity of individual adaptation from infancy to kindergarten: A predictive study of ego-resiliency and curiosity in preschoolers. *Child Development, 1979, 50,* 950–959.

Bentler, P. M. The interdependence of theory, methodology and empirical data: Causal modeling as an approach to construct validation. In D. B. Kandel (Ed.), *Longitudinal research on drug abuse: Empirical findings and methodological issues.* New York: Wiley, 1978.

Bischof, N. A. A systems approach toward the functional connections of attachment and fear. *Child Development, 1975, 46,* 801–817.

Blehar, M. C., Lieberman, A. F., & Ainsworth, M. D. S. Early face to face interaction and its relation to later infant–mother attachment. *Child Development, 1977, 48,* 182–194.

Bolz, C. R. Typological theory and research. In R. B. Cattell & R. M Dreger (Eds.), *Handbook of modern personality theory.* Washington, D. C.: Hemisphere Publishing Corporation, 1977.

Bowlby, J. *Attachment.* New York: Basic Books, 1969.

Bowlby, J. *Separation: Anxiety and anger.* New York: Basic Books, 1973.

Bowlby, J. *Loss: Sadness and depression.* New York: Basic Books, 1980.

Cairns, R. Attachment and dependency: A psychobiological and social-learning synthesis. In L. Gewirtz (Ed.), *Attachment and dependency.* Washington, D. C.: V. H. Winston,, 1972.

Connell, D. B. *Individual differences in infant attachment: An investigation into stability, implications, and relationships to structure of early language development.* Unpublished doctoral dissertation, Syracuse University, 1976.

Connell, J. P., Goldsmith, H. H., & Buhrmester, D. *Alternative approaches to the ABC classification system in the study of attachment.* Paper presented at the meetings of the International Conference on Infant Studies, New Haven, Conn., March 1980.

Connell, J. P., Goldsmith, H. H., & Gaensbauer, T. *Relationships between dimensions of affect and attachment during separation and reunion episodes of the strange situation.* Paper presented at the Developmental Psychobiology Research Group Conference, Estes Park, Col., May 1980.

Gaensbauer, T., Schultz, L., & Connell, J. P. *Contextual and temporal influences on the stability of affect and attachment behaviors in a modified strange situation.* Paper presented at the meeting of the Society for Research in Child Development, Boston, April 1981.

Gewirtz, J. L. Attachment, dependence, and a distinction in terms of stimulus control. In J. L. Gewirtz (Ed.), *Attachment and dependency.* Washington, D.C.: V. H. Winston, 1972.

Goldberger, A. S. Structural equation models: An overview. In A. S. Goldberger & O. D. Duncan (Eds.) *Structural equations models in the social sciences.* New York: Seminar Press, 1973.

Horn, J. L., & McArdle, J. J. Perspectives on mathematical/statistical model building (MASMOB) in research on aging. In L. W. Poon (Ed.), *Aging in the 1980's: Psychological issues.* Washington, D. C. American Psychological Association, 1980.

Jöreskog, K. G. A general approach to confirmatory maximum likelihood factor analysis. *Psychometrika*, 1969, *34*, 183–202.

Jöreskog, K. G. & Sorbom, D. *LISREL-IV: Analysis of linear structural relationships by the method of maximum likelihood.* Chicago: National Educational Resources, 1978.

Kenny, D. A. *Correlation and causality.* New York: Wiley, 1979.

Lamb, M. E. Quantitative aspects of mother– and father–infant attachment. *Infant Behavior and Development*, 1978, *1*, 265–273.

Maccoby, E. E., & Masters, J. C. Attachment and dependency, In P. H. Mussen (Ed.), *Carmichael's manual of child psychology* (Vol. 2). New York: Wiley, 1970.

Matas, L., Arend, R. A., & Sroufe, L. A. Continuity of adaption in the second year: The relationship between quality of attachment and later competence. *Child Development*, 1978, *49*, 547–556.

Spearman, C. *The abilities of man.* New York: Macmillan, 1927.

Sroufe, L. A. The coherence of individual development: Early care, attachment, and subsequent developmental issues. *American Psychologist*, 1979, *34*, 10, 834–841.

Sroufe, L. A., & Waters, E. Attachment as an organizational construct. *Child Development*, 1977, *48*, 1184–1199.

Thompson, R. A., Lamb, M. E., & Estes, D. Stability of infant mother attachment and its relationship to changing life circumstances in an unselected middle-class sample. *Child Development*, in press.

Thurstone, L. L. *Multiple factor analysis.* Chicago: University of Chicago Press, 1947.

Vaughn, B., Waters, E., Egeland, B., & Sroufe, L. A. Individual differences in infant–mother attachment at 12 and 18 months: Stability and change in families under stress, *Child Development*, 1979, *50*, 4, 971–975.

Vaughn, B., Egeland, B., & Sroufe, L. A. *The coherence of maternal caregiving and the continuity of infant adaption in the first two years of life.* Symposium presented at the meetings of the International Conference on Infant Studies, New Haven, Conn., March 1980.

Waters, E. The reliability and stability of individual differences in infant–mother attachment. *Child Development*, 1978, *49*, 483–494.

Waters, E., Vaughn, B., & Egeland, B. Individual differences in infant–mother attchment relationships at age one: Antecedents in neo-natal behavior in an urban, economically disadvantaged sample. *Child Development*, 1980, *51*, 1, 208–216.

Waters, E., Wippman, J., & Sroufe, L. A. Attachment, positive affect, and competence in the peer group: Two studies in construct validation. *Child Development*, 1979, *50*, 821–829.

CHAPTER 16

Infant's Differential Social Response to Mother and Experimenter

RELATIONSHIPS TO MATERNAL CHARACTERISTICS AND QUALITY
OF INFANT PLAY

George A. Morgan, Nancy A. Busch-Rossnagel, Rex
E. Culp, Annette K. Vance, and Janet J. Fritz

INTRODUCTION

Overview

This chapter focuses on infants' socioemotional reactions to their mother and
to a relatively unfamiliar experimenter during a structured social interaction
sequence similar to the one developed by Klein and Durfee (1976). Infants
were divided into two groups based on their differential (comparative) pattern of reaction to experimenter and mother rather than the more common
procedure (e.g., Morgan & Ricciuti, 1969) of using only the reaction to the
experimenter or analyzing the reactions to the two adults separately. We felt,
based on a study by Harmon, Suwalsky, and Klein (1979), that grouping infants by the type of differential social reaction they showed could provide a
meaningful index of the quality of the infant–mother relationship. Furthermore, we hypothesized that the type of differential social response would be
related on the one hand to maternal characteristics and on the other hand to
the quality of infant play. Thus differential social response is conceptualized

George A. Morgan, Nancy A. Busch-Rossnagel, Rex E. Culp, Annette K. Vance, and Janet J.
Fritz • Department of Human Development and Family Studies, Colorado State University,
Fort Collins, Colorado 80523. Supported in part by a Faculty Research Grant from Colorado
State University and the Developmental Psychobiology Research Group Endowment Fund.

as an intervening variable mediating the relationships between maternal variables and child variables.

The approach of the present study is similar to that advocated by Sroufe and Waters (1977) as the organizational view of attachment. They contrast this organizational construct with the view of attachment as a trait that varies in strength and can be measured by counting the frequencies of discrete "attachment" behaviors such as touch, approach, cling, and cry. Critics (e.g., Masters & Wellman, 1974) have argued that since such discrete behaviors are not highly intercorrelated or stable over time, the study of individual differences in infant–adult ties is not likely to be a productive research strategy. However, Sroufe and his colleagues and Ainsworth and her colleagues have persuasively argued, based on a number of recent studies (see Ainsworth, 1979; Sroufe, 1979), that when emphasis is placed on the organization of behavior, stable individual differences and meaningful correlates are evident.

Strange Situation Studies

Ainsworth and her colleagues (e.g., Ainsworth, Blehar, Waters, & Wall, 1978) developed the now widely used standard laboratory procedure, the strange situation, to assess attachment in 1-year-olds. The patterns of behavior shown in this series of episodes, especially the reunions following brief, but often stressful, separations from mother, are used to classify the attachment of the infant to the mother. Eight patterns were identified, falling into three main groups labeled A, B, and C. To simplify and summarize, Group A infants are said to be *avoidant*; they rarely cry during separation, and in the reunion they avoid proximity with mother. Group B babies are said to be *securely attached*; they may be distressed upon separation, but seek proximity or at least interaction with their mothers upon reunion. Group C babies have been labled *ambivalent* in their attachment; they tend to be intensely distressed by separation and then both resist and seek contact with mother during reunion. Both A and C infants are said to be anxiously attached as contrasted with the securely attached Group B infants.

Ainsworth *et al.* (1978) have examined the at home behavior of the mothers of these babies and conclude that the securely attached (Group B) babies had mothers who were, throughout the first year, more sensitively responsive to the infants' signals than the two anxiously attached groups. Mothers of avoidant (Group A) babies did not like body contact and were more rigid and rejecting. From these findings it may be speculated (but there does not seem to have been any direct measure) that the mothers of A and C babies were more anxious, at least about caregiving. At any rate, Group A and Group C infants fell more to the anxious as opposed to the secure end of a factor-analytic dimension of infant home behaviors (Stayton & Ainsworth,

1973). In addition, there is now considerable evidence (summarized in Ainsworth et al., 1978 and Sroufe, 1979) that securely attached infants are more competent in play and social relations later in infancy and childhood.

Reactions to Stranger and Mother, Attachment and Competence

The present study also draws on a strategy used by Harmon, Morgan, and Klein (1977) to "tease out" determinants of individual differences in infants' reactions to strangers. Previous studies (see review in Morgan, Levin, & Harmon, 1975) had found few consistent correlates of reactions to strangers, but regularities emerged when scores from several settings and times were used. Furthermore, dichotomizing and then combining several potential determinants or sensitizing factors led to greatly increased predictive power.

The social interaction sequence and differential response classification used in the current study is based on one used by Harmon, Suwalsky, and Klein (1979). They found that different patterns of social reactions to mother and an unfamiliar adult were associated with later differences in attachment behaviors, when mother left the room and then returned, and in competent infant functioning. Thirty-six 12-month-old infants were classified into one of four groups (labeled *fearful, wary, no preference,* and *mother avoiding*) on the basis of the infant's positive and negative reactions to mother and a stranger in a structured social interaction sequence with both adults present. This classification of differential reaction to mother and stranger was meaningfully related to attachment groupings similar to those described by Ainsworth. That is, the wary and fearful babies in the Harmon et al. study had patterns of behavior in the separation and reunion episodes similar to those of two of Ainsworth's securely attached subgroups, that is, B2 and B3 babies, respectively. The mother-avoiding infants had attachment behaviors similar to Ainsworth's A1 subgroup. The no-preference infants, who probably should have been labeled *no-difference* because the infants did not have the occasion to choose between mother and experimenter, were somewhat similar to Ainsworth's A2 subgroup. Both of these types of A babies are felt by Ainsworth to be less securely attached than B babies.

Although there were some important differences between each of the four groups in the Harmon et al. (1979) study, the wary and fearful babies were similar in that they reacted less favorably to the experimenter than to the mother and both of these groups appeared to be more securely attached than those infants who showed no difference or reacted more positively to the experimenter. This interpretation of the Harmon et al. finding suggests that a two-part classification, based on the infant's differential reaction in a social interaction sequence, could provide a meaningful secondary index of the security of attachment to mother. If this proves to be the case, it would be a briefer and a less stressful measure of attachment than that provided by the Ainsworth strange situation because the mother was present during the whole social sequence. Thus this type of procedure could have advantages when assessment time was limited and/or there were reasons not to stress the infants.

Harmon et al. (1979) also found that the wary and fearful groups scored higher than the other groups (no preference and mother avoiding) on the Bayley Mental Development Index (MDI) and on a set of mastery tasks. These same infants were somewhat higher in the amount of mature play, but were lower in the total amount of active play (mostly simple manipulation/exploration) in a laboratory spontaneous play session. Thus a higher proportion of the active play of these wary and fearful (more securely attached) infants was mature.

Studies of Maternal Characteristics

There has been considerable research on normal adult personality and motivation, but little of it has been done with mothers of young children. In examining the relationship of maternal characteristics to infant development, researchers have usually focused on maternal behaviors or attitudes associated with caregiving, for example, maternal attitudes toward children or the amount of social stimulation. Little research has considered the relationship between infant development and characteristics of the mother as a person, apart from her role as a mother. Clarke-Stewart (1973), in a study of interactions between mothers and their infants, did assess four of Cattell's personality factors: ego strength, imaginativeness, experimentingness, and self-control. Mother's ego strength was correlated with the infant factor of object orientation, and imaginativeness was correlated with infant competence. In another such study, Busch-Rossnagel and Peters (1980) examined changes in Cattell's second-order factor of anxiety and Cattell's motivation sentiments during the first few months following the birth of normal, handicapped, and at-risk babies. Career interest was associated with low selfishness in mothers of handicapped children. In mothers of normal infants there was some indication that higher maternal anxiety was tied to low expectations for infant development, but the relationship of anxiety to competency in mothering was not examined. Hazaleus (1970) found that mothers (not necessarily of infants) who were more satisfied with their jobs were also less anxious and more satisfied with their role as homemaker/mother than mothers who had lower job satisfaction. Finally, Ottinger and Simmons (1964) found that highly anxious mothers had neonates who were more fussy, perhaps starting the mother–infant relationship off poorly. Little is known, however, about how these personal, as opposed to child-oriented variables, relate to infant–mother attachment or to infant play.

In addition to studies based on the Ainsworth strange situation, there have been a number of studies relating various maternal childrearing characteristics to infant and child development. In an overview of this topic, Kagan (1979) notes that one of the few replicated generalizations is that variety of experience promotes cognitive development. For example, Gaiter, Morgan, Jennings, Harmon, and Yarrow (1982) have found that the variety of cognitively oriented maternal play is related to both the infant's contemporaneous and later cognitive development. There does not appear to be any direct evidence about whether variety of maternal stimulation is related to security of attachment. However, because secure attachment, as well as variety of maternal play, is related to cognitive development (Ainsworth & Bell, 1974), variety and attachment may be related to each other.

METHOD

Subjects

Two samples of normal, white, middle-class infants and their mothers from a small city in Colorado were used as subjects. One sample consisted of 15 infants observed at 12 months of age; this is called the "12-month-only" sample. Corresponding data were obtained from 14 other infants observed at 9 and at 12 months of age; this is called the "longitudinal sample."

Procedure

Each infant and mother came to a human development laboratory for a maternal interview, 10–15 min of simultaneous free play by the infant, and a social interaction sequence involving the infant with both the experimenter and mother. Sessions were videotaped in a 3 m × 3 m playroom. The mothers were also asked to complete, at home, brief questionnaires.

Seven scores, each described below, plus three demographic variables (infant sex, number of siblings, and whether the mother worked) were used in this study. Because the scores on several of the measures were not distributed normally and the meaning of extreme scores was not always clear, it was decided to dichotomize each of the variables and use nonparametric statistics. This type of analysis enables us to view each variable as a factor (+ or 0) which might facilitate the infant–mother social relationship or not. In order to get the most stable measure on each of the variables, the 9- and 12-month scores for infants in the longitudinal sample were averaged before the dichotomization was done. Because the samples were so small, the samples were combined for most analyses.

Differential Social Response to Experimenter and Mother

After 10–15 min of free play, first the experimenter and then the mother performed a brief two-interval, social interaction sequence. During Interval A, which lasted 30 sec, the adult offered the infant a squeeze toy and then attempted to play "give and take" with the infant. In Interval B, also 30 sec, the adult offered to and then did pick up the infant, attempting to elicit a smile and/or wave by the infant at the reflections in a mirror.

The differential social response groups used in this chapter were formed from the following four types of behavior which were coded during each interval: (a) smile, (b) fuss/cry, (c) positive postural behavior (reaches toward, touches adult, takes toy, or waves), and (d) negative postural behavior (pulls back, withdraws, pushes adult away, stiffens when held, gaze aversion). From these behaviors, the differential response groups were formed using the following steps:

1. Separate scores for Intervals A and B to both experimenter and Mother were computed.

+ 2 = Both smile and positive postural behavior

+ 1 = Smile or positive postural behavior

  0 = No marked affect or postural behavior

− 1 = Fuss/cry or negative postural behavior

− 2 = Fuss/cry and negative postural behavior

+ / − = Both positive and negative behaviors coded in the same interval (counted as equivalent to zero in computing the algebraic differential response score).

2. The scores from Intervals A and B were algebraically summed to get an overall score (+ 4 to − 4) in response to each interactor.

3. The overall score to mother was subtracted from the overall score to experimenter in order to obtain an algebraic differential response score.

The infants were then divided into two groups: Group I, whose infants were then equally sociable, that is, they showed no difference in response to experimenter and mother or in some cases reacted more positively to the experimenter; and Group II, whose infants were more sociable to mother, that is, they reacted in a more positive or less negative way toward the mother. Twenty tapes were scored by two coders. Exact interobserver agreement on the algebraic differential response score was 80%. There were no disagreement as to which group those 20 subjects should be classified in.

Only 2 of the 14 infants (14%) in the longitudinal sample changed group (one from the equally sociable group to the more-sociable-to-mother group and one vice versa). This degree of stability would not be expected to occurr by chance. A nonparametric measure of association or correlation (tau) was used in this and other analyses reported in the paper (tau = .71, $p < .01$). Individual social behaviors and even the overall social response scores to experimenter and mother were not as stable over time as was this pattern or categorization of differential reaction. Because of this consistency and the supposition that the best predictability would occur with stable measures, the two longitudinal sample infants with inconsistent differential social response group classifications were omitted from all further data analyses. The longitudinal sample was thus reduced from 14 to 12.

Maternal Charcteristics

Responsivity to Infant Signals. During the free play, several types of infant signals (fuss/cry, bids to mother, and social use of a toy) were recorded. Responses by the mother in which she stopped talking to the interviewer and did something with or to the infant were also recorded. The ratio of the latter divided by the former was used as an indication of maternal responsivity to infant signals. Scores of the infants who had no signals were not used because their mothers did not have an opportunity to be responsive in this 10-min session. There was interobserver agreement on 17 out of 17 tapes about whether this score was high or low.

Variety of Cognitively Oriented Caregiver Activities. Using a refinement of an interview question developed by Gaiter et al. (1982), the mothers were asked to describe the most frequent types of noncaregiving social activities they had with their infants. All mothers named at least 5 types of activities. These were categorized by the interviewer as not-cognitively-oriented (roughhousing, cuddling, pushing in a stroller) or as one of the following four types of activity presumed to be cognitively enriching: (a) relational play such as helping the infant combine or stack objects, (b) pretend/adult-imitation activities such as talking on the telephone, (c) verbal play such as naming objects, and (d) cause and effect play such as peek a boo or playing together with responsive toys. Mothers who mentioned 3 or 4 *different types* of cognitively oriented activities, out of the first five activities described, were said to be high on variety of cognitively oriented activities.

Maternal Anxiety. The mothers completed, at home, a short form of the Cattell 16 Personality Factor Test, the Institute for Personality and Ability Testing Anxiety Scale Questionnaire (Cattell, 1976; Krug, Scheier, & Cattell, 1976). On the basis of responses to this scale, the mothers were divided into two groups at the mean of the national adult norms.

Mother's Career Interest. A shortened form of Cattell's Motivation Analysis Test (LMAT, 1975) was also answered at home by the mothers. It provides an indication of the mother's relative interest in career and personal development. Again, the scores were dichotomized.

Mother's Parental/Home Interest. The LMAT (1975) was also used to assess the mother's interests in matters related to her parents and home. The scores were, again, dichotomized.

Quality of Infant Play

The first 10 min of free play with a wide variety of toys and household objects was coded using a slightly modified version of a system developed by Morgan, Harmon, and Bennett (1976). Counts were made of the number of 10-sec intervals (out of 60) in which a type of behavior occurred. The quality of infant play was the ratio of the number of intervals of mature play (appropriately combining objects, using cause and effect toys, and elementary pretend sequences) to intervals of simple exploration or manipulation. These scores were divided to form two groups: high and low quality of play. Two observers agreed on the group assignment on 88% of the 17 tapes used for reliability.

RESULTS

Patterns of Infant Reaction to Experimenter and Mother

Table I provides descriptive data about how the infants responded when the experimenter and the mother picked them up, that is, during Interval B of the social sequence. Reactions during this interval, rather than to Intervals A

Table I. Reactions of 9- and 12-Month-Old Infants to Interval B (Pickup) by the Experimenter and the Mother

	Group I		Group II	
			More sociable to mother	
	Equally sociable			
	To experimenter	To mother	To experimenter	To mother
9-month-old infants	N = 5	N = 5	N = 7	N = 7
Positive response(s)	60%(3)[a]	20%(1)	0%(0)	71%(5)
No clear affect	20%(1)	60%(3)	71%(5)	29%(2)
Both + and − responses	20%(1)	20%(1)	14%(1)	0%(0)
Negative response(s)	0%(0)	0%(0)	14%(1)	0%(0)
All 12-month-old infants	N = 11	N = 11	N = 16	N = 15[b]
Positive response(s)	64%(7)	45%(5)	13%(2)	73%(11)
No clear affect	27%(3)	36%(4)	38%(6)	36%(4)
Both + and − responses	9%(1)	9%(1)	0%(0)	0%(0)
Negative response(s)	0%(0)	9%(1)	50%(8)	0%(0)

[a] Number of subjects in this group with this type of response.
[b] One subject who was clearly upset by the experimenter was not tested by mother, but calmed when held by mother.

and B combined, are shown because they present a clearer summary of the data and still accurately reflect the main differences between the two experimental groups (equally sociable and more sociable to mother), and between 9- and 12-month-old infants.

Although there was variability between infants in their reactions, all equally sociable (Group I) infants except one 12-month-old had qualitatively similar reactions to experimenter and mother. With this exception, it would not be accurate to label any of these babies as *mother-avoiding,* and this baby was very positive to both mother and the experimenter at 9 months. Two Group I babies did exhibit both positive and negative behaviors when picked up by mother and several were not very responsive to either mother or experimenter.

Group II infants also varied in their reaction to the experimenter, but by definition all reacted relatively more positively to their mother. Only a few of these babies voluntarily approached when the experimenter offered to pick them up, and few smiled or waved after being picked up by the experimenter. At 12 months, half could clearly be labeled as *wary* toward the experimenter, but only four showed frank distress, indicating that this procedure was indeed less stressful than the Ainsworth strange situation.

Maternal Characteristics and Infant's Differential Response

Table II shows the relationships, for the combined samples, between the scores on each of the maternal characteristics and the infant's differential social response group. Note that the Group I (equally sociable) babies have a low probability of having a mother who shows any of the first four hypothesized positive maternal characteristics. Mothers of Group II (more positive to mother) babies are significantly more likely than Group I mothers to (a) be responsive to their infants' signals during free play, (b) do a variety of cognitively oriented types of play with their infants at home, (c) be low on maternal anxiety, and (d) be high on career interest. There was not a significant relationship between differential social response and parental/home interest. Some additional evidence for the stability of these findings is the fact that three out of the four maternal characteristics that were significant in the combined samples had tau's significant at $p < .07$ on the separate small ($N = 15$ and 12) samples. The fourth variable in each case had a tau with $p < .20$.

There were no significant differences between Group I and II families on the three demographic variables. There were no differences related to the infant's sex or the number of siblings in the family. Few of the mothers worked outside the home, and there was no difference between the groups related to whether they did.

Table II. Relationships between Infants' Differential Social Response and Each of Five Maternal Characteristics (Longitudinal and 12 Month Samples Combined)

Maternal characteristic	Group I Equally sociable	Group II More sociable to mother	Tau[b]	Eta Squared[a]
High responsitivity to infant signals	10%(10)[a]	75%(12)	.65[e]	42%
High variety of cognitively-oriented caregiver play	0%(10)	56%(16)	.58[e]	33%
Low maternal anxiety	27%(11)	81%(16)	.54[e]	29%
High career interest	11%(9)	53%(15)	.42[d]	18%
High Parental/home Interest	44%(9)	53%(15)	.09	1%

[a] Group size for this variable. Tau and eta squared were computed using frequencies, not percentages.
[b] Tau is a nonparametric measure of association or correlation.
[c] Eta squared ($\times$ 100) is an estimate of the percentage of variance in differential social response explained by or associated with variation in the maternal characteristic.
[d] $p < .05$.
[e] $p < .01$.

In order to test how a combination of the four significant variables shown in Table II would discriminate the differential social response groups, the number of such "positive" maternal characteristics in the environment of each infant was computed. Table III shows the results of this analysis for the combined samples. The percentage of Group II (more sociable to mother)

Table III. Prediction of Infants' Differential Social Response Group from Maternal Characteristics (Combined Samples)

Number of positive maternal characteristics[a]	Group I Equally sociable	Group II More sociable to mother	Percentage more sociable to mother[c]
	N = 11	N = 16	
4	0%(0)[b]	6%(1)	100%(1)
3	0%(0)	44%(7)	100%(7)
2	9%(1)	38%(6)	84%(7)
1	27%(3)	13%(2)	40%(5)
0	64%(7)	0%(0)	0%(7)

[a] The four characteristics are: low anxiety, high responsivity to infant signals, high variety of cognitively-oriented caregiver activities, and high career interest.
[b] Number of subjects in this group with this number of maternal characteristics.
[c] The percentages in this column are based on the number of infants (in parentheses) whose mothers' had that number of positive maternal characteristics, 0–4. Percentage = $N_{II} + N_I + N_{II} \times 100$.

infants increases progressively as the number of positive maternal character-istics increases. This relationship is significant not only for the combined samples ($\tau = .88$, $p < .001$), but also for the two separate small samples ($\tau = .75$, $p < .02$ for the longitudinal sample and $\tau = .96$, $p < .001$ for the 12-month-only sample). Replication of the findings in these two independent samples strengthens the argument that this is a stable finding and that taken together, these four maternal characteristics provide a high degree of dis-crimination between the groups. The percentage of variance in differential response predictable by these four maternal variables is 68%, 54%, and 100% for the combined, longitudinal, and 12-months-only samples, respectively.

Quality of Play, Differential Response, and Maternal Characteristics

Table IV shows that the proportion of all active play which was high quality (i.e., functional or appropriate use of a toy) was significantly related to the infants' differential social-response group. Group II (more sociable to mother) babies were more likely to have high quality play.

Table IV also shows the relationship between each of the maternal char-acteristics and infant play. Only maternal anxiety and responsivity to infant signals were related to quality of play. When these two maternal characteris-tics were combined, 8 out of 9 of the infants whose mothers had neither posi-tive maternal characteristic showed relatively low-quality free play. More than one such maternal environmental factor did not seem to increase the probability of high-quality infant play; only 10 out of 18 babies with one or

Table IV. Relationship between the Quality of Infant Play, Differential Social Re-sponse, and Each Maternal Characteristic (Combined Samples)

Differential social response	Low quality of play	High quality of play	Tau[b]	Eta squared[c]
Group II - More sociable to mother	38%(16)[a]	91 %(11)	.53[e]	29%
Maternal characteristics				
High responsivity to infant signals	29%(14)	75 %(8)	.45[d]	20%
Low maternal anxiety	44%(16)	82 %(11)	.38[d]	15%
High Career Interest	28%(14)	50 %(10)	.22	5%
High parental/home interest	57%(14)	40 %(10)	-.17	4%
High variety of caregiver play	33%(15)	36 %(11)	.03	0%

[a] Group size for this variable.
[b] Tau is a nonparametric measure of association or correlation.
[c] Eta squared ($\times$ 100) is an estimate of the percentage of variance in quality of play explained by or associated with variation in the other variable.
[d] $p < .05$.
[e] $p < .01$.

both maternal characteristics had high-quality play. This relationship was significant ($\tau = .45, p < .05$), but was not an improvement on the relationship between quality of play and the more differentiating of the two factors, mother's responsivity to infant signals. Furthermore, neither one of the maternal characteristics alone nor the two combined leads to as high a degree of discrimination between the two levels of play as differential social response.

DISCUSSION

Differential Social Response as a Useful Way of Grouping Infants

Our findings support those of Harmon et al. (1979). We too found meaningful results by grouping infants based on their differential reactions to mother and experimenter in a brief, standardized social sequence. Both studies indicate that this general procedure and classification scheme should lead to fruitful future research and possible clinical applications.

In the present study, relationships were found with four maternal characteristics which seem to have influenced the pattern of reaction to mother and experimenter. Although no such relationships to the maternal social environment were reported in the Harmon et al. study, there is some relevant literature which was mentioned in the introduction and will be discussed below in the section on maternal and demographic factors.

Both the present study and Harmon et al. found relationships with infant competence. The findings are consistent with followups of the children used in several strange situation studies. Relationships have been found between earlier secure attachment and Development Quotient (DQ) (Ainsworth & Bell, 1974), quality of exploration and play (Main, 1973), enthusiasm, persistence, and ability to use the caregiver for help with a difficult task (Matas, Arend, & Sroufe, 1978), and peer group competence (Waters, Wippman, & Sroufe, 1979) in toddlers and preschoolers.

Attachment and Differential Social Response

As described in the introduction, Harmon et al. (1979) found that their wary and fearful infants, who are operationally similar to our Group II (more sociable to mother) infants, responded during an independently assessed separation and reunion episode much like the Ainsworth securely attached infants. Likewise, the Harmon et al. no preference and avoidant infants, who are operationally similar to our Group I (equally sociable) infants, responded to the reunion like Ainsworth's insecurely attached infants. Although there is no direct evidence in the current data, it might be inferred that, if our infants had been tested in the strange situation, most group I infants would have been classified as insecurely attached and most Group II babies as securely attached.

Our findings of relationships with the positive maternal variables and quality of play give further credence to thinking of Group I as insecurely and Group II as securely attached. However, examination of the literature and the social sequence reactions themselves raise some questions about that interpretation. On the one hand, since a sizeable proportion of Group II infants were wary toward the experimenter, it might be assumed that wariness would interfere with quality of spontaneous play as it apparently does with cognitive test performance (e.g., Stevenson & Lamb, 1979). On the other hand, Harmon *et al.* (1979) have argued that those Group II infants who reacted negatively to the experimenter are showing the normal developmental avoidance of strangers which accompanies the onset of attachment and that they could use the mother as a secure base for exploration. Those Group II infants who showed little or no negative behavior to the experimenter may have entered a more consolidated stage of secure attachment during which they can interact more freely with the stranger, the nearby mother again providing a secure base. Nevertheless, they still prefer the mother and react more positively to her.

Some of the patterns of social sequence behavior shown by Group I infants are less clearly interpretable, by themselves, as reflecting insecure attachment. As indicated in the Results section, one infant could be described as avoidant, at least at 12 months, and five other 12-month-old infants did show either some ambivalence (both + and − behavior) or affectively flat behaviors in interaction with mother. These reactions could reflect less than optimal mother–infant relationship but could also have been related more to the infants' temperament or current state because they reacted in a similar way to the experimenter. The remaining 5 (out of 11) 12-month-old Group I babies were quite positive toward both mother and experimenter. The reactions of these five infants could be interpreted as being quite sociable. Sociable babies have been shown by Stevenson and Lamb (1979) to be high on cognitive performance and to have maternal and home characteristics thought to be desirable on the basis of other research. Our findings for these particular five infants are not consistent with those of Stevenson and Lamb; these five babies had low-quality play and few, if any, "positive" maternal characteristics. Thus they do seem to belong, as placed, with the other Group I babies in our study.

Harmon *et al.* (1979) point out that their no-preference group seemed to be more heterogeneous than their other three groups. They felt that if the social sequence had been more stressful, these infants might well have shown differential response patterns similar to one of their other three groups. The avoidant behavior of most of these no-preference infants during reunion and their relatively poor performance during tests suggests that most might have become mother-avoiding under greater stress.

It seems likely that, although our differential social response groups have some correspondence to Ainsworth's attachment groups, we are not measuring exactly the same concepts. Likewise, we are not measuring absolute sociability as, for example, Stevenson and Lamb (1979) did; there were infants in both Groups I and II who were affectively positive to the experimenter. The important point for us is the infant's response to experimenter relative to the response to mother. Our data suggest that what we are measuring is an aspect of the mother–infant relationship that is influenced by the sensitivity, skillfulness, and perhaps spontaneity of the mother's approach to the infant and by the infant's feelings about relatively unfamiliar adults. Contrasting responses to experimenter and mother may serve as a sort of control for variation in infant temperament and certain situational factors such as fatigue or interest in objects in the environment.

Maternal and Demographic Factors

Our finding that mothers of Group II infants are more likely to be responsive to their infant's signals is consistent with the major finding of the Ainsworth et al. (1978) study. The relationship of maternal anxiety with apparently insecure attachment is not a direct replication of any known attachment studies, but seems in keeping with the general pattern of findings by Ainsworth. The other two "positive" maternal factors in our study (variety of caregiver play and maternal career interest) appear not to have been studied before in relation to attachment.

The significance of the relationship of infants' differential response to the cluster of maternal characteristics containing responsivity, variety of cognitive play, low anxiety, and career interest may be evidence of an underlying maternal competency. Whereas caregiving behaviors have been examined in relation to infant development, there has been little research or discussion of the role of personality and motivation. According to the data here, maternal personality and motivation have a significant relationship to infant development. This relationship is apart from the caregiving characteristics because the four maternal variables were not highly interrelated. This does not imply that each maternal characteristic is necessary; rather a combination of two or three appears to be sufficient. This idea is supported by the significant relationship of only two of the maternal characteristics to quality of play.

Ainsworth et al. (1978) found, as we did, that slightly but not significantly more boys than girls are categorized as securely attached and that there are no consistent differences between working and nonworking mothers in security of attachment. No findings about birth order or the number of siblings seems to be reported by Ainsworth *et al.* so it would appear that they too found no relationship.

Differential Response as an Intervening Variable

The differential social response group can be predicted quite well from the positive maternal factors, and quality of play can be predicted, in turn, from differential social response. However, only at the low end (no positive maternal factors) can we predict quality of play directly from the environmental variables. These findings are consistent with the notion, diagrammed in the introduction, that the quality of mother–infant interaction serves a mediating or intervening function between more solely maternal and child characteristics.

Infant Effects

The discussion so far as assumed that it is primarily the mother who affects the infant; however, at least in some instances the effects may be in the other direction. For example, it could be argued that mothers who are generally more anxious tend to be stiff in the experimental situation and thus less likely to elicit positive responses from their children. On the other hand, it may be that in some way the lack of preferential response by the infant may cause insecurity and anxiety in the mother rather than vice versa. Perhaps mothers of year-old infants expect them to show fear of strangers, and if they do not, the mother may feel threatened and anxious.

The direction of effects in parent–child relationships is hard to substantiate, probably because mother and child are both affecting each other in a dynamic interaction. Some notion of direction might be obtained by measuring maternal expectations (e.g., about infants' fear of strangers) prenatally, before they can be influenced by their child, and also assessing maternal anxiety at earlier periods.

Future Research Directions

Research extending and expanding the work of Harmon *et al.* (1979) and of this current study should be conducted. We plan to assess the effectiveness of a variety of structured social interaction procedures and their temporal sequencing. Further, we will continue to "tease out" the maternal and demographic factors which contribute to the differential social interactions of infants with their mother and other adults. We will also continue to investigate the behvioral correlates of differential social responsiveness. Because we have found meaningful results using a relatively unstressful social sequence, we intend to continue to focus on this type of sequence rather than using the

more stressful strange situation procedure that has proved useful in the previously cited studies by Ainsworth, Sroufe, and others.

In conclusion, we feel that this procedure and type of analysis has
already proved quite productive and will, when elaborated, lead to a
better understanding of the causes and outcomes of good infant–mother
relationships.

ABSTRACT

Twenty-seven infants were divided into two groups based on their differential reaction to their mother and an experimenter in a brief, structured
social sequence. The 16 infants who were more sociable to mother (Group II)
had mothers who were more likely to be: (a) high on responsivity to infant
signals, (b) high on variety of cognitively oriented play with the infant, (c) low
on anxiety, and (d) high on career interest. All seven of the mothers who
showed none of these "positive" maternal characteristics had infants who
were in Group I (equally sociable to mother and experimenter). The Group II
infants were more likely to have a high proportion of mature play during a
spontaneous play session. Harmon, Klein, and Suwalsky (1979) found that
infants who had differential social responses similar to those of our Group II
babies were more likely to be securely attached to their mothers. Thus this
brief, relatively unstressful social sequence seems to tap an important aspect
of the mother–infant relationship that is meaningfully related to several maternal characteristics and to the quality of infant play.

Acknowledgments

We wish to acknowledge the assistance in data collection and coding of
Ron Kirkegaard, Sallie Wetherbee, Betsy Stewart, and Norris Bakke. Joseph
Campos, R. Brooke Jacobsen, and Barbara McCornack made helpful com-
ments about earlier versions of the manuscript and the data analysis.

REFERENCES

Ainsworth, M. D. S. Infant–mother attachment. *American Psychologist,* 1979, *34,* 932–937.
Ainsworth, M. D. S., & Bell, S. M. Mother–infant interaction and the development of compe-
tence. In K. J. Connolly & J. S. Bruner (Eds.), *The growth of competence.* New York: Academic
Press, 1974.
Ainsworth, M. D. S., Blehar, M. C., Waters, E., & Wall, S. *Patterns of attachment.* Hillsdale, N. J.:
Lawrence Erlbaum, 1978.
Busch-Rossnagel, N. A., & Peters, D. L. Parental development in first-time mothers of handi-
capped, at-risk, and normal children. *International Journal of Rehabilitation Research,* 1980, *3,*
229–230.

Cattell, R. B. *Self analysis form.* Champaign: Institute for Personality and Ability Testing, 1976.

Clarke-Stewart, K. A. Interactions between mothers and their young children: Characteristics and consequences. *Monographs of the Society for Research in Child Development,* 1973, *38,* (6–7, serial No. 153).

Gaiter, J. G., Morgan, G. A., Jennings, K. D., Harmon, R. J., & Yarrow, L. J. Variety of cognitively-oriented caregiver activities: Relationships to cognitive and motivational functioning at 1 and 3 ½ years of age. *Journal of Genetic Psychology,* in press, 1982.

Harmon, R. J., Morgan, G. A., & Klein, R. P. Determinants of normal variation in infants' negative reactions to unfamiliar adults. *Journal of the American Academy of Child Psychiatry,* 1977, *16,* 670–683.

Harmon, R. J., Suwalsky, J. D., & Klein, R. P. Infants' preferential response for mother versus an unfamiliar adult: Relationship to attachment. *Journal of the American Academy of Child Psychiatry,* 1979, *18,* 437–449.

Hazaleus, M. B. *Inter-role conflict of employed mothers.* Unpublished masters thesis, Colorado State University, 1970.

Kagan, J. Family experience and the child's development. *American Psychologist,* 1979, *34,* 886–891.

Klein, R. P., & Durfee, J. T. Infants' reactions to unfamiliar adults versus mothers. *Child Development,* 1976, *47,* 1194–1196.

Krug, S. E., Scheier, I. H., & Cattell, R. B. *Handbook for the IPAT Anxiety Scale.* Champaign: Institute for Personality and Ability Testing, 1976.

LMAT. Champaign: Institute of Personality and Ability Testing, 1975.

Main, M. *Exploration, play, and level of cognitive functioning as related to child–mother attachment.* Unpublished doctoral dissertation, Johns Hopkins University, 1973.

Masters, J., & Wellman, H. Human infant attachment: A procedural critique. *Psychological Bulletin,* 1974, *81,* 218–237.

Matas, L., Arend, R. A., & Sroufe, L. A. Continuity of adaptation in the second year: The relationship between quality of attachment and later competence. *Child Development,* 1978, *49,* 547–556.

Morgan, G. A., & Riccuiti, H. N. Infants' responses to strangers during the first year. In B. M. Foss (Ed.), *Determinants of infant behavior* (Vol. 4). London: Methuen, 1969.

Morgan, G. A., Levin, B., & Harmon, R. J. Determinants of individual differences in infants' reactions to unfamiliar adults. JSAS *Catalog of Selected Documents in Psychology,* 1975, *5,* 277. (Ms. No. 1006)

Morgan, G. A., Harmon, R. J., & Bennett, Ca. A. A system for coding and scoring infants' spontaneous play with objects. JSAS *Catalog of Selected Documents in Psychology,* 1976, *6,* 105. (Ms. No. 1355)

Ottinger, D. R., & Simmons, J. E. Behavior of human neonates and prenatal maternal anxiety. *Psychological Reports,* 1964, *14,* 391–394.

Sroufe, L. A. The coherence of individual development: Early care, attachment, and subsequent developmental issues. *American Psychologist,* 1979, *34,* 834–841.

Sroufe, L. A., & Waters, E. Attachment as an organizational construct. *Child Development,* 1977, *48,* 1184–1199.

Stayton, D. J., & Ainsworth, M. D. S. Individual differences in infant responses to brief, everyday separations as related to other infant and maternal behaviors. *Developmental Psychology,* 1973, *9,* 226–235.

Stevenson, M. B., & Lamb, M. E. Effects of infant sociability and the caretaking environment on infant cognitive performance. *Child Development,* 1979, *50,* 340–349.

Waters, E., Wippman, J., & Sroufe, L. A. Attachment, positive affect, and competence in the peer group: Two studies in construct validation. *Child Development,* 1979, *50,* 821–829.

CHAPTER 17

Attachment Behavior in Abused/Neglected and Premature Infants

IMPLICATIONS FOR THE CONCEPT OF ATTACHMENT

Theodore J. Gaensbauer and Robert J. Harmon

Bowlby (1969) put forth the concept of "attachment" as a model of the mother–infant relationship which could account for clinical observations indicating that separation of the infant from its mother had quite detrimental short-term and potentially long-term effects. By integrating points of view derived from psychoanalysis, ethology, and systems theory, this construct has proved to be extremely fruitful in stimulating developmental research. The work of Bowlby, Ainsworth, Sroufe, and their respective colleagues has produced convincing evidence for viewing attachment as an organizational construct that reflects qualitative aspects of the parent–infant relationship (Ainsworth,Blehar, Waters, & Wall, 1978; Lamb, Chapter 14; Sroufe & Waters, 1977). Although originally formulated based on observations of clinical populations, most of the empirical work on attachment has been conducted on normal, middle-class groups of infants and their parents. In this chapter we would like to return to the clinical realm in order to emphasize the value of clinical study for broadening and clarifying the concept of attachment.

Theodore J. Gaensbauer and Robert J. Harmon, ● Department of Psychiatry, University of Colorado School of Medicine, Box C 268, 4200 E. Ninth Avenue, Denver, Colorado 80262. Dr. Gaensbauer is supported by Research Career Development Award 1–K04–HY–214–5. Dr. Harmon is supported by Research Career Development Award 1–K01–MH–00281–02. Portions of this work were supported by grants to both authors from the Grant Foundation Endowment Fund of the Developmental Psychobiological Research Group of the Department of Psychiatry, University of Colorado Health Sciences Center, Denver, and from BRSG RR–05357 awarded by the Division of Research Resources, National Institutes of Health. Dr. Harmon is supported by Research Grant No. 1–R01–MH34005–02 from the National Institutes of Mental Health.

Most of the empirical work based on the attachment construct has focused on the first two years of life and has been conducted using a structured laboratory paradigm—the strange situation (Ainsworth & Wittig, 1969). Patterns of infant behavior in response to a series of brief separations and reunions with the mother have been associated with the quality of caretaking in the home environment, with a variety of measures of cognitive development, and with competence in peer relationships at older ages (Ainsworth *et al.*, 1978; Bretherton, Bates, Benigni, Camaroni, & Volterra, 1979; Harmon, Suwalski, & Klein, 1979; Matas, Arend, & Sroufe, 1978). Evidence for the validity of the concept has accumulated to the point where investigators are currently utilizing the strange situation and its variants to assess the quality of parent–infant relationships and the effectiveness of therapeutic interventions in clinical populations (Chichetti & Serafica, 1981; Gaensbauer & Harmon, 1981; Gordon & Jameson, 1979). In this chapter we will address a number of the important issues raised by the application of these methods of studying attachment to clinical situations. We will be emphasizing clinical observations and case material which, while less amenable to rigorous control of experimental conditions, can highlight variations and suggest determinants of attachment behavior in ways that are often not possible in controlled experimental studies.

Two clinical populations are represented in this chapter. Each has unique background characteristics highlighting important factors presumed to influence attachment behavior. The first sample consists of infants who have experienced disturbed parenting, including physical abuse and neglect, chaotic and inconsistent caregiving environments, multiple caregivers, frequent separations, and foster home placements. This sample has provided an opportunity to examine the effects of extreme environmental stress on attachment behavior. The second sample consists of extremely low birthweight premature infants (weighing less than 1500 g) whose early life experiences involved both extreme physiological as well as psychological stresses. This sample has provided an opportunity to examine the importance of an intact biological organization at birth and the effects of disruption in early parent and infant contact on subsequent attachment behavior (Kaplan & Mason, 1960; Koops & Harmon, 1980; Leiderman, Leifer, Seashore, Barnett, & Grobstein, 1973). The samples include over 80 abused/neglected infants between the ages of 3 and 30 months observed with natural parents, foster parents, and/or other primary caregivers, over 200 normal infants between the ages of 12 and 18 months from a broad range of socioeconomic backgrounds, and 30 12-month-old premature infants.

The infants were observed utilizing a modification of the Ainsworth-Wittig strange situation, as described in Table I. Our rationale for the clinical use of this modified paradigm can be found in Gaensbauer and Harmon (1981). The sequences most pertinent to the discussion of attachment include

(1) a free-play period in which the spontaneous interaction of the mother and her infant may be observed; (2) a graduated stranger approach, followed by an approach by the mother in a similar manner, allowing for a comparison of the infant's affiliative behavior to the mother and to the stranger; (3) a brief maternal separation and reunion episode, followed by (4) a stranger separation and reunion episode, again allowing for a comparison of the infant's attachment behavior to a familiar and a relatively unfamiliar adult. Although there are a number of obvious differences between our modified paradigm and the Ainsworth and Wittig strange situation—primarily in our use of one separation instead of two—our paradigm nevertheless provides abundant opportunity to observe attachment behavior. A number of studies have indicated that valid judgments about the quality of attachment can be made based on a single separation (Harmon *et al.*, 1979; Matas *et al.*, 1978).

VALIDITY OF AINSWORTH'S CONCEPTS OF SECURE VERSUS INSECURE ATTACHMENT

Ainsworth *et al.* (1978) have developed a three-part classification system based on the infant's responses to separation from and reunion with the mother in the strange situation paradigm. Group A, "avoidant," babies are described as explicitly avoiding proximity to or interaction with the mother during reunion. In general, they are not distressed by their mother's absence. In addition, they show little or no tendency to seek contact with the mother at any time; if picked up, they do not actively resist contact. Both mother and stranger are treated in similarly indifferent manners; often there is less avoidance of the stranger. Group B, "securely attached," infants demonstrate proximity and contact-seeking behaviors toward the mother upon her return following separation. After gaining contact, they seek to maintain it, often by resisting being put down by the mother. Distress during separation is variable, but clearly related to the mother's absence. During reunion with the mother, the infant may show either positive greeting behavior or crying; in either case there is a tendency to approach the mother and little or no tendency to resist contact with her. Although some infants may be friendly toward the stranger, they are clearly more interested in interacting with the mother, especially during the reunion sequences. Group C, "resistant," infants show intense conflicts between strong desire for contact and clear resistance of contact and/or interaction with the mother. The resistant behaviors have an unmistakable angry quality, and are particularly prominent during the separation episodes. They may also be seen in preseparation episodes and toward the stranger as well as the mother.

There has been a clear inference, both from Ainsworth's original longitudinal study and subsequent correlational studies, that the avoidant and

Table I. Two Examples of the Use of a Structured Experimental Situation for Clinical Assessment in Infancy.

One-Session Paradigm[a]		
1. Mother & infant enter: "make infant comfortable"		2 min
2. Infant free play with mother present		5 min
3. Stranger enters, stranger approach		4 min
a. Talk to mother	1 min	
b. Talk to infant	1 min	
c. Give-and-take	1 min	
d. Pick up infant	1 min	
4. Mother approach (similiar to stranger approach)		2 min
a. Give-and-take		
b. Pick up infant		
5. Developmental testing with mild frustrations		15–30 min
6. Stranger & infant engage in interactive play		1 min
7. Mother leaves - separation		3 min
8. Mother returns - reunion		2 min
9. Stranger leaves - separation		3 min
10. Stranger returns - reunion		2 min

Two-Session Paradigm[b]		
1. Mother & infant enter: "make infant comfortable"		2 min
2. Infant free play with mother present		2 min
3. Stranger enters, stranger approach		4 min
a. Talk to mother	1 min	
b. Talk to infant	1 min	
c. Give-and-take	1 min	
d. Pick up infant	1 min	
4. Mother approach (similiar to stranger approach)		2 min
a. Give-and-take		
b. Pick up infant		
5. Free play and maternal interview		20 min
6. Stranger & infant engage in interactive play		1 min
7. Mother leaves - separation		3 min
8. Mother returns - reunion		2 min
9. Stranger leaves - separation		3 min
10. Stranger returns - reunion		2 min

Mastery Motivation Testing Session

A. Tasks

Nine tasks are given in the same order to each infant for a 3-min trial. The tasks are divided into 3 conceptual clusters: (1) effectance production, or tasks which allow the infant to produce interesting effects (surprise box, toaster, forest); (2) problem solving, or tasks in which the infant seeks a toy from behind a barrier (barn door, object permanence testing, barrier box); (3) practicing emerging skills, which are tasks in which infants put one object into another (pegs in boat, drop-a-ball, and shape sorter).

Our key measure on these tasks consists of the percentage of time each infant engages in persistant goal directed behavior (Jennings, Harmon, Morgan, Gaiter, & Yarrow, 1979).

Table I. (*Continued*)

Mastery Motivation Testing Session
B. Adminstration of Object Permanence Scales (Uzgiris-Hunt)
C. Adminstration of Bayley Scales of Mental Development

[a] One-session paradigm was designed to study the regulation of affective expression in normal and abused/neglected infants.

[b] Two-session paradigm was designed to study attachment, cognitive-motivational development, and affective development in term and preterm infants.

resistant infants have experienced less optimal caretaking than the securely attached infants. Group A and C infants and mothers have been found to be similar on many home environment measures. They are often grouped together as being "anxiously" or "insecurely" attached. Group B infants are considered to be securely attached.

In our studies of normative infants the patterns of attachment behavior most commonly observed have been consistent with those described by Ainsworth as reflecting secure attachment. In general, during the brief separation the infant shows some evidence of missing the mother. Reactions may range from a very mild reduction in positive mood and a transient letdown in play, to intense distress and disrupted play. On reunion, most infants greet their mothers positively and/or show some degree of proximity-seeking and proximity-maintaining behavior.

In the abused/neglected sample, the pattern of responses has been consistent with those described by Ainsworth *et al.* (1978), as indicative of a less than optimal attachment relationship. For example, of the 14 infants observed between the ages of 12 and 21 months living with their natural mothers at the time of testing, 11 showed either resistant or avoidant behavior upon reunion. An avoidant pattern was by far the most common. Similar patterns have been observed in older infants as well as in infants observed with foster mothers.

Although our findings provide support for the validity of the inferences made by Ainsworth, Sroufe, and others regarding indicators of problematic attachment, a number of caveats must be kept in mind. The fact that extremely stressful caretaking conditions produce patterns of behavior considered to be indicators of insecure attachment does not automatically imply that the presence of such a pattern is indicative of physical or emotional abuse and/or neglect. Most of the findings reported to date on attachment behavior in the strange situation have been based on group data. The meaning of avoidant and/or resistant behavior in an individual infant is an entirely different question. One cannot always infer from the presence of attachment behavior that all is well, nor does the presence of an avoidant or resistant pattern automatically mean that serious difficulties are present. We would therefore like to enumerate several principles based on our work with clinical populations which emphasize that, for the individual infant, assessment of attachment behavior alone may not adequately describe the quality of the caregiver–infant relationship.

THE STRONG PREDISPOSITION OF INFANTS TO SHOW ATTACHMENT BEHAVIOR

Although one usually assumes that the presence of a reaction to separation from the mother and positive greeting and proximity-seeking behavior upon her return are indicative of a secure mother-infant relationship, our work with populations at risk for disturbances in attachment has impressed on us that infants may show secure attachment behavior toward surrogate or foster mothers, toward receptive unfamiliar adults, and in situations of inconsistent mothering. Such experiences have emphasized to us the high adaptability and resilience of this behavioral system, at least as it is manifested in the laboratory situation. They have also caused us to be hesitant in always assuming that the parent–child relationship is without difficulty when a normative pattern of attachment behavior is present.

A number of infants observed in the laboratory with their natural parents had, because of parenting disturbances, been placed in foster homes for weeks to months prior to the visit. Contact with the parents involved one-hour supervised visits once or twice a week. Such brief contact was sufficient in at least nine infants to produce a pattern of attachment behavior in the laboratory consistent with secure attachment. If one had looked only at attachment behavior and did not have the historical information, it would have been easy to assume that these infants were currently being home-reared in an optimal family setting.

The motivation to demonstrate attachment behaviors to a responsive adult is perhaps most dramatically evidenced by infants who have shown preferential indicators of attachment to the experimenter rather than to the mother. In our situation, the infant has an opportunity to interact with the stranger for approximately 20 to 30 minutes preceding the separation episode. In 3 out of the 14 abused/neglected infants referred to earlier, the emotional availability of the stranger was sufficient to produce an incentive in the infant to maintain the interaction with him during the stranger-separation sequence. These infants evidenced disappointment and some form of search behavior after the stranger's leaving and positive greetings on the stranger's return. Perhaps the most dramatic example was a 12-month-old infant who went to the door after the stranger's departure, remained there for a minute or so calling out, and on the stranger's return smiled and crawled over to the stranger's lap. When the mother left, the infant had continued his play with no reaction.

A not uncommon example of the readiness to attach to an available caretaker was a 22-month-old infant who had been found by the police abandoned with his $3\frac{1}{2}$ year-old sibling in a bedroom full of feces, dirt, and garbage. His previous history had included a hospitalization, inconsistent caretaking, experience with neglect, and brief foster home placements. He was then moved to a very responsive foster home; within 2 days he showed a clear differentiation in favor of the foster mother. When observed in our playroom laboratory one week later, he showed a distinct preference for the foster mother, with a marked distress response when she left the room. On her return, he immediately ran over to her to be soothed, quieting promptly. Although one might suspect the presence of a previous attachment bond as a prototype for the current relationship with the foster mother, the readiness to attach to the new caretaker was striking. Five additional infants between 12 and 26 months of age, in foster placements for less than three weeks, have shown similar patterns of secure attachment to the new caretaker in the laboratory situation.

The strong predisposition toward attachment behavior is also illustrated by premature infants. These infants are not only physiologically immature and stressed at birth, but their 2 to 4 month average hospitalization results in obvious interferences in the degree to which their parents are able to visit and care for them. Even when parents can visit at any time, their interaction with their infant is often limited by the infant's medical condition. In spite of these physiological and environmental stresses, these infants, in preliminary analyses, have shown lesser amounts of avoidance or resistance and increased proximity seeking and contact-maintaining behavior during reunion than a group of matched controls (Harmon & Culp, 1981).

THE SPECIFICITY OF ATTACHMENT BEHAVIOR

Although infants may show a strong predisposition toward attachment behavior, they are by no means indiscriminate. Ainsworth et al. (1978) considered it likely that the relationship with each attachment figure would depend on the history of the interaction between the child and that particular figure. Data comparing attachment responses to fathers versus mothers have illustrated the validity of this point (Cohen & Campos, 1974; Lamb, 1977; Lamb, Chapter 14). In our work with children of disturbed parents we have had occasion to compare infants' responses to a variety of caretakers, for example, fathers versus mothers, mothers versus grandmothers, and mothers versus foster mothers. We have been impressed by the degree to which the attachment behaviors shown reflect the quality of the infant's relationship with a particular person. To cite one example among many, a 17-month-old child placed in foster care immediately after his birth had had ongoing supervised weekly one-hour visits with his parents. Home observers had noted that his mother was quite insensitive to his needs; his father, although a rigid disciplinarian, had a capacity for warmth and affection. In the laboratory, the child showed little response to his mother leaving the room, continuing to play with the examiner. When his mother returned he gave her a mild smile, but immediately turned away, showing behavior which would have classified him as an "avoidant" infant. When his father entered the room at the end of the session, the child immediately crawled across the room into his father's arms. When the father left the room several minutes later, the child began to cry and crawled over to the door. When the father returned the second time, the child immediately went to him to be held and remained in the father's proximity for several minutes. Such differentiation between individuals has been a frequent enough finding for us to utilize such information in making clinical judgments about the child's relationships with the various caretakers in his or her life.

We have been impressed that specificity in attachment behavior is seen not only in relation to particular individuals but also in relation to particular situations. This is important to keep in mind, since the assessment of attachment behavior in the laboratory is weighted toward behavior during episodes of maternal separation and reunion. The separation situation itself may have special meaning to the child. The child's response based on this specific meaning might or might not be characteristic of the overall relationship with the caretaker. An obvious example would be the case of the working mother, where the child's extensive experience with separations and reunions might well influence his reactions in the laboratory. Although some investigators have found differences in attachment behavior based on the amount of day care (Blehar, 1974), others have not (Caldwell, Wright, Honig, & Tannenbaum, 1970; Kagan, Kearsly, & Zelazo, 1978; Portnoy & Simmons, 1978). In either case, the implications for the overall quality of the relationship are far from clear.

Conversely, attachment behavior in the specific context of the separation–reunion paradigm may appear optimal, yet not capture all elements of the attachment relationship. Put more precisely, behavior indicative of secure attachment cannot be considered synonymous with optimal development. This was seen most dramatically in a 15½ month-old infant who had experienced severe abuse culminating in a skull fracture which resulted in hospitalization and foster home placement at 10½ months of age. The child saw his parents for weekly supervised visits over the next several months, leading up to the laboratory evaluation at 15½ months of age. During the session he showed all the indicators of a well-attached infant, including frequent interaction with the mother during the free-play session with much smiling and vocalizing, a mild letdown during the maternal separation, and positive greeting and proximity-seeking on reunion. Contrasting with this optimal picture was his behavior during developmental testing. On at least two occasions when the examiner attempted to illustrate a task to be done with an open-handed gesture, the child eyed the examiner fearfully, froze in his posture, cringed as if anticipating a blow, and began to cry. During the face-to-face encounter of the testing situation he was inhibited and hypervigilant; consequently, his performance and capacity to cooperate were seriously impaired.

Another example was a 12-month-old infant who had been placed in foster care two weeks prior to the laboratory visit. His separation and reunion behavior to the foster mother was consistent with secure attachment. At the same time, he exhibited clear evidence of depression and withdrawal intermittently throughout the session, most notably in the minutes immediately following the reunion. These affective responses would not be captured utilizing the attachment classification alone. In our experience, even when the responses to separation and reunion would seem to indicate a secure attachment, infants who have experienced disturbed parenting will often demonstrate affective behavior during other portions of the session indicative of possible developmental disturbance. The area of disturbance has usually been quite specific to the particular caregiver–infant dyad. For this reason, we have emphasized the importance of assessing multiple lines of development, with the pattern of attachment behavior being one area of assessment among many (Gaensbauer & Harmon, 1981).

Although there is a high degree of specificity in attachment behavior, we would not want to imply that attachment experiences have no generality. Extensive research work has indicated that the infant's attachment relationship with his primary caretakers has important implications for social development, such as the capacity to cooperate, acceptance of discipline, quality of gestural communication, and competence in play and peer relations (Ainsworth et al., 1978; Bretherton et al., 1979; Harmon et al., 1979; Lamb, Chapter 14; Main, 1973; Matas et al., 1978; Sroufe & Waters, 1977). In our experience the likelihood of transferring positive expectations to new social relationships is greater when the child's experiences with different caretakers have been consistently positive. In our normal samples, we have been impressed with the extent to which a positive social relationship with the mother can carry over to the experimenter after any initial wariness has worn off. Similarly, in those clinical populations involving infants placed in foster homes, we have found that positive experiences during brief weekly visits with the natural parents, may result in the expression of secure attachment behavior to the natural parents during the laboratory evaluation. In these instances, the attachment behavior to the natural parents has most likely been a consequence of excellent foster care rather than a true reflection of the parent's caregiving ability. This tendency to transfer has at times made it difficult to predict how well an infant and his or her parents will do when the parents resume full-time care.

We believe that specificity in attachment behavior is more likely when there have been significant differences in the qualities of caregivers, with both positive and negative experiences capable of being transferred. The infants who showed the most dramatic evidence of attachment behavior toward the experimenter have in each case had highly positive prior relationships with fathers and foster fathers. On the negative side are those infants who interact with the examiner in manners which have grown out of their previous distorted interactions with caretakers (Gaensbauer & Sands, 1979). The most dramatic examples of such generalizations have been infants who were abused by their fathers and exhibited extreme fear of the male stranger.

STABILITY OF ATTACHMENT: ATTACHMENT BEHAVIOR AS REFLECTING RECENT CARETAKING EXPERIENCES RATHER THAN PAST EXPERIENCES

The question of the specificity of attachment behavior is closely related to the question of stability. Sroufe and his colleagues have reported that the attachment group classifications (A,B,C) are consistent over the 12 to 18 month period (Vaughn, Egeland, & Sroufe, 1979; Waters, 1978; Waters, Wippman, & Sroufe, 1979) while Ainsworth has reported continuity between attachment behavior at 12 months and such antecedent caregiving variables as responsiveness to infant crying signals, careful and tender handling, pacing of feeding, and face-to-face interactions during the first quarter of life (Ainsworth et al., 1978). Whether or not sensitive, responsive caregiving in the early months of life is necessary for the establishment of an attachment relationship at 12 months, or whether an attachment relationship at 12 months derives from the fact that in a particular mother–child dyad there tends to be continuity from past to present, is a question which has not been definitively answered. Our own experience suggests that attachment behavior in the laboratory seems a better reflection of the relatively recent quality of the infant–caregiver relationship as opposed to the remote past. As was pointed out on p. 271, from the study of infants with both their natural and foster mothers, we have learned that in regard to attachment behavior, a satisfactory current relationship can overcome past experiences of a high traumatic nature.

At the same time, we would not want to imply that previous experiences have no enduring effects. In certain infants whom we have followed longitudinally the emergence from social withdrawal has been painfully slow. It is our impression that a number of complex interrelated factors will determine whether, and over what period of time, a previously withdrawn child will be able to establish a meaningful attachment to the current caregiver. Contributing elements would include the degree of previous trauma, the extent of withdrawal or other developmental disturbances, behaviors in the infant which interfere with the caregiver's ability to respond to the infant, and factors related to the caregiver's sensitivity and investment in the child. The establishment of an attachment relationship as defined by the presence of attachment behavior is relative, and certainly does not indicate a full recovery to normal developmental status. The establishment of a specific attachment relationship is probably only the first step to developmental recovery, serving as a vehicle for undoing or modifying the effects of previous difficult experiences in a broad variety of areas.

The persisting vulnerability of these children, despite a capacity for differential attachment, is illustrated by the 12-month-old infant described earlier who showed depression and withdrawal but who had clearly established an attachment relationship after two weeks with his sensitive and involved foster mother. During developmental testing, he had performed above the norm and we were quite optimistic about his chances for developmental progress. Unfortunately, during the third month of his stay in the new home, an acute illness of the foster father and difficulties with her own children began to drain the foster mother's attention. When observed in the laboratory at 17 months, he seemed quite withdrawn, showed attachment behavior which would have classified him as avoidant, and did less well on developmental testing than he had done earlier. The foster mother contrasted his behavior with the behavior of her 13-month-old granddaughter, who was also living in the home but who had not experienced such trauma. The granddaughter took the initiative in engaging her grandmother's attention in spite of the grandmother's preoccupation with her husband's illness, whereas her foster brother reacted to her preoccupation by withdrawing. As the situation in the foster home stabilized and the foster mother had more energy to direct toward him, he began to emerge from his withdrawal and his development began to pick up again. However, one might hypothesize that he will continue to be quite vulnerable to stress in future attachment relationships.

THE ROLE OF PLEASURABLE INTERACTION IN FACILITATING ATTACHMENT BEHAVIOR

What can observations of these clinical populations tell us about the motivational factors underlying attachment behavior observed in the laboratory? Ainsworth *et al.*, (1978), have pointed to the mother's sensitive responsiveness to infant communications across multiple situations as a crucial factor in the bringing about of an attachment relationship. Thompson, Lamb, and Estes (1982) have also recently focused on the specific contribution of maternal contingent responding and comforting of infant distress. They suggest that an expectation of comforting may be the most important determinant of the pattern of attachment observed in the laboratory.

Our experience, however, would lead us to emphasize that the opportunity for pleasurable interchange is in itself an important motivating factor for attachment behavior, independent of previous experiences with contingent comforting. As mentioned on page 268, several infants have shown preferential attachment behavior to the experimenter, even though their prior experience with him had been one of pleasurable interaction and had not involved comforting from distress. The importance of pleasurable interchange is also demonstrated by those infants who were being cared for in foster homes because of problem parenting, yet who showed secure attachment behaviors during the laboratory separation and reunion episodes with their natural mothers. In most cases, the infants' contact with their parents during the previous several months had consisted of weekly supervised play sessions designed to emphasize pleasurable interchange. These relatively brief positive contacts appeared to be sufficient to sustain secure attachment behavior toward the natural parent, if not produce it. These observations have emphasized for us the important motivational qualities of pleasurable interaction in facilitating attachment behavior.

In thinking about the various possible motivational factors underlying attachment behavior, one must keep in mind the specific situation and context in which the behavior is occurring and the affective meaning of the situation for that particular child. It is likely that attachment behavior shown in nonstressful contexts might have very different determinants and implications than attachment behavior shown in more stressful contexts. For example, abusing and/or neglecting parents do not abuse or neglect their children 24 hours a day. Under specific conditions and for specific reasons disturbances may occur; at other times, the parent–child interaction may be very positive. In the laboratory situation, a not infrequent observation has been that during nonstressful play periods interaction between parent and child may appear quite positive and indistinguishable from normal samples. One might see spontaneous approaches, vocalizations, reciprocal play, mutual pleasure, and sustained interaction. In these cases, only under stress, such as is occasioned by mild frustrations during developmental testing, by pressures to complete a cooperative task, or by the maternal separation, are disturbances likely to be observed.

ATTACHMENT BEHAVIORS MUST BE SEEN IN DEVELOPMENTAL PERSPECTIVE

Our last point relates to the importance of having a sense of the developmental progression of attachment behavior and the openness of this system to change over time. This is particularly important in judgments about the status of the caregiver–infant relationship in premature infants. Whereas in a homogeneous full-term, middle-class population there is likely to be considerable consistency in attachment behavior shown at particular ages, in premature infants a variety of factors may make conclusions less definitive. For example, one premature infant who showed little evidence of attachment to the mother at 12 months (corrected for gestational age) showed clear evidence of attachment when seen again at 15 months. The change during this period seemed to reflect the infant's growing maturity as well as the mother's realization that she may have felt differently about this infant as a result of his long hospitalization. During the 12-month laboratory visit the infant had shown a clear preference for the male stranger over his mother. Although this behavior seemed to reinforce in this mother's mind that she was a "poor mother," by history it became clear that his father had taken a major role in his care and that he often showed a preference for men. As the interview with the mother continued, it was obvious that she cared for him greatly, but was not getting the necessary reinforcement from him that he knew her as someone "special." It seemed that although this infant could discriminate his mother from the stranger, he had not yet developed a strong affective differentiation. Our assessment was that this resulted from maturational delays in the child, as well as experiential factors involving the mother. This assessment was shared with her and a second session was scheduled at 15 months to determine if changes in the infant's attachment behavior would occur with time. During this subsequent visit, when the mother left the room the infant burst into tears and tried to follow her. During reunion, both mother and infant were in tears, reflecting the consolidation of their relationship and the meaningfulness of the infant's expression of his attachment for the mother.

The evaluation of this mother–child dyad required a sense of the importance of the timing of their coming together and the dynamic and maturational factors operating in their relationship. Without this understanding, one would have had less confidence in the eventual outcome.

CONCLUSION

Our experience with clinical populations has provided considerable evidence for the validity of the concept of attachment as a qualitative measure of the infant's relationship with his caregiver. Research evidence, clinical experience, and common sense would suggest that the mother or primary caregiver should be meaningful enough to the infant to produce some degree of letdown in response to her departure and some incentive to resume interaction on her return. The intensity of this letdown and the motivation to regain proximity may vary greatly. Infants at the extreme ends of this continuum—who either show no evidence of missing the mother and who "snub" her on her return, or who show anger and distress which carry over to the reunion in the form of maladaptive resistance to the comforting of the mother—may be showing indicators of a less than optimal attachment relationship. Our work with abused/neglected infants has supported this hypothesis.

At the same time, we have emphasized a number of caveats which should be kept in mind when using the strange situation paradigm to make inferences about the quality of the mother–infant relationship. Attachment behavior may or may not be a true reflection of the caretaker–child relationship. Infants show a strong predisposition to show attachment behavior, even in circumstances which one would have thought might mitigate against such behavior. Thus one cannot assume that because secure attachment behavior is present, that all is well in the caregiver–child relationship. Attachment appears to be highly specific in its expression, relating to specific experiences that a child has had with a particular individual. The nature of the attachment behavior appears in the main to reflect relatively recent experiences in caregiver–infant interaction, and can only with great care be utilized to draw inferences about past experiences. Finally, it is important to consider attachment behavior as part of the developmental progression and to appreciate the resiliency characteristic of caregiver–infant relationships.

Based on our experiences in applying the attachment construct to our work with clinical populations, there are two potential pitfalls which need to be avoided. First the concept of attachment promotes a tendency to think of caregiver–infant relations in dichotomous terms—"well-attached" versus "not well-attached," thereby potentially over-simplifying and reifying what are in reality enormously complex relationships. Second, the operationalization of the concept in terms of behaviors which either promote or interfere with proximity-seeking, while furthering empirical research, has had a tendency to obscure other manifestations of the caregiver–infant relationship (Bernal, 1974). Indeed, the emphasis on operational definitions has led to such unproductive positions as concluding that the notion of an attachment bond is invalid because consistent behavioral measures cannot be found (Maccoby & Feldman, 1972; Rosanthal, 1973; Weinraub, Brooks, & Lewis,

1977), or writing that attachment to the caregiver wanes toward the end of the second year because proximity-seeking diminishes as the child becomes older (Clarke-Stewart, 1977; Feldman & Ingham, 1975).

In their original formulations Bowlby (1969) and Ainsworth (1973) did not have a restricted concept in mind. Attachment was defined as an affective bond, implying "strong emotions, not only security, anxiety, and anger, but also love, grief, jealously, and, indeed the full spectrum of emotion and feeling" (Ainsworth et al., 1978, p. 23). We find it ironic that, despite this definition, there has been so little direct study of the role of emotion in the caregiver–infant relationship. In our own approach, we have found it much more fruitful to think in terms of the variety of discrete emotions which may come into play during affective exchanges between infant and parent, and the ways in which the particular quality of these affective exchanges have shaped the infant's emotional responsiveness, (Gaensbauer & Sands, 1978; Gaensbauer, 1981). We believe that a more direct focus on the qualitative affective experience of the infant growing out of caretaker–infant interaction will expand our understanding of the emotional underpinnings of attachment behavior as observed in the laboratory, avoid some of the potential blind alleys into which the attachment concept can lead, and at the same time provide richer and broader conceptualizations of the caregiver–infant relationship.

ABSTRACT

In this chapter, observations of the attachment behavior of abused/neglected and premature infants in a structured laboratory paradigm are used to broaden and clarify the concept of attachment. Utilizing clinical examples, the strong predisposition of infants to show attachment behavior, the specificity versus generality of attachment behavior, issues of stability, the role of pleasurable interaction in facilitating attachment behavior, and the need to view attachment behavior in developmental perspective are discussed. Experience with these clinical populations has indicated that while the concept of attachment has validity, attachment behavior as observed in the laboratory may not be a true reflection of the caretaker–child relationship. It is suggested that a more direct focus on the emotional interchanges occurring between caregiver and child may ultimately be more productive in qualitatively describing caretaker–infant relationships.

Acknowledgments

The authors would like to thank Mrs. A. Culp and Ms. L. Schultz for their contributions to many aspects of the work. We would also like to thank

Dr. I. Bretherton and Ms. D. Rosenberg for their critical comments on an earlier version of the manuscript.

REFERENCES

Ainsworth, M. D. S. The development of infant–mother attachment. In B. Caldwell & H. Ricciuti (Eds.), *Review of child development research*(Vol. 3). Chicago: University of Chicago Press, 1973.

Ainsworth, M. D. S., Blehar, M. C., Waters, E., & Wall, S. *Patterns of attachment.* Hillsdale, N.J.: Lawrence Erlbaum, 1978.

Ainsworth, M. D. S., & Wittig, B. Attachment and exploratory behavior of one-year-olds in a strange situation. In B. M. Foss (Ed.), *Determinants of infant behavior.* New York: Wiley, 1969.

Bernal, J. Attachment: Some problems and possibilities. In: M. Richards (Ed.), *The integration of the child into the social world.* Cambridge: Cambridge University Press, 1974.

Blehar, M. D. Anxious attachment and defensive reactions associated with day care. *Child Development*, 1974, *45*, 683–692.

Bowlby, J. *Attachment.* New York: Basic Books, 1969.

Bretherton, I., Bates, E., Benigni, L., Camaroni, L., & Volterra, V. Relationship between cognition, communication, and quality of attachment. In E. Bates, L. Benigni, I. Bretherton, L. Camaroni, & V. Volterra, *The emergence of symbols: Cognition and communication in infancy.* New York: Academic Press, 1979.

Caldwell, B. M., Wright, C. M., Honig, A. S., & Tannenbaum, J. Infant day care and attachment. *American Journal of Orthopsychiatry,* 1970, *40*, 397–412.

Chichetti, D., & Serafica, F. C. Interplay among behavioral systems: Illustrations from the study of attachment, affiliation, and wariness in young children with Down's syndrome. *Developmental Psychology,* 1981, *17*, 36–49.

Clarke-Stewart, A. *Child care in the family.* New York: Academic Press, 1977.

Cohen, L. J., & Campos, J. J. Father, mother and stranger as elicitors of attachment behaviors in infancy. *Developmental Psychology,* 1974, *10*, 146–154.

Feldman, S., & Ingham, M. Attachment behavior: A validation study in two age groups. *Child Development,* 1975, *46*, 319–330.

Gaensbauer, T. J., & Sands, K. Distorted affective communications in abused/neglected infants and their potential impact on caretakers. *American Journal of Child Psychiatry,* 1979, *18,* 236–250.

Gaensbauer, T. J., & Harmon, R. J. Clinical assessment in infancy utilizing structured playroom situations. *Journal of the American Academy of Child Psychiatry,* 1981, *20* (2), 264–280.

Gordon, A. H., & Jameson, J. C. Infant–mother attachment in patients with nonorganic failure to thrive syndrome. *Journal of the American Academy of Child Psychiatry 18* (2), 251–259.

Harmon, R. J., & Culp, A. M. The effects of premature births on family functioning and infant development. In I. Berlin (Ed.), *Children and our future.* Albuquerque: University of New Mexico Press, 1981.

Harmon, R. J., Suwalski, J. D., & Klein, R. P. Infants' preferential response for mothers versus an unfamiliar adult: Relationship to attachment. *Journal of the American Academy of Child Psychiatry,* 1979, *18*, 437–449.

Jennings, K. D., Harmon, R. J., Morgan, G. A., Gaiter, J. L., & Yarrow, L. J. Exploratory play as an index of mastery motivation: Relationships to persistence, cognitive functioning, and environmental measures. *Developmental Psychology,* 1979, *15* (4), 386–394.

Kagan, J., Kearsley, R. B., & Zelazo, P. R. *Infancy-its place in human development.* Cambridge: Harvard University Press, 1978.

Kaplan, D. N., & Mason, E. A. Maternal reactions to premature birth viewed as an acute emotional disorder. *American Journal of Orthopsychiatry*,1960, *30*, 359–552.

Koops, B. L., & Harmon, R. J. Studies on long-term outcome in newborns with birth weights under 1500 grams. In B. Camp (Ed.), *Advances in behavioral pediatrics*. Greenwich, CT.: JAI Press, 1980.

Lamb, M. E. Father–infant and mother–infant interaction in the first year of life. *Child Development*, 1977, *48*, 167–181.

Leiderman, P., Leifer, A., Seashore, M., Barnett, C., & Grobstein, R. Mother–infant interaction: Effects of early deprivation, prior experience and sex of infant. *Research Publications for Research in Nervous and Mental Disease*, 1973, *51*, 154–175.

Maccobby, E., & Feldman, S. Mother attachment and stranger reactions in the third year of life. *Monographs of the Society for Research in Child Development*, 1972, *37* (1, Serial No. 146).

Main, M. *Exploration, play and cognitive functioning as related to child–mother attachment*. Unpublished doctorate dissertation, Johns-Hopkins University, 1973.

Matas, L., Arend, R. A., & Sroufe, L. A. Continuity of adaptation in the second year: The relationship between quality of attachment and later competence. *Child Development*, 1978, *49* (3), 547–556.

Portnoy, F. C., & Simmons, C. H. Day care and attachment. *Child Development*, 1978, *49*, 239–242.

Rosenthal, M. Attachment and mother–infant interaction: Some research impasses and a suggested change in orientation. *Journal of Child Psychology and Psychiatry and Allied Disciplines*, 1973, *14*, 201–207.

Sroufe, L. A., & Waters, E. Attachment as an organizational construct. *Child Development*, 1977, *48* (4), 1184–1199.

Thompson, R. A., Lamb, M. E., & Estes, D., *Stability of infant–mother attachment and its relationship to changing life circumstances in an unselected middle class sample*. Manuscript in preparation, 1982.

Vaughn, B., Egeland, B., Sroufe, L. A. Individual differences in infant–mother attachment at 12 and 18 months: Stability and change in families under stress. *Child Development*, 1979, *50* (4), 971–975.

Waters, E. The stability of individual differences in infant–mother attachment. *Child Development*, 1978, *49*, 483–494.

Waters, E., Wippman, J., & Sroufe, L. A. Attachment, positive affect, and competence in the peer group: Two studies in construct validation. *Child Development*, 1979, *50*, 821–829.

Weinraub, M., Brooks, J., & Lewis, M. The social network: A reconsideration of the concept of attachment. *Human Development*, 1977, *20*, 31–47.

CHAPTER 18

Maternal Referencing in Normal and Down's Syndrome Infants

A LONGITUDINAL ANALYSIS

James F. Sorce, Robert N. Emde, and Mark Frank

Researchers interested in the developing mother–infant relationship have observed that beginning in early infancy there is already a complex nonverbal communication system (Bowlby, 1969; Brazelton, Koslowski, & Main, 1974; Stern, 1977). We agree with Darwin (1872) that a critical aspect of this "first language of infancy" is that *emotional* signals are reciprocally exchanged between mother and infant.

Most investigators have focused on the infant-to-mother aspect of this communication. Studies have investigated the emotional information communicated by infants' facial expressions, and have shown that mothers do recognize these discrete emotional signals (Emde, Katz, & Thorpe, 1978; Sorce & Emde, 1982), and they also monitor these emotional expressions in order to guide their caregiving activities (Stechler & Carpenter, 1967; Emde, Gaensbauer, & Harmon, 1976; Sorce & Emde, 1982). Thus maternal abilities in "reading" and in reacting to infant's emotional expressions may not only be vital for ensuring that the infant's physical needs will be met. but also may be important for ensuring that a relationship conducive to social and cognitive growth will develop (Goldberg, 1980).

James F. Sorce, Robert N. Emde, and Mark Frank ● Department of Psychiatry, University of Colorado School of Medicine, 4200 E. Ninth Avenue, Denver, Colorado 80262. This research was supported, in part, by the Grant Foundation Endowment Fund of the Developmental Psychobiology Research Group of the University of Colorado Medical School, Department of Psychiatry. Dr. Sorce is supported by PHS–MH–15442, Development of Maladaptive Behavior. Dr. Emde is supported by Research Scientist Award 5–K05–MH–35808 and NIMH Project Grant 2–R01–MH–22803.

Surprisingly little is known about the mother-to-infant aspect of this communication. Although research has documented the infant's early visual interest in human faces, less is known about their developing awareness of the emotional meanings communicated by adult facial expressions. For example, even minutes after birth, infants prefer to fixate on stimuli that resemble the human face (Goren, Sarty, & Wu, 1975). However, throughout the first 2 months, it appears that the face is attractive because it is a perceptually interesting stimulus (e.g., Haith, Bergman, & Moore, 1977; Haith, 1980; Salapatek, 1975). After two months of age, infants begin to discriminate between different adult facial poses when a few discrete emotional expressions are presented (i.e., happy vs. surprise is discriminated by 3-month-olds, Young-Browne, Rosenfeld, & Horowitz, 1977; and happy vs. anger is discriminated by 4-month-olds, LaBarbera, Izard, Vietze, & Parisi, 1977), although there is no evidence that infants at these ages respond to the emotional messages conveyed by these facial poses. However, during the next months, infants do become aware that these patterned configurations represent *affective* information. Hetzer & Buhler (1928) indicated that as early as five months of age, infants began reacting emotionally when a "live" experimenter displayed a smiling or angry expression. At this time the posed expression must involve both a facial display combined with a vocalic expression to ensure that infants will react positively to the smiling expression and negatively to the angry expression. At 6 months of age this emotional discrimination occurred to voice alone, and by 7 months of age infants reacted emotionally when facial expressions alone were posed for the infant. More recently, Kreutzer and Charlesworth (1973) had a "live" adult experimenter pose facial-vocal combinations of not only happy and angry expressions, but also of sad and neutral expressions. They too found that at 6 months of age infants reacted emotionally with more positive responses to happy or neutral expressions, and with more negative responses to angry or sad expressions.

Therefore, during the second half-year of life, evidence suggests that infants do understand the emotional meaning of a few discrete emotions when communicated by adult facial expressions. We postulate that once infants are aware of these emotional communications they actively seek out this information to help guide their own behaviors, especially in situations of uncertainty. When confronted with a situation beyond their capacity to understand, infants may look to mother (or other trusted adults) to gain information about the likelihood of pleasant or unpleasant consequences. Information is then communicated by mother through her own emotional reactions to the situation. We, along with Joseph Campos and Mary Klinnert have termed this phenomenon *maternal referencing.*

Although there are anecdotal reports that infants "spontaneously" look to their mother's face when confronted with unfamiliar people, objects, or events, there is no research evidence indicating whether infants, in the natural course of daily events, attempt to seek out mother's emotional reactions in times of uncertainty. To this end, we have undertaken a retrospective analysis of maternal referencing from films of 13 normal and 6 Down's syndrome infants that had been taken during two previous longitudinal studies (Emde *et al.*, 1976, 1978). Assuming that the approach of a stranger presents some uncertainty to an infant in the second half-year of life, we reviewed these films at each month from 6 to 12 months of age and analyzed whether infants, in the presence of both mother and stranger, actively looked to mother's face after noticing the stranger's presence.

In order for maternal referencing to occur we are assuming that three basic competencies are present. First, when infants experience uncertainty we assume that they reference their mother's face. Second, we assume that when they see their mother's reaction they are capable of understanding the meaning of her emotional expression and will also react emotionally. Third, we also assume that infants can use this emotional information to guide their own behavior with respect to the ambiguous stimulus. This report will provide evidence supporting the first assumption: that during the second half-year of life infants do reference their mother's face in the midst of uncertainty.

In this study, we tested three hypotheses related to this assumption: (1) that maternal referencing does occur in infants during the first year of life when uncertainty is produced by an approaching stranger; (2) that the pattern of emotional behaviors accompanying maternal referencing changes from 6 to 12 months as a function of the different quality of uncertainty produced by a stranger over this time period; (3) that since maternal referencing involves a cognitive-affective response it should also be present, but delayed, in Down's syndrome infants whose cognitive-affective organization is similar to normal infants but "lags behind" ontogenetically (Cicchetti & Sroufe, 1976, 1978).

METHODS

Subjects

The 13 normal (7 females, 6 males) and 6 Down's syndrome (3 females, 3 males) infants who comprised the sample for this study had participated in two previous longitudinal studies on emotional expression in infancy (Emde *et al.*, 1978; Emde, Gaensbauer, & Harmon, 1976). These were primarily middle-class families with all mothers having completed high school and none working when the study began. Mothers of Down's syndrome infants were referred to us by hospital personnel based on a clinical and chromosomal diagnosis of Down's syndrome soon after delivery.

Procedure

Monthly home visits were made by two and occasionally three investigators. Visits lasted about 1 1/2 hr and included a maternal interview, a filmed social interaction sequence, informal observations of mother–infant interactions, and developmental tests. This study reanalyzed infants' reactions during the social interaction sequence which was designed to highlight the developmental course of stranger distress. This standardized sequence provided infants with two opportunities for maternal referencing. The normal group was filmed monthly from 6 to 12 months, while the Down's group was filmed at 3-month intervals from 6 to 18 months.

The social interaction sequence began when mother briefly left her infant alone in the living room of their home while an adult male stranger approached the infant, first walking silently to within 3 ft., then talking to, and finally picking up the infant. After approximately 3 min mother returned, thus providing the first opportunity for maternal referencing (mother approaching while the infant is with Stranger 1). Next, Stranger 1 departed and a second adult male stranger approached while mother remained. This provided the second maternal referencing opportunity (Stranger 2 approaching while infant is with mother). The entire social interaction series lasted approximately 8–10 min.

Because of our interest in infants' *initial* reactions to uncertainty when mother is available, only the first 30 sec after infants realized that both stranger and mother were present were analyzed. Thus a total of 60 sec from each social interaction sequence was analyzed for maternal referencing: (1) the 30-sec interval following the infant's awareness of mother approaching while in the presence of Stranger 1; and (2) the 30-sec interval following the infant's awareness of Stranger 2 approaching while in mother's presence. Second-by-second analyses were performed to assess whether infants looked at mother, stranger, or neither. In addition, we scored other behaviors related to infants' emotional reactions. These included the presence or absence of (a) smiling, marked frowning, or crying and (b) approaches to mother or to stranger by leaning toward, touching, grabbing or snuggling. A maternal referencing episode was defined as an infant's initially focusing on the stranger's face for an uninterrupted time followed immediately by fixating on mother's face. The initial referencing episode within each 30-sec interval provided the primary data for this study.

A 5-sec period prior to each of the two 30-sec intervals was employed as a baseline for assessing the infant's prior emotional state. A 3-point scale for hedonic tone was utilized: (1) *Obviously Happy* (frequent smiling and/or positive vocalizations; (2) *Alert/Attentive* (predominantly interested and motorically quiet, although blends with curiosity and surprise could occur); (3) *Obviously Distressed* (predominantly sober or wary and/or fussing or crying).

Reliabilities. One judge, naive to the hypotheses of this study, rated all filmed sequences of the 13 normal and 6 Down's syndrome infants. A second naive judge independently rated 25% of the 30-sec intervals (randomly selected from individuals in each infant group and from various ages). In all cases reliabilities were calculated as the number of agreements about the presense of a behavior divided by the number of agreements plus disagreements. Reliability for judging the presence of maternal referencing episodes during a 30-sec interval was high (.88 and 1.00 for the normal and Down's groups). For each 1-sec interval in an initial referencing episode judges reached high agreement about whether an infant looked at stranger or mother (.82 and .80 for the normal and Down's groups). During maternal referencing episodes, judges also agreed about the presence of specific emotional behaviors directed to either stranger or mother (.81 and 1.00 for normal and Down's groups).

RESULTS

Presence of Maternal Referencing

At each month the proportion of infants who exhibited maternal referencing in either 30-sec interval was calculated. Figure 1 illustrates that maternal referencing (defined as looking back-and-forth from stranger to mother)

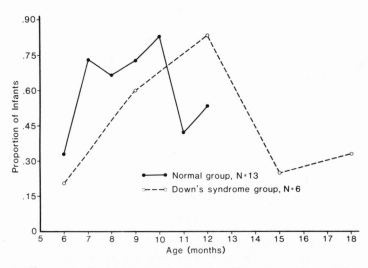

Figure 1. Changes in the proportion of normal and Down's syndrome infants who exhibited back-and-forth looking from stranger to mother's face as a function of age.

did occur and that a developmental function with an inverted U-form is suggested for normal infants. When normal infants did reference mother, 47% did so during both 30-sec intervals of a social interaction sequence, while 31% referenced only in the first interval and 22% referenced only in the second interval.

Down's syndrome infants also showed maternal referencing although it seemed to occur approximately two months later. It appears that maternal referencing occurred less frequently in the Down's syndrome group. These infants were more likely to reference only in the first interval (55%) or the second interval (27%) of a social interaction sequence, but not during both intervals (18%). This conclusion receives additional support from an analysis of multiple referencing episodes. Although 35% of the normal infants exhibited more than one referencing episode during a 30-sec interval, only 16% of the Down's infants did so.

Visual Fixation Patterns

An analysis of the duration of looking from stranger to mother during infants' initial referencing episodes changed as a function of age. Figure 2 presents the distribution of looking time between stranger and mother for

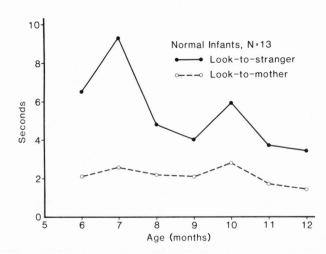

Figure 2. Changes in the length of time normal infants spent looking at stranger and then mother during initial referencing episodes as a function of age.

normal infants during the *initial referencing episode*. (For those infants who referenced in both 30-sec intervals during a social interaction sequence, their initial referencing responses in each interval were averaged to produce a single looking time from stranger to mother.) Notice that across the 7-month period, infants consistently looked longer to the stranger's face than to mother's face, but that looking to the stranger was especially dominant at 7 and again at 10 months of age. (There were too few referencing episodes at each 3-month interval to perform similar analyses for the Down's infants.) We believe that these two peaks represent times when a stranger presents heightened uncertainty, but that the context of the uncertainty differs between these two time periods. This interpretation is based on an analysis of the emotional behaviors that the normal infants exhibited during these periods while looking at mother versus strangers.

Emotional Behavior Accompanying Referencing

Figure 3 presents normal infants' emotional preferences for mother versus stranger during initial referencing episodes. Infants were scored as indicating emotional preference for mother if while looking at her they smiled, showed positive vocalizations or attempted to reach out and touch or grab her, without having shown similar behaviors while looking at the stranger.

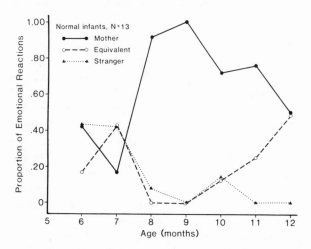

Figure 3. Changes in the proportion of normal infants who exhibited emotional preferences for mother versus stranger during initial referencing episodes as a function of age.

Infants were scored as preferring the stranger if they exhibited these same behaviors while looking at the stranger, without also exhibiting them while looking toward mother. Infants were judged as showing equivalent emotional response if they showed either positively toned approach or negatively toned avoidance behaviors to both mother and stranger during a single referencing episode. As a group the normal infants did not show emotional preferences during the 6- and 7-month periods; however, in months 8–11 there was clear emotional preference for mother. For the 6- and 7-month-olds checking back and forth appeared to be a comparing of faces which occurred in the context of interest and novelty. It was likely to be accompanied by positive emotional reactions to both mother and stranger. Later, in months 9, 10, and 11, infants' looking back and forth seemed to be in the context of sober or negative emotional reactions to stranger. It was as if later on infants were clearly aware that this was a stranger, and their uncertainty concerned whether they were safe or not and how they should behave to protect themselves. At this time there was clear evidence for positive emotional reactions to mother, and sober reactions to each of the two strangers. (Although Down's syndrome infants also exhibited emotional behaviors while referencing, there were too few observations at each 3-month interval to perform similar analyses.)

Emotional State Baseline

Infants' prior emotional state influenced both (1) the likelihood of subsequent referencing and (2) the length of looking during referencing. Normal infants were most likely to reference mother in either 30-sec interval if they had been alert/attentive during the baseline period (66%), and were less likely to reference if they had been distressed (24%) or happy (10%). In addition, during initial referencing episodes, infants spent a longer time looking at the stranger than at mother if they had been alert/attentive during the baseline period (average total = 9.1 sec; 6.8 sec to stranger and 2.3 sec to mother) and less time looking if they had been distressed (average total = 4.9 sec; 2.4 sec to stranger and 2.5 sec to mother) or happy (average total = 7.7 sec; 6.1 sec to stranger and 1.6 sec to mother). Thus those infants who remained curious, interested, and motorically calm prior to the 30-sec intervals were most likely to react to the stranger by referencing mother.

For Down's syndrome infants, prior emotional state also influenced the likelihood of subsequent referencing since 80% of the referencing episodes were exhibited by infants who had been alert/attentive during the baseline, with only 20% following happy baseline ratings and no referencing following distress baseline ratings.

DISCUSSION

These results indicate that maternal referencing (fixating on an uncertain stimulus, then checking back to view mother's face) did occur in both normal infants and Down's syndrome infants when the uncertain stimulus was an unfamiliar adult. These referencing episodes were characterized by longer periods of viewing the stranger, particularly at 7 and 10 months, immediately followed by briefer looks toward mother's face. An analysis of the emotional behaviors occurring during these referencing episodes revealed that 6- and 7-month-old infants were likely to respond positively to both stranger and mother during these referencing episodes. In contrast, the 8 to 11-month-olds often moved toward mother and away from stranger while exhibiting positive emotional responses toward mother and negative or neutral responses toward stranger. These two developmental phases for maternal referencing are remarkably similar to what Mahler and Fuhrer (1968) have described as (1) a "checking back" phenomenon to mother which occurs at about 6–8 months of age and then (2) a reoccurrence of the "checking back" at 10–16 months of age in the context of "emotional refueling" (p. 17). Interestingly, these authors also observed the checking back pattern primarily in response to adult strangers. During what they have designated as the "differentiation subphase" (7–8 months) infants appeared to take special interest in learning about mother. Here, the stranger's presence enabled infants to engage in a feature-by-feature comparison of mother and stranger to better familiarize themselves with mother. Later, during the period they designated as the "practicing subphase" (10–16 months), locomotor infants periodically oriented to mother when at a distance from her and even "the wilting and fatigued infant 'perks up' in the shortest time of following such contact; then he quickly goes on with his explorations and once again becomes absorbed in his pleasure in functioning" (Mahler, Pine, & Bergman, 1975, p. 69). In spite of the poignancy of these observations these authors fail to mention (a) the immediate causes that motivate infants to "check" and (b) how mothers communicate to their infant during checking so that "emotional refueling" can occur.

Not only did infants in this study exhibit emotional behaviors during initial referencing episodes, but their prior emotional state was also related to maternal referencing. Infants who remained curious and attentive during previous approaches and departures of the stranger were most likely to exhibit maternal referencing and produced longer initial referencing episodes.

These findings are compatible with our hypothesis that maternal referencing is an important component of an infant's attempt to cope with uncertainty. We believe it is useful to think that the infant calls on *intrinsic appraisal processes* (Arnold, 1960) to evaluate whether the ambiguous stimulus event is likely to lead to pleasant or unpleasant consequences. Further, if the infant concludes that the stimulus is not harmful, positively toned emotional states like interest and enjoyment will be experienced. Such emotions are likely to promote approach, exploratory, and playful activities. On the other hand, if the appraisal outcome leads the infant to expect possible harm then negatively toned emotions like distress, fear, or anger will be experienced. These emotions serve to terminate exploration activities and are likely to promote retreat and avoidance. In other words, when the infant's intrinsic appraisal processes can adequately evaluate the ambiguity, feelings of uncertainty are eliminated, and internal emotional signals are available for guiding adaptive coping behaviors. However, when the infant's intrinsic appraisal processes fail to resolve the ambiguity, we believe he turns to mother (or another adult caregiver) and attempts to benefit from her appraisal capabilities. The infant "checks" for her emotional reaction and uses this to guide his own behavior. Thus the infant not only responds to his own emotional activity, but comes to respond emotionally to the emotional activity of others. As Campos and Stenberg (1981) have recently stated, an infant who is capable of maternal referencing is no longer tied to the firsthand experiencing of positive or negative consequences for each unfamiliar stimulus. He can now make use of mother's knowledge base by deciding to approach or avoid in an ambiguous situation based solely on his awareness of her emotional reactions in those situations. This is a very adaptive form of learning, especially during the time when extremely curious infants are becoming more mobile, but are seriously limited in their ability to foresee the potential dangers present in their surroundings.

Although the results of this study indicate that infants do seek out mother's face in times of uncertainty, we have no information about what emotional expressions mothers communicated to their infants, and whether these emotions influenced the infant's subsequent behaviors. It is interesting that in Figure 3, 12-month-old infants showed an increase in equivalent emotional responses to strangers during maternal referencing. We speculate that at this time, infants can quickly look to mother and decide based on her positive reaction, that they are safe and can explore and cope. We are currently presenting three different situations of uncertainty to infants (stranger approach, visual cliff, and a toy-play situation) to investigate whether infants reference mothers in these ambiguous situations, and in addition, whether infants react differently depending on the specific emotion expressed by mother during a maternal referencing episode. These experimental conditions will include relatively neutral as well as intense emotional expressions by mothers, and infants will have the freedom to engage in a variety of exploratory, playful, and/or attachment behaviors as they cope with these uncertainties.

ABSTRACT

Maternal referencing is defined as the infant's back-and-forth looking from an ambiguous stimulus to mother's face. This "checking back" phenomenon is viewed as the infant's active attempt to seek out mother's emotional reaction and utilize this information in deciding whether approach or avoidance behaviors are warranted. As an initial step in understanding the developmental course of maternal referencing we assessed whether infants would spontaneously "check" mother's face when confronted with the uncertainty of an approaching stranger. Films of 13 normal and 6 Down's syndrome infants from two previous longitudinal studies were analyzed by microanalytic techniques. Results indicated that maternal referencing did occur in normal infants during the second half-year of life, and it also occurred in Down's syndrome infants somewhat later in development. Maternal referencing initially appeared to involve a "comparing of faces" which occurred in the context of interest in inspecting novel stimuli; later referencing appeared to involve a concern for safety which occurred in a context of wariness and avoidance of the stranger.

Acknowledgments

We wish to acknowledge our collaborators, Joseph Campos and Mary Klinnert, for their contributions in formulating these ideas.

REFERENCES

Arnold, M. *Emotion and personality* (Vol. 1 & 2). New York: Columbia University Press, 1960.

Bowlby, J. *Attachment.* New York: Basic Books, 1969.

Brazelton, T. B., Koslowski, B., & Main, M. The origins of reciprocity: The early mother–infant interaction. In M. Lewis & L. Rosenblum (Eds.), *The effect of the infant on its caregiver.* New York: Wiley, 1974.

Campos, J. J., & Stenberg, C. R. Perception, appraisal and emotion: The onset of social referencing. In M. Lamb & L. Sherrod (Eds.), *Infant social cognition.* Hillsdale, N.J.: Lawrence Erlbaum, 1981.

Cicchetti, D., & Sroufe, L. A. The relationship between affective and cognitive development in Down's syndrome infants. *Child Development,* 1976, 47, 920–929.

Cicchetti, D., & Sroufe, L. A. An organizational view of affect: Illustration from the study of Down's syndrome infants. In M. Lewis & L. Rosenblum (Eds.), *The developmental of affect*. New York: Plenum Press, 1978.

Darwin, C. *Expression of emotion in man and animals*. London: John Murray, 1904. (Originally published, 1872.)

Emde, R. N., Gaensbauer, T. J., & Harmon, R. J. Emotional expression in infancy; A biobehavioral study. *Psychological Issues, A Monograph Series, Inc.* (Vol. 10), No. 37. New York: International Universities Press, 1976.

Emde, R. N., Katz, E. L., & Thorpe, J. K. Emotional expression in infancy: II. Early deviations in Down's syndrome. In M. Lewis & L. Rosenblum (Eds.), *The development of affect*. New York: Plenum Press, 1978.

Goldberg, S. Some biological aspects of early parent–infant interaction. In S. G. Moore & C. R. Cooper (Eds.). *The young child: Reviews of research*. Washington, D.C.: National Association for the Education of Young Children, 1982.

Goren, C. G., Sarty, M., & Wu, P. Visual following and pattern discrimination of face-like stimuli by newborn infants. *Pediatrics*, 1975, *56*, 544–549.

Haith, M. M., Bergman, T., & Moore, M. J. Eye contact and face scanning in early infancy. *Science*, 1977, *198*, 853–855.

Haith, M. M. *Rules that newborns look by*. Hillsdale, N.J.: Lawrence Erlbaum, 1980.

Hetzer, H., & Buhler, C. Das erste Verstandnis fur Ausdruck in ersten Lebensjahr. *Zeitschrift für Psychologie*, 1928, *107*, 50–61.

Kreutzer, M. A., & Charlesworth, W. R. *Infants' reactions to different expressions of emotions*. Presentation at the biennial meeting of the Society for Research in Child Development at Philadelphia, March 1973.

LaBarbera, J. D., Izard, C. E., Vietze, P., & Parisi, S. A. Four- and six-month-old infants' visual responses to joy, anger, and neutral expressions. *Child Development*, 1976, *47*, 535–538.

Mahler, M. S., & Fuhrer, M. *On human symbiosis and the vicissitudes of individuation*, Vol. 1, *Infantile psychosis*. New York: Basic Books, 1968.

Mahler, M. S., Pine, F., & Bergman, A. *The psychological birth of the human infant: Symbiosis and individuation*. New York: Basic Books, 1975.

Salapatek, P. Pattern perception in early infancy. In L. B. Cohen & P. Salapatek (Eds.), *Infant perception: From sensation to cognition* (Vol. 1) New York: Academic Press, 1975.

Sorce, J. F., & Emde, R. N. The meaning of infant emotional expressions: Regularities in caregiving responses in normal and Down's syndrome infants. *Journal of Child Psychology and Psychiatry*, in press, 1982.

Stechler, G., & Carpenter, G. Theoretical considerations. *Exceptional Infant Normal Infant*, 1967, *1*, 165–189.

Stern, D. *The first relationship. Infant and mother*. Cambridge: Harvard University Press, 1977.

Young-Browne, G., Rosenfled, H. M., & Horowitz, F. D. Infant discrimination of facial expression. *Child Development*, 1976, *48*, 555–562.

PART THREE

COMMENTARIES

Attachment Research and Mental Health

A SPECULATION

Nicholas J. Anastasiow

The research questions dealt with in this volume can be grouped into several areas of speculation, which, although generally related on a continuum of infant development, tap into quite diverse issues. Vernadakis and Timiras look at neural growth and the influence of hormones on brain development; they are willing to make the largest inference as to the impact of environmental experiences, or their lack, on the developing brain. Another major portion of the volume contains chapters examining the nature of the influence of the caretaking environment on the development of attachment systems (Gaensbauer & Harmon, Chapter 17; Konner, Chapter 12; Morgan, Busch-Rossnagel, Culp, Vance, & Fritz, Chapter 16; Sander, Chappell, & Snyder, Chapter 11).

From the major chapters on attachment systems it can be concluded that the authors do not disagree that attachment systems have a genetic base, an evolutionary survival value, and a genotypic mode of expression. They make the point, however, that while earlier research on attachment has advanced our understanding, the focus on bonding is a misleading metaphor. (See particularly Svejda, Pannabecker, & Emde). The preference for the concept of *attachment systems* rather than *attachment* allows for fuller exploration of the roles of maturational factors, individual differences in temperament, and the responsiveness of the environment, particularly the childrearing techniques used by primary caretakers (Gaensbauer & Harmon, Chapter 17; Morgan *et al.*, Chapter 16; Lamb, Chapter 14). The authors stress that an attachment system develops over time and that both parents play an important role in its

Nicholas J. Anastasiow • Special Education Program, Hunter College of the City of New York, New York, New York 10010.

development (see particularly Lamb). They believe the appropriate subject of study is the nature of the caretaking environment. The majority of chapters on attachment focus on the environmental experiences that facilitate or distort the development of attachment systems as they are theoretically supposed to appear in humans. To summarize these essays, they emphasize the importance of the following factors: the timing of experience in relation to the appearance of the fixed behavioral patterns; the infant's cognitive state at the time; and the potential impact experiential factors have on the ultimate expression of the total functioning of the infant, specifically in the infant child's affective communications.

Undergirding the majority of the chapters is the basic inference, based on the work of Spitz (1965) in particular and Eric Erikson (1950) in general, that the development of attachment systems is necessary for the human acquisition of autonomy and competence, and that there are "good" attachments and healthy attachment systems. Note that the word "acquisition" is used rather than "development." The authors in this volume argue that there is a genetic predisposition for the development of an attachment system that has survival value beyond the infancy period and that the display of this survival value takes form in later complex behavioral systems, such as autonomy and competence. That is, caretaker attachment serves the infant by relieving his distress and providing the basic care needed for survival. Infant attachment grows out of this relieving of distress, which is basically pleasurable, and the attached figure is used for referencing as the infant learns about the environment (Sorce, Emde, & Frank, Chapter 18). Thus, the attachment system, having evolved as an adaptive characteristic of humans, is attained by many mechanisms, particularly during infancy. By this action, researchers can question the evolutionary function of the system and its role in human development.

If there is a theme that cuts across the wide array of basic research, behavioral research, and speculation presented in this book, it is in the transactional roles of the environment in relation to genotypic expression during development. This transaction can be seen somewhat indirectly in the chapters on attachment (particularly that of Gaensbauer & Harmon) and temperament (Goldsmith & Campos, Chapter 13) and more directly in the Timiras chapter, supported by the chapters by Vernadakis, Tennes, Konner, and Sackett. The generalization to be drawn regards the critical role of experience in the development of the genetically programmed brain system and, thereby, the brain-system development that can be inferred from behavioral display. The Timiras chapter is a good illustration of this theme and generalization. Timiras stresses that the young human brain is plastic and that, in achieving optimum potential in performance (here I read autonomy and competence for optimum), "events which occur in early development have long term effects on the subsequent developments of the whole individual and the psychophysiological competence of the adult" (p. 59). Stated in other terms, the basic research question is: How does a child become independent (autonomous) and secure and confident in his or her own talents (competent)?

From Vernadakis's and Timiras's work, it is possible to generalize that: experience is necessary for the full maturation of brain and/or behavioral systems; the nature of the experience influences the development of what has been genetically programmed; and the timing of the experience has its greatest impact during periods of accelerated brain development and during the course of the maturation of related brain systems. Thus while one cannot separate after birth the genetic force from the environmental influence, one can detect the strong genetic push toward a certain level of development, perhaps displaying behavior in the form analogous to a fixed pattern (for example, the social smile at 2 to 3 months, as previously demonstrated by Emde, Gaensbauer, & Harmon, 1976). After such a fixed pattern appears, it is suggested that the environment completes the development through the caregiver's transactions with the child. Vernadakis's work indicates that neurons can be influenced by the environment before they are set into action to do what it is they are genetically programmed to do. She suggests that neurons can respond to brain damage and take over the function of another area. Also, given ecological changes, inhibitory neurons can become excitory neurons. In essence, Timiras and Vernadakis provide a model for influence on brain development that can be used to explore what types of environmental experiences influence the nature of the development, and at what times and to what results.

What concerns me about many of the chapters in this book is the conservative stance of most of the authors, with the notable exception of Timiras and Vernadakis. As a teacher of child development, rather than a person doing research on attachment systems, I keep wanting to ask how these research findings go together, what they mean, how they can be placed in perspective. I feel the balance of the transactional model shift heavily to the environment and the techniques of the caregiver and away from focusing on what the infant brings to the setting other than some expectable, potential, universal patterns, such as the social smile. Perhaps coffee-break discussions have no place in a research volume. I would, however, have been appreciative if the scholars in this volume had been a little more speculative, a little more involved in the complexity of the system. These authors deal with the development and origins of complex behavioral systems, and while it is important to look at discrete events, such as the potential effects on mothers and fathers upon seeing a wide-eyed baby compared to a baby with silver nitrate in its eyes (Butterfield, Emde, Svejda, & Neiman, Chapter 9), I have the uneasy feeling that after the discrete event is explained, we are left with the findings of a single event which have not been related back to the so-called transactional system. These findings become isolated, lying out there exposed. They need to be tied back to the complexity of the system and to the child state. Further, on the other end of the continuum from discrete events, we are left with global constructs, such as enriched environments, early experience, activity levels, and a response to children's needs. Hopefully, someone, a modern-day Spitz, will be courageous and arise to tell us the significance of all this isolated data; what it means beyond the first 2 years of life to other major developmental events—the 5-to-7 integration, the 9-to-11 integration.

Perhaps what I am asking from these authors are some advance organizers of some encompassing theory or model that would allow me to get a perspective on and integrate the various themes.

In the absence of such direct guidance, I will construct my own theme. Readers beware that it is my construction and not necessarily the authors. And perhaps that is the best model after all—to make us, the readers, construct our own unifying meanings.

In any event, although most of the data in this volume are on infants and their caretakers, one can feel the speculation underlying this research as to the implications of the development of infant attachment systems for mature adult functioning. At this point, it is relevant to recall Freud's definition (as found in Vaillant) of the two major themes of mental health and human development: "the ability to love" and "the ability to work" (Vaillant, 1977). Actually, as Vaillant notes, Tolstoy said it more eloquently, when Freud was only 6 months old: "One can live magnificently in this world if one knows how to work and how to love, and how to work for the person one loves and to love one's work" (Vaillant, p. 8). The research of the authors in this volume can be interpreted as falling into the category of the "ability to love" rather than the "ability to work."

Dynamically oriented research workers have kept alive the need to search for the origins of mental health. Many of the authors of this volume can be viewed as searching for the sources related to the affective nature of mature adult functioning. They are doing so by examining the early infant–caregiver transactions, which lead to the development of an attachment system. Each author can then be seen as having explored a discrete area which in the long run should fit into a model of the sources of human adaptation to complex human environments. To be sure, the mosaic is incomplete, but one feels the press toward a future predictive model, such as Connell and Goldsmith suggest in their chapter. It would appear that the model would include the infant's capacities at birth, the maturational level, the level of cognitive development, the caregiver's skills and needs, and the environmental opportunities or the disadvantages.

REFERENCES

Emde, R. N., Gaensbauer, T. J., & Harmon, R. J. *Emotional expression in infancy: A biobehavioral study.* New York: International Universities Press, 1976.

Erikson, E. H. *Childhood and society.* New York: W. W. Norton, 1950.

Spitz, R. A. *The first year of life: A psychoanalytic study of normal and deviant development of object relations.* New York: International Universities Press, 1965.

Vaillant, G. E. *Adaptation to life.* Boston: Little, Brown, 1977.

Attachment Research

PROSPECT AND PROGRESS

Marshall M. Haith

I suppose there is some virtue in having an "outsider" comment on contributions to a volume that is meant to capture the state of the art in a particular area. A fresh eye, lack of investment in theoretical positions, awareness of a literature that may be at least tangentially relevant, are all reasonable reasons. Although only an extremely isolated psychologist could remain unaware that interesting work has been going on in the area of attachment, my own area of expertise in infant visual perception is quite distant from this discipline. A possible virtue for the "outsider" is that he may learn something from having to read the volume on which he is to comment. In fact, I have learned a great deal, both about how far the area of parent–infant relations has advanced over the past two decades and about how similar are the problems that seemingly distant disciplines face.

The contributions to this volume cover an impressive range. We have discussions of developmental issues relating to hormonal factors, neuronal plasticity, anatomy, animal models, perception, social interaction and social class, infant temperament, and parenting styles and personality. Interestingly enough, issues that were raised in one domain were often echoed, albeit in slightly different form, in a quite different domain.

An important example is the theme of barrenness in single-factor theories, a refrain that was repeated from the first paper through the last. Whether the discussion focused on behavioral isolation, hormones, the pleuropotential neuron, cross-cultural or socioeconomic influences, "bonding" or baby or parent effects, the message was always the same: single-factor theories will

Marshall M. Haith • Department of Psychology, University of Denver, Denver, Colorado 80210.

not work. Okay, that is not news, but the diversity of contexts in which that theme was replayed certainly sharpened the point.

The term *system* was used frequently throughout this book; no other word captures better the notion of sets of organized, multiple influences that affect everything of any interest that people want to study these days. First, I want to discuss the various components that comprise the infant relational system and were alluded to in this volume. Then I will move along to some comments and reactions I had about how the infant's relations to adults have been evaluated.

THE "SYSTEM" OF INFANT SOCIAL RELATIONS

Let us start with the baby. The baby's role in the infant–other relation was acknowledged in several papers. Sackett described sex differences in monkeys' reactions to isolation, and Lamb reported that the baby's gender affects parental involvement in infant care. For monkeys, evidence implies that fetal-gender influences on the parent predate birth, affecting the mother's social interactions with other monkeys. This intriguing finding suggests that, for example, "rebound" effects could bias the mother's treatment of her infant, postnatally, based on differential treatment of her by her peers during pregnancy. Missing from the discussions, however, was a detailed treatment of how individual baby characteristics might affect the relation between infants and others. A start in this direction was made by Tennes who reported some interesting data that suggested that babies with chronically high cortisol-hormone levels tend to react more strongly to mother's absence. Further work should evaluate whether cortisol level is a "constitutional given" or whether maternal style affects chronic cortisol level as well as baby's response to absence. I would also find it interesting to know whether all affective states, both positive and negative, are accentuated by high cortisol levels.

Perhaps the absence of more discussion of the role of infant personality in social relations reflects measurement problems. The Goldsmith and Campos chapter testifies to the struggle involved simply in separating out conceptual components of infant "personality" as well as some of the measurement problems involved. As they point out, however, temperament may affect both the mother's behavior toward the infant and the psychologist's assessment of attachment. I would add that differences in temperament may affect the relative *importance* for the baby of the quality of relations with others. Frequently described are the cuddly versus tense babies and the reactions these babies produce in adults around them. I think it not daring to suggest that these types of babies "value" different aspects of their social relations differently. Critical for our future understanding of the system is progress in evaluating individual difference components among infants and their consequences.

A second component of the infant social-relation system is the social sphere. Sander, Chappell, and Snyder described an elegant procedure for evaluating the role that caretakers play in synchronizing infant biological rhythms to external periodicities. And Haynes, Wade, and Cassel alerted us to the fact that the organized activity of a social group can influence the activity of infants in that group, a directive role that cannot simply be described only in terms of imitation or physical constraints. Finally, Gaensbauer and Harmon reminded us of the huge variation that exists in the social spheres among abused, neglected, and "normally" treated infants. Still, I would have enjoyed more discussion of the fact that the infant is but a part of the whole social system involving mother, father, grandparents, siblings, nonrelated caretakers, neighbors, friends, and so on. The structure of this social array must play a role in any specific relation between the infant and another on which we may want to focus.

Still a third component of the system involves the particular characteristics of the social agents in the infant's world. There are fairly consistent reports of parent-gender effects: father is more the play figure and mother the caregiver, for example. The data of Butterfield, Emde, Svejda, and Naiman suggest that variations in newborn responsiveness may affect fathers more than mothers. And Lamb, Frodi, Hwang, Frodi, & Steinberg, despite heroic efforts at deconnecting gender and parent attitude toward infants, found parent gender to be a strong predictor of behavior toward the infant. Personality and motivational characteristics of parents seem less well explored. The Morgan, Busch-Rossnagel, Culp, Vance, and Fritz chapter is a welcome exception and seems to be a step in the right direction. For their effort, I think important information could be garnered by interviewing mothers prior to birth. Also, by evaluating mother's behavior toward the baby's siblings, one might begin to disentangle the role of infant "personality" from mother's attitudes and behavior toward her infant. Finally, Gaensbauer and Harmon have presented some rich clinical impressions of the impact of parental and caregiver characteristics on infant social relations; some followup detailed observations are needed.

More effort should be directed toward describing characteristics of the social sphere *qua* sphere. The quality of interaction among social agents in the infant's life probably plays an important role in the infant's "attachments" to those agents. Gaensbauer and Harmon warned us that the affective context of the interaction plays an important role: some families are under chronic stress, others are not. There must be ways to characterize the infant's social world along meaningful dimensions that will permit a reasonable attack on this issue.

Then there is the relation of parent to infant and the parent's caregiving style. This component has been most heavily researched. Svejda, Pannabecker, & Emde abused us of the notion that an attachment relation, from the mother's vantage, strikes like lightning. From the baby's perspective, the suggestion is that the infant develops a strong relation with a caregiver who is sensitive and responsive (Ainsworth) through predictable, consistent, and appropriate behavior (Lamb). A consideration that I see to be missing from current thinking is the *developmental* context of relations in infancy. Haynes *et al.* reported a declining influence of the social group on infant activity and the rising role of individual differences with development. And Gaensbauer and Harmon asserted the importance of focusing on the fact that relations do change. These statements about the course of social relations seemed all the more striking by virtue of their rarity in the volume, which is somewhat of an irony. Whereas there is reasonable agreement regarding which factors lay the base for strong infant–caregiver relations, how the relation changes has been virtually ignored. Repeated observations of caregiver and infant appear to have been carried out to examine stability in measures, rather than normal and abnormal progression in social coupling. Surely, more theoretical and empirical consideration needs to be devoted to the progression of infant–other relations.

The melding of these various components into a workable conceptual system is a large task, indeed. No models seem available. Ironically, I have found similar problems in dealing with what should be a much simpler behavioral domain—infant visual scanning (Haith, 1980). The problem is that thinking in psychology has been fairly strongly conditioned, through both experimental paradigms and statistical tools, to deal with single behavioral events. Multivariate or sequential-analysis conceptions are not completely satisfying because the single-factor, single-behavior prototype is simply concatenated to generate multi-factor analyses or analyses that handle single behaviors, sequentially ordered over time. Connell and Goldsmith described conceptual and statistical tools for characterizing the structure of relations of variables at a given moment, and this approach could be helpful. However, I still feel there is something missing in describing the activity of the system and wonder how one talks about both a system and its change over time. We seem to be stuck with state-change characterizations in psychology when we really need something akin to a system calculus.

If the reader feels that I am simply arguing for analyses that utilize multiple independent and dependent variables, then one or both of us has not been up to the communication task. If we are going to talk about systems, then our deterministic, vector-oriented "set" in psychology may have to go. Galactic systems, for example, can not be talked about in cause-effect, independent-dependent variable terms. Rather, notions are used that deal with the properties of all the elements "behaving" in concert; systems talk is going to require systems thinking and analyses.

I do not mean to belittle the contributions to this volume; the problem transcends virtually every field of psychology I know anything about, and I am sure that I am not unique in feeling frustration at the discrepancy between our single-factor measures and the system characterization for which we need to aim.

CONCEPTUALIZING AND EVALUATING THE RELATION BETWEEN THE INFANT AND SOCIAL AGENTS

Attachment and Other Relations

Several chapters discussed conceptual issues concerning the attachment relation between mother and infant, notably Svejda *et al.*, Lamb, and Gaensbauer and Harmon. The opinion was clearly expressed that in a strong attachment relation the caregiver serves as a source of security and warmth for the infant. Attachment in the other direction, from mother to infant, was discussed by Svejda *et al.*, and I think the highly skeptical attitude concerning the question of maternal bonding is healthy and definitely warranted.

The use of relatively dichotomous terms such as *bonding* and *attachment* to describe caretaker–infant relations reflects a poverty of theory and creates some problems. Gaensbauer and Harmon warned of the reification of the term attachment; as an outsider, I was confused by usage of the term. At times, attachment is a label for a special subcategory of relations that the baby has toward social agents (baby is "attached" to mother but not sister), but at other times attachment is synonymous with *relation* and refers to a dimension, such as when authors refer to "secure" and "insecure" attachments (or relations). Of course, discussion of attachment of mother to infant adds still other considerations in how we are to interpret this term. (The term *bonding* seems much more definite, making its inadequacy for describing complex relations readily apparent.) The term *attachment* might either be discarded or reserved for relations that satisfy a special set of conditions, but I see no merit in using the term to refer to a dimension when the term *relation* serves the same purpose.

Lamb and Gaensbauer and Harmon dealt with the issues of the quality and predisposing circumstances of attachment relations. Lamb argued that time was the most important component for an attachment relation but included the qualitative aspects that must be considered, namely predictability, consistency, and appropriateness of the caretaker's behavior. Consistency was held to foster in the infant feelings of effectance, appropriateness, and trust. Conceptual specificity along the lines that Lamb is pursuing is laudable and should generate testable propositions and better articulation of what the mother–infant relation is all about. Consideration of the affective context in which caregiver and infant interactions occur was stressed by Gaensbauer and Harmon. There is disagreement between Lamb and others about what the most important contexts are. Lamb argues that distress–relief or stress situations have heaviest weighting in the establishment of attachment, whereas Gaensbauer and Harmon, for example, emphasize the importance of positive situations. My guess is that both types of situations will turn out to play an important role in the relation and that the assumption of a state of attachment is forcing theorists to think too categorically. It would be hard to argue that either exclusively stress–relief or exclusively positive events would not matter for a caregiver–infant relation if we think of relation in multidimensional rather than dichotomous terms. If we were to take three sets of infants differing in their experience—one experiencing only distress–relief relations, one experiencing only positive-affect relations, and still a third, as most often happens, exposed to a balance of the two—I am sure we would find perhaps strong, but very different, kinds of attachments in those three sets of infants. And our "evidence" for attachment would probably emerge in different settings; most notably, exclusive experience with distress–relief settings would play a major role when, as is conventional, attachment is evaluated in a stressful situation.

Proximity-Seeking as an Indicator of Attachment

Proximity-seeking appears to be used almost universally as an indicator of infant attachment. Gaensbauer and Harmon raised a number of interesting problems with this index and cited several instances for which it was unfaithful. Connell and Goldsmith suggested that investigators take a much more comprehensive approach to evaluating behavior in the strange situation. We need better documentation of the Gaensbauer/Harmon observations, and I hope they will be forthcoming.

Even considered in the abstract, however, the proximity measure raised questions for me. Does not the infant's threshold for distress matter as well as his or her experience with the stressor itself? Goldsmith and Campos raised this issue. It is hard to believe that these factors do not matter as well as a particular infant's current "need" for cuddling as opposed to independence. These matters were ignored in most discussions about age changes in proximity-seeking. At some point, proximity-seeking is not an indication of a strong infant– or child–caretaker relation. If so, should we not expect age functions concerning the attachment/proximity relation?

There is a pressing need for the development of converging operations for assessing the infant's relations to others. We would never assume that we could portray the intricacies of the relation among two adults by assessing one or even a few behaviors in a single, untypical setting. Other types of stressful situations should be devised for which neither the mother's actions nor those of a stranger serve as the stressor; there is a potential for some complicated confounds in the situations that have been used between: prior separation experiences in which the mother serves as a distress-reliever, the mother–infant relation, the relation of infants to others, the experience of infants with strangers, and so on. Furthermore, situations should be devised for evaluating attachment in exclusively positive situations. The maternal referencing behavior of young infants discussed by Sorce and Emde provides some suggestions of revealing behaviors other than proximity-seeking and, thereby, of more positive situations than have been used in the past. A broader based, converging-operation strategy is crucial to progress in this field.

Finally, to reiterate a point I made in a narrower context before, I found it striking that more attention was not given to age changes both in attachment and to the relation that is presumed to exist between attachment and its indices. Gaensbeuer and Harmon raised the question of the need for considering attachment relations in a developmental context. They discussed the fact that both the infant and the caregiver change with time depending both on internal and external factors. Speaking from my own experience, babies differ as "criers" or "noncriers" from the start. One of my children was never a crier, the second was a crier to 5 months of age and then suddenly became a smiling "buddha," and the third was a crier until 17 months of age and then reversed. The differences in behavior among these three infants as well as the sudden change in behavior with age in two of them strikingly affected the infant–caregiver relation. (I guarantee it!) Gaensbauer and Harmon pointed to relations outside of the mother–infant sphere that affect the attachment relation. More attention needs to be given to the *plasticity* of the relation and to its natural course to complement the over-concern with its *stability*. Conceptual effort needs to be devoted to what aspects would be expected to remain stable and which should change.

CONCLUDING COMMENT

It is no difficult task to stand to the side of a field, especially one in which the critic has no research investment, and cast stones. That was not my goal, and I fully acknowledge the distance between verbiage and implementation. I have focused on hopes for the future of the field; it is worthwhile to close by taking a look also at the accomplishments this volume documents. Investigators have clearly moved well beyond the metaphorical descriptions of the mother–infant relation that characterized earlier decades of writings. We

have moved through various phases with the "critical period notion" currently giving way to a more reasonable and supportable stance in the form of
"sensitive periods" and variable "rates of development." Sensitivity to the
fact that the baby grows up in a complex social network, not only in a bound
mother–infant interaction, is evident. Clearly, the appreciation that the father
plays an important role, a recent "discovery," is a solid move in this direction.
Adding to the appreciation of complexity is the awareness that individual
characteristics of the infant are important as well as individual characteristics
of the caretakers and, most importantly, how these profiles mesh.

The availability of animal models has contributed a great deal both
methodologically and conceptually. The early separation work of Harlow
(Harlow & Harlow, 1965) established the base for a score of monkey studies
and helped to shape the focus on response to separation in infants. Finally,
the attempts to operationalize procedures and concepts by such pioneers as
Ainsworth and her coworkers (Ainsworth, Blehar, Waters, & Wall, 1978)
have moved the field well beyond what was possible in the early 60's.

Thus this volume stands as testimony both to what is possible and what
is desirable. If the next 20 years of work in this field is as productive as the last
20 years has been, a future "neutral" commentor should have quite an interesting story to tell.

REFERENCES

Ainsworth, M. D. S., Blehar, M., Waters, E., & Wall, S. *Patterns of attachment*. Hillsdale, N.J.:
    Lawrence Erlbaum, 1978.
Haith, M. M. *Rules that babies look by: The organization of newborn visual activity*. Hillsdale, N.J.:
    Lawrence Erlbaum, 1980.
Harlow, H. F., & Harlow, M. K. The affectional systems. In A. M. Schrier, H. F. Harlow, & F.
    Stollintz (Eds.), *Behavior of nonhuman primates* (Vol. II). New York: Academic Press, 1965.

Index

Abused and neglected infants, 263–277
Animal models
  advantages, 34
  attachment, 31–32, 36–37
  in developmental psychobiology, 43–45
  homology versus nonhomology, 33–34
  in maternal-infant behaviors, 75–76
  risks, 34–35
Attachment, infant
  ABC typology, 216–221
  abused and neglected infants, 263–277
  animal models, 31–40
  bonding model, 87–89
  caretaking experiences in, 89–90,
    272–273
  clinical assessment, 265–268, 276–277
  definition, 36–37
  depression and, 43–45
  developmental perspective, 109–117,
    119–136, 275
  differential social response, 197,
    245–261, 269–272
  early contact, 86–87
  evolution and, 33–34, 36–38, 45, 295–297
  father-to-infant, 89–91, 109–117
  individual differences, 195–202
  infant effects, 259
  initial social interaction, 95–106, 119–136
  !Kung and, 138–141
  maternal characteristics and, 248–249,
    251–256, 258–259
  mental health, 295–298
  mother-to-infant, 84–89. See also
    Mother–infant relationship
  organizational construct, 214–215

Attachment, infant (cont.)
  path analysis and latent variables,
    237–241
  play and, 252–256
  pleasure and, 274–275
  predictive validity, stability, 206–208,
    217–219
  predisposition for, 268–269
  proximity seeking, 306–307
  recent caretaking experiences and,
    272–273
  relationship to maternal anxiety,
    248–249, 251
  security, 206–208
  sex differences, 109–117, 198–199
  silver nitrate
    effects of, in eyes of newborn, 95–106.
      See also Silver nitrate
  social relations, infant, 302–306
  strange situation behavior, 202–205,
    215–241, 246–248, 252–253
  structural modeling, 221–241
  system theory and, 302–305
  temperament
    and attachment, 185–188
    infant, 113, 161–189

Bassinet monitor, 123–130
Bonding
  father bonding, 89–91
  frequent infant nursing and, 138–141
  maternal and infant physiology, 153–154
  maternal bonding research, 84–86
  shortcomings of bonding model, 87–88,
    91–92

Cortisol
  in mother–infant relationship, 78
  separation and, 76–78
Critical periods, 47, 50–51, 308. *See also*
    Hormones

Depression, 43–45
Distress
  infant and cortisol, 76–78
Down's syndrome infants, 281–291

Early experience, 3–5
Eye contact
  en face mother–infant, 85
  and parental behavior, effects of silver
    nitrate, 95–106,

Father–infant relationship
  caregiving, 89–90, 109–117
  father bonding, 90–91
Fearfulness
  development of, in infants, 149–153
Fetus, effects on mother, 8–11

Gender and caretaking role, 109–117
Glial factors and neuronal growth, 70–71

Homology, 33–34
Hormones
  critical periods, 47, 50–51
  effects on brain development, 47–60
  effects on developmental processes,
    48–49
  as epigenetic growth factors, 68–69
  in mother–infant transactions, 75–79
  regulation of growth, 59
  sex hormones, 51–55
  thyroid hormones, 55–59

In vitro studies, 65–71
Infant–caregiving system, 119–136
Isolation syndrome, 5–8

Maternal referencing
  emotional behaviors, 287–288, 289–291
  in normal and Down's syndrome infants,
    281–291
  visual fixation patterns, 286–287
Monkeys
  crabeater, 6–7
  in isolation, 5–8

Monkeys (*cont.*)
  pigtail macaques, 5, 16–18, 44–45
  rhesus, 5–11
  squirrel, 76
Mother–infant relationship
  animal models, 75–76
  attachment, 84–89
  biological aspects, 137–155
  caretaking, 109–117
  cortisol, effect on, 78–79
  hormones, 75–79
  infant play, 252–256
  maternal bonding research, 84–86
  maternal characteristics, 248–249,
    251–256, 258–259
  neurobehavioral growth, 142–144
  nursing, 138–141
  separation, 75–79

Neurohumor substances as growth factors,
    69–70
Neuronal differentiation
  epigenetic factors, 65–71
  role of microenvironment, 66–68

Parent–infant interaction. *See also*
    Attachment, infant; Father–infant
    relationship; Mother–infant
    relationship
  bassinet monitor, 123–130
  caretaking role, 109–117, 119–136
  development of attachment, 196–202
  first week of life, 119–136
  gender identify, 109–117
  infant state and, 130–135
  silver nitrate effects, 95–106
  strange situation behavior, 202–205,
    213–241, 246–247
  Sweden, traditional and nontraditional
    parents, 109–117
Play
  infant, 252–256
  monkeys in isolation, 6–7
Primate development
  activity rhythms, 13–15
  early experience, 3–5
  isolation rearing, 5–8
  prenatal sex differentiation and behavior,
    8–11

Rats, 32, 37, 39, 51–56, 66–67, 76

Rhesus monkey
 fetus, effects on mother, 8–11
 hormones, 53
 isolation rearing effects, 5–8

Self regulation, 120
Separation
 brief infant separations and cortisol,
  75–79
 factor analytic model and, 222–228
 in monkeys, 43–45
Sex differentiation
 hormones, 51–55
 parental effect on behavior, 8–11
Silver nitrate
 behaviors of parents, 103
 effects on newborn eye openness and
  visual tracking, 95–99
 effects on parent–infant interaction,
  99–106
 visual behaviors of newborn, 101
Social fears, 149–153
Social smiling, 145–149
Social groups
 adult behaviors, 17–18

Social groups (*cont.*)
 dyads, 27
 group state, 19–21, 23–24
 infant behaviors, 18–19
 primate model, 15
 temporal adaptation, 26–27
 temporal coherence
  adult group state, 23–24
  infant with adult group state, 24–26
Social withdrawal, 273

Temperament
 adult personality and, 163–174
 affect and, 180–182
 attachment and, 185–188
 critical approach, 166–169
 definition, 174–178
 effect on caretaking, 113, 115
 infant, 174–189
 measurement, 182–184
 neonatal approach, 171–174
 origins of, 180
 psychobiological approach, 169–171
 style approach, 164–166